British Steel
An Industry between the State and the Private Sector

Heidrun Abromeit

British Steel

An Industry between the State
and the Private Sector

BERG
Leamington Spa/Heidelberg

Berg Publishers Ltd
24, Binswood Avenue, Leamington Spa,
Warwickshire CV32 5SQ, UK

Panoramastr. 118, 6900 Heidelberg,
West Germany

First Published 1986
© Heidrun Abromeit and Berg Publishers 1986

All rights reserved. No part of this publication
may be reproduced, stored in a retrieval system, or
transmitted in any form or by any means, electronic,
mechanical, photocopying or otherwise, without the
prior permission of Berg Publishers Ltd.

British Library Cataloguing in Publication Data

Abromeit, Heidrun
  British Steel : an industry between the state
  and private sector.
  1. Government business enterprises—Great
  Britain
  I. Title
  338.0941   HD4145

ISBN 0–907582–43–5

Printed in Great Britain by Billings of Worcester

Contents

Foreword	vii
Introduction	3

I The Benefits of Public Enterprise
1 Why Nationalise? The Goals of Public Enteprise	15
2 The Problem of Efficiency	23
3 The Problem of Control	32

II Nationalised Industries in Britain
4 The History of Nationalisation	45
5 The Organisational Formula: the Public Corporation	50
6 Problems of Ministerial Control	54

The Statutory Powers 54
Aims and Policies 57
Finance and the Role of the Treasury 61
'Government Interference' 62
The Deficits 65
The Position of the Boards or: Who is in Power? 71

7 A History of Reform	74

Excursus: Experiences Abroad 75
Reforms and Reform Proposals 79
The Thatcherite System 87

8 Ministerial Control and the British Political System	93
9 Nationalised Industries and the Private Sector	98

III British Steel: a Public Corporation Between the State and the Private Sector
10 History and Organisation of the British Steel Industry	111

Developments before Re-Nationalisation and the Role of ISB and BISF 111
The Re-Nationalisation of 1967 118
Organisation and Reorganisation 123
Fighting for the Ten-Year Development Strategy 129
The Remaining Private Sector 135
The Steel Industry in a Declining Market 138

11 Ministerial Control and the Industry's
    Decision-Making   145
        Statutory Rights and Duties   145
        Aims, Policies and Joint Planning   151
        Power on the Board   160
        Financial Control   167
        Government Interference   176
        The Impact of Policy Changes   183
        Sponsor Department and Treasury: a Source of
            Conflict   188
        Conflict or Harmony: the General Relationship   195
        Job Rotation and the Amount of Expertise   202
        The Effectiveness of Control—Seen from Two Sides   208
12 The BSC and the Private Steel Companies   218
        An Involved Relationship   218
        The Personal Relationship or: Remnants of the Past   220
        Conflicts — Past and Present   223
        Joint Interests and Joint Ventures   230
        The Phoenix Projects   235
        Cooperation, Coordination and the Role of BISPA   241
        The 'Real Interest Divide' — and the Benefit of Dividing
            an Industry   246
13 The BSC and the Private Economic Sector   253
        General Relationships   253
        The Role of BRISCC   256
        Strategies for a State-owned Industry in a Private Enterprise
            Environment   262
        The BSC in the CBI   266
14 Attitudes towards Nationalisation   269
        The Civil Servants' Views: the Controller as
            Banker   269
        The Private Steelmen's Attitudes: Nationalisation a
            Benefit or a Disaster?   272
        How Public Steelmen Define their own Role:
            'Convergence' or an Alternative?   277
IV **The Meaning of Nationalisation**
    15 Summary   289
    16 The Future of the BSC and of the Nationalised Industries 300
    17 The Meaning of Nationalisation in Capitalist Societies 306

Appendices   I BSC Management organisation, April 1985   313
            II Steel production of individual countries (% of
                    world production)   314
Abbreviations   315
Bibliography   317
Index   323

Foreword

The problem with studying the British nationalised industries, and writing about them, is that things seem to change with breakneck speed — at any rate since 1979 when I got interested in the subject (not long before the first Thatcher government came into office). Not all the intended policy changes, or the changes of framework, made an impact; all the same, it has not been easy to keep pace with changing events, and to sort out mere window dressing from seriously-meant answers to pressing needs, and 'day-to-day crisis management' from reforms of longer-term importance. The task of keeping up has been the more urgent since the present government has not been concerned with reforms of the institutional framework but has put the existence of the nationalised industries as a whole in jeopardy. Add to this the dire situation of the steel industry in Western Europe, and you may imagine the somewhat desperate sense of hurry imposed on an author who must fear that the very subject of her writing is disappearing from this world even as her work nears completion.

I have tried to keep up with events until December 1984, when two things seemed clear to me: firstly, that the BSC is meant to survive; and secondly, that the government's privatisation policy, radical though it is, proves to be more pragmatic than at first appeared, being used as a means of raising money rather than a structural overhaul.

Since then, the BSC has achieved its best operating result since 1976/7 and 'would have made an operating profit of £40m after interest'; unfortunately, with an estimated cost to the corporation through the NUM strike of £180m and other 'exceptional costs' its losses for 1984/5 again rose, to a total of £409m.[1] Its 'vigorous policy of disposing of its non-mainstream activities' continued; disposals since 1980/1 now number up to forty-one, joint ventures to eleven. As a consequence of this policy, manpower is now down to 64,500. Ravenscraig is still operating (in fact, in the August 1985 agreement

1. BSC, *Report and Accounts* 1984-85, pp. 2f.

Foreword

between the government and BSC it got 'another three-year reprieve';[2] in compensation, Gartcosh rolling mill (not far from Ravenscraig) is to be closed in the spring of 1986. Once more BSC has bought a private sector steel plant only to close it down (Alphasteel hot-strip mill in South Wales). Phoenix II, over which the BSC and GKN had reached an agreement by March 1984, has not yet spread its wings (the government still being slow to provide funds), but should do so in April 1986; it will — inter alia — result in the closure of BSC's Tinsley Park plant in Sheffield.

As for the rest of the nationalised industries, the threat to their existence seems to be more serious, after all, than I had thought when writing the last chapter (see pp. 303ff.). Since the sale of BT only the 48 per cent government share of British Aerospace has been sold; BA's flotation had to be postponed again and again. But now British Gas is at the head of the government's privatisation list; its fierce opposition against the government's policies appears to have been overcome. Sir Denis Rooke is said to have 'qualms', but may have acquiesced in view of the impending new legislation on the control of nationalised industries, announced (more precisely: leaked) in the autumn of 1984. Concerning two aspects of the privatisation policy, however, I seem to be proved right by events: firstly, privatisation will not be coupled with 'liberalisation' and the restoration of competition; monopolies such as BT or British Gas will remain intact, being placed under the supervision of regulatory bodies on whose structure and functions they will have considerable influence (and whose effectiveness is in doubt). Hence, secondly, privatisation is reduced to a purely redistributive measure, especially since the privatised companies, in which the government retains a 'golden share', will remain hybrids.

The legislation mentioned is a long time coming. As Peter Rees, from the Treasury, said in an answer to a parliamentary question in March 1985, 'no final decisions have been taken on the timing and content of any legislation' — apart from that *not* to include in them any 'powers to wind up existing corporations or to change their status'.[3] Meanwhile two decisive features of British nationalised industries and their control appear wholly unchanged: the industries still overdraw their ELFs, and continue to accuse their ministers of 'meddling'.

2. *The Economist*, 10 August 1985, p. 18.
3. Hansard, 19 March 1985, col. 465.

This book rests primarily on information gleaned through interviews. Hence I owe a tremendous debt to all those people, in the public and private steel industry as well as in Whitehall, who patiently answered all my questions and who have, partly, supported my work over years; I may proudly say that over the time some of them have become dear friends.

I am equally grateful to the colleagues who discussed the subject with me and whose criticisms proved of valuable help; these have been George Bain, Volker Berghahn, Gerhard Himmelmann, Les Metcalfe, Claus Offe and Jeremy Richardson. Further thanks are due to the RIPA Research Group on Public Enterprise and to the Gesellschaft für öffentliche Wirtschaft und Gemeinwirtschaft (GÖWG), both of whom provided a forum where I could discuss some of my ideas.

Finally, I wish to express my gratitude to Juliet Standing and Janet Langmaid, who undertook the tedious task of streamlining my English prose.

Wuppertal, November 1985   H. Abromeit

Introduction

This study was originally intended as part of an ambitious programme of research into the general problem of public enterprise and to compare such enterprises in several countries. The question was to examine how they work in different settings, how they are influenced by politics and how effectively they are controlled in different political systems. Events have dictated that the case study on the British Steel Corporation (BSC) must stand on its own, with only an occasional glance at the comparative aspect. From the beginning of my research programme, however, it was clear that, for a number of reasons, the BSC offered a particularly intriguing example of a West European state-controlled enterprise.

Firstly, the nationalisation of steel, as a key industry, has been a major political issue for several decades (and not only in Britain). Secondly, in Britain, this old debate has been renewed within the last two decades, when steel was re-nationalised in the mid-1960s; since then the pros and cons of nationalising a major industry have become a live issue again. Thirdly, the steel industry is a manufacturing industry rather than a public utility; in the latter case nationalisation is accepted without undue debate — presumably because civil servants are seen as better able to 'manage' water or electricity than a 'real' industry. Fourthly, we are dealing here with a declining industry, which is making heavy losses and suffering from over-capacity all over Western Europe. The result everywhere is that even those businessmen and economists who are strongly orientated towards free enterprise are calling for state aid from their respective governments. Finally, and specific to the British situation: in contrast to most other West European countries, nationalisation in Britain did not mean that the state took over single firms (whether whole or in part); instead it absorbed a whole industry and thereby created a public monopoly. In this respect Britain provides an exception to the rule. In a specifically British context, however, the steel industry in its turn provides the exception, because it is the only nationalised British industry which was not nationalised in toto; hence the BSC is not a state monopoly but a public corporation, forced to compete with a considerable private sector.

All this does not imply, though, that the main interest of this study now focuses on the problems of the steel industry: the main interest remains the study of public enterprise as such or, more precisely, of public enterprises in predominantly private enterprise economies in which they occupy a minority position. This position, together with the contradiction between public ownership and private enterprise environment, inevitably leads to the question of how they ought to behave: as agents of public policy, or 'commercially' (as demanded by the great majority of state enterprise managers, not only in Britain). In all Western economies where public enterprises exist their founders and those who have to deal with them have tried continually to find the 'correct' mixture between these alternatives. What prompted this study, then, was the question of whether the proper balance between both elements can be theoretically determined; put differently, the task is to find out how, within the context set out above, public enterprises *ought* to behave and how they behave in reality. Hence, in the last resort, this book is about the *meaning* of nationalisation.

Of course many authors, most of them economists, have tried to tackle these questions. They have come to rather divergent, if not contradictory conclusions which varied with the political outlook of the individual author, the political as well as the economic situation of the country concerned, and a host of other factors. Austen Albu, for instance, writing in 1963, came to the conclusion: 'The theory that the boards [of the nationalised industries, H. A.] are independent commercial enterprises has been shown not only to be unreal in practice, but also undesirable in principle.'[1] For various reasons and from totally different standpoints this hypothesis is being widely debated today.

Interestingly enough, for more than a decade public enterprises have not been a subject of scholarly analysis at all, even though it can hardly be said that the problems raised by their mere existence had diminished during that period. Nor is it possible to say that they had become an economic irrelevance. On the contrary, in spite of first attempts at reducing the public sector through privatisation its economic impact throughout Western Europe in 1979 was as great as ever. In that year state enterprises in the European Community:

1. Austen Albu, 'Ministerial and Parliamentary Control', in Michael Shanks (ed.), *The Lessons of Public Enterprise*, London, 1963, p. 111.

employed 11.9 per cent of the total working population in employment (excluding agriculture), compared with 8.3 per cent in 1973;

had a share of 22.5 per cent of gross fixed capital formation (again excluding agriculture and non-commercial services) (compared with 22 per cent in 1973, but 24 per cent in 1976!);

contributed 13.2 per cent to the net domestic product,[2] (compared with 11 per cent in 1973).

The impact of the public sector of the economy was greatest in Italy, where more than a third of total investment takes place in state enterprises, followed by France and Britain. In Britain the public corporations and enterprises in 1979 contributed:

11.1 per cent to the gross domestic product (8.8 per cent in 1960);

8.1 per cent to total employment (7.7 per cent in 1960);

20.0 per cent to the gross domestic fixed capital formation (18.8 per cent in 1960).[3]

Yet the importance of public enterprises is not reflected merely in these statistics. In most of the West European countries they clearly dominate the energy, communication, and transport sectors; in some countries they are also heavily involved in banking and insurance and, in Britain, France and Italy, in iron and steel as well. In other words, state enterprises dominate at least some of what were once the 'key industries'. They have a strategic position in the economy as a whole and could use this position to influence or even direct national economic development. One should (and in fact used to) think that this economic weight opens considerable opportunities for economic policy and national economic planning; but reality lags far behind what seems theoretically possible. In all West European countries the complaints are the same, not only about the alleged inefficiency of public enterprises but also about the difficulties of having them properly controlled and about their tendency to achieve considerable autonomy, even in the face of financial dependence.

In view of all this the lack of scholarly interest in the topic is difficult to understand. However there is now a renewed interest in public enterprises, even to the level of discussing principles. The reasons for

---

2. See CEEP, *Die öffentliche Wirtschaft im Europa der Gemeinschaft — Bilanz und Ausblick. Dokumentation: IX Kongress der CEEP Athen '81*, Berlin, 1982, p. 136.
3. See CEEP, *Jahrbuch 1981: Die Öffentlichen Unternehmen in der Europäischen Gemeinschaft*, Brussels, 1981, p. 93. For the figures for 1960, see NEDO, *A Study of UK Nationalised Industries, Appendix Volume*, London, 1976, pp. 11ff. The figures Richard Pryke (*The Nationalised Industries. Policies and Performance since 1968*, Oxford, 1981, p. 2) gives for 1977 are higher throughout: 12.7 per cent share of gross domestic product, 9.4 per cent of employment, 22.6 per cent of gross domestic capital formation.

this are not difficult to see. In the Mediterranean countries the public sector is expanding and further sectors of the economy have been nationalised, in Britain and Germany developments have been moving in the opposite direction. The debate about privatisation in the latter two countries has led to the re-emergence of the fundamental question of whether or not it is necessary that some key or service sectors of the economy (the public utilities at least) should be owned and controlled by the public. The recent nationalisations in France, on the other hand, have heightened the interest in the question of how public enterprise can be effectively controlled and its tendency to become autonomous be stopped or reversed; for what use can be seen in further nationalisation if nationalised industries evade control and behave as any other 'normal' enterprise?

A third factor may have contributed to the renewed interest in the problems of public enterprise. For a long time there existed a firm belief, at least with left-of-centre politicians and economists, that in times of crisis public enterprises would prove to be indispensable because they could be used by governments as tools to counteract a recession. In the world-wide recession since the mid-1970s, however, state enterprises did not act anywhere as the saviours people had hoped for them to be. Instead, many of them were hit more severely by the recession, or responded to it more restrictively, than their private counterparts. After this experience it is not surprising that the existing system of public enterprise has been described as a 'fair-weather system'[4] which now, together with the economy as a whole, is 'in crisis'.[5]

The general question underlying this study is that about the meaning of nationalisation. It should be noted from the start, however, that this question will be tackled not from the economist's point of view, but from that of the political scientist. This means that the study deals mainly with processes of goal definition, decision-making, and influence *in* a nationalised industry as well as *concerning* a nationalised industry. No attempt will be made to dive into subtleties of definition — whether such as, for instance, for an enterprise to be classified as 'public' it ought to be *owned* 100 per cent, 51 per cent or only 25 per cent by public agencies, or only to be 'publicly controlled', whatever that might mean.[6] However, one crucial distinction between a public

---

4. John B. Heath, in: SCNI (Sub-Committee E), Session 1978–79, *The Relationships between Ministers, Parliament and the Nationalised Industries. Minutes of Evidence*, London, 1979, p. 2.
5. See, e.g., John Redwood, *Public Enterprise in Crisis*, Oxford 1980.
6. See, e.g., Charles Beat Blankart: *Ökonomie der öffentlichen Unternehmen*, Munich,

and a private enterprise should be pointed out: for the 'normal' private enterprise the goals are usually assumed to be given (profit maximisation); for the 'normal' public enterprise, even if market-dependent, this is not the case. When the management of the latter attempts to define its goals and strategies, there are always the political controllers to be taken into consideration. The ensuing negotiations and resulting decision-making process will be the more complex since (1) the public agencies as owners of the enterprise are themselves complex social entities, usually not speaking with one voice; (2) other social groups and interests will try to use their political influence to profit in some way or other from the enterprise's policies; and (3) influences from different directions usually do not restrict themselves to formal channels. In the words of John B. Heath: 'The state is a single owner but it lacks a single corporate presence'.[7] What follows from this is (1) that the market behaviour of a public enterprise is not in principle determined (and hence predictable); and (2) that it is clearly not sufficient to study public enterprise solely from the economist's point of view and with the economist's tools of analysis. Hence examining a nationalised industry to some extent is tantamount to 'studying . . .the process of government',[8] and this requires the tools of the political scientist.

The juxtaposition of the two types of enterprises, of course, holds true only on the theoretical and conceptual level. It has to be modified when it comes to dealing with real corporations. Since Berle and Means investigated, in 1945, the behaviour of large joint-stock corporations, various versions of a 'theory of the firm' turned away from the neoclassical concept of the market-orientated, 'entrepreneurial' firm in which 'rational behaviour' is axiomatically equated with profit maximisation and whose behaviour is therefore calculable and predictable. They started from the assumption that (1) the behaviour of large organisations comprising different groups with differing interests (e.g., owners and managers) *cannot* be deduced from axioms of rational behaviour in individuals; and that (2) managers definitely develop utility functions *of their own*, not necessarily in harmony with those of the owners, nor necessarily identical with those of the classical 'entrepreneur'.[9] Consequently, these new theories (such as the 'agency theory') became preoccupied with complementing neo-

---

1980, pp. 1–9.
7. John B. Heath, *Management in Nationalised Industries*, Second NICG Annual Lecture (25th March 1980), NICG Occasional Papers No. 2, London, 1980, p. 6.
8. David Coombes, *State Enterprise. Business or Politics?* London, 1971. p. 15.
9. See, e.g., Robin Marris, *The Economic Theory of 'Managerial' Capitalism*, London, 1964, pp. xi, 5, 13ff., 47ff.

classical microeconomic theory with findings from the sociology of organisations; they were concerned with internal processes of information, communication, decision-making and so on, as well as the various motives which led managerial action. The goals of the private firm, they concluded from all this, are not, in fact, 'given', but result, through more or less complex processes, from the different goals and motives of, and from the interactions between, its various members.[10]

This would seem to indicate that the difference between private and public firms is not so decisive after all. Still, there remains the systematically important distinction that in private firms such social processes are essentially *internal* (and, incidentally, lose much of their behavioural impact the more the firm is under competitive pressure); in the case of public enterprise these processes amount essentially to dealings with *external* (political) agents.

This distinction can be exemplified by the recent study of Jonathan Boswell who professes to analyse the complex process of decision-making in three (pre-nationalisation) steel companies.[11] In fact he analyses the impact of managerial motivation on corporate decision-making; his study is about how small management teams, or even individuals (mostly the chairmen of the boards of the three companies) arrived at their decisions and whether they followed a more rationalistic or a more behavioural approach. Underlying is the tacit assumption that a large company is a centralised structure having one will and speaking with one voice — that of the chairman or chief executive: to explain its behaviour you must know what the top management is thinking. This is why Boswell talks of 'managerial regimes'.[12] What does *not* come into the picture are external influences. External agents do not appear to have any impact of their own on the company's decision-making — that is, an impact distinct from what filters through into the management's thinking, via unknown channels. But such a state of affairs is what *cannot* be assumed in the case of public enterprises, not even for the BSC under Ian MacGregor.

While many authors agree that, in theory, this is indeed the crucial distinction between public and private enterprise, there are, surprisingly, few studies investigating how it affects a public enterprise's behaviour *in practice*, and analysing the political and economic processes which public enterprise decision-making is subjected to. Certainly no such study has as yet been undertaken that relates to Britain's

10. See, e.g., Andreas Schuke, *Theorie des Unternehmens*, Frankfurt/New York, 1977, pp. 219ff.
11. Jonathan S. Boswell, *Business Policies in the Making*, London, 1983.
12. Ibid., p. 211.

nationalised industries; in Germany there is a single monograph dealing with Prussian state-owned firms in the Weimar Republic.[13] In it, H.-J. Winkler describes how the Prussian Diet and the government, mainly by sending their representatives to the supervisory boards, tried to influence the firms' policies. These attempts were usually hampered by the political heterogeneity of the prevailing governing coalitions as well as by the public managements' expertise, esprit de corps, and their solidarity with the private sector. The bulk of Winkler's book, though, deals with the existing *formal* channels, i.e. with the possibilities of political influence; he concludes that the dominance of the *Bergassessoren* asserted itself in *informal* processes, a hypothesis which cannot rely on written or oral material and hence must remain unconfirmed.

Our case study of British Steel represents an attempt to fill this gap, at least partially, remembering at the same time that it is not only govenment which may play a part in public enterprise decision-making. It looks for answers to the following questions:

(1) What objectives is a nationalised industry to follow, how are they defined and agreed upon and who participates in this process;

(2) to what degree are government officials (formally or informally) incorporated in the decision-making structure of a nationalised industry and to what extent do they *actually* influence its decision-making;

(3) how developed is the ability, as well as the will, to control the policies and performance of a nationalised industry on the part of the public authorities;

(4) to what degree is a nationalised industry interlocked with private industry and to what extent can private industrialists influence its decision-making;

(5) how do leaders of a nationalised industry define their own role, especially with regard to their position between state and private industry, and what do they think about the 'meaning of nationalisation'?

With these questions in mind, a number of hypotheses were formulated to guide the investigation. It was expected that:

(1) interactions between public authorities and public enterprises do not follow strictly what is prescribed by the statutes, but vary with government policies, political and economic situations and — a factor not to be underestimated — with personalities;

(2) public control lacks consistent policies and objectives specific to the single nationalised industry; government officials lack the expert-

---

13. Hans-Joachim Winkler, *Preußen als Unternehmer. 1923–1932*, Berlin, 1965.

ise to develop such policies; and in the last resort even the *intention* to control may be lacking;

(3) a considerable part of the much complained-about inefficiency of public enterprise is due to exactly these deficiencies of public control: to the lack of insight into the close connection between efficiency, on the one hand, and clear guidance and control, on the other;

(4) decision-makers in nationalised industries choose their own strategies and objectives rather autonomously, and quite successfully try to exclude external influences, using their superior expertise as a sort of shield against government officials;

(5) the managements of nationalised industries are eager to establish good relations with private industry and to appear as 'one of them' — not least with a view to winning them as allies against the politicians;

(6) the self-definition of those managers runs in the direction of their leading 'normal commercial enterprises'; but the secret wish (at least of the technocrats among them) is to be free not only from public, but also from market control.

To sum up: the contribution this study hopes to make to the theory of public enterprise is (1) to reconsider the question of the benefits of nationalisation from the angle of the political scientist; (2) to find empirical evidence about how the processes of joint decision-making and public control of public enterprise actually work; (3) to see and study a public enterprise in its triangular relationship with government *and* the private sector; and (4) to reflect on the relevance of the attitudes of (public) businessmen, and on the impact of the notions of 'managerial autonomy' and 'commercial' behaviour in the context of a nationalised industry.

The questions and hypotheses are easy to enumerate, however, but not so easy to answer. The economist studying public enterprise may feel justified in confining his attention to the final decisions and to their consequences; both are matters which lie comparatively in the open. The difficulty for the political scientist studying public enterprise with an eye to processes of influence and decision-*making* is to locate the evidence. This is why we shall also have to say something about the methods applied.

In a case such as that of the BSC, the obvious choice of method would seem to be, first, to single out controversial or otherwise interesting decisions, then to investigate them in the archives of the participating agencies and, finally, to round off the investigation by interviewing some of the individuals involved. Unfortunately the

Introduction

archives required for the present study are not open to the public.[14] Hence the main sources of information for this investigation (apart, of course, from studies already published on the subject) were (1) all reports, White Papers etc. and, as far as attainable, unofficial papers and documents; and (2) what individuals involved in the steel business told me. Indeed, many of the findings of the present study rest very largely on interviews.

Three groups of persons were approached for interviews: leading members of the Corporation, senior government officials dealing with British Steel, and private industrialists (steelmen and steel consumers). The first two groups presented no problem of selection: all BSC board members, plus some executives and an ex-chairman were written to (Ian MacGregor, chairman at the time of the investigation, was not available). A majority, twelve in all, agreed to meet me and patiently answered a host of questions; some were interviewed several times. The same applies to some of the government officials, of whom the Under Secretaries and Assistant Secretaries dealing with iron and steel both in the Department of Industry and in the Treasury were questioned. The effects of job rotation in the British Civil Service explains why those interviews ultimately totalled eight. Where the private-sector steelmen were concerned, the British Independent Steel Producers' Association (BISPA) helped to select suitable interviewees by naming, from their members' list, those steel managers who had either particularly close connections with the corporation or particularly pronounced views against state-owned steel. Of the twelve members thus selected, ten agreed to being interviewed; of these, I was able finally to meet nine, as well as two BISPA representatives. As for selecting steel consumers, the Confederation of British Industry (CBI) was unable to help. The Steel Consumers' Council (BRISCC) furnished me with a list of its member firms (which was unfortunately a short one). Of these, only the management of GKN agreed to answer my questions. Thus I was able to arrange a total of thirty-three interviews — twelve at BSC, eight in Whitehall and thirteen in the private sector (including GKN and BRISCC). To round off the picture, I was able to talk with some individuals from outside the steel industry — in the NICG, at the Ashorne Hill Management Training

---

14. It should be noted that the perusal of archive materials such as letters, memos and minutes of proceedings is frequently less rewarding than expected; the FBI/CBI papers, for instance, now open to the public in the Modern Records Centre, University of Warwick, reveal very little about the interests leading to and the conflicts arising from the inclusion of the nationalised industries into the CBI membership.

Introduction

College, in the NCB and at the Department of Energy.

The conversations at those meetings were guided by an open questionnaire, in order to guarantee a reasonable degree of comparability. For the three different groups of addressees questionnaires were different, but related to each other in such a way that each question put to one group concerning its relations to the other had as its counterpart a question put to that other group; by this means it was hoped to achieve comparability of answers not only within the groups, but between groups as well.

Relying to such a large extent on what people *tell* you raises certain dangers which must not be overlooked. The first of these, that people do not know what they are talking about, did not apply in this case. The second danger, of getting biased views, ought to be balanced out by an advantage — the opportunity of contrasting the biases of one group with those of the other. Yet with quite a range of questions in this study personal, subjective and 'biased' answers are exactly what was desired: to find out about processes of influence (such as whether A feels dominated by B) and, even more, about people's perception of their own role, subjective views are needed; impartial and detached answers, in this case, would arouse suspicions that something is being hidden. A third danger is that answers will vary with the overall situation at the time of the interview. Asking people about their inter-personal relationships in times of abounding problems will inevitably lead to an overstressing of conflicts and difficulties. In the context of the present study this holds true in particular for the group of private steelmen. Although the danger of overstressed problems should be borne in mind, it should not be exaggerated. The conflicts mentioned in hard times will as a rule be those which have been latent before, glossed over in good times or hidden behind a veil of outward harmony.

The first part of the book attempts to determine theoretically the core questions of the meaning of nationalisation and of the interdependence of political guidance, public control and efficiency in public enterprise. The second part will give a short survey of the British system of nationalised industries, highlighting its general features and most obvious drawbacks. The third and main part will deal with the unique situation and specific problems of British Steel — a public corporation between the state and the private sector. This part will present the results of the interviews described before. Finally, after a summary of the findings, the last chapter will return to the question of what benefits might arise from public enterprise in a private-capitalist environment.

I

The Benefits of Public Enterprise

Why Nationalise? The Goals of Public Enterprise

1

To the naive observer it seems self-evident that, if there *are* enterprises or whole industries to be nationalised, there must be certain goals to nationalisation. After all, if an enterprise, once nationalised, is to behave exactly as it did before, then nationalisation is meaningless, apart, of course, from certain fiscal effects. 'Simply to behave commercially', as public enterprise managers like to describe their task, hardly seems to justify state ownership. Equally, economists trying to define the specific notion of 'public enterprise' tend to concentrate upon outlining the essential *differences* between public and private enterprise, which they detect in the difference of goals. Even authors who define public enterprise primarily by formal criteria, such as ownership and statutory rights of intervention,[1] usually end up by naming the public agencies' 'power of direction' (Jarass)[2] — the collectively, politically found goals (Blankart) — as the crucial criterion.

In Germany there is an influential school of economists who defend public enterprise under the banner of *Gemeinwirtschaft*. They believe that public enterprises must be judged from what they contribute to the 'commonweal'; that their raison d'être lies in their fulfilment of 'public tasks'. Public enterprises, in the words of Gerhard Weisser, are 'enterprises whose institutionally established meaning is *directly* to serve public purposes'.[3] This instrumentalist view of public enterprise, which at-

---

1. See Charles Beat Blankart, op. cit., pp. 1–9; Hans D. Jarass, 'Der staatliche Einfluß auf die öffentlichen Unternehmen in Frankreich', in *Archiv des öffentlichen Rechts*, 106/3, pp. 407ff.; from the legal point of view Karl Wenger, *Die öffentliche Unternehmung*, Vienna/New York, 1969, Part II.
2. This is the definition used by the Centre Européen de l'Entreprise Publique (CEEP) as well; see CEEP (ed.), *Les Entreprises Publiques dans la Communauté Européenne*, Paris, 1967, p. 575.
3. Gerhard Weisser, *Gemeinwirtschaftlichkeit bei Einzelwirtschaften*, Schriftenreihe Gemeinwirtschaft Nr. 11, Frankfurt a.M., 1974, p. 13. The school of *Gemeinwirtschaft* has a long tradition in Germany, starting with the *Katheder-Sozialisten*. It was of particular importance during the Weimar Republic when the notion of *Gemeinwirtschaft* was coupled with ideas of national economic planning (W. v. Moellendorff)

15

tempts to bind it closely to public policy, has been criticised because of its inability to enumerate the specific public tasks which are to distinguish the public enterprise from other types of enterprise. Indeed most catalogues of 'genuine' public tasks hardly make convincing reading, and appear the more arbitrary the more general they are. Nor do they lose their arbitrariness by the specification that public tasks are usually those not, or not sufficiently, fulfilled by private enterprise; after all, the contents of the tasks fulfilled by private or public enterprise will vary with time and from society to society.

There are two ways of solving the problem of how to define the specific goals of public enterprise. One is to go back to the old tradition of *Gemeinwirtschaft*, which links it closely to the broader concept of democratic socialism. The alternative is to develop another, equally comprehensive concept which allots to public enterprise its rightful and legitimate place within it. Only such a concept is able to provide a rigorous criterion with which to determine and measure the *Gemeinwirtschaftlichkeit* of an enterprise and allows us to escape the vicious circle of defining the activities of public enterprises, whatever they may be, as *gemeinwirtschaftlich*, since they are, *per definitionem*, said to contribute to the commonweal. Unfortunately, for such concepts to be of practical relevance, they require a broad consensus, a prerequisite which, in its turn, brings forth anew the dangers of overgenerality and arbitrariness which have been criticised above. The only other solution to the problem — pragmatic, if theoretically not quite as satisfactory as it may be — is to concentrate *not* on the *contents* of the specific goals of public enterprise but on the *process* by which they have been arrived at. Here the assumption is that they are not prescribed quasi-automatically by market forces but that they are decided upon in a political process, under the dominant influence of public agencies. Obviously the task of defining their specific public goals cannot be left to the leaders of public enterprises themselves. Such a definition, undertaken necessarily from a microeconomic point of view, would contradict the notion of 'public interest' as a macro-economic, or societal, category.[4]

— which in the early days of the Republic were put into practice (e.g., in the organisation of the coal mining and the potash industry) — and with the idea of economic democracy (F. Naphtali). Only after the Second World War was *Gemeinwirtschaft* stripped of its macroeconomic context and reduced simply to denote a certain type of enterprise. This isolation from broader concepts of *Gemeinwohl* explains the arbitrariness of the various catalogues of public tasks ascribed to this type of enterprise.

4. See Eberhard Witte and Jürgen Hauschildt, *Die öffentliche Unternehmung im Interes-*

Accordingly, whatever the problems of specification, the notion of politically found goals used here does imply that they are bound *somehow* to the interests of society as a whole. So we propose to insist that the benefit of public enterprise, and its crucial distinction from private enterprise, should lie in its directly contributing 'to the objectives of the society as a whole, *beyond* those factors that contribute ... to the profitability of the enterprise'.[5] Interestingly enough, this is just what economists with a more conservative market-orientated point of view insist upon as well. They argue that (1) it depends on their fulfilment of public tasks whether public enterprises essentially differ from private enterprise; that (2) without such a 'public commission' they are just like ordinary private enterprises; and that (3) in a private capitalist and market-orientated economy such pseudo-public enterprises ought to be privatised.[6] Hence, from the theoretical point of view, there is agreement that, unless it is bound by politically determined goals, public enterprise is meaningless. This agreement extends to naming the 'inherent antagonism between political and economic goal realisation'[7] as being an essential feature of public enterprise; but it stops where the possible contents of those political goals are involved. Concepts concerning the latter range from an enumeration of specific aspects of the common good to a purely formal definition, i.e., to the statement that the public purpose of public enterprises can be served by their mere existence and their behaving 'as an enterprise' and that, once they are founded, no additional specification of public purposes is required.[8]

Indeed, possible objectives of nationalisation and, hence, possible goals of public enterprise vary widely. They can be listed under various headings.

Socialism. Public enterprises are to be established in order to help bring about the step-by-step transformation of capitalist society.

Planning. Public enterprises are to be established 'on the commanding heights of the economy' in order to further control of basic industries or to allow strategic investment control and generally make

---

senkonflikt, Berlin, 1966, p. 25.
5. William G. Shepherd et al., *Public Enterprise: Economic Analysis of Theory and Practice*, Lexington (Mass.), 1976, p. 173.
6. See Peter Eichhorn et al., 'Probleme der Eigenwirtschaftlichkeit öffentlicher Unternehmen', in *Politische Vierteljahresschrift*, Sonderheft 8/1977, *Politik und Wirtschaft*, Opladen, 1977, p. 67; Karl Oettle, *Grundfragen öffentlicher Betriebe*, I, Baden-Baden, 1976, pp. 57ff. Similarly William G. Shepherd et al., op. cit. p. xiv.
7. Jürgen Backhaus, *Öffentliche Unternehmen*, Frankfurt a.M., 1977, p. 402.
8. Ibid., p. 87.

the steering of the economic process more successful.

Structural policy. Public enterprise is to be used either as a means of economic development, i.e., to further new and coming industries; or as a means of rationalisation and 'clearing up' in declining industries; or, more generally, as a means of furthering coordination and cooperation in certain industries.

Social policy. Public enterprises are used as a tool of redistribution, or to counteract unemployment, or as models of industrial democracy; by dint of the supply of 'public utilities' they may further correct social inadequacies.

Anti-monopoly policy. Pronounced adherents of the free-market economy point out the use of public enterprise in counterbalancing oligopolistic tendencies in important markets.

Defence. Public enterprise is a useful device where interests of national security and strategic interests are at stake (especially, as happened more than once in France, when multinational concerns threaten to take over strategically important firms).

Service for private enterprise. Public enterprise is to be used to provide the private sector of the national economy with the infrastructure it needs, with the basic utilities, with cheap raw materials etc.; this sees public enterprises as agents of (private sector) economic development in the widest sense.

Adjustment of market failure. This is the widest category and can mean very different things:
— public enterprise is to be used as repairing agent of the external costs resulting from private sector market processes;
— public enterprises will provide the 'public goods' not provided by private enterprise;
— public enterprise is to be used to overcome private enterprise rivalries and/or to soften the social impact of seemingly necessary processes of rationalisation or restructuring of whole industries;
— public enterprise will generally be used as a sort of fire-brigade when nationally important concerns threaten to go bankrupt (in which case, quite frequently, such enterprises are sold back to the private sector after their recovery).

Fiscal goals. Public enterprise is to be used to further redistribution between the public and the private sphere, or to make up for budgetary losses incurred elsewhere.

It seems obvious that, according to the different types of objectives set for public enterprise, a different behaviour on their part and different types of control on the part of their public owners are to be expected. The latter will vary quite widely, depending on whether

public enterprise is supposed
— to alter the economic system as a whole, or
— to complement the private enterprise economy, to help its results approach Pareto-optimum and to improve its efficiency, or
— to play the role of the fire-brigade (arriving at the last minute to prevent complete disaster), or merely
— to contribute to the exchequer.

In the first place, public control and public accountability depend upon the mere existence of identifiable objectives, against which the performance of public enterprise can be assessed. Without such goals not only nationalisation, but the whole concept of public accountability is meaningless. Secondly, public control will be the better feasible the more it has to deal with political goals, as the criteria for appraisal as well as the relevant data lie comparatively in the open in this case. On the other hand, the more intertwined the political and the economic objectives of the public enterprise are, the more difficult it will be to assess both aspects of goal realisation, because deficiencies with regard to one aspect can be explained away by necessities arising from trying to achieve satisfying results with regard to the other.

Thirdly, the concept of public accountability and ministerial control becomes dubious again when the objectives of public enterprise are defined, as is done by Jürgen Backhaus[9], by it being an efficient unit competing with others. The consequence of such a view (as Backhaus himself admits) is the negation of public control of single public enterprises. If they are to behave as normal enterprises, without any additional objectives, they ought to be controlled normally, i.e., by the capital market and not by public agencies. This, by the way, is the way the central government in West Germany deals with its shares in manufacturing industries. They are not used as policy-making tools in any way; their sole objective is to make a profit. Consequently they are not guided in any way by the Ministry of Industry but merely supervised by the Ministry of Finance; actual control lies 'with the market'.

In other Western countries, including the UK, trends point in the same direction. This is probably due to the fact that in the majority of cases nationalisation did *not* take place in accordance with any clear political concept, but more or less in response to varying practical needs of the day. Hence complaints are now heard everywhere about politicians being loath to define specific objectives for public enterprises, thus leaving open a wide field of action for their managements.

9. Ibid., pp. 44ff., 87.

Not always is such a lack of guidance seen as a deficiency, though. Ministers like to point out that 'managerial autonomy' is a necessary condition for reaching an economic efficiency in state enterprises that enables them to compete with their private competitors and/or to react flexibly to market changes; and that it would damage their efficiency and their proper role in the economy if they were to be set objectives other than those of private enterprise.[10]

Understandably, the necessity of managerial autonomy is stressed even more urgently by public enterprise managers themselves, who tend to see themselves as the permanent victims of erratic politicians. Wherever they are brought to reflect in public on their own tasks and policies, they invariably concentrate upon their kinship with private sector managers and their necessarily 'commercial' orientation.[11] Sir William Barlow summed up this attitude quite neatly when he stated: 'My own position is quite simply: we've got nationalised industries . . .; they have to be managed; the best method is to operate them as businesses at arm's length from Government and with minimum interference.' He followed this with the warning that it was not 'reasonable and logical for politicians to seek to exercise close control on the management of nationalised industries in order to achieve ends which suit their particular policies'.[12] This is a clear enough refutation of the idea that politicians should be called upon to define the tasks that state enterprises are to fulfil.

This explains why 'the search for elbow room has been a persistent characteristic in the behaviour of state-owned enterprises'[13]. In this they seem to have been remarkably successful throughout Western Europe, with the result that economists for some time now have been prone to talk about a 'convergence' of public and private enterprise, which they see as inevitable or even as a law of development. Indeed, the question has to be asked whether or not such a convergence is forced by necessity upon public enterprises acting in private-capitalist competitive markets. After all, how can they survive in this environment without being economically strong — that is, without trying to

10. As examples see Pietro Sette (Italy) and Oskar Grünwald (Austria) in GÖWG (ed.), *Entstaatlichung, Verstaatlichung, Status quo — Europa wohin?*, Baden-Baden, 1982, pp. 61ff., 29ff.; Erwin Stahl (Ministry of Research and Technology, FRG) in CEEP, *Die öffentliche Wirtschaft im Europa der Gemeinschaft—Bilanz und Ausblick*, op. cit. p. 25.
11. See practically all contributions by practitioners in CEEP, ibid.
12. Sir William Barlow, 'The Problems of Managing Nationalised Industries', lecture to the RIPA, London, 26 January 1981 (ms), p. 1.
13. Raymond Vernon, Introduction, in Raymond Vernon and Yair Aharoni, *State-Owned Enterprise in the Western Economies*, London, 1981, p. 13.

maximise profits and without adapting to the behaviour of their (private) competitors?[14] It is a plausible assumption that in the conflict of interests between politicians (as the 'owners' of state enterprise) and the managements of the latter (as actors in a private capitalist economy) the managements' interests will prevail.

It should be noted, however, that the tendency of managers to gain autonomy, and to develop utility functions of their own and goal systems distinct from those of the owners, is a feature not specific to public enterprise, but a more general feature of 'managerial capitalism' (Marris); still more generally, it is one of all large organisations. One might even argue that the phenomena of goal replacement, (internal) coalition formation etc. which the 'theory of the firm', inspired by the theory of organisations, has for some time now detected in private corporations, do not point in the direction of public enterprises adapting to private, but of private enterprises getting 'politicised' and adapting to public enterprises. This argument is reminiscent of socialist authors (such as R. Hilferding) who, some sixty years ago, visualised the advent of the joint-stock corporation as the first step towards socialism — an obviously erroneous assumption. The notion of convergence as a two-sided process of public and private enterprises gradually assimilating to each other (converging, perhaps, in A. A. Berle's concept of 'corporate responsibility'), or even of private firms adapting to public ones, might be equally erroneous. It overlooks (a) that managerial autonomy in the private sector is usually very firmly based on a strong identification of managers with the class of owners, and (b) that, whatever the degree of managerial autonomy, they still follow the essentially micro-economic rationale (whether profit-maximising or expansion-orientated) of actors in capitalist markets. By contrast, it has to be emphasised that the rationale of public enterprise, and its systematic difference *vis-à-vis* private enterprise, is to overcome just this micro-economic orientation and to be related to the macro-aspects of the commonweal. That is why the raison d'être of public enterprise is related to its fulfilment of politically defined tasks and why its benefits rest essentially on external political guidance. If both are, for systemic reasons, not to be achieved, then the whole concept of public enterprise becomes dubious. *The Times* once commented on this as follows: 'If what we want to do is to make the state undertakings resemble private corporations as closely as poss-

---

14. For this subject see especially Theo Thiemeyer, 'Privatwirtschaft und Gemeinwirtschaft', in Lothar F. Neumann (ed.), *Sozialforschung und soziale Demokratie*, Bonn, 1979, pp. 317ff.

ible, then the obvious way to do it is to turn them into private corporations . . . '.[15]

Hence the first conclusion of our theoretical deliberations on the subject is: If societies are to benefit from public enterprise, *qua* public enterprise, the trend towards (one-sided) convergence ought to be stopped. The question is, whether it is realistic to hope to do this.

---

15. *The Times*, 14 September 1968 (quoted in Friedmann, W. G. and J. F. Garner (eds.), *Government Enterprise. A Comparative Study*, New York, 1970, pp. 89ff.).

The Problem of Efficiency

2

If the benefits of public enterprise are to be judged only against the goals set for them, the same holds true for the question of their efficiency. This should be borne in mind when we come to deal with the widespread prejudice that public enterprise is inefficient — not accidentally but *per se*. This prejudice originates in the belief, firmly held by liberals, that the work of non-owners is inferior: 'How inferior is the quality of hired servants, compared with the ministrations of those personally interested in the work'.[1] Yet (what most of his followers seem to forget), when John Stuart Mill stated his dogma he did not think of 'bureaucrats' as leaders of state enterprise, but rather of managers of joint-stock companies which, after all, are private. And do not forget that Mill's statement is followed by the conclusion: 'And how indispensable, when hired service must be employed, is "the master's eye" to watch over it'. This points to the interdependence of efficiency and control — and not only in public enterprise.

The prejudice about the inherent inefficiency of state enterprises seems to be well-founded; do they not, after all, have access to a 'bottomless purse' (since no government would let its own enterprises go bust)? Do they not lack the strict 'discipline of the market'? Is not 'political interference' the direct opposite of commercial efficiency? Charles K. Rowley[2] tries to work out the notion of inevitable inefficiency logically and scientifically. His main argument is that public enterprise does not exist in a vacuum but is 'subjected to all the pressures of the political market place', with the result that its performance will not (as it ought to) be determined 'by the calculus of welfare economics'. By necessity, governments 'will tend to retain the closest grip of all upon those areas of public enterprise activity which are most sensitive to voter preferences, viz. the price and capital

---

1. John Stuart Mill, *Principles of Political Economy*, London, 1865, p. 86.
2. In his book, *Steel and Public Policy*, London, 1971, pp. 268ff.

formation decisions'; and where the voter preferences collide with the 'marginal rule' (which ought to be obeyed in those decisions), 'the state will not hesitate to intervene to ensure that voter preferences are observed, even at very considerable costs in terms of sacrificed social welfare'. This reasoning does, in fact, imply that it is impossible to run a state enterprise efficiently in a democracy.

Of course there is a certain force in Rowley's argument: the 'exigencies of the political market' are certainly a factor not to be underestimated. But there are other factors to be taken into account before the question of 'inevitable inefficiency' can be decided. Thus the efficiency problem is distorted by the threefold handicap under which most public enterprises (and nationalised industries especially) are labouring. The first handicap follows from the fact that, as a rule, enterprises/industries become nationalised only when they are declining or even threatened by bankruptcy — that is when, in private ownership, they would be considered as beyond being restructured and rescued. Not only in Britain there exists a 'philosophy. . .that the State may own and operate industries which are unprofitable and declining. . .but that it may not be left in undisturbed possession of those which are new, expanding, and profitable'.[3] This 'philosophy', which William A. Robson once characterised as 'a perverse and malign conception of public enterprise,[4] means that it is primarily the losses that are being nationalised.[5] For private industry, having shed the declining and retaining the prospering industries, it is then easy to point at the 'inefficiency' of the public sector.

A second handicap results from the way in which the former owners are paid compensation for handing over their (loss-making) assets to the public. It seems to be a typical feature of nationalisation in Western economies that such assets are overvalued, a fact which can be explained by a strong urge on the part of the nationalisers that a measure conforming so little with the prevailing economic ideology as nationalisation needs overlegitimation. The private entrepreneurs are thus over-compensated for the damage done to the private enterprise system. It is consequently very hard for public enterprises thus founded ever to get 'out of the red'. The great debt incurred at the

3. William A. Robson, *Nationalized Industry and Public Ownership*, 2nd ed., London, 1962, p. xxx.
4. Ibid.
5. An extreme example for this policy is the West German Ruhrkohle AG for which the socialising of the losses is the only maxim; should the RAG make a profit, this would be distributed between the *Altgesellschaften*, as the former pit-owners. See Peter Schaaf, *Ruhrbergbau und Sozialdemokratie*, Marburg, 1978.

time of their birth must always distort their balance-sheets, to say nothing of the high annual interest rates they are forced to pay.

The third handicap seems to be as prevalent as the other two: most public enterprises feel obliged, even without overt government pressure, to support the private sector by charging low prices, 'buying British' and so on. Although the Nationalisation Acts sometimes lay down various other 'social obligations' which do not always have much of an impact upon policies, this particular obligation is usually taken seriously; otherwise it would be enforced (as has frequently been demonstrated) by government intervention. This intervention is probably due to the same urge for overlegitimation which has been mentioned before.

In the face of all these handicaps, it is rather surprising that some of the existing public enterprises/nationalised industries have done remarkably well over the years; most of them are not nearly as inefficient as is made out by their critics. For the UK, where complaints about the loss-making state industries seem to be particularly bitter, the studies by William G. Shepherd (1965), Richard Pryke (1971) and even the famous NEDO study of 1976 have demonstrated this. In his very thorough early investigation Pryke established that in the decade from 1958 to 1968, which he called the 'productivity decade', productivity in the nationalised industries rose by about 5.3 per cent annually, compared with a mere 3.7 per cent in private manufacturing industries; there was only one nationalised industry where productivity gains lay below the level of those in the private sector; and the highest productivity gains in the private sector — 6.9 per cent for the chemical industry — were topped by an 8.0 per cent in the nationalised electricity industry and an 8.9 per cent in the nationalised air corporations.[6] Pryke could refute the charges of heavy losses and misallocation in the nationalised industries, and summarised his findings as follows:

> 'After reviewing the evidence the conclusion seems irresistible that the technical efficiency of the public enterprise sector has been rising more rapidly than that of the private sector, and that this must in part have been due to the way in which it is organised and managed. . . . Because of their heavy interest payments the nationalised industries often appear to be making losses when, if they were financed on an equity basis like private firms, they would be shown to be profitable.'[7]

6. Richard Pryke, *Public Enterprise in Practice*, London, 1971, pp. 103ff.
7. Ibid., pp. 436f.

In his recent book, Pryke draws a much more negative picture of the nationalised industries.[8] However, in the last decade, indicators of economic success saw a downturn for the private sector as well, and no less drastically so — not only in the UK; furthermore, nationalised industries had been used by governments to make amends for some of the more obvious failures of (private sector) economic development, by keeping plants open in otherwise depressed areas. Even so, in 1976 NEDO was still able to report that, albeit figures looked much worse than in the 1960s, only the National Coal Board and British Rail made substantial losses; for all the other nationalised industries in the years between 1969 and 1974, interest and tax payments and dividends to the Exchequer still exceeded the revenue subsidies and capital write-offs they had been granted.[9] In the early 1980s, the NCB, British Rail, the BSC and British Shipbuilders were said to be the real loss-makers. In 1983, British Rail at least, was out of the red again, having made an overall profit of £8m and a profit of £62m on its railway operations (while receiving government subsidies of £856m to run uneconomic lines which the government wants to be kept open).[10]

Shepherd could refute the reproach of the (allegedly inevitable) tendency of misallocation and over-expansion in nationalised industries;[11] his investigation, though, was restricted to the fuel industries. However, the most interesting study in this respect is that of Jonathan Aylen, in which he proves the enormous progress, by international comparison, which the BSC, this seemingly 'black sheep' of public enterprise, has made with regard to productivity and modernisation. Whereas under private ownership, Aylen infers, the British steel industry and its investment policies were 'technically conservative', it required nationalisation for it to reach the technological standard set by its international competitors.[12] It seems, therefore, that the thesis of the inevitable inefficiency of public enterprise has to be modified.

Sometimes the latter thesis is based on another argument, i.e., that it is necessarily 'soft' management control which characterises public enterprise. As John B. Heath argues, the 'dilution of business with politics suggests that the control system for achieving positive busi-

---

8. *The Nationalised Industries*, op. cit.
9. NEDO, *A Study of UK Nationalised Industries, Appendix Volume*, op. cit., p. 74.
10. See *The Economist*, 21 April 1984, p. 25.
11. William G. Shepherd, *Economic Performance under Public Ownership*, New Haven/London, 1965.
12. Jonathan Aylen, 'Innovation in the British Steel Industry', in Keith Pavitt (ed.), *Technical Innovation and British Economic Performance*, London/Basingstoke, 1980, pp. 200–34.

ness performance is likely to be relatively soft, compared with the private sector. No chairman is going to be penalised for failure to reach his financial target when politics have intervened . . .'.[13] The mixture of business and politics would result in a complexity making it 'difficult to devise fair rewards for good performance', and where incentive schemes for the achievement of targets are lacking, efficiency must suffer. Another argument which reaches the same conclusion rests on the assumption that in the case of public enterprise 'major decisions are typically made at a political level', which leaves only marginal and routine decisions for the management.[14] Whereas this also points in the direction of 'lacking incentives', Raiffa goes on to argue that the responsibility of the 'political level' furthermore leads to (1) a very specific kind of dependence of the manager: his performance will be 'judged largely by his ability to stay out of trouble', i.e., his policies must not do 'any discernible harm to any identifiable group' relevant at that level; and (2) to a diffuse set of objectives, since they will tend to be the result of conflict-minimising processes of compromise. As a consequence of (1) the management will be conservative and avoid risks, while (2) will lower its efficiency — 'a multiplicity of vague objectives serves to protect the inefficient'.[15]

Now it is the assumption of 'major decisions' being made by politicians which must be doubted for the majority of cases when it comes to the practice of public enterprise; following Raiffa's arguing, objectives set on the political level would not do much damage, anyway, if they were precise, clear and unambiguous. On the other hand, those authors mentioned above, who demonstrated that public enterprise was much less inefficient than had been suspected, explicitly led back their positive findings to good management: industries nationalised (at least partly) because of their inefficiency under private ownership obviously profited from the ensuing 'managerial shake-up and clear-out'; their successes with respect to rationalisation and modernisation are seen 'not just as a question of managerial economies of scale, but also as a result of the Corporation's *management ethos*.[16]

Richard Pryke mentions a specific reason why management performance was so satisfactory: permanent public scrutiny was 'a signifi-

---

13. John B. Heath, *Management in Nationalised Industries*, op. cit., p. 9.
14. Howard Raiffa, in Vernon and Aharoni (eds.), *State-Owned Enterprise in the Western Economies*, op. cit., p. 55.
15. Ibid., p. 57.
16. Richard Pryke, *Public Enterprise in Practice*, op. cit., p. 446; Jonathan Aylen, 'Innovation in the British Steel Industry', p. 202.

cant contribution towards efficiency'.[17] Most authors, however, and even more so public enterprise managers themselves, maintain just the opposite. There is a widespread belief that public sector managers, if left to themselves, would act in a way to guarantee economic efficiency and social welfare, but that ministerial control and other government interference perpetually intervene to stop them doing so. Government influence, parliamentary (and other) scrutiny, the necessity of constantly bargaining with politicians and/or civil servants — so the complaints run — were the main reason for public sector inefficiency. They implied (1) delays where it was important to react quickly to market developments; (2) the obligation to follow short-term and frequently changing political instead of purely commercial guidelines; and hence (3) deviations from economically optimising strategies. All this — as Pryke admits in his second book on the subject — had a 'demoralising' effect on public managements.[18]

The flaw in such arguments is that two different things are being conflated: government intervention in previously agreed policies of public enterprises, on the one hand, and *ex ante* political guidance and *ex post* public accountability (both of which are included under the heading 'ministerial control'), on the other. Whereas complaints about short-term political intervention (or interference with day-to-day management, as it is called in Britain) are understandable, as it can in fact damage nationalised industries' performance, complaints about political guidance and control (in so far as it is their existence, rather than their absence, which is criticised!) are usually much less well-founded. The object of ministerial control is, after all, to ensure the efficiency of public enterprises: to make sure that they reach their political objectives as well as their financial targets; it is to act (with respect to the latter) as a substitute for the discipline of the market. Where it works, it should make itself felt as such a discipline and therefore should not be judged (as Pryke rebukes the SCNI for doing) from the point of view of whether the enterpises' chairman were 'happy' with it.[19] There is a close connection between control and efficiency (always assuming that the control systems work): the less ambiguous the political guidance, the closer the scrutiny, the better the methods of joint investment appraisal etc., the more efficient public enterprises will be.

As may be seen from what has been said above, the debate about the

17. Pryke, *Public Enterprise in Practice*, op. cit. p. 450.
18. Richard Pryke, *The Nationalised Industries*, op. cit. p. 262.
19. Pryke, *Public Enterprise in Practice*, op. cit. p. 457.

The Problem of Efficiency

efficiency or inefficiency of public enterprise suffers from some serious misconceptions. The first of these is that there is one, and only one, notion of 'efficiency', and that this can be clearly defined, is objectively identifiable and scientifically measurable. In fact there is no such thing; those who accuse the nationalised industries of inefficiency and those who defend their efficiency usually have quite different objects in view. Some deal with 'the marginal problems of allocational efficiency' (living in the 'fine-tuned world of reducing departures from Pareto-optimality'),[20] others have a broader notion of macroeconomic or social efficiency; others, again, simply confuse notions of efficiency and profitability. But these two notions are clearly distinct: an enterprise can be so profitable as to be able to 'afford' inefficiency, while some public enterprises which are very efficient will never be profitable because they will never be fully paid for their services.

Obviously private and public sector efficiency comparisons[21] based on a concept of efficiency-as-profitability will lead to even more massive distortions than those mentioned earlier in this chapter. The narrow microeconomic notion of commercial efficiency, however, seems to be as inadequate when it comes to judging public enterprise performance; unfortunately it is just this concept that is used by most of the critics of the British nationalised industries, including the SCNI. It does not consider technological, innovative efficiency and long-term efficiency (which might call for short-term cross-subsidisation etc.); it does not consider the social costs arising from the achievement of commercial efficiency, nor the social obligations public enterprises ought to meet; and it does not account for the internalities and interdependencies where whole industries, instead of single firms, are nationalised.[22] Judging public enterprises by such a yardstick (which W. A. Robson once characterised as 'abysmally narrow and rigid')[23] implies that they are in no way different from private firms. As a consequence, if commercial efficiency is considered as the only real criterion of success for public enterprises, they had better be privatised.

20. William G. Shepherd et al., *Public Enterprise*, op. cit., p. xi.
21. The fact that most efficiency comparisons between private and public sector are not very reliable because of unclear notions of efficiency was demonstrated recently by Eberhard Hoffmann, *Zur Aussagefähigkeit von Vergleichen über die Erstellung kommunaler Leistungen durch Verwaltungen und private Unternehmen*, Speyerer Arbeitshefte 51, September 1983.
22. See Alec Nove, *Efficiency Criteria for Nationalised Industries*, London, 1973, pp. 73, 77ff.
23. W. A. Robson, 'Ministerial Control of the Nationalised Industries' (1969), reprinted in Friedmann and Garner (eds.), *Government Enterprise*, op. cit., p. 87.

This leads to a second misconception about the efficiency problem which is as fundamental as the first: that it is possible to measure a public enterprise's efficiency without knowing its specific objectives. The main mistake made by many critics of public enterprise is that they treat 'efficiency' as an end in itself; whereas the crucial criterion by which to judge a public enterprise's performance is whether it reaches its objectives — financial, economic *and* social — 'efficiently', i.e. with minimum costs. Since the essential feature of public enterprise is its public purpose, its performance and efficiency can be assessed properly only with respect to this criterion. This is why formalised concepts, such as 'break even' or 'make a profit taken one year with another', are inadequate yardsticks.

Leonard Tivey once remarked that it was impossible 'to answer questions about the general "success" of nationalization. There is no obvious criterion of success'.[24] He may be right in so far as a clear and consistent political guidance of nationalised industries is lacking; but theoretically such an 'obvious criterion' does exist: it is provided through their public purpose. Incidentally, strict adherence to the latter might offer the answer to the problem outlined by Rowley (see above, pp.23f.). A publicly agreed, consistent, long-term set of objectives specified for each public enterprise should be able to neutralise the 'exigencies of the political market' — provided, of course, politicians as well as managements felt bound by it.

Still, even where such clear and unambiguous sets of objectives do exist, there remain the problems of how to measure target fulfilment, and how efficiently it is achieved. In other words, what are still lacking are consensual efficiency criteria for the *Gemeinwirtschaft* (social economy). Though Alec Nove, for example, wrote a whole book on precisely this subject, he confined his work to criticising the prevailing use of conventional micro-economic efficiency criteria, instead of himself offering a new approach to operationalising specific efficiency criteria for nationalised industries. A way suggesting itself for arriving at such a new and comprehensive set of efficiency criteria is to elaborate on the more or less rudimentary systems of 'social accounting' which are either in existence (as in France, since 1977) or have been debated for some years now in several countries. As yet, these systems suffer from various shortcomings: the social audit, *bilan social* or *Sozialbilanz*, where it is put into practice (1) affects only a part of the firm's activities — usually those concerning employment or activities that can be classified as 'social'; (2) in most cases it is a mere

24. Leonard Tivey, *Nationalization in British Industry*, rev. ed., London, 1973, p. 73.

regrouping of figures which would appear in the 'normal' accounts anyway, it being left to the management to define which part of the firm's activities, and in which way, might be said to contribute to a rather nebulous 'social welfare'; (3) there is obviously no agreement on how to define social costs and social benefits, which figures/ actions/costs/damages to include under those headings or how to evaluate them and derive from them a total of social costs and benefits.[25] A move to solve these problems by developing a comprehensive system of 'social indicators' in those countries where the social audit has been under debate, seems to have foundered — not least because of the opposition of private business against having their social accounting put on a more objective basis. Yet such social indicators might prove to be the solution to the problem of how to judge the overall efficiency of a public enterprise.

There are three conclusions to be drawn from the points raised in this chapter: firstly, that as regards efficiency public enterprises do not get a fair deal when they are judged according to a narrow, microeconomic, commercial concept of 'efficiency'; secondly, that the efficiency concept needed adequately to assess their performance as a minimum ought to include the notion of *social* costs and benefits; and thirdly, that the efficiency problem cannot be tackled separately, without dealing with their objectives and the control they are subjected to at the same time.

---

25. See Klaus v. Wysocki, *Sozialbilanzen*, Stuttgart/New York, 1981; Wolf Fischer-Winkelmann, *Gesellschaftsorientierte Unternehmensrechnung*, München, 1980; James S. Shulman and Jeffrey Gale, 'Laying the Groundwork for Social Accounting', in *Financial Executive*, March 1972, pp. 38–42.

The Problem of Control 3

The usual starting-point of theorists as well as of practitioners of public enterprise, when debating adequate manners and amounts of control, is the question of how best to balance whatever control system is envisaged with a modicum of managerial autonomy, how 'to achieve equilibrium between autonomy and control'.[1] The usual answer to this question is that in all Western economies practitioners struggle with this problem with but indifferent success; that the 'proper balance' has as yet proved elusive.[2] Before tackling such a problem, however, one should be perfectly clear about what is meant by 'control', and for which purposes it is proposed to apply it. This in turn depends on what purposes the public enterprise itself is to serve: if it is to achieve nothing but profitability other types of control will be required than if it is to meet specific social obligations.

On a very general level two different notions of control can be distinguished (which might roughly be described as the Anglo-Saxon vs. the Continental): (1) *ex ante* control, in the sense of guidance or direction (goals are fixed and their implementation continually monitored); and (2) *ex post* control, in the sense of supervision (performance is checked after the event). The latter can be either goal-orientated or purely financial and thus in a narrow sense 'efficiency'-orientated, whereas *ex ante* control implies by definition that goals play a major role. Performance indicators which are under debate as a new control instrument in the UK would be an example for goal-orientated *ex post* control (only they seem not to be easily operationalised).

For these three types of control (which other authors name as 'strategic', 'tactical' and 'operational' control)[3] various institutional devices are at hand, albeit differently suited to them. (1) The most

---

1. Friedmann and Garner (eds.), *Government Enterprise*, op. cit., p. 123.
2. See, e.g., ibid., p. 335.
3. See Dieter Brümmerhoff and Heimfried Wolff, 'Aufgabe und Möglichkeit einer Erfolgskontrolle der staatlichen Aktivität', in *Zeitschrift für die Gesamte Staatswissenschaft*, vol. 130, 1974, pp. 477ff.

far-reaching variety would be that of state agencies being directly and continually involved in the process of leading the enterprise/industry, by dint of government officials sitting on the board. (2) Equally continual influence might be achieved, in a two-tier system, by government representatives sitting on the supervisory board, or with the creation of special controlling agencies, such as the *Contrôleur d'Etat* in France. (3) Quite a different way of control is that of binding major management decisions to government approval, or of establishing a responsible minister with the right of veto. (4) Similarly, managements can be bound by special contracts; here again France, with its system of *Contrats d'Entreprises*, may serve as an example. In a more formalised way, managements can be confronted with specific sets of targets which have to be met within fixed time-spans. (5) Governments may restrict themselves to issuing general directives and check periodically as to whether these have been followed. (6) Governments may restrict themselves even further to appointing the personnel whom they believe able to guarantee the 'right' management policies without special guidance; this was obviously Herbert Morrison's ideal. (7) Control can be delegated to a state holding (the Italian model) which itself is subject to more or less detailed ministerial supervision. (8) Financial control especially can be delegated to authorities separate from government, like the *Corte dei Conti*, the *Cour des Comptes*, or the *Bundesrechnungshof*. (9) Of course, there is always the possibility of trying to maintain control via 'backstairs pressures', through informal channels. (10) Finally, even public enterprise can be subjected to market control, particularly to control through the capital market. All of these institutional control systems (whose enumeration here is certainly not complete)[4] promise different degrees of effectiveness, pose different problems and tend to degenerate in different ways. To start with the last point: to rely solely on the capital market may have an effect on the profitability of public enterprises; but with regard to their achievement of public goals such reliance will be not only ineffective, but even counter-productive; it will certainly provide managements with strong arguments against 'meddling politicians'. Financial 'efficiency' controls by means of special courts usually have the drawback of coming much too late, of providing by necessity more or less random checks (the famous 'candle-ends' method) and of

---

4. What has not been mentioned, for instance, is *wirtschaftliche Mitbestimmung* (the German version of industrial democracy) which F. Naphtali and other theorists of *Gemeinwirtschaft* envisaged as part of a control system extending over *private* enterprise as well. As this variety means control with a specific interest in view, and is (usually) not identical with *public* control, it has not been dealt with here.

scrutinising only a small part of entrepreneurial activity; in all countries where such systems are applied they have proved to be rather ineffective.[5] This is particularly true of West Germany where the *Bundesrechnungshof* merely scrutinises the activities of the central authority with regard to its enterprises, i.e. the state's actions as a shareholder, but not the activities of the enterprises themselves.[6] Equally ineffective is the Morrisonian method of restricting control to the appointment of individuals who are then left 'free to manage'; this illusory method is surpassed only by the idealistic view some German theorists have of *Gemeinwirtschaft*, earnestly believing that managers in *gemeinwirtschaftlichen Unternehmen* will not need any external guidance because they will obey the requirements of the 'commonweal' by ethos and free will.[7]

External guidance might be given through 'general government directives', if only these were not, by definition, too unspecific to provide any real check on managerial autonomy. By contrast, methods (3) and (4) can both be said to be effective in the sense that they do bind managements to the will of the government. However, the trouble with contracts or sets of targets is that they may promote a propensity for devising simple formulae on the part of the controllers and further inflexibility on the part of the managements. Neither is likely to enhance either social or economic efficiency. For such a control system to be practicable one needs targets that can be calculated and the realisation of which can be easily checked — if possible by non-experts; as a consequence, the stress will tend to be placed on indicators that can be looked up in balance-sheets and profit-and-loss accounts. The difficulty which has been described above in the context of 'social accounting', of finding comprehensive as well as practicable criteria for the measurement of performance against targets in respect of social costs and benefits (macroeconomic, structural/regional development, longer-term development of the industry itself, consumer needs and policy goals, such as redistribution and environment protection) will favour such 'abysmally narrow' concepts of efficiency as yardsticks of control, for which W. A. Robson rebukes the SCNI. At the same time, the conventional, microeconomic type of targets will not even guarantee economic efficiency. As Redwood and Hatch point out, 'even if the industries follow the pricing and investment

5. See Vernon and Aharoni (eds.), *State-Owned Enterprise in the Western Economies*, op. cit., pp. 145ff.
6. See Jürgen Backhaus, *Öffentliche Unternehmen*, op. cit., pp. 277f.
7. As an example see Achim von Loesch, *Die gemeinwirtschaftliche Unternehmung*, Cologne, 1977, p. 27.

guidelines, and meet their profit and cashflow targets, they may still be ineffective or inefficient . . . . They are heavily weighted towards trying to deter unproductive investment; they place far less emphasis on improving current operations and encouraging genuinely useful investment'.[8] Conservative, not innovative management strategies will be rewarded, to say nothing of the danger that rigid cash-flow targets (like the British EFL), so far from improving efficiency, might lead to rising prices.

The tendency recognisable behind the 'set of targets' type of control is the wish to keep politicians from 'meddling' by inventing processes which are largely self-operating, without the 'need for ministerial scrutiny except as a check on whether the formulae were being strictly applied'.[9] This tendency, albeit understandable, does not seem to be the obvious solution to the control problem. There remain the 'personal' types of control (1, 2, 3, 9 as well as 7) to be discussed. They imply different degrees of involvement and influence. Government representatives on supervisory boards are not involved in the decision-making process itself, hence they are less influential than representatives on boards in one-tier organisations; this is particularly true if representation is limited, as it is in Germany, where members of (federal) government are always in a minority position (whether the federal state is the majority shareholder or not).[10] Equally, the amount of ministerial influence might be debated where it is mediated through, for instance, state holdings. In the case of direct involvement actual influence will depend on the government officials' degree of expertise (the ambivalence of which will be discussed below) as well as on the strength of personalities. Assuming this influence to be sufficient for real *ex ante* control, however, these types of control pose two specific problems. The first is that the controllers will tend to be incorporated in the dealings of 'their' enterprise/industry in a way that makes them unfit for adapting the latter's interests to the wider aspects of economic/social development and, more specifically, for coordinating the policies of various public enterprises. In most Western economies such a lack of coordination is deeply felt; only very few

8. John Redwood and John Hatch, *Controlling Public Industries*, Oxford, 1982, p. 105.
9. W. A. Robson, 'Ministerial Control of the Nationalised Industries', l.c., p. 85.
10. H. J. Winkler shows, by reference to the Prussian state enterprises, that even where government (or Parliament) representatives are in a majority position, their influence is limited: (1) because of the structural disadvantage of supervisory boards in relation to the management; (2) because of the various interests which MPs and civil servants in the supervisory boards are representing; (3) because of their limited tenure of office and other 'checks and balances' operating on them. *Preußen als Unternehmer*, op. cit., pp. 39ff., 51ff., 63ff.).

countries have as yet made attempts to find institutional means of coordinating controls over state enterprises. If anything of that nature takes place at all, it is 'occasional and secret'.[11] The second problem, and one that is the source of much complaint, is that ministers have a propensity to override economic efficiency considerations in the interests of narrow party interests. Public enterprise managers would identify a third problem: that the control which binds major decisions to government approval inevitably leads to economically damaging delays.

Despite these problems, the only control system likely to guarantee that public enterprises live up to their public purpose is that of direct involvement, or, more precisely, one which allows for genuine political guidance. Most people will agree that such a control-cum-guidance system will be the more necessary the more 'political' the objectives of public enterprise and hence the more important its performance for government policy. But since we started from the assumption that the only justification for the existence of public enterprise lies in its politically determined goals, the notion of political guidance *on principle* holds for every public enterprise. The nature of those goals (whether they are of the reform or of the 'fire brigade' type, for instance), will then determine how detailed the guidance is or how far it is actualised in single decisions.

However, some important prerequisites have to be given to allow any political *ex ante* control system to achieve any sort of success. The first and major prerequisite is, of course, that governments must have clear and consistent concepts about the purpose and objectives of the enterprises they own; this implies that the objectives are specific enough to bind both managements and controllers and that they are made public to allow for public accountability of both managements and controllers. Although there may be difficulties in expressing political objectives in operational terms, since usually they cannot be condensed into simple formulae like financial targets, they will none the less make public control comparatively easy. This is because objectives as well as criteria for appraisal will be collectively agreed, lie in the open and be understood by the general public, whose judgement therefore will not be liable to be overruled by an economic expertise which only too frequently disguises economic interests.

Combined with this major requirement is the necessity of keeping political and financial objectives well apart, so as not to hinder the assessment of both aspects of goal realisation; otherwise they could be

---

11. Friedmann and Garner (eds.), *Government Enterprise*, op. cit., p. 329.

played off against each other, thus obscuring the enterprise's total performance. Financial objectives are not made superfluous by the existence of clear concepts about the public purpose of state enterprise; at the least, they will provide a check to the recklessness of politicians (exposed to the pressures of the political market) and to managerial ineffectiveness. Hence it seems reasonable to suggest a combination of political guidance, social indicators *and* sets of financial targets to optimise the control of public enterprise.

Another important qualification concerns the institutional requirements of public control which mainly refer to the 'exigencies of the political market', but also to the structure of government and to the notorious 'backstairs pressures'. If, for instance, the latter are not shut out, political guidance may soon get lost in blurred responsibilities. Equally, the uncontrolled influence of various interested parties may counteract ministerial control and condemn it to failure. If, on the other hand, the government structure is highly fragmented (either vertically, as in federal systems, or horizontally, with no coordination between ministries, as in clientelistic systems), political guidance will not come about; and the inevitable 'adversary politics' of political parties alternately in power, will make it a short-term, and therefore futile device. This last factor indicates that, beyond institutional arrangements, the success of ministerial control as well as of public enterprise will depend, to a considerable degree, on the existence of a broad consensus among the public as to the exact purpose of public enterprises.

Finally, the success of ministerial control will vary with the determination of ministers to have public enterprises comply with their political guidelines as well as with the actual power they possess over their managements. The trouble with the latter is that generally ministerial power over managements grows with their financial dependence. This leads us to the 'paradox of public enterprise';[12] it means that the fulfilment of public tasks can best be brought about in the case of financially dependent enterprises, i.e., those which do not have the resources to fulfil those tasks. If there is a way to overcome this paradox, again the only chance would seem to be that of direct involvement of the public authorities in the decision-making processes of the public enterprise concerned — provided they are determined enough to make the proper use of the respective institutional arrangement.

12. Eberhard Witte/Jürgen Hauschildt, *Die öffentliche Unternehmung im Interessenkonflikt*, op. cit., p. 69.

Yet, as mentioned before, direct involvement is in itself problematical. One major problem of public enterprise practice, as things stand, is the emancipation of the controllers, and/or their becoming 'house-trained' in the respective industries. The latter problem aroused attention in France, where the *Contrôleur d'Etat* is an institution with considerable powers, but with ill-defined functions and responsibilities. As D.M.G. Lévy put it: 'No one is charged with coordinating the instructions they receive, their activities are not supervised and are scarcely controlled at all'; his conclusion is that, in this specific institution, the 'control tends to substitute itself for the direction of the enterprise', without being itself subjected to control.[13] Control by ministers, who in France seem to have extensive statutory rights by comparison with their British colleagues, has likewise been subjected to criticism, though from a slightly different angle; here it is judged to be 'impossible to assess accurately the real, as distinct from the theoretical, extent of the powers because relations between the corporation and the competent minister are inevitably close and continuous; in many cases it may be that ministerial direction is not exercised openly, but behind closed doors, that it does not take the form of a directive but of mutual consultation . . . '.[14] So the question is that of who actually controls whom, after all.

Indeed, this seems to be the main problem with *ex ante* controls, and not only in France; government officials' involvement in the decision-making of public enterprises necessarily implies very close contacts, a mingling of controller and controlled which inevitably leads to a certain blurring of responsibilities and — not inevitably, but probably — to a certain alienation of controllers who may lose sight of the original object of control. Such alienation, furthermore, is one of the likely results of acquiring expertise which, on the one hand, is necessary for a proper understanding of what managers are talking about in order to be able to exercise control at all, but which on the other hand quite frequently goes hand-in-hand with internalising the group norms of the 'experts'[15] and with adapting to their ideas and interests. In short, the phenomenon of 'goal displacement', that seems

13. D. M. G. Levy, in Friedmann and Garner (eds.), *Government Enterprise*, op. cit., pp. 129f.
14. W. Friedmann, ibid., p. 326.
15. See Theo Thiemeyer, in GÖWG (ed.), *Kontrolle öffentlicher Unternehmen*, vol. I, Baden-Baden, 1980, p. 11. See for this, again, the experience of the Prussian state enterprises. *Landtag* members who sat on the supervisory boards of those enterprises, with the express object of controlling them, soon proved to be valuable lobbyists for the latter's interests in the *Landtag* (Winkler, *Preussen als Unternehmer*, op cit., p. 40).

to be so typical of the behaviour of large organisations, affects the behaviour of their controllers in the same way.

The obvious way of stopping these tendencies would be 'to control the controllers' — a task partly and until recently tackled by the SCNI in Britain, albeit with varying success. The problem, however, is a general one, and not specific to the control of public enterprise; as yet it has not been solved, either in the political system or in the economy. Economists dealing with joint-stock companies and their control, for instance, seem to have despaired of finding a way out of the situation where members of supervisory boards are either unable to check managerial autonomy because of their lack of expertise, or they are sufficiently expert to make common cause with managements and hence become unwilling to provide that check.

Thus, the question of how to control the controllers is closely connected with that of how to control the experts, which brings us to the second problem of public enterprise practice, that of the 'emancipation of managements'. While this is a feature not necessarily *specific* to public enterprise, but one that can be observed wherever ownership and management are separated, it needs to be reemphasised that it appears to be of greater and more *systematic* importance in public enterprise. A public enterprise's essence and *raison d'être* lies in its public purpose; with public sector managements emancipating themselves, it is this specific purpose which tends to get lost. In Germany such emancipation is clearly intentionally promoted, not only by managements but also by politicians, who thus pride themselves in having achieved a state of affairs between governments and their enterprises which is 'free of conflict'.[16] The West German central government even grants the managements of companies where it is the majority shareholder a degree of autonomy unheard of in those private joint-stock companies similarly dominated by a main shareholder. The theoretical justification of this strategy is advanced by economists, who generally postulate an incompatibility between entrepreneurial activity on the one hand and control, or mere supervision, on the other. To act in an entrepreneurial way, as Karl Oettle argues,[17] implies that managements are able to choose the objects of their activity freely and to react flexibly to competition and market development. Supervising them effectively (to say nothing of political guidance) would, by contrast, imply that important decisions were

16. Ernst Pieper (Ministry of Finance), in CEEP, *Gegenwärtige Probleme der öffentlichen Unternehmen in der Europäischen Gemeinschaft. Dokumentation. VII. Kongreß CEEP, 16.–19.6.1975 in London*, p. 118.
17. Karl Oettle, *Grundfragen öffentlicher Betriebe*, op. cit., pp. 59f.

left to the supervising government officials. This has the further implication that in some areas at least the managements could no longer make decisions in a way which could be classified as 'entrepreneurial'; this, in turn, would allow managements to explain away failures (whether rightly or wrongly), as due to their reduced freedom of entrepreneurial action. In other words, it would allow them to minimise their own responsibility. Again we are back at the 'blurring of responsibilities'. The conclusion to be drawn from this argument (albeit not one drawn by Oettle himself) is that, to evade the damaging effects of blurred responsibilities, public sector managements should be granted full autonomy.

Other authors (similar to theorists of the 'soulful corporation' in the private sector) justify the necessary managerial autonomy more emphatically by stating a basic identity of public and management interests;[18] it is derived from the assumption that, after all, the public purpose of the latter can be achieved only by entrepreneurial success, for otherwise they would not exist as *enterprises*. This rather naive supposition overlooks the mundane occurrence of interest clashes between managements and owners — and not only in public enterprise. It was this very fact that prompted John Stuart Mill, in the passage quoted above, to insist that, wherever 'hired servants' instead of owners led a firm, the strictest control over them was necessary. Yet while it is obvious from public enterprise practice that these enterprises, as much as any other, typically develop 'a strong and continuing set of interests'[19] neither necessarily nor automatically identical with that of their public owners, it is equally obvious that their managements are well able to evade such control, by dint of their superior expertise and information. This indeed appears to be the feature most characteristic of state enterprise all over Western economies. It is detrimental to the respective societies in more than one way: to begin with, the public purposes of public enterprise tend to be reached underoptimally; secondly, these enterprises, shielding themselves from government influence and, through state support, from competitors' influence, tend to act like 'profit-maximising monopolists'.[20]

The problem is more complex than appears at first sight. Naturally a certain amount of managerial autonomy is necessary, otherwise it would be futile to let public tasks be fulfilled by enterprises. It would

18. See Bruno Kropff in Peter Eichhorn (ed.), *Auftrag und Führung öffentlicher Unternehmen*, Berlin, 1977, pp. 85f.
19. William G. Shepherd et al., *Public Enterprise*, op. cit., p. 42.
20. Charles Beat Blankart, *Ökonomie der öffentlichen Unternehmen*, op. cit., p. 129.

seem that the necessary margin for 'entrepreneurial' action, as well as the necessary public control, were best guaranteed (1) by fixing specific and unambiguous objectives for each state enterprise and (2) by substituting 'supervision' for joint decision-making on major subjects, thus circumventing the problem described by Oettle. There are some snags, however, in what, on a theoretical level, suggests itself as the obvious solution. The first is still that of how to control the experts. 'Joint' decision-making will be more or less a sham, if managements are able to take advantage of their superior knowledge, either by talking the participating government representatives into compliance with their designs, or by withholding information at board meetings to achieve the decisions they want. Should the government representatives themselves have sufficient expertise to outmanoeuvre such tactics, this would constitute the second snag: that of controllers becoming 'house-trained', adapting to managements and hence forgetting that the state enterprise's *raison d'être* reaches beyond the mere pursuit of commercial or technological ends.

The theoretically as well as practically unsolved dilemma of how to prevent controllers from emancipating themselves from the original purpose of control, thus rendering public control impossible as well as evading public accountability, is related to a third snag which is of a more political nature: the lack of intent or willingness to control — especially at the top of the body politic where the more general directives of how to guide the public enterprise sector ought to be decided. This is another common feature of ministerial control of state enterprise in most Western countries, which seems to indicate that it is not accidental, but rather the result of constraints inherent in the political system: 'For the time that can be devoted to public enterprise affairs by busy politicians is inevitably strictly limited and the political incentives to do so are often slight'.[21] As long, at least, as the subject of public enterprise is not a major concern of public opinion, does not play any significant role in voter preferences and is not ascribed a strategic value in the overall programmes of political parties, the lack of intent to control will be hard to overcome. Incidentally, the most typical way in which this lack expresses — or rather conceals — itself is, again, that of the all-pervasive 'blurred responsibilities'.

Hence the final snag rests with the political market. Yet, contrary to Rowley's assumptions,[22] the main problem with regard to its 'exigencies' is less that of governments, reacting in accord with voter prefer-

---

21. Charles K. Rowley, *Steel and public policy*, op. cit., p. 270.
22. See above pp. 23ff.

ences, being pressured to interfere heavily and in the wrong way and the wrong places, but rather that of governmental inertia. To this may be added the problem of institutional and ideological fragmentation as well as of interest clashes. All three are apt to enhance an already existing tendency towards inertia and immobilism by suggesting strategies of conflict-avoidance, postponement and dubious compromise. Resulting from this is not only the danger of public sector managements being left 'free to manage', but equally that of leaving a wide twilight zone of informal and hidden clientelistic influences, mainly coming from the business community — to which the managers of state enterprise, feeling abandoned by the politicians, aspire in any case.

To conclude these theoretical considerations on the subject of the benefits of public enterprise: principally, from whichever angle one looks, one must always return to the crucial question of political guidance. Most problems of existing public enterprises, including that of efficiency, would be better tackled, if not solved, by the existence of, and adherence to, a clear, specific and publicly agreed set of goals. Without it, without such guidance public enterprises cannot be led out of the twilight they are in at present; certainly the same result will not be achieved by making them as similar to private enterprise as possible (whether that makes 'their chairmen happy' or not), for in this case their public enterprise status becomes superfluous. However, it is the political guidance itself, fraught with the weaknesses of the political system, which poses one set of problems as yet unsolved. The other set, equally unsolved, centres round the dilemma of how to control the experts — and how to control the controllers once they are experts themselves. Since economic expertise, in the private capitalist system, is concentrated in the private sector of the economy, this dilemma has a considerable bearing on the trend towards convergence discussed above. In other words, as long as this dilemma cannot be solved in such a way as to regain autonomy, not for managements but for the political authorities who are bound to control, there seems to be no reasonable hope of halting that trend, and state enterprises will continue to gravitate towards their private-capitalist counterparts, thus perpetually providing the argument for their own privatisation.

The problems of the British steel industry discussed below may serve as an example of such mechanisms at work, and show what their results are, regardless of all the good intentions of all the individuals involved in the control of a major public enterprise.

II

Nationalised Industries in Britain

The History of Nationalisation

4

To a considerable degree, the specific problems faced by public enterprises in any given country are due to the reasons for, and the way in which they were nationalised. Where, for example, a consistent political concept was lacking at their birth it seems unreasonable to expect one when they mature.

In Britain, as in most other Western countries, no 'socialisation', in the true, political meaning of the term, has ever taken place, and in only a few cases was nationalisation prompted by political (let alone socialist) reasons at all. The workers' movement itself had taken a long time to reach any agreement on the subject of socialisation — and in fact there is disagreement still, opposition to it coming mainly from the unions. Instead it was from other quarters that, at the end of the nineteenth century, the impulse to nationalisation came: from the 'radicals', for example, who called for 'municipal socialism' as well as for the nationalisation of land and railways.[1] Later further impulses were to emanate from the consumers' movement, from guild socialists who aimed at workers' control, and from a conglomerate of socialist, 'technocratic' and even managerial circles who either believed in the necessity of national economic planning or who wished for more 'rational' and coordinated investment policies.[2]

These different forces eventually (and at least outwardly) concentrated around the Labour Party which, after all, had officially adopted the demand for public ownership in its programmes. Yet with respect to this demand its programmes restricted themselves to 'the barest minimum;'[3] furthermore they gave no answers to the crucial questions of how to implement nationalisation and what the future 'nationalised industries' should be like. In the 1930s this gap was filled by Herbert Morrison's concept of the 'public corporation' (see below),

1. See E. Eldon Barry, *Nationalisation in British Politics*, London, 1965, pp. 130ff.
2. See Leonard Tivey, *Nationalization in British Industry*, op. cit., pp. 19ff.
3. Barry, op. cit., p. 281.

45

which implied that the idea of nationalisation had been stripped of practically all 'socialist' meaning and content. So that by the time the Labour Party was able to put its programmes of 'socialisation' into practice these had been doubly minimalised: in scope as well as by the choice of the organisational formula. Even so, when the Labour Party came to power in 1945 there were no ready plans waiting to be implemented; even the nationalisation of the coal mines, which had been an official Party demand since 1919, existed as 'nothing but a crude scheme'.[4]

The first nationalisations to be undertaken in Britain had nothing to do with socialist policy, anyway, but were carried out for purely pragmatic reasons; the Labour Party was not even concerned with most of them: the Port of London Authority, for instance, was created in 1908 by the Liberals, the Central Electricity Board (1926) and BOAC (1939) by the Conservatives. Not only then but after 1945 as well, the initiative often came from the reports of government commissions who recommended radical measures for the industries in question since they were in need of fundamental reorganisation; such was the case with the Royal Commission on Transport in 1930, the Committee on Electricity Distribution in 1936, the Technical Advisory Committee on Coal Mining (Reid Report) and the Committee of Inquiry into the Gas Industry, both in 1945.[5] Hence the majority of the nationalisation acts passed by the Labour Government between 1945 and 1951 also came about 'in the main for practical reasons that bore only an incidental relationship to ideological principles'.[6]

The principal argument for nationalisation after the Second World War was the inefficiency of whichever industry was in question, which accounts for the almost total lack of antagonism aroused in the great majority of cases, even in the private sector. In other cases — like that of the former Imperial Airways, which was in fact flourishing, or, more recently, that of Aerospace — the argument of safeguarding 'national interests' explained wide and non-socialist support for what was (in terms of a private capitalist economy) so drastic a measure. Furthermore, most industries earmarked for nationalisation were already subject to far-reaching controls and/or regulations, so that nationalising them seemed to be not so great a step after all. A further reason for the general wide acceptance of nationalisation

---

4. R. Kelf-Cohen, *Twenty Years of Nationalisation*, London, 1969, p. 42.
5. See H. A. Clegg and T. E. Chester, *The Future of Nationalization*, Oxford, 1955, pp. 20f.
6. R. M. Punnett, *British Government and Politics*, 3rd ed., London, 1976, p. 346.

measures was the experience of the government-controlled war economy, where people had become used to the state playing a major part in the economy. Thus if ideological influences concerning nationalisation during this period are to be appraised, the prevalent ones were technocratic rather than socialist.

Most of the nationalisation bills proposed by the Labour government after 1945 therefore appeared in the Statute Book without much opposition. Among the more important of these were the Civil Aviation Act, in 1946, and the Nationalisation Acts — for coal in 1946, electricity and transport in 1947 and gas in 1948. Although the very question of the nationalisation of coal, advocated by the miners themselves since the middle of the nineteenth century, had been for decades 'a political football in Britain',[7] it no longer met with any opposition to the principle, but merely with criticism on points of detail. The only Nationalisation Act that provoked genuine controversy was that of the iron and steel industry (which will be discussed at length in Part III); consequently this industry was de-nationalised after the Conservatives had regained power in 1951 — and re-nationalised when Labour returned to office in the mid-1960s.

With this sole exception, nationalisation since the early 1950s has not really been a political issue, but 'increasingly a technical subject';[8] there seemed to exist a broad consensus that the basic industries, at least, should remain nationalised. Of course the Conservative manifesto of 1951 announced de-nationalisation measures; these, however, were much less far-reaching than had been hoped for by more radical party members and feared by their opponents. The measures were put into practice with a great deal of caution; only the steel industry (which in any case was nationalised on paper only) and the most profitable part of the transport industry, long-distance road haulage, were de-nationalised in 1953 (and in both cases the government experienced some difficulty in selling the shares).

So while there continued to be controversy over *further* nationalisation the existing nationalised industries, until very recently, on the whole were never threatened. A Labour government, had it stayed in office after 1951, might have embedded them in a planned economy, thus attaching a specific content to nationalisation as such. But, as has been stated above, neither in programme nor in practice was Labour very clear about this; and as, on the other hand, the heads of the nationalised industries very soon developed quite distinctive ideas of

7. Israel Berkovitch, *Coal on the Switchback*, London, 1977, p. 45.
8. David Coombes, *State Enterprise: Business or Politics?*, op. cit., p. 13.

their own about their proper role in the economy, it seems to be over-stretching the point when Michael Shanks concludes: 'The disappearance of the Labour government left the nationalised industries in limbo, survivors of a vanished world trying to adjust themselves to a new environment'.[9] From the beginning the Conservatives declared that their aim was 'to make public industries as similar to private firms as possible'[10] and hence in principle to leave them to themselves. Contrary to Shanks' belief this seems to have suited them, for they made irritated noises only when Conservative governments departed from official party doctrine and tried to use them as instruments of Conservative economic (especially prices and incomes) policy.

When the Labour Party returned to power in 1964, it immediately started to fulfil its promise to re-nationalise the iron and steel industry, but otherwise kept its 'socialist' energies for building up a planned economy (though it is worth noting that it was a Conservative government, with the founding of the National Economic Development Council, that initiated this process). It was not until the early 1970s that the public sector of the economy found further additions — ironically enough under the Heath government which went into office under the motto of 'disengagement', promising not to support 'lame ducks', not even public ones, any longer, and envisaging the first steps of de-nationalisation.[11] Shortly afterwards it was faced with the bankruptcy of Rolls-Royce and the near collapse of the Mersey Docks and Upper Clyde Shipbuilders. So the policy of disengagement duly came to an end with the nationalisation of Rolls-Royce and with massive injections of public capital into the other threatened companies which, a few years later, were nationalised and combined to form British Shipbuilders.

On the whole, therefore, nationalisation policies in Britain have never really been a matter of doctrine and socialist principle. Hence every now and again leftist politicians claim that it is high time for 'socialising public ownership'.[12] It was not until Mrs Thatcher took office in 1979 that nationalisation became not only a political issue, but

---

9. Michael Shanks, 'The Aims and the Problems', in Shanks (ed.), *The Lessons of Public Enterprise*, op. cit., p. 18.
10. See Nigel Harris, *Competition and the Corporate Society. British Conservatives, the State and Industry 1945–1964*, London, 1972, p. 182.
11. For instance it demanded de-nationalisation of the NCB's non-coalmining activities, which led the NCB's chairman, Lord Robens, to resign under protest, though the planned measures were, after all, carried out to only a limited extent. See I. Berkovitch, op. cit., p. 160.
12. As an example, see Martyn Sloman's *Socialising Public Ownership*, London, 1978.

a matter of doctrine as well — though this time in the negative sense of de-nationalisation, now called privatisation. And it took her vigour to stick to the de-nationalisation and disengagement programme (contrary to her conservative predecessor, Ted Heath); yet even she has had to realise that such programmes are neither put into practice as smoothly as she would have wished, nor are they always the obvious solution to existing problems, as she might have thought.

The Organisational Formula: the Public Corporation 5

While this history of nationalisation, with its prevalence of pragmatist/technocratic over socialist impulses, appears to be typical for nationalisation in Western economies, British nationalisers in the 'public corporation' created an organisation that is unique. The underlying concept of the 'arm's-length approach', formulated by Herbert Morrison, for some time was controversial within the Labour Party and was attacked particularly by unionists who favoured joint control by government and workers. Nevertheless Morrison's concept was put into practice with the foundation of the London Passenger Transport Board (LPTB) in 1933 and has prevailed ever since, the argument in its favour being that public managements should aim to be as efficient as possible and are therefore better not hampered by worker participation.[1] Furthermore, the concept recommended itself by finding wide acceptance by the non-socialist public. Thus adopting this organisational formula meant adopting a conflict-minimising strategy and helped in allaying suspicions of nationalisation as such. As Maurice Garner recently put it, by creating this specific organisation

> it was possible to allay the trade unions' fears of placing industries in the hands of bureaucrats . . .; it was possible to persuade the managerial and technical classes that the directing staff would remain business men . . . ; it was possible to satisfy politically neutral opinion convinced of the need for restructuring some of Britain's industries that these industries were not being socialized but would be run very much on business principles; and yet, by stressing that the new organizations were not companies but public corporations from which private capital had been eliminated, it was possible to present the new organizational form to the partisans of socialism as the fulfilment of their aspirations.[2]

1. See Tivey, *Nationalization in British Industry*, op. cit., pp. 35ff.
2. Maurice R. Garner, 'Auditing the Efficiency of Nationalized Industries: Enter the

The 'public corporation' thus established can be defined as a juristically independent public trading body, created by, but not directly responsible to Parliament, which has to carry out specific functions (more or less precisely prescribed) in the national interest, and to this end enjoys a substantial degree of financial independence and managerial autonomy, whilst the public control it is subjected to is limited to the appointment (and dismissal) of board members and to certain other rights (of direction and approval) fixed in the statutes. Hence the typical shape that a British public enterprise takes is that of a big 'public concern' (usually uniting the whole industry in question) in its own right (that is, for instance, no 'Companies' Act company'), run by an independent board of experts and subject to public scrutiny only in the form of an (originally) relatively distant ministerial control.

The aim of such a construction was to bring important industries within public control without making them part of the government; the Morrisonian corporation is intended as 'a kind of half-way house' between the spheres of business and government, 'attempting to combine public responsibility with freedom for day-to-day operation';[3] its twofold duties are to be responsive to the public interest and to operate as an efficient commercial body. It seems obvious that those two duties are not always and not easily reconcilable — at least not if one does not assume a pre-stabilised harmony between the public and the board's interests. The Morrisonian concept of substantial managerial autonomy, whilst part of the conflict-minimising strategy towards nationalisation, in itself was (and is) at the root of much confusion and conflict, especially if, as is frequently done, managerial freedom to act and public accountability are seen as potentially antithetical. Interestingly enough, from the beginning opinions differed less concerning the necessity of the former, but mainly with regard to the necessary extent and appropriate form of the latter.

The dividing line between both (and therefore the core of the 'arm's-length' concept) was fixed as that between 'general policies' (as the sphere of ministerial guidance) and their implementation in 'day-to-day management', which was to be left free from governmental interference. But this dividing line is not as easy to define as may at first appear. In the first place, it can mean a range of different things:[4] (a) ministers are restricted to a strictly *political* role, whilst manage-

---

Monopolies and Mergers Commission', in *Public Administration*, vol. 60, Winter 1982, p. 424.
3. W. Thornhill, *The Nationalized Industries*, London, 1968, p. 20.
4. For the following enumeration I am indebted to Leonard Tivey.

ments occupy the economic and commercial field; (b) ministers are concerned with the general *economic* purpose of the industry, managements with target fulfilment (or, more or less, with routine implementation); (c) ministers set *financial* targets which managements have to meet (regardless of how they otherwise act in their economic surrounding); (d) managements may be used as instruments of the economic/social policies of the day and have to mould their investment, pricing and other policies to fit in with these. Depending on which of these possible interpretations one chooses, ministerial control will vary from distant to very close, and the role of the boards from that of near civil servants to nearly unchecked businessmen.

Secondly, even if the dividing line were clear in theory, in practice it would none the less result in conflict and confusion and, hence, in a blurring of responsibilities. For, on the one hand, you cannot set up a nationalised industry with an 'independent board of experts' expected to run the industry as an efficient business and then leave it with no say in the definition of its 'policies': 'if day-to-day work is all that is to be left to corporations, then it is hard to see why they have high-powered boards or quality staff at all.'[5] On the other hand, you cannot exempt day-to-day operations from ministerial influence altogether, because they also should be carried out with due regard to the public interest: 'it is just not possible to put them into a "commercial" box and at the same time expect them to add up to a total performance which equates by some mysterious process of addition with the "national interest"'.[6]

Taking all this into account, it is small wonder that the Morrisonian corporation met with severe criticism from the beginning. Critics from the right as from the left judge it 'an unsatisfactory hybrid'[7] which, incidentally, even Herbert Morrison in 1950 acknowledged had 'not fulfilled our hopes'.[8] From one side it is criticised as allowing the boards too little independence; from the other side, by a false analogy with private enterprise, of allowing for too little control. The concept of a 'half-way house' probably was not the best solution if 'public enterprise' is to live up to its true meaning; in any case, as may be seen from the following discussion of the problems of ministerial control, such problems might have been less pungent had the public

5. Leonard Tivey, 'Structure and Politics in the Nationalised Industries,' in *Parliamentary Affairs*, vol. 32, no. 2, 1979, p. 165.
6. Thornhill, *The Nationalized Industries*, op. cit., p. 187.
7. Nevil Johnson, '*The Public Corporation: An Ambiguous Species*', in Butler and Halsey, (eds.), *Policy and Politics. Essays in honour of Norman Chester*, London, 1978, p. 124.
8. Quoted ibid., p. 123.

corporation been 'given its rightful place in the public sphere where it truly belongs'.⁹

---

9. Thornhill, *The Nationalized Industries*, op. cit., p. 189.

Problems of Ministerial Control

The Statutory Powers

Each public corporation deals with a 'sponsoring minister' whose task it is 'first to secure the wider public interest, and secondly to oversee, and if possible to ensure, the efficiency of the industries'.[1] Each minister is to guarantee 'that wider industrial, social and national interest considerations are taken into account', he is 'advising on and implementing government policies, including those for whole sectors', while making sure that public funds are applied appropriately and, last but not least, acting 'as advocate[s] for [his] corporation[s]' in dealing with government, Parliament and the public.[2] To fulfil these comprehensive tasks, the Nationalisation Acts provided ministers with surprisingly few powers. Identical for each nationalised industry, the statutory powers are quickly listed:

(1) ministers appoint and dismiss board members (and fix the level of their salaries);

(2) ministers issue general directives to the boards when this is required by the 'national interest' (the exact wording used in most of the Acts is: 'directions of a general character as may appear to the Minister to be requisite in the national interest');

(3) ministers approve the general investment, research, development and training programmes of the nationalised industries;

(4) ministers, in collaboration with the Treasury, approve any loans for which the nationalised industries apply and can instruct their boards as to the handling of funds and profits;

(5) annual balance sheets as well as reports of the nationalised industries are subject to examination by an auditor appointed by the minister, before being presented to Parliament;

---

1. First Report from the SCNI, Session 1967–68: *Ministerial Control of the Nationalised Industries*, London, 1968, vol. I, p. 9.
2. NEDO, *A Study of UK Nationalised Industries*, op. cit., p. 25.

(6) ministers are entitled to get adequately informed by the boards.

In practice these statutory powers developed in a way different from that envisaged by the legislators. First of all, the power to appoint and dismiss board members, originally regarded as the most effective weapon of ministerial control,[3] turned out to be a blunt one. Since the nationalised industries are to be run as commercial enterprises, appointments are governed by 'management considerations', meaning that ministers mostly rely on information provided by the boards themselves or their chairmen (the work of the Public Appointments Unit notwithstanding). Indeed it has proved nearly impossible to force even non-executive board members upon unwilling chairmen. Equally difficult to enact is the power of dismissal. Trying 'to sack the chairman' would cause a public outcry which ministers tend to avoid. There have been cases when such an outcry was brought about by a minister's not renewing the appointment of a chairman at the end of his first 5-year term of office. Hence chairmen appear to have gained a fairly untouchable position; and certainly, as the NEDO stated in its report of 1976, till then there had been hardly any 'publicly available evidence that reappointment is linked to a chairman's or a corporation's performance'.[4] In this, the chairmen profit not only from the public's tendency to shield 'chairmen under pressure', but also from the undeniable difficulty of *finding* suitable candidates. Salaries, which in most cases are still considerably lower than those in the private sector, as well as the ambiguous responsibilities of public sector managers, apparently do not make those posts sufficiently attractive; consequently, an energetic minister who sacked an obstinate chairman would find himself at a loss for a likely successor.

The other main control mechanism laid down in the statutes, the power of issuing 'general directions', likewise proved to be ineffective. Except on finance and accounting matters, the corporations received very few directions — a measure of restraint on the part of ministers to be explained only by the fact that such directives would have to be published and would therefore be open to public scrutiny. Instead ministers have tried to implement government policies through less formal means, such as persuasion or 'private arm twisting', which can be controlled neither by Parliament nor in any other public manner.

---

3. 'Herbert Morrison seems to have believed that the most important thing was to choose the right man and then let him get on with the job.' (C. D. Foster, *Politics, Finance, and the Role of Economics*, London, 1971, p. 68).
4. NEDO, *A Study of UK Nationalised Industries*, op. cit., p. 35.

The remaining statutory powers of ministers are mainly financial and rather imprecise. The latter provided a further incentive for the development of more or less informal arrangements, which vary from corporation to corporation. Added to this is the fact that the ministerial powers enumerated in the statutes are by no means comprehensive, a fact which prompted governments to act in accordance with a 'theory of implied powers' and which led eventually to the uncoordinated system of interventions discussed below. Hence, as the SCNI summed up in its 1968 Report, ministerial control 'is something that has grown up in a somewhat haphazard way'[5] and certainly cannot be adequately described by reference to the statutes.

In a parliamentary system, ministerial control of a public enterprise, whatever it is like, ought to be complemented by parliamentary control. Yet from the very beginning the development of such a 'triangular' relationship has been hampered by the construction of the public corporation as a semi-independent body. This implies that (theoretically) it is not the performance of the *corporation* that lies open to parliamentary scrutiny, but only the performance of the *minister* dealing with it. Even in the latter case parliamentary control can effectively be blocked by a minister pointing out to MPs that the issue raised by them lay entirely in the responsibility of the management, and that ministerial interference would be not only illegal, but also most inopportune, as it would be certain to attract criticism from other MPs 'who would say that that was unwarranted interference with the day-to-day management . . .'.[6] As this tactic has been the one usually employed to fend off parliamentary questions, virtually the only control mechanism that remained open to Parliament for a long time was legislation and as this, in its turn, has been restricted to nationalisation, de-nationalisation and capital restructuring, parliamentary control over the actual operation of nationalised industries has been negligible.

The setting up of a permanent parliamentary committee for the nationalised industries, with the object of obtaining at least some information about them, was resisted by both Labour and Conservative governments for a considerable time. When a first Select Committee on Nationalised Industries (SCNI) came into being in March 1955, its powers were so restricted that it was hard pressed to find

5. First Report from the SCNI, Session 1967–68: *Ministerial Control* . . . , op. cit. vol. I., p. 12.
6. Thus the Minister of State in the Department of Industry, Gerald Kaufman, when asked about the BSC; see Second Report from the SCNI, Session 1977–78, *The British Steel Corporation*, London, 1977, p. 80.

anything of relevance to examine: questions of ministerial responsibility, of day-to-day management, of wage policy and terms of employment, and questions 'of relevance to formal statutory machinery' were removed from its reach.[7] Consequently this first SCNI declared that it could not operate on such terms. In 1956, after a further tug-of-war, a new SCNI was appointed with 'virtually unrestricted powers' of investigation, whilst at the same time 'warned' against dealing with the above-listed problems.[8]

After that, the SCNI operated successfully in so far as, bit by bit, it subjected all the nationalised industries to detailed scrutiny and also tackled some of their more fundamental problems, including that of ministerial control itself. Yet as, according to the Nationalisation Acts, it is the minister and *not* Parliament who is responsible for the nationalised industries, the Committee's activity amounted to very little more than supplying the public with information; it certainly did not constitute any new 'accountability to Parliament' on the part of the corporations. Furthermore, its work necessarily suffered from the basic problem mentioned above, that due to the imprecise definition of 'policies' and 'day-to-day management', ministers hid behind boards and boards behind ministers and both combined to shut out parliamentary scrutiny and to keep certain topics out of public debate. By tacit agreement ministers and nationalised industries thus managed to prevent Parliament from adopting a more integral role in industrial affairs.

At the end of 1979 the SCNI was dissolved and its specialised expertise, accumulated over years, dispersed. Parliamentary scrutiny of single nationalised industries now rests with the committees concerned with the respective sponsoring departments, a measure in line with the Thatcher government's policy of treating public enterprises as in no way special or distinct from any other enterprise. Their control by parliament, and public insight into the problems common to them all, is certainly not made easier by this.

Aims and Policies

Yet the essential feature of public enterprise and its main difference from private enterprise lies (as has been argued in Part I) in its aims, which ought to be decided in the political sphere. The Morrisonian concept clearly followed the same line of thought when it separated

---

7. See A. H. Hanson, *Parliament and Public Ownership*, London, 1961, pp. 142f.
8. See Albu: 'Ministerial and Parliamentary Control', l.c., p. 102.

the 'policies' from 'day-to-day management' and ascribed the decision over them to ministers. Hence not only the meaning of nationalisation as such, but the successful operation of the 'arm's-length approach' depends to a considerable degree on the political authorities setting the necessary objectives and providing long-term direction.

Unfortunately, right from the beginning political action concerning the nationalised industries suffered from a lack of purpose. The aims connected with nationalisation as such were already vague and diverse; they ranged from the reduction of the income gap, the realisation of industrial democracy and the introduction of national economic planning, to simply increasing the efficiency of the industries in question — though (as has been shown above) as early as 1945 the latter aim seems to have taken precedence over the others. Of course the Labour Party's concept of nationalisation was at the time strongly influenced by a belief in planning; in this concept, the ministerial power to issue directions was meant to 'make sure that each nationalised industry could be made to comply with cabinet decisions concerning national economic policy'.[9] But the priority of the 'efficiency' objective, combined with the specific form of the public corporation, caused a dilemma all subsequent governments found themselves in: while too many directives might interfere with efficient management, too little direction would render nationalised industries useless as tools of economic policy and planning.

The objectives which the individual corporations were given to pursue were hardly any clearer. The aims laid down in the Nationalisation Acts are typically restricted to general statements about guaranteeing adequate supply to the population, securing the efficient development of the industry itself, and generally acting in a way 'to further the public interest' — a stipulation which, in the absence of continual political guidance, would imply that the public interest in each single case is defined by the management itself. Added to these general aims is a financial objective which (originally) states that costs and returns ought to be balanced 'on an average of good and bad years' — again a stipulation not really restricting managerial autonomy, because it is vague enough to allow for a whole range of financial strategies. Finally there are some 'social obligations' imposed on most nationalised industries, and here the Acts likewise fail to offer anything in the nature of clear directions.

The Nationalisation Acts then did not furnish the industries with any useful economic, financial and social guidelines. They left it to the

---

9. Clegg and Chester, *The Future of Nationalization*, op. cit., p. 143.

boards themselves to resolve the conflict between furthering the national interest or paying attention to social costs, on the one hand, and creating or securing commercial profitability and cost-effectiveness on the other. Of course, acts and statutes of necessity have to be general rather than precise, to a certain degree at least. Hence the importance of the guidance coming from the government of the day, which steps into the gap and defines the national interest in varying situations.

Such guidance could take the form of general directives — which is, as has been shown, most unusual — or materialise in the less formal, but the more continuous 'everyday' contacts between ministers and boards. After all, the sponsoring minister, being responsible for the success or failure of his nationalised industry (in theory at least), ought continually to review its board's programmes and policies, for how otherwise would he be able to secure that those policies do take the 'wider industrial, social and national interest considerations' into account? At the core of this continuous supervision lie investment control, usually (and not insignificantly) called investment appraisal, and joint planning.

Investment appraisals were systematised during the 1960s (see below), but only in the sense of financial control: there are annual investment reviews and new investment projects are approved if they promise to reach a 'required rate of return'. *Not* reviewed in this context, according to all the evidence, are matters of demand development, economic/social desirability of the project and so forth. Obviously, ministers in this respect act as bankers, not as politicians. Furthermore, a notable precedence is given to the Treasury — that is, the 'banker' dealing with the investment appraisals is one whose main interest is to cut expenses. If there *are* policy inputs to be detected they have mostly been connected with short-term considerations of economic, mainly incomes, policy; at the moment investment appraisals do seem to be politically influenced, but only in the negative sense of avoiding the danger of 'crowding out' private investment.

What clearly has been lacking, so far, is the determination to influence *positively* a nationalised industry's development; ministers do not take initiatives, they restrict themselves to 'approve' what a corporation's experts lay before them. As the (then) Department of Trade and Industry stated to the SCNI, in its Memo of 25 May 1972, it limited itself to: '1. achieve a full understanding both of the [investment] programme itself and of the industry's circumstances; 2. satisfy itself that the programme is related to a sound strategy for the industry . . .; 3. ensure that the projects comprising it have been fully and effectively appraised'.[10] The snag in the laudable intention to judge the 'sound strategy' is that the DTI civil servants, as Mr Bullock admitted freely before the same committee, 'would not claim to be expert practitioners' of, for example, technological forecasting.[11] It might even be questioned whether they are always fully informed. Hence departments fall back on satisfying themselves that certain financial stipulations are met,[12] and this only for a limited number of projects (that is, for 'major projects', which are differently defined in each industry).

It should be clear from the above that corporate planning (which itself was formally introduced only in the early 1970s) very rarely is real 'joint planning' — frequent meetings between boards and ministers notwithstanding. The boards develop more or less long-term strategies for their industries (in the case of British Gas, for instance, up to twenty-five years), ministers agree — albeit, sometimes, after long and hard battles — but usually make no contribution of their own and 'modify' or reject only when parts of those strategies crop up in the annual investment reviews. The latter accounts for some of the resentment felt in the boards, for how can you implement an 'approved' strategy if you cannot go ahead with the individual projects comprising it? The only exceptions, where ministerial input is concerned, occur from time to time with respect to the social services some of the corporations are to provide; and these exceptions are now a further source of resentment, for the boards, left alone in all other respects to define strategies of their own, have come to see themselves in a purely commercial role.

It might be concluded that the Morrisonian dividing line between 'general policies' and 'day-to-day management' is hardly existent in so far as ministers usually refrain from laying down such 'general policies'. From the beginning government policies concerning the nationalised industries suffered from a 'lack of clarity of objectives':[13] governments of both colours did not really know what to do with the public corporations or what they were there for. Consequently, the NEDO report's severest criticism of subsequent governments 'was not of bad policy but of no policy'.[14]

10. First Report from the SCNI, Session 1973–74, *Capital Investment Procedures*, London, 1973, p. 27.
11. Ibid., p. 33.
12. See, for further evidence, the Memo of the Department of Environment, ibid., p. 69.
13. Foster, *Politics, Finance and the Role of Economics*, op. cit., p. 19.
14. Tivey, 'Structure and Politics in the Nationalised Industries', l.c., p. 166.

Finance and the Role of the Treasury

There may be no control in the sense of guidance, but certainly there is financial control of the nationalised industries. Though its basis lies in the statutes (see above), government attained a firm grip on the corporations' finances only when, in 1956, the Finance Act decreed that the corporations were to borrow no longer on the capital market but from the Treasury, and made their capital requirements part of the Public Sector Borrowing Requirement. This measure was the product of necessity rather than of a determination to develop tighter control, since in those first years the nationalised industries had proved unable to raise sufficient funds for their investment programmes; however, it turned out to be the crucial step that made them really dependent on government, and immediately led to a series of attempts to bring various mechanisms of financial control into a tight and comprehensive system. It started in 1961 with the setting of financial targets and ended with the additional fixing of cash limits (first in 1976) for each corporation (this is discussed further below). This indeed put the whole financial structure of the nationalised industries into a straitjacket — though it should be noted that the degree to which these controls provide actual restraints on the corporations' activities varies with their financial situation; it grows in proportion to their losses.

The development of the system of financial control may be looked upon as overwhelming evidence of the fact that it is much easier to invent uniform criteria for the financial control of each industry, and put them on an easily-checkable and calculable basis, than it is in the spheres of economic performance and social benefits. Accordingly, the three main elements of the current system — investment appraisals based on the uniform 'required rate of return' of 5 per cent, medium-term financial targets in terms of current cost operating profit earned on net assets (valued at current costs), and short-term operating control in the shape of the EFLs — are based on comparatively elaborate and widely accepted criteria and are apparently practicable, at least in the sense of making the financial structure of the corporations open to scrutiny. By contrast, the fourth element meant to complete this system, the performance targets, as yet seem rather under-developed, though it is an equally widely acknowledged fact that 'by themselves, financial targets do not necessarily guarantee that nationalised industries are efficiently run'.[15]

15. Eighth Report from the Treasury and Civil Service Committee, Session 1980–81: *Financing of the Nationalised Industries*, London, 1981, vol. I, p. xii.

On the one hand, the comparative easiness of finding and calculating criteria of financial control gave rise to a precedence, not only of this over other types of control, but also of the Treasury over the sponsoring departments — though, on the other hand, one might argue that the specific precedence of the 'cash limit' type of control has its basis in the unwillingness of sponsoring ministers really to bother about the nationalised industries and their policies. The precedence of the Treasury, in its turn, has had serious consequences for the operation of the system of ministerial control as a whole, and on the relationship between boards and government. The Treasury has other interests at heart than the sponsoring ministers who in most cases act as advocates, or even lobbyists, for their industries; its main tasks are either to keep public expenditure down, to consider balance of payments questions and to reach and maintain macroeconomic equilibrium — or to implement the economic philosophy of the government of the day. With these ends in view it has frequently interfered with agreements between sponsoring departments and corporations: more precisely, it has axed investment already approved by a minister. Not unnaturally this has led to resentment on the part of the boards, especially as such expenditure cuts are usually based to a lesser degree on consistent concepts about the development of the industry in question than are interventions by the responsible minister. Furthermore, in most cases such cuts have not been discussed on a face-to-face basis by the corporation and the Treasury; contacts between the two are typically mediated by the sponsoring department, with the result that often the Treasury appears as an anonymous but threatening power 'behind the scenes'. If Parliament and public are to complain about the constant 'blurring of responsibilities' between boards and ministers so, with equal right, boards themselves can complain about the blurred responsibilities between the sponsoring department and the Treasury. In the frequent conflicts between them both, it seems to have been often the corporations who have 'lost' in the end.

'Government Interference'

The finding that ministers have so far refrained from formulating policies for their nationalised industries does not mean that, apart from financial control, the corporations have been left wholly in peace to pursue their own strategies. In fact, there is a long and much criticised history of government interference into the 'day-to-day management', of 'backstairs pressures' on boards, and of 'private arm twisting' of chairmen. From the beginning, in dealing with the corporations, governments relied heavily on *ad hoc* as well as informal means of influence (instead of on continuous and open guidance), which may be explained firstly by the obvious lack of consistent and long-term concepts for these industries, and secondly by the common tendency of governments in parliamentary systems 'to get their own way without wanting to be held publicly responsible for the results . . .',[16] that is, to avoid public commitment and to minimise parliamentary accountability.

The main excuse for the use of such influence was, of course, that all governments wished to make the nationalised industries comply with the short-term goals of their economic policy; in particular, the battle against inflation led to their 'use as a battering ram'[17] against the wage claims of their employees and as a means of keeping producers' prices down. There is abundant evidence of government interference in the corporations' prices policies. Though no mention of price control is made in any of the Nationalisation Acts, boards have been obliged throughout to ask for ministerial approval before altering their prices and rather frequently have been induced at least to postpone the proposed increases. As the SCNI stated in 1968, such interventions 'appear to have been ad hoc rather than in conformity with any common principle', and were brought about by 'political reasons' (in contrast to 'the Board's commercial judgment on prices').[18] The 'political reasons' were not only those of an anti-inflation policy, but also stemmed from a general policy of support to private industry, or from social considerations. According to the NEDO evidence, the nationalised industries most affected by price restraints were electricity, postal communications, railways and the BSC.[19] In the case of the latter the wish to further private sector interests was particularly obvious and bred general illwill, not only within the BSC itself: meanwhile the remaining private steel companies complain bitterly about the BSC's 'under-pricing'.

The National Board for Prices and Incomes, while it was in existence (1965–70), tried to put price controls on a more systematic basis. The same institution, however, recognised the conflict between its

16. William A. Robson, *Nationalized Industry and Public Ownership*, 2nd ed., op. cit., p. 147.
17. Edmund Dell, *Political Responsibility and Industry*, London, 1973, p. 22.
18. First Report from the SCNI, Session 1967–68: *Ministerial Control* . . ., op. cit., vol. I, pp. 85ff.
19. NEDO, *A study of UK Nationalised Industries*, op. cit., pp. 36f.

own policy of price restraint, on the one hand, and the statutory duty of the nationalised industries to balance profits and costs, together with the financial targets invented to increase their (financial) efficiency, on the other: it suggested that price controls were useless as long as the financial targets had to be accepted as given.[20] None the less, in May 1969 it asked, for balance of payments reasons, for a 25 per cent reduction of steel prices. Though the BSC, supported by its sponsoring minister, managed to tone down this somewhat radical request, it seems obvious that such interventions did not contribute to its profitability. In fact, the governments' deflationary policies, which continued during the 1970s, impaired the financial soundness of at least some of the nationalised industries to such a degree that there were discussions about the necessity of the government's compensating them for price interventions.[21]

Under the current (1984) government the policy of price restraint seems to have been stopped; on the part of some of the corporations this has led to immediate and considerable price increases in order to make good losses previously incurred. But the government has not abandoned price intervention altogether; on the contrary, in 1983/4 the gas and electricity industries were asked to raise prices *above* the level indicated by their 'commercial judgment'.[22] Hence it is the motive and direction of interference that has changed, not the politics of interference itself.

Though prices policy is the most conspicuous field of government interference it is by no means the only one. When the Labour government started its great National Plan in 1965 it expected the nationalised industries to comply with its objectives and to act in accordance with its growth forecasts — with the result that the corporations soon found themselves burdened with over-capacity.[23] This was an experiment which lasted only a few years; yet there have been other instances of governments trying to bring the nationalised industries into line with whatever pressing needs of economic/anti-cyclical/structural/social policy were suddenly felt. In principle one would think that this is exactly what public enterprises are there for; the snag,

20. See Coombes, *State Enterprise*, op. cit., p. 129.
21. See NEDO, *A Study of UK Nationalised Industries*, op. cit., Appendix vol., p. 73.
22. In fact the CEGB and the Department of Energy felt obliged to 'remind the treasury of the limits, imposed by nationalised industry statutes, on their power to set prices' (*The Economist*, 17 March 1984, p. 32; see also John Morris's column in the *Guardian*, 26 March 1984.)
23. See Michael Shanks, *Planning and Politics: the British Experience 1960–1976*, London, 1977, pp. 43ff.

however, is that ideas about such pressing needs can change with dazzling rapidity.

Another line of interference was to induce corporations to 'buy British', a policy which seems to have impaired their technological competitiveness and, hence, profitability; the case of British Airways is particularly relevant here.[24] The BSC, to give another example, has suffered repeatedly from delays in planned plant closures and capacity reductions. At the moment, government — or more precisely the Treasury — intervenes mainly with the aim of keeping total public expenditure down or, in the case of the few profitable corporations, of bringing cash to the exchequer.

The Deficits

All in all, the British system of ministerial control does not strike one as being well adapted to its tasks: the Morrisonian concept of 'arm's-length', with its division into 'policies' and 'day-to-day management', seems to be neither an adequate nor even a practicable one. The division, ambiguous already in theory, in practice got muddled past recognition.

The main deficits of the prevailing situation are:

(1) No government seems to have had any consistent concepts about the meaning of nationalisation as such and the benefits of the nationalised industries taken together, nor have there been clear (non-financial) objectives, or formulated 'general policies', for each *individual* nationalised industry.

(2) This lack accounts for a prevalence of short-term interventions (though the latter have another cause in a feature of the political system, which is the generally short-term view forced upon party politicians by electoral pressures); it clearly contradicts the need for industries to develop long-term strategies.

(3) Also derived partly from the lack of consistent concepts and/or 'general policies' and partly from more general features of the politico-administrative system, is a lack of co-ordination between the policies of the different nationalised industries. The most conspicuous example here is the apparent inability of the Department of Energy, in charge of the three nationalised fuel industries, to formulate an energy

---

24. See Chris Harlow, *Innovation and Productivity under Nationalisation*, London, 1977, pp. 11ff., 45ff.

policy which embraces all three, and to co-ordinate their activities.[25] Passiveness in this respect goes to such lengths that the efforts of the Electricity Council, that is, of one single nationalised industry, to coordinate the investment strategies of the CEGB's area boards, found no support in government.[26] And it is not only ex ante coordination that is lacking: ministers have done hardly anything to try to reconcile the conflicting interests of the nationalised industries; as yet they hardly seem to have realised that decisions affecting one industry might also affect others.[27]

(4) The only control mechanisms that exist and work (to a degree at least) are financial; there is still a lack of (economic) efficiency and (economic and social) performance control.

(5) As a consequence of the predominance of financial control, and of the inclusion of the corporations' capital expenditures in the PSBR, the Treasury has gained a pre-eminent role without being a real 'partner' of the boards, thus complicating the relationship between boards and government: the 'power behind the scenes' blurs responsibilities and renders long-term corporate planning yet more difficult.

(6) Yet such 'blurred responsibilities' seem to be of the essence of the British system of ministerial control: too many institutions are concerned with the dealings of the public corporations; there is no clear demarcation line between the business of ministers and the business of the boards; and, last not least, there is the (statutorily) undefined role of Parliament in this respect. As a result, no individual or single body accepts responsibility for anything — each participant in this complicated structure is able to use another as a scapegoat.

(7) Finally, there is the problem of expertise: those in charge of the nationalised industries are not expert professionals but civil servants (as Maurice Garner, when head of the Electricity Division in the DTI, stated before the SCNI in 1972: 'I start by disclaiming being an expert. I am only a civil servant'.),[28] which in Britain means that they have not been reared as specialists of any kind, but as 'generalists' ('we are administrators trying to cope with whatever jobs we are given from

25. See First Report from the SCNI, Session 1973–74, *Capital Investment Procedures*, op. cit., p. xxxv.
26. See *The Economist*, 11 October 1980, p. 75.
27. See, for instance, the criticism of British Aerospace's chairman in the Sixth Special Report from the SCNI, Session 1977–78, *Comments by Nationalised Industries and Others on the Government White Paper on the Nationalised Industries*, London, 1978, p. 1; see also the NEDO report, op. cit., p. 26.
28. In First Report from the SCNI, Session 1973–74: *Capital Investment Procedures*, op. cit., p. 64.

time to time'.).[29] Now the matter would certainly be mistaken, and the aims of ministerial control misunderstood, if departments were to build up 'a vast army of expertise to rival that which the industries have under their own command',[30] because such a strategy would not only imply 'double-guessing' the boards (which ought to raise the question of why the boards were being set up as separate bodies, in the first place), but also evoke the danger of controllers becoming 'house-trained' and, hence, forgetting their primary task of controlling and bringing the industries' policies into line with the public interest. Yet it must remain in doubt as to whether, for the latter purpose, it suffices to be equipped with only 'a certain amount of informed scepticism'[31] and to be able, every now and again, to pose some intelligent questions, without really being able to judge the quality of the answers — as R. H. W. Bullock (DTI) once admitted: 'If they [the boards] say black is white...I do not know how anyone could prove that the contrary is true'.[32] Obviously it is very difficult to determine the right amount of expertise even theoretically (as has been shown in Part I); the practice of ministerial control in Britain, though, leaves one with the impression that the prevailing danger is that of too little expertise rather than that of too much.[33]

The main deficit of ministerial control, however, and the cause of most of the others, is a lack of purpose and specific objectives. The Morrisonian concept, with its aim of combining managerial autonomy and public accountability, could only operate in that sense when boards have been given clearly defined as well as comprehensive sets of objectives; that is, it calls strongly for ministers to take the task of formulating their corporations' policies seriously. It is debatable whether the relationship between corporations and ministers then could still be called 'arm's-length'; yet it is equally debatable whether the present relationship, with its lack of policy formulation but abundance of 'interference', can be so called.

Critics from different sides (and different interested parties) will, of course, differently accentuate the deficiencies and detect still more of

29. W. J. Sharp, ibid., p. 71.
30. J. G. Liverman (DTI), ibid., p. 53.
31. Ibid.
32. Ibid., p. 39.
33. 'It is not necessarily clear to anyone really that the people you put in charge of a nationalised industry are less able to determine the investment worth of a project than arts graduates in the Civil Service . . .'; Mr English, in Eighth Report from the Treasury and Civil Service Committee, Session 1980–81, *Financing of the Nationalised Industries*, op. cit., vol. II, p.73.

them. Economists tend to stress the lack of efficiency control and the inadequacies of the methods of investment appraisal and financial control. As Richard Pryke argues, the result of these shortcomings is that the use of capital in the public enterprise sector has been poor throughout; though the Treasury tried hard to weed out ill-judged investment projects, its efforts frequently failed when such expenditure was backed by sponsoring ministers.[34] The other main criticism from this side is that the government hinders the boards' efforts to follow their 'commercial judgment' (and not only in their pricing policies) by dint of unwarranted and arbitrary intervention, which has hampered the industries' efficiency and, worse still, 'demoralised' the boards and 'reduced their sense of responsibility'.[35] Hence the popular complaint about abundant government intervention in, and 'short-term political manipulation' of,[36] the policies of public firms is coupled with the equally popular one of blurred responsibilities, with their negative consequences for efficiency and 'management ethos' as well as public accountability. On the other hand, it is also coupled with deploring the lack of 'discipline' ('although the nationalised industries have been subject to many constraints they have been under remarkably little discipline')[37] and, sometimes, the lack of objectives. This is only a surface contradiction; for the laying-down of rules for the boards and formulating policies for them might render ad hoc interference with their management superfluous.

It may be surprising that there are also voices which do not find much fault with the British system of ministerial control and which should not be suppressed here. This system, William G. Shepherd wrote in the mid-1970s, was characterised by 'a nice balance between the firms' independence and outside guidance by the government. By 1970 a careful, even sophisticated, set of supervisory arrangements had been worked out between public firms and their ministries. There was autonomy but also a responsiveness to larger interests'.[38]

The SCNI, one of the severest critics of ministerial control in most of its reports, certainly did *not* take this view. The tenor of its criticism has been that, in general, ministers gave too little policy guidance to their industries, choosing to become too 'closely involved in many aspects of management'[39] instead, with the main emphasis lying on

34. Pryke, *The Nationalised Industries*, op. cit., p. 249.
35. Ibid., p. 262.
36. Shepherd et al., *Public Enterprise*, op. cit., p. 110.
37. Pryke, op. cit., p. 263.
38. Shepherd et al., op. cit., p. 109.
39. First Report from the SCNI, Session 1967–68, *Ministerial Control* . . ., op. cit., vol.

the latter. In the eyes of the SCNI 'the industries should . . . be left as free as possible to carry out the policies required of them as efficiently as possible'[40] (while the question of how such efficiency could be guaranteed was left open). Critics of the SCNI, in their turn, like to point out that its criticism was somewhat one-sided, its main yardstick being not what impact ministerial control had on the nationalised industries, but 'whether their chairmen were happy'; its main concern, it has been argued, was 'happiness and tidiness instead of efficiency'.[41] As shall be seen below there is some truth in this argument, although it is only partly valid since the SCNI throughout complained about the lack of clarity of objectives and the damaging effects of blurred responsibilities as well.

While in Whitehall itself one might hear criticism of some of the nationalised industries, but hardly a single critical word about ministerial control (indeed one could say that here the old Morrisonian concept is defended tooth and nail), the boards' complaints about the latter have been both massive and bitter and not restricted to the overriding one that government interference upsets the boards' own commercially and economically sound judgement and greater insight. The inevitable delay that ministerial control causes in the nationalised industries is a more specific criticism. It is aimed not only at 'interference' but at most forms of financial control, especially at the established routine of investment appraisal and approval. According to the derogatory remark of a BA director, made in 1973, 'to have to put up a detailed submission on this to the DTI, to go through all this rigmarole, and delay the whole thing, . . . is not satisfactory'.[42] Quite obviously such remarks reveal a wish for as little supervision as possible; accordingly, each time a new control instrument is under debate (as, for instance, in recent years the performance indicators or 'specific directives'), the boards, or at least their majority, try to fight back with the standard argument that they would cause additional and detrimental delays.[43]

Other common criticisms from the board's personnel are: that there is a lack of expertise in their sponsoring departments which, they feel,

---

I, p. 10.
40. Ibid., p. 35.
41. Pryke, *Public Enterprise in Practice*, op. cit., pp. 457f.
42. D. H. Glover, in First Report from the SCNI, Session 1973–74, *Capital Investment Procedures*, op. cit., p. 192.
43. See various statements in the Sixth Special Report from the SCNI, Session 1977–78, *Comments by Nationalised Industries and Others on the Government White Paper on the Nationalised Industries*, op. cit.

is aggravated by the British Civil Service's habit of rotating civil servants around divisions and departments every three to five years; about the role of the Treasury as the 'power behind the scenes' and the sometimes disruptive effects of its measures; about the frequent incompatibility of the economic policy of the day with the long-term programmes agreed between boards and sponsoring ministers (and, hence, about the impossibility of successful planning by the corporations); and, in particular, about the general lack of a bi-partisan approach to nationalisation and the nationalised industries. The prevailing 'political see-saw' is seen as one of the major reasons for a range of disadvantages in the current system of ministerial control, especially for the most irritating tendency to short-term intervention. Hence the demand that 'the importance of these industries should preclude their being used as political footballs, and the fundamental responsibilities of both parties to the public should command their attention to the development of an effective bi-partisan policy'.[44]

There is less agreement on the issue of policies and objectives. Some of the boards feel that defining their own policies and strategies is an essential part of the managerial autonomy they claim for themselves — the more so because of the 'inability of Government . . . to appreciate the scale and range of problems involved in running a major industry'[45] — and particularly oppose their being used as tools in the execution of 'political' ends of whatever persuasion. But other boards would rather 'welcome a stronger lead from Government on a number of strategic aspects'[46] and favour a more seriously coordinating role on the part of the government. So the pattern emerging from the boards' complaints is that, on the one hand, they wish to minimise ministerial scrutiny and, certainly, short-term interference but, on the other hand, are not averse to being set clear objectives and to succumb to (bi-partisan) long-term guidance — or, in other words, to have a certain security of orientation with (and this is by no means of the least importance) ministers *openly* taking responsibility for it.

44. Sir Francis Tombs (Electricity Council), 'The Role of the Nationalised Industries', Bristol Lecture to the Local Centre of the Institute of Bankers, 11 November 1980, ms., p. 29.
45. The North of Scotland Hydro-Electric Board, in Second Special Report from the SCNI, Session 1976–77, *Comments by Nationalised Industries on the NEDO Report*, London, 1977, p. xiv.
46. The South of Scotland Electricity Board, in Sixth Special Report from the SCNI, Session 1977–78, *Comments by Nationalised Industries and Others* . . ., op. cit., p. 61.

The Position of the Boards or: Who is in Power?

In one respect at least, the boards succeeded in bringing round the whole public, committees and all, to their views: that they were suffering from 'excessive government intervention'; that the degree of managerial autonomy amounted to almost nothing; and that their role had degenerated, more or less, to that of civil servants. The frequent use of the expression 'double-guessing the management', when debating certain control procedures, is one of numerous examples which show how completely the public has adopted the boards' view (it expresses, after all, no more than the boards' distaste at having their judgments exposed to informed scrutiny). The general conviction is that 'the Government is usually in so powerful a position and has so many opportunities for persuasion or inducement at its disposal that it can almost always influence a public enterprise to do what it wants whatever the legal text may say';[47] that boards 'will more and more become executants of policy laid down centrally — even if it is a policy which they dislike';[48] that 'if anything was wrong with the nationalised sector it was that governments were interfering too much rather than too little';[49] and that this was exactly why the nationalised industries had proved to be so unsatisfactory — 'ailing and inefficient giants'.[50]

As has been mentioned already, the SCNI shared this conviction, which is quite in line with the doctrine, equally commonly shared, that nationalised industries should work along commercial lines and that, consequently, any political influence that interfered with their 'commercial judgment' was an aberration to be held at bay. Yet not all the boards present the same dreary picture of their being pushed around and 'arm-twisted' to do what ministers (or civil servants) want. Sir Jack Hawkins (ex-chairman of the CEGB) was able to say at the end of his five years (in 1979), 'that we had not done a single thing in spite of all the arm-twisting which we had [had] no intention of doing';[51] and BA's Sir Henry Marking stated on the same occasion:

---

47. William A. Robson, 'Ministerial Control of the Nationalised Industries' (1969), l.c., p. 79.
48. Kelf-Cohen, *Twenty Years of Nationalisation*, op. cit., p. 191.
49. John Redwood, *Public Enterprise in Crisis*, op. cit., p. 179.
50. George and Priscilla Polanyi, in Rhodes Boyson (ed.), *Goodbye to Nationalisation*, Enfield, 1971, p. 36.
51. The SCNI (Sub-Committee E), Session 1978–79, *The Relationships between Ministers, Parliament and the Nationalised Industries*, op. cit. p. 27.

'If the Chairman is worth his salt he will not succumb to the pressures which the Minister puts on him unless he thinks they are right'.[52] There are still other examples which bear out the view that the more a chairman 'knows his long-term strategy, and the shape of the agreements he wishes to make, the more likely it is that he will be able to persuade his sponsoring department . . . that there is no sensible alternative but for him to go ahead'.[53]

This is a clear admission of the fact that, after all, the boards are the experts and therefore in the stronger position — whatever the minister's powers to control might be. As long as the managements know what they want and are intent upon their plans — and which manager 'worth his salt' would not? — they will always have the better arguments and, as likely as not, succeed in carrying their plans through *in the end*, particularly when confronted with controllers who, instead of expertise, have only a vague 'informed scepticism' to bring to the battle and, with respect to their own industry, have no long-term perspective of their own, anyway. But even those ministers who are really determined to implement certain policies can meet with serious difficulties when these do not appeal to the boards; hence the proposal of a Conservative MP that state chairmen should offer their resignation to any incoming government in order to end 'British Gas-style opposition to government policy'.[54] Of course, the boards' powers decrease when their industries make losses and 'live in the government's pocket'; yet there are enough examples of even unprofitable corporations having their own way with their ministers. The NEDO seems to have been right when it expressed doubts as to whether the nationalised industries were, in practice, in any way effectively controlled and held accountable for their performance.[55] Similarly, there is some truth in C. D. Foster's observation, when trying to describe the role of the sponsoring minister, that it was less that of a majority shareholder, or a [merchant] banker, but rather that of a 'lawyer administering a family trust fund'.[56]

However, while this applies to the sponsoring ministers, the Treasury is in a somewhat different position. Its dealings with the corporations are only a part of its more general and (mostly, at least) clearly

---

52. Ibid., p. 40.
53. J. D. M. Bell (Electricity Council), 'The Development of Industrial Relations in Nationalized Industries in Postwar Britain', in *British Journal of Industrial Relations*, vol. XIII, 1975, p. 11.
54. See *The Economist*, 29 May 1982, p. 41.
55. NEDO, *A Study of UK Nationalised Industries*, op. cit., p. 38.
56. Foster, *Politics, Finance and the Role of Economics*, op. cit., pp. 57ff.

defined task of keeping public expenditure down and implementing certain strategies of national economic policy. It has quite distinctive ideas of its own to hold against those of the industries — and, furthermore, it is only rarely subject to the boards' attempts at persuasion. Hence, if a board's plans are thwarted, it is usually through the intervention of the Treasury.

As to the questions of 'who is in power?' or 'too much or too little control?', some qualifications need to be made in order to distinguish between control and interference, as well as between *ex ante* and *ex post* control. Whereas there has been a great deal of interference and ministers have had the power to force upon the corporations price reductions (or increases, as recently), delays of plant closures, and so on, the boards in most cases had the power to push through their long-term strategies and investment programmes. And whereas the Treasury can and does subject the corporations to expenditure cuts, and stop single investment projects, ministerial control so far seems to have failed to bring the investment programmes as a whole into line with (non-existent?) government policies beforehand. Hence the power potential of the government has been used only *ad hoc*, on a single-case basis, and *ex post*, but not for a systematic and continuous *ex ante* control, that is, for a guidance which might have rendered unnecessary the *ad hoc* interventions by ministers and *ex post* curtailings of investment plans by the Treasury.

A History of Reform

7

The criticisms dealt with here (to which many more could be added) provide evidence of widespread dissatisfaction with the practice of ministerial control. Whenever something went wrong in or with the nationalised industries, such as their investments failing to bring the expected return, or their losses not diminishing within a 'reasonable' time, this was and still is ascribed to a failure of ministerial control. Indeed there is some reason to be dissatisfied, for it cannot be denied that the performance of some of the nationalised industries, albeit not quite so black as it is usually painted, has been rather disappointing — particularly during the 1970s. As Richard Pryke has pointed out, by the middle of the decade their finances were 'in chaos', their total call on public funds in the financial year 1974/5 amounting to over £2,750 m.[1] Though the Thatcher government tried hard to reduce the deficits, by 1983 the total figure was still roughly the same.[2] An attempt to put the corporations under the strict financial discipline of annual cash limits did not improve matters significantly, for the main loss-making industries (British Rail, NCB,[3] BSC and British Shipbuilders) repeatedly overdrew their EFLs and had to be given additional credit.

Even in the case of profitable and seemingly efficient corporations, such as British Gas and the CEGB, a firm of accountants and the Monopolies and Mergers Commission respectively discovered inefficiencies, especially with respect to strategic planning, pricing policies and the calculation of future costs as well as future demand.[4] Furthermore the nationalised industries have been accused of 'chronic over-investment'[5] and misallocation. Since at least some of these faults can

1. Pryke, *The Nationalised Industries*, op. cit., p. 261.
2. See *The Economist*, 14 May 1983, p. 31.
3. In the year 1980–1, however, NCB doubled its operating profit (to £69m); it was only the high interest payments which again caused a deficit (of £58m) — see *The Economist*, 1 August 1981, p. 42.
4. See *The Economist*, 27 August 1983, p. 17; 23 May 1981, pp. 31ff.
5. *The Economist*, 20 June 1981, p. 14.

be put down to the effects of government interference, and those which are due to 'bad management' ought to be eliminated by ministerial control, it is small wonder that for more than two decades there have been various attempts to sharpen the tools of control and to render the whole system more effective.

Excursus: Experiences Abroad

The series of reforms and reform proposals which started around 1960 was influenced partly by the experiences of other Western countries with their public enterprises. The types of organisation and control of public sector economy that seemed to be of particular interest to Britain were those of France, Italy and West Germany (at federal level), while the predominant *absence* of public enterprise in the United States seems to have inspired the reform strategies of the Thatcher government.

The French model is of particular interest here because, albeit there were versions of public enterprise as early as the 1920s, the bulk of nationalisation took place immediately after the Second World War, with the expressed purpose of using public enterprises as instruments of planned economic and social change. Meant to be leading agents in the implementation of the French system of 'planification', the *entreprises publiques* (which cover a wide range from public utilities, the banking system and key industries, such as coal mining and steel, to manufacturing concerns such as Renault) were made subject to strict government control. This was to be achieved by a rather complex system of internal and external controls:[6]

(1) The great majority of public enterprises has, as a supervisory board, a *conseil d'administration* composed of representatives of various interests, including workers and consumers, of experts (*'personnalités compétentes'*), and of government representatives. But the fate of these supervisory boards is similar to that of the boards of most private corporations: lacking the information and expertise of the management, and hampered by their divergent interests, they are permanently at a disadvantage and usually not very influential.

(2) The enterprises are supervised by sponsoring ministers who have to approve major decisions and can issue directions, especially

---

6. See Friedman and Garner (eds.), *Government Enterprise*, op. cit., pp. 107ff., 123ff.; Shepherd et al., *Public Enterprise*, op. cit., pp. 123ff.; Jarass, 'Der staatliche Einfluß auf die öffentlichen Unternehmen in Frankreich', op. cit.

with respect to the aims of the general economic planning.

(3) For each of the enterprises there is a *commissaire du gouvernement* as a permanent link between minister and management; since 1955 there are, with roughly the same function, additional *contrôleurs d'état*, appointed by the ministers of industry and of finance. The problem with these special controllers is that their rights and functions are ill defined and vary in practice with each public firm. They seem to lack any overall control, which suggests their becoming 'house-trained' in their specific industries.

(4) After the Nora Report (1968) had criticised the *entreprises publiques* for lack of efficiency and, in order to improve matters, had recommended programme contracts (*contrats d'entreprises*) between government and individual firms, several such contracts have been negotiated and now serve as a control by way of fixed indicators and sets of targets. Yet this new system is spreading rather slowly; obviously ministers have not been very eager to relinquish their right to intervene, which would be the reverse side of this type of control.

(5) Finally, public enterprises are to be controlled by the ministry of finance and the *commission du plan*.

This rather elaborate system of different controls has not proved as successful as might have been expected; on the contrary, it was the managements who succeeded in establishing and defending a considerable autonomy. In their endeavour to gain a freedom of action similar to that of private capitalists they were sometimes supported by their own ministers, particularly in conflicts with the *commission du plan*. As John B. Sheahan put it, the practice of French public enterprise 'has demonstrated the power of the individual firms to assert their own independent interests and in some cases to exert pressure on national policy decisions'; they even seem to have contrived to return the planning system 'from coordinated policy towards plans determined by the firms themselves'.[7] This development may be partly due to a lack of (social) purpose assigned to public enterprises and to a failure of governments to formulate clear functions for them. But the first experiences of the Mitterrand government with (even the newly) nationalised firms provide evidence that their managements are particularly resistant to having their proper functions formulated for them.[8]

7. John B. Sheahan, 'Experience with Public Enterprise in France and Italy', in Shepherd et al., *Public Enterprise*, op. cit., p. 166.
8. In the summer of 1983 this resistance led to the unseating of the Minister of Industry, whose interference the public firms' managers had strongly resented. See *The Economist*, 1983 July 16, pp. 87ff.

The Italian system of nationalised enterprise developed in a much more haphazard way, with a considerable number of public firms resulting from economic crises and, initially, not expected to remain public. The state holding IRI, after which later holdings were modelled (ENI in 1953, ENEL and EFIM in the 1960s), was founded in 1933 in response to certain bank collapses which caused a vacuum of ownership in various industrial and financial companies; it was meant to sort things out, to keep the companies going and, after having restored them to health, to sell the shares back to private investors. The construction of the Italian model is simple:[9] the state owns holdings which in their turn own widely varying proportions of equity in operating firms spread, more or less, across the whole economy. The holdings are bound by law to follow entirely commercial lines in their control of the operating firms; the latter, being 'normal' corporations, follow these lines in any case. Because of the varying stakes the holdings have in them, it is quite often not at all clear whether the firms are to be classified as public or private — the Italian system renders sharp distinctions between the two nearly impossible.

Originally ministerial control of Italian public enterprise was practically nil, apart from the power to appoint the chairmen of the holdings. In 1956 a Ministry of State Holdings was created, with powers of direction and control over the public sector; as far as the operating firms are concerned, its influence is restricted to making general policy recommendations. Though the holdings are responsible to the ministry, the snag lies in the fact that it is *their* ministry — not one of industry (or economic affairs) in general. As a consequence the ministry has developed into a spokesman *for* the holdings within government, and has never made the effort to become an agency of government control over the public holdings: 'Hence the impression that the public economic power has not only succeeded in freeing itself to some extent from political power, but is getting the upper hand over the latter'.[10] In view of this development it is somewhat surprising that it is the Italian formula which so frequently serves as the admired pattern ambitious reformers try to follow, and not only in the UK.

The same almost total absence of general policy direction of a public enterprise which characterises the Italian system is a conspicuous

9. See Sheahan, op. cit.; Friedmann and Garner (eds.), *Government Enterprise*, op. cit., pp. 133ff.
10. G. Treves, in Friedmann and Garner (eds.), op. cit., p. 148.

feature of the West German model, though West German public enterprises ought not to be dealt with in terms of 'model' or 'system': the principles governing the organisation and control of public firms on different state levels (*Gemeinde, Land, Bund*) and in different sectors (manufacturing industries, public utilities, Bundesbahn and Bundespost) are too different. Yet what seems to have interested British reformers at some stage was the two-tier structure of companies owned by the federal state (*Bund*) (apart from the post and railways, which are organised as government departments and financially treated as *Sondervermögen*). Like the Italian operating firms, these are usually 'normal' corporations with varying proportions of equity held by the state and operating entirely on commercial lines, but only partly bound together in holdings (VEBA and VIAG). The corporations are supervised in exactly the same way as private corporations, that is by supervisory boards composed of bankers and experts from other corporations; since 1974 the federal government has taken care that there are no more than two government representatives on each of those boards, so that the state, even if majority shareholder, is always in the minority position.

In line with this obvious strategy of 'indirect privatisation' of state enterprise is a marked lack of an in any way systematised or centralised ministerial control: 'Eine zentrale Steuerung der Bundesbeteiligungen im Sinne einer Konzernführung findet nicht statt'.[11] Public enterprises are to be controlled solely by the market; even the barest minimum of public accountability, financial control by the *Bundesrechnungshof*, does not extend to their entrepreneurial activities, but is restricted to the federal state's activities as a shareholder.

Not much need be said about the American model, since there are hardly any public enterprises to speak of; even the 'public utilities' are operated on the basis of private ownership and 'free enterprise'. This does not mean that in America the state does not interfere in the business sphere at all: instead of direct involvement it has set up a whole range of semi-independent regulatory commissions (as, for instance, the Interstate Commerce Commission) to bind the otherwise free enterprises to the public interest. In this task the commissions have been hardly more successful than the various types of ministerial control over public enterprise.[12] Their critics unite in the verdict that, so far from protecting consumer interests and forcing

11. Fritz Knauss (Federal Ministry of Finance), in GÖWG (ed.), *Kontrolle öffentlicher Unternehmen*, vol. I, op. cit., p. 34.
12. See Paul W. MacAvoy, *The Regulated Industries and the Economy*, New York, 1979.

private firms to behave strictly competitively (the main reason for their existence), the commissions have developed into a means of protecting the respective industries' interests and of stabilising private market power. With a lack of centralised control over the commissions, the private firms have proved so capable of dealing with their commissions (using them not only to achieve prices considerably above competition level, but also to keep new competitors out of the market), that the latter sometimes are dubbed the 'puppets' of their industries. Still, there might have been a benefit in their existence had they, within their industries, pushed for coordinated modernisation and developed some sort of joint long-term planning that took into consideration the 'national interest'; but if one is to believe the evidence, they have also failed in that.[13]

The conclusion to be drawn from these models, apparently, is that there is no obvious solution to the problem of how to control enterprises, private or public, and of how to make them operate in keeping with the public interest. The models recommended by various reform proposals have not as yet met with significantly more success than has the British model itself.

Reforms and Reform Proposals

The series of major reforms of ministerial control of nationalised industries in the UK started with the White Paper of 1961. Until then (apart from the Finance Act of 1956, which transferred the corporations' borrowing from the capital market to the Exchequer) reforms had been limited to single nationalised industries and had mostly concerned themselves with questions of centralisation and decentralisation. But the 1961 White Paper on Financial and Economic Obligations of the Nationalised Industries concerned them all and for the first time tried, with the invention of financial targets, to put financial control of them on a systematic and calculable basis. With the 1967 White Paper on the same subject the attempt to commit the corporations to quantitative objectives was continued, and completed by the introduction of uniform criteria for investment appraisal (the test discount rate, TDR) and of the marginal cost pricing rule. There was some debate then as to whether both new instruments would not render the existing financial targets superfluous. The question was

---

13. There seems to be a parallel to the former BISF in Britain, as will be shown in more detail below.

answered, if not in principle, then by the practice of price control and price restraint which lasted until the mid-1970s; since under such conditions the corporations were not free to charge the prices they thought appropriate to earn a profit, the financial targets (usually expressed in terms of profit) had to be abandoned — only to be re-introduced in the late 1970s.

There were also debates on the usefulness and practicability of TDR and marginal cost pricing. The latter especially was criticised as impracticable for, quite apart from price controls, which obviously render any pricing rule futile, it is apparently difficult (if not dubious) to determine in practice what marginal cost prices really are. Furthermore, had the corporations strictly applied that rule, it would have conflicted with their financial targets: if the industry as a whole is to make a profit, some prices at least must exceed costs.[14] Criticism of TDR was not only that the rate of return was fixed on too high a level but, even more, that it did not reflect upon what sort of investment there should be and that it discouraged projects with a higher long-term pay-off; in short, that it was by no means a guarantee of optimal factor allocation. What most critics as well as the corporations themselves appreciated, however, was that according to the White Papers both of 1961 and 1967 the nationalised industries were to be treated as unequivocally *commercial* enterprises whose primary duty was to make a profit. Should politicians decide that unprofitable services should be offered in the 'public interest', then the nationalised industries should be financially compensated.

At roughly the same time, 1965 to 1970, there was the short interlude of the NBPI. Though its task was to control price and wage increases over the economy as a whole, it was of specific relevance for the nationalised industries because of its right to subject single corporations to efficiency controls. But its efforts to complement ministerial control did not meet with success. In the first place, neither its role between ministers and industries nor its proper functions towards the latter were ever made quite clear; hence its interventions exacerbated the general problem of muddled responsibilities and caused a great deal of resentment. Secondly, its concept of efficiency, and how it was related to the purpose of the industry, was not very clear either.[15] The foundation of the National Consumer Council in 1975 might have been another step in the direction of performance and efficiency

14. For the criticism see (*inter alia*) Redwood and Hatch, *Controlling Public Industries*, op. cit., pp. 66f.
15. For the role of the NBPI see Coombes, *State Enterprise*, op. cit., pp. 126ff.

control. Yet the Council does not have any real powers of 'control': it is restricted to making recommendations.

Instead, the line pursued in subsequent reforms was that of elaborating on the system of financial control. The next step in that direction was the introduction of cash limits in 1976.[16] Whilst before that, only the capital expenditure of the corporations was included in the PSBR, now their working capital was included as well. And what was, and still is, important is that even money borrowed from the private sector counts as public spending, so that the cash limits cannot be dodged by applying to other sources.

In the White Paper of 1978[17] the system of financial control found its last and still valid formulation: the TDR (of 8 per cent) was substituted by the required rate of return, RRR (fixed at 5 per cent in real terms); the rule of marginal cost pricing was abandoned but financial targets reintroduced; the annual cash limits were firmly established. It promised, in addition, the publication of non-financial targets for each nationalised industry; financial controls were to be supplemented by an efficiency control via performance indicators. Yet while the instruments of financial control have been in use long since, there is still much doubt as to how to find and define suitable performance targets for each industry — especially since the government does not like to be 'bothered' with the task of defining the purpose of each.

Another non-financial proposal of this last White Paper was that the composition of the boards should be made more flexible; that is, it encouraged attempts to find ways of control 'from inside' by having government representatives as part-timers on the board, or to supplement ministerial by consumers' or workers' control by appointing consumer and/or worker representatives as part-time members. There are only a few instances where this proposal has been put into practice, and these show that such new categories of part-timers do not have much impact on the boards' decision-making — an experience quite in line with those of the French *conseils d'administration* or with the German version (in private enterprise) of *Mitbestimmung*: board members representing interests alien to, or conflicting with, those of the business in question, and without the specific expertise and camaraderie of businessmen, tend to be second-class members.

One should perhaps mention, as a further reform concerning the control of public enterprise, the establishment of the National Enter-

---

16. *White Paper: Cash Limits on Public Expenditure*, Cmnd. 6440, London, 1976.
17. *The Nationalised Industries*, Cmnd. 2131, London, 1978.

prise Board; particularly since, for some time, it seems to have been fashionable to recommend modelling the state's dealings with its enterprises after the Italian IRI formula.[18] There is indeed a similarity of construction between the NEB and the IRI, yet its main purpose was, like that of its predecessor the Industrial Reorganisation Corporation, to support private firms, to save them from bankruptcy, help them to modernise and reorganise, further mergers and so on. With respect to public enterprises its role is restricted to dealing with those few that do not have the status of a nationalised industry; as *The Economist* put it, 'it owns the state's shares in national disasters'.[19] The specific organisation of the 'public corporation' by definition precludes the NEB, as a holding, from having anything to do with the nationalised industries.

Reforms have been brought about not only by governments but by the corporations themselves. Mostly these have had to do with the reorganisation and restructuring of their industries. However, a major step towards improving the situation of them *all* was made by building up an association designed to work out a common stance on questions of joint interest and to act as the corporations' spokesman, mainly towards government. The origins of this association lay in informal meetings held from the end of the 1950s and initiated by Lord Robens ('Alf Robens' Think Tank'); gradually, and partly because of protests from the chairmen of smaller corporations who felt passed over, those meetings developed into something more formal until, in 1976, the Nationalised Industries' Chairmen's Group was founded officially. Though the NICG takes some pains to retain a certain informality of character (it has hardly any staff, for instance), and is particularly anxious not to be looked upon as a 'public sector CBI',[20] it does in many respects perform the functions of a normal business association. The Group meets regularly and is advised by the Finance, Personal, and Economic Panels formed by the respective experts of the boards. Its main addressee is the government — especially the Treasury, which is, as the NICG see it, one of the reasons why it is not particularly liked in the other departments — and its main concerns are: (1) to restrict the power of the ministers; (2) to influence the financial framework (to have the corporations' interests in this respect permanently represented a joint working group with the Treasury has been established); and (3) — and not least! — to raise

18. See, for instance, Stuart Holland (ed.), *The State as Entrepreneur*, London, 1972.
19. *The Economist*, 6 May 1978, p. 115.
20. Thus James Driscoll (NICG) in March 1981.

board salaries which, according to the NICG, are so poor by private sector standards that they fail to attract really capable men to the public sector. The NICG claim not to interfere in the dealings of an individual corporation with its minister — unless those dealings do 'not get through to the heart of the matter'.[21] This might mean that in cases of severe conflict between a chairman and his minister the NICG would try to stiffen the chairman's stance.

Though the bulk of the NICG's activities are concerned with dealing with the government there are other spheres of activity. The Group has contacts with the TUC, for instance, particularly close ones with the CBI, contacts with the NEDC and, on the European level, with the CEEP. One thing the NICG does not concern itself with is the 'commercial' affairs of the individual corporations: it is not an agent of co-ordination and it does not try to solve conflicts arising between its members; its activities are directed entirely to the outside world. Probably this stance is the only means of maintaining a modicum of coherence within the group itself; for the main problem of the NICG, and the main hindrance to its greater effectiveness as a pressure group, is the heterogeneity of its members' interests. Concerning a limited range of issues, however, it has proved to be a sufficiently effective lobby in recent years, fending off an extension of the Comptroller and Auditor General's (C&AG) power of scrutiny over the nationalised industries, and just now drawing the teeth of Treasury plans to reshape ministerial control (see Part IV). For some time, in 1981 and 1982, it even looked as though it might succeed in loosening the nationalised industries' ties with the PSBR.

In addition to the reforms mentioned various proposals have come to nothing because of determined opposition from different sides. One such was the SCNI's suggestion, in 1968, to form a separate Ministry of Nationalised Industries, in the hope that such a centralised authority would improve the efficiency of ministerial control and allow both for more coordination in the policies towards nationalised industries and for more cooperation between them. The latter argument would seem to be a valid one, though the example of the Department of Energy shows that the concentration of responsibility for several nationalised industries in one department does not necessarily imply a higher degree of coordination. But as for the higher efficiency of control, the SCNI might have learned from the Italian experience with the Ministry of State Holdings that, so far from exerting control, such a ministry would be in perpetual danger of

21. Ibid.

becoming the instrument of the enterprises it ought to control, to be their spokesman in government and to further their interests. The criticisms the SCNI's proposal met with in Britain, however, did not refer to the Italian example but expressed serious misgivings that such a new super-ministry, instead of solving the problem of blurred responsibilities, would only add to them, especially as the SCNI had not, at the same time, suggested that the responsibility of the various sponsoring departments for their nationalised industries were to come to an end.

In 1976 the NEDO made another move to solve the problems of ministerial control by proposing a restructuring of the public corporations after the two-tier model of French (and German) state enterprises: each nationalised industry was to have, separate from the corporation board, a 'policy council' which was to include representatives of the management, of government, trade unions and consumers, as well as 'an independent element'.[22] While the corporation board was to be responsible to the Council, the latter's tasks were visualised as restricted to the development of 'strategies'; the distinction of the 'arm's-length' concept between policies and day-to-day management was to be transferred to the nationalised industries. The government's part in the new system suggested by the NEDO was limited to co-operation with the policy councils; government was *not* to interfere any longer with the work of the corporation boards.

Like the proposal of a separate ministry for all the nationalised industries, the construction of a separate policy council for each of them was rejected almost unanimously by ministers and boards alike. The government was not prepared to renounce its influence over the executive of the nationalised industries and the boards,[23] aware of what to expect from government, feared that the restructuring, so far from clarifying responsibilities, would cause a still greater muddle. Furthermore, the boards' comments made it abundantly clear that the NEDO's proposal was felt to be a (much resented) attack upon their own role and raison d'être. Seeing themselves as distinct from the executive management, theirs were the functions now ascribed to the new councils; so it was either the councils or they themselves who were superfluous. Accordingly they argued that at best the councils would be irrelevant because of 'lack of specialist knowledge'[24]

22. NEDO, *A Study of UK Nationalised Industries*, op. cit., p. 12.
23. See Second Special Report from the SCNI, Session 1976–77, *Comments by Nationalised Industries on the NEDO Report*, op. cit.
24. Ibid., p. xvi.

(a probable outcome, as the French example shows); at worst the proposed construction would prove to be 'a fertile source of discord and animosity'.[25]

It was probably unfortunate that the NEDO had suggested this new institutional device, for public debate focused on it and tended to neglect the other, useful recommendations the NEDO had given. It had, for instance, criticised the inadequacy of concentrating on the financial side of control and suggested: (1) a closer involvement of government in the strategic planning process of the corporations; and (2) the development of 'guidelines packages' (including guidelines referring to standards of service and social objectives) 'specifically tailored to the situation of each nationalised industry'.[26] It is one of the major deficiencies of the British system of ministerial control that such guidance is still lacking.

In its reaction to the NEDO Report the 1978 White Paper had, apart from the improvements of financial control already discussed, suggested that ministers ought to have the power to issue not only 'general directions' but also 'specific directives' which were to be made public and open to parliamentary scrutiny. This further effort to tackle the problem of blurred responsibilities has not yet met with success, either, opposition from both sides again being the cause. Ministers are naturally reluctant to have their own parliamentary accountability tightened; and the majority of the boards feared that 'the appetite for detailed intervention might grow in line with the power to intervene'.[27] In this case, however, the boards' opposition was by no means unanimous;[28] a substantial minority hoped that the proposed device might end the informal processes of 'nudge and fudge' and, because of the reluctance of ministers to be publicly committed, decrease the amount of government interference. Probably the most characteristic comment was the remark by Sir Keith Granville, ex-chairman of BA, to the effect that 'it is just as bad to be threatened over lunch with a direction as it is to have your arm twisted over the second glass of brandy'.[29]

---

25. Ibid., p. ix.
26. NEDO, *A Study of UK Nationalised Industries*, op. cit., Appendix vol., p. 114.
27. NICG Memo, in the SCNI (Sub-Committee E), Session 1978–79, *The Relationships* . . ., op. cit., p. 76.
28. See Sixth Special Report from the SCNI, Session 1977–78, *Comments by Nationalised Industries and Others on the Government White Paper on the Nationalised Industries*, op. cit.
29. In the SCNI (Sub-Committee E), Session 1978–79, *The Relationships* . . ., op. cit., p. 51.

Lately there have been two further proposals for reform (apart from the general privatisation policy). One of these was the Think Tank's suggestions in 1981: (1) to set a clear strategic objective for each chairman; (2) to appoint a majority of non-executive members to each board, with the task of supervising efficiency; and (3) to establish a group of businessmen in each sponsoring department to improve its expertise. The last suggestion met with so much opposition that the Report of the Central Policy Review Staff was not even published. Though there was a passing reference to proposal (1) in the parliamentary debate on the budget in 1982,[30] the line of agreeing 'strategic objectives' with each corporation did not, at first, seem to have been followed up, thus reminding one strongly of the typical fate of reform proposals which ventured to suggest, *inter alia*, institutional rearrangements: the latter were usually opposed so intensely that the public debate was wholly focused on them and the rest of the recommendation, however sensible, fell into oblivion. In this case, however, the proposal is said to have resulted, meanwhile (1984), in the 'new approach' to agree such objectives whenever a new chairman is appointed.

The other recent proposal seeks to extend the competence of the Comptroller & Auditor General over the public corporations. It was part of the St John Stevas Bill (which originated in the Public Accounts Committee), and was — once again — opposed by the government as well as by the boards. The idea is rather an old one: as early as 1960 William A. Robson had asked for an Efficiency Audit Commission as the only means to improve the corporations' efficiency.[31] Now the PAC's claim for 'independent' efficiency control is supported by Maurice R. Garner (former DTI) who, for some time past, has kept pointing to the fact that the problem of efficiency audits has been sadly neglected.[32] The boards' opposition in this case rested mainly on the not exactly original argument that any additional control would cause further 'delays' in their decision-making and hamper their commercial efficiency; they feel that, as things stand, there are more than enough controlling agencies consuming their time and meddling with their affairs. The government, on the other hand, agreed in principle with the need for efficiency auditing but main-

---

30. House of Commons, *Parliamentary Debates*, Hansard, vol. 20, no. 77, 15 March 1982, p. 24.
31. See, for instance, the First Report from the SCNI, Session 1967–68, *Ministerial Control* . . ., op. cit., vol. II, p. 534.
32. M. R. Garner, 'Auditing the Efficiency of Nationalised Industries: Enter the Monopolies and Mergers Commission', l.c.

tained that this task should better rest with the Monopolies and Mergers Commission (which, since 1980, has investigated the efficiency of several of the nationalised industries). Yet there is an important snag in the solution favoured by the government: the MMC, in the first place, can act only when commissioned to do so by government while the C&AG acts autonomously; and secondly, the MMC's power to investigate is restricted to the corporations while the C&AG may scrutinise the sponsoring departments as well. There is obviously some point in suggesting that, for efficiency control to be effective, it should not be dichotomised into one for the industries and one for their sponsoring ministries, for such a separation inevitably leaves room for the well-tried tactical ploy of each side pointing to the other as causing the inefficiencies they are both accused of. Equally, the interests of boards and governments being what they are, it is quite understandable that they are both opposed to having this useful tactical ploy barred to them. Small wonder, then, that the House of Commons eventually dropped all reference to the nationalised industries from the Bill. So here we have another example of the somewhat unfortunate tendency characterising British efforts to reform the system of ministerial control: that all reform proposals reaching *beyond* the mere improvement of financial control, whether they are sensible and promising or not, are frustrated by the combined resistance of boards and governments.

The Thatcherite System

Since the Thatcher government came into office in 1979, its policies towards the nationalised industries have been guided by three principles: (1) to improve and tighten financial control over them (based on the proposals of the 1978 White Paper); (2) to treat them as entirely commercial undertakings and, hence, abstain from all intervention into their management; and (3) wherever possible, to de-nationalise them, or at least break their monopoly power.

The first principle has led to the current system of financial control already outlined above (pp. 61f.). Although in theory this system tries to find a nice balance between long- (investment appraisal based on RRR), medium- (financial targets) and short-term (EFL) elements, its practice is characterised by a much-criticised dominance of the short-term 'financial discipline'. This preponderance is only partly due to some difficulties in the application of investment appraisals which, furthermore, still differ from industry to industry; rather, the main reason for the lopsidedness of the financial control system must be seen in the Treasury's determination to keep public expenditure down and to control the growth in the money supply. Now, annual EFLs are by no means a bad thing in themselves, provided that there is some built-in guarantee that they genuinely operate as the intended 'spur to efficiency'; unfortunately they can be met, not only by lowering costs but equally by increasing prices or by cutting or postponing investment. So far there is no evidence that the EFLs were, in fact, the cause of price increases; but there have been many complaints that they tend to reduce investment below the level suggested by other (economic) criteria, and that this tendency will of necessity adversely affect the infrastructure of the nationalised industries as well as the growth of the economy as a whole.[33] Though the Treasury not unjustly points to the fact that the amount of *de facto* frustrated investment during recent years was much less than the public impression indicated, there can be no doubt that inflexible EFLs lead to an under-valuation of long-term aspects. Furthermore, in some cases the EFLs seem to have collided with the financial targets set for the same industry.

Obviously the main snag in this type of 'financial discipline' lies in the EFLs being tailored less with a view to the specific needs and objectives of each industry than with a view to the Treasury's monetarist policies; hence the complaint that 'the most disturbing thing is that in Years 5, 4, 3 and 2 you can agree your capital programme with your department and with the Treasury and then in Year 1, just when you are actually about to start it, suddenly you are told, "Oh no, the PSBR restraints are set, you cannot go ahead . . ." '.[34] Because of it being 'unreasonable to ask nationalised industries to forego desirable investment projects because the government itself has overspent'[35] the NICG has asked long since that the corporations' investment expenditure be taken out of the PSBR and that they be given access to private finance, but so far to no avail. One of the main arguments of the Thatcher government against this claim has been that of 'crowding out', that is, that public investment hinders private investment. While the argument has not been proved to be valid or even likely, it is in line with the Thatcherite belief that public sector economic activity is undesirable *per se*, whatever its nature, efficiency, growth effect or profit potential.

33. See the various statements, in Eighth Report from the Treasury and Civil Service Committee, Session 1980–81, *Financing of the Nationalised Industries*, op. cit., vol. II.
34. Mr P. Shelbourne (BNOC), ibid., p. 17.
35. Memo. of the British Gas Corporation, ibid., p. 172.

The politics of emphasising the EFLs are *not* in line, however, with the second principle of Conservative policies toward the nationalised industries: that of treating them 'commercially'. If there is something the EFLs do achieve it is that the corporations are not in a position to implement long-term corporate planning and that they do not have the room for manoeuvre their private sector counterparts usually have; 'rigid adherence to the EFL on a financial year basis is . . . certainly not a reflection of normal commercial practice'.[36] In view of the effects of the EFLs on investment policies especially it is not surprising that members of the boards of nationalised industries comment somewhat sarcastically on the government's professed policy of non-intervention: 'This government is perhaps not quite clear about the meaning of the word non-intervention'.[37] Yet there are other instances of government interference, for example, into the pricing policies of the profitable corporations, trying to squeeze out more cash for the Exchequer (which now is labelled 'negative EFL').[38] So, as has already been mentioned, and contrary to all non-interventionist doctrines, it is at best the nature and direction of government intervention that has been altered, not the politics of intervention itself.

What has indeed changed, most radically, is the attitude towards nationalisation as such. Whereas previous Conservative governments broadly accepted the public/private split and restricted themselves to stressing the commercial orientation of the existing nationalised industries, the Thatcher government attempts to undertake a drastic roll-back of public sector economy and, in fact, is ideologically committed, in the long run, either to return *all* public enterprises to private ownership, or to close them down. Yet the policy of denationalisation has not only an ideological but also a budgetary dimension: the sale of nationalised assets raises cash and, at the same time, reduces the size of the PSBR.

At the time of writing the first sales have taken place,[39] though the process of privatisation has been moving much less quickly and

36. Ibid., p. 173.
37. Jim Driscoll, March 1981.
38. In November 1983 the EFL of the CEGB was fixed at −£740m, which meant an increase of 70 per cent in electricity's contribution to public funds over 1983–84 (see *The Economist*, 17 March 1984, p. 32).
39. The measures up to December 1983 were:
    (1) the state's stake in BP is reduced to 31.7 per cent;
    (2) BNOC's oil fields and exploration and drilling business are hived off, put into the new company Britoil and sold to the private sector;

smoothly than the government might have thought. In some of the earlier cases the stumbling block lay in the fact that private investors were not over-enthusiastic to buy the shares offered, since the industries in question did not seem profitable enough. To find a remedy for such cases the government have fallen back upon the Heathite formula of 'hiving off' the profitable bits of those industries, that is, to sell bits and pieces to the private sector; another strategy is, instead of 100 per cent sales, to form 'hybrid companies' with government stakes of 50 per cent or less.

Although the corporations' chairmen usually resent their subjection to ministerial control and to the rules of the PSBR, the majority of them do not seem to be altogether happy with the privatisation programme. Opposition is particularly strong to the 'hiving off' strategy; in some cases it has already led chairmen or board members to retire in protest. Furthermore, there are sharp differences of opinion on these policies between the Treasury (and the PM) and sponsoring ministers. Yet the policy of privatisation does not only encounter difficulties of implementation (which, however, seem to have been overcome), worsen the situation of the remaining public corporations (who are left with the unprofitable bits), and lead to a deterioration in the relationship between boards and government, which is already precarious enough; with its side-strategies of hiving off, of injecting private capital into public firms and encouraging joint ventures, it blurs the borderline between the public and the private sectors. This is the more problematic as there are hints (although this is denied by the Treasury) that the government have supplied hybrids as well as the privatised companies with public money — that is, have placed public funds in private hands over which they no longer have any power of control. Hence the suspicion that privatisation may neither stop public sector economic activity, nor relieve the tax payers' burden; it does, however, put an end to public accountability and ministerial control.[40]

 (3) the state's stake in Cable and Wireless is reduced to 23.1 per cent;
 (4) British Aerospace is sold to 51 per cent;
 (5) Amersham International is sold;
 (6) the National Freight Corporation is transferred 'to a consortium led by its own management' (to be sold thereafter);
 (7) British Airways is transformed into a 'Companies' Act company' to be sold (but no investors yet found).
In other cases legislation is under way or on the Statute Book enabling the government to sell. (See *The Economist*, 3 December 1983, p. 44; Hansard, vol. 19, no. 73, 9.3. 1982, p. 791). For developments since then see Part IV, Chapter 16, below.
40. For a further discussion of the problems of the privatisation policy, see Part IV,

A History of Reform

To summarise these remarks on the British system of ministerial control:

(1) The statutes (as the starting point) prescribe a combination of *ex ante* ('general directives', approval of investment programmes) and *ex post*, albeit in both respects a somewhat distant control; what they did not envisage was continual guidance and supervision, and what they particularly neglected was efficiency control.

(2) The practice of ministerial control developed into a somewhat contradictory combination of great distance where 'policies' are concerned — more precisely, a lack of policy guidance — and great closeness in day-to-day management, that is, frequent government interference by way of 'backstairs pressures'. The interference itself usually had little to do with the corporations' specific situation, but much with the various governments' day-to-day economic policies. The conclusion to be drawn from this development is that the Morrisonian concept of 'arm's length', though still the prevailing doctrine for the governments' dealings with their public corporations, has from the very start existed on paper only.

(3) Reforms in the last two decades were attempts to find a system of 'control by formulae' and, mainly because of this, were restricted to a continuous tightening of financial discipline, the instruments of which are problematic in so far as they are one-sided as well as applied regardless of the purpose and nature of the individual nationalised industries. The problems the reforms have not yet tackled are those of the lack of clear objectives for each industry as well as the lack of long-term consideration of their development, the lack of policy coordination the lack of efficiency (or performance) control, and the pervasive problem of 'blurred responsibilities'. Apparently these are just the problems (apart, perhaps, from that of efficiency control) which are not to be solved by the application of simple formulae and easily calculable criteria.

If one of the reasons for relying so heavily on the 'set of targets' type of control was to circumvent the dilemma of how to control the experts, then the reformers were over-optimistic. To undertake investment appraisals requires expertise and simply to axe investments, through cash limits, and regardless of their possible benefits, will provoke highly undesirable reactions by the 'experts' as well as equally undesirable economic results. Yet it is doubtful whether the reformers spent much thought on the problem of expertise. Instead, the ideology underlying the reforms since 1961 has been that public

---

Chapter 16, below.

firms are commercial undertakings which must operate commercially and must be treated as such — without being 'double-guessed' by controllers. This analogy to the private sector has barred the view to the vital question of what public enterprises are, and should be, there for; and it has given governments a permanent excuse for never wasting a serious thought on what they wanted to achieve with (and through) them. Hence it is only to be expected that at the end of this history of reform we find that the decision has been to de-nationalise.

Ministerial Control and the British Political System

8

Though most of the problems that we have described here are by no means unique, there are some that are certainly aggravated by specific features of the British political and administrative system. One of these is a lack of coordination, and a habit of 'blurring responsibilities', not only in the government's dealings with outside groups, but within the machinery of government itself. Not even Mrs Thatcher, who in various cabinet reshuffles tried to drive the 'wets' out of government, seems to have succeeded in fundamentally altering the traditional character of the cabinet of being '*not* an institution for co-ordinating policies. It enforces collective responsibility but not collective decision-making'.[1] There are attempts on the part of the Treasury to bring the other ministries into line with the 'general policies' agreed between the PM and the Chancellor, and there have been various 'steering committees' (on economic policy, for instance) for the same purpose, but such attempts at coordination are frequently, and not altogether unsuccessfully, resisted by ministers defending the interests of their clientele. Below the ministerial level there are a lot of interdepartmental contacts, of course, and in the Treasury even a Nationalised Industries' Policy Committee, set up to combine the respective efforts of various departments; yet these contacts and committees seem to be no more successful than those on the highest level. Although it would be plausible to expect that civil servants, because of their job rotation, would be interested in at least a modicum of coordination of departmental policies, the effects of such an interest, if it does exist, are elusive; judging from the examples of the Department of Energy as well as of the Department of Environment, where coordination of policies does not occur even between the various divisions within the department,[2] the existence of the interest itself must be doubted.

1. Richard Rose, *Politics in England Today*, London, 1974, p. 310.
2. See Martin J. Painter, 'Policy Co-ordination in the Department of the Environ-

The effects of the lack of co-ordination are the more detrimental because of overlapping responsibilities, especially in the field of economic policy — and, of course, concerning the nationalised industries: the respective functions are distributed over quite a number of departments and institutions. Though the overlap was worse in the 1960s, when the Treasury and the (then) Department of Economic Affairs fought a battle over which of them was to have the last word in questions of economic policy and there was, in addition, the NBPI to be reckoned with, it may still be seen in the distribution of economic functions between the Department of Industry and the Department of Trade (which have been merged recently into a new DTI) and the Treasury — to say nothing of the various sponsoring ministers who have a say in economic matters by reason of their influence over the public sector economy.

The manifold institutional changes indicated by this brief sketch of administrative functions moving between old and newly-created, merged, separated and again merged departments point to another specific feature of the British system of government: the urge 'to move the institutional furniture around'.[3] There seems to be hardly any other Western country where, over the last two decades, departments and other quasi-governmental institutions have changed with such a 'dazzling rapidity'.[4] Apart from such major changes, this institutionalism has found its expression in an inclination, whenever a new problem has turned up or old, unsolved ones became urgent again, to set up a commission or similar body in the hope of thus, if not to solve yet to get rid of them. Countless commissions have absorbed their members' time and energy but, instead of bringing about the necessary action, have exhausted themselves with conferences and reports — while yet other commissions have busied themselves with collecting and evaluating the comments to the reports by those concerned. In the case of the nationalised industries, especially, the setting up of new agencies has usually only imperfectly concealed a basic unwillingness to make decisions about purposes and policies. More generally, the tendency to institutionalism, or over-institutionalisation, which results in a 'proliferation of overlapping and rival bodies',[5] is the specifically British type of government inertia,[6] of a

---

ment, 1970–1976', in *Public Administration*, vol. 58, Summer 1980, pp. 135–54.
3. An expression ascribed to Sir Geoffrey Howe when he was Chancellor of the Exchequer.
4. Samuel Brittan, *Steering the Economy*, London, 1969, p. 39.
5. Ibid., p. 186.

resistance to any real change and innovation. Politics, not only concerning the nationalised industries, confine themselves to minor alterations and window-dressing; innovative impulses get lost in a chaos of confused responsibilities.

The tendencies to uncoordinated fragmentation, over-institutionalisation and the distribution of functions between a multitude of rival bodies should be counterbalanced by the reigning Whitehall principle of 'generalists'. Not only functions and the institutional furniture are moved around, but the civil servants as well, who usually spend no more than three to five years in any one department or division of a department. From this job rotation several beneficial results are to be expected: (1) it ought to guarantee a modicum of inter-ministerial communication and cooperation, as civil servants from different departments are (or should be) versatile enough to understand each other's problems and interested, for the sake of their own further progress, in the successful running of other departments; (2) civil servants are prevented from becoming too deeply involved with their clientele and, hence, from 'going native' and neglecting the wider aspects of public welfare; (3) by the end of their career they are presumed knowledgeable in all possible fields of government activity and competent to deal with any problem they encounter.

While the actual achievement of these beneficial results must remain in doubt, job rotation has at least two serious drawbacks. The first is that the clientele of the civil servants are constantly confronted with new colleagues, which is less a personal problem than one of making expert communication possible. The nationalised industries, forced into continuous and close contact with their sponsoring departments, suffer especially from the frequent changes of personnel and the resultant lack of continuity. It is difficult to imagine how, in this way, civil servants will ever gain the expertise needed for the task of controlling public enterprise. The other, even more serious drawback of the rotation principle is that it contributes to the institutional inertia mentioned above. Frequent changes leave no incentive to civil servants to enter wholeheartedly into the problems they deal with in each position, nor do they allow for commitment to programmes, or for a sense of responsibility for programme results. Instead, civil servants tend to define their tasks in very limited terms ('administering the statutes') and, because of the limited base of knowledge they operate from, to take the 'safe course' of avoiding risks and postponing

---

6. See, specifically, Jack Hayward, 'Institutional Inertia and Political Impetus in France and Britain', in *European Journal of Political Research*, 4 (1976), pp. 341-59.

decisions[7] — hence to cling to the status quo.

Finally, the efficiency of governmental action in general and ministerial control in particular suffers from the British political parties' addiction to adversary politics, leading to a 'reversal and re-reversal and re-reversal of policy'[8] on the part of each incoming government. On the surface this seems to contradict the tendency to inertia given here as one of the main characteristics of the British politico-administrative system. However, the typical result of adversary politics is an extreme short-term orientation which renders the formulation and implementation of consistent and necessarily long-term programmes for real (structural) innovation impossible, prompting a mere change of institutions instead — the sort of window-dressing described above.[9] What is more, such concealed immobilism tells most strongly on those who depend on government — who, like the nationalised industries, need government approval for going ahead with their programmes. The 'disruptive effects of political change',[10] restricted though they are, with institutional rearrangements, nationalisation, de-nationalisation, re-nationalisation,[11] the curtailing of investment programmes, constant alterations of target systems and so forth, make themselves felt drastically in the public corporations and hardly allow for any long-term planning. So far from furthering a commercial outlook and innovative entrepreneurial strategies they should rather be expeced to lead to a 'civil service mentality' in public sector managers, passively awaiting the next U-turn of government policy. The political immobilism, that is, becomes infectious.

Of course the short time-horizon of politicians, albeit in not quite that radical way, must be seen as a common feature of all parliamentary democracies, the more so when coupled with a two-party system. Party competition forces politicians to look first, and above all, to the next election, to do everything they deem necessary to get (re-) elected, to react to short-term pressures and not to think beyond that date. Hence the clash between the politicians' short-term orientation and the public enterprises' need for long-term planning is one of the

7. See the severe criticism by Harold Seidman, 'Ministers, Departments and Public Enterprise', paper presented to the RIPA Research Group on Public Enterprise, 27.6. 1980, pp. 6ff.
8. S. E. Finer (ed.), *Adversary Politics and Electoral Reform*, Anthony Wigram, 1975, p. 16.
9. Or to 'reforms without change'; see Dennis Kavanagh and Richard Rose (eds.), *New Trends in British Politics*, London/Beverly Hills, 1977, p. 15.
10. Coombes, *State Enterprise*, op. cit., p. 13.
11. The Labour Party have already announced their determination to reverse all the present (1984) government's privatisation measures.

more general problems faced by any public enterprise in parliamentary systems.

There is yet another feature common to these systems which is also detrimental to the interests of ministerial control of public enterprises: the reluctance of politicians to be publicly committed. Public commitment lays them open to criticism; they may be held responsible in case the policies they are committed to fail; and this, in turn, may weaken their chances of re-election. Consequently, they tend not only to refrain from formulating long-term programmes, but if possible to avoid public approaches to the problems presenting themselves altogether. This explains the pervasive lack, in practically all Western economies, of clear, publicly-stated policies for the public enterprises: the often complained about 'lack of clarity and purpose' concerning them is by no means accidental.

While the deficiencies of ministerial control may be the result of general as well as specific features of the politico-administrative system, they may themselves influence the way in which the latter operates. Since sponsoring departments, in spite of the effects of job rotation, tend to identify with their nationalised industries when dealing with other ministries and (particularly) with the Treasury, one is justified in supposing that the conflicts between individual nationalised industries and between them and the Treasury will aggravate and intensify the conflicts and problems of coordination within the machinery of government. Thus, under the Thatcher government, *The Economist* feared that Britain's nationalised industries might be 'undermining' the Prime Minister's control over her cabinet, their chairmen having 'recruited wetter ministers into an unholy alliance against the beleaguered treasury . . .'.[12] The close and continuous contact between the corporations and their sponsoring departments — more precisely, the latter's divisions dealing with them — can be said to enhance an already existing tendency in Whitehall to the emancipation of functional sub-units, or to the 'relative . . . self containment of policy sub-systems'.[13] The phenomena of fragmentation, colonialisation and particularisation, which some authors[14] detect as characteristic of the administration in its dealings with a private capitalist economy, obviously exist in its dealings with the public sector of that economy to at least the same extent.

12. *The Economist*, 20 June 1981, p. 14.
13. Painter, 'Policy Co-ordination in the Department of the Environment, 1970–1976', l.c., p. 152.
14. See Joachim Hirsch, *Staatsapparat und Reproduktion des Kapitals*, Frankfurt a.M., 1974, pp. 62ff., 234ff.

Nationalised Industries and the Private Sector 9

Public enterprises not only have to struggle in and with the political system, but must make their way in an economic environment dominated by private enterprise. This does not necessarily imply that they find themselves in a hostile environment, nor even in one more hostile than an entirely public sector environment would be. The relationship, at least in Britain, between the various nationalised industries is by no means harmonious — a fact which, considering the lack of coordination between their 'sponsors', is hardly surprising; left to themselves they develop, like any other enterprise, distinct interests of their own.[1] Conflicts arise, typically, when one corporation depends on deliveries from another, particularly if the latter is in a monopoly position. For example, during the years when the gas industry depended on coke, relations between British Gas and the NCB were notoriously bad. The situation between the NCB and the BSC is similar, complicated by the latter threatening to import not only part, but all of its coke requirements — a threat which confronted the government with the dilemma of having to decide whose losses it wished to increase, those of the BSC or of the NCB.[2]

Whatever the conflicts between them, however, the various nationalised industries find themselves in the same structural position, particularly *vis-à-vis* the government: they are all dependent on the Treasury, suffer from government interference and so on. In this respect private firms are in an entirely different position; hence, underlying the relationship between the two sectors of the economy is a slight feeling of mingled envy and resentment (albeit seldom openly expressed). The public corporations envy private firms their freedom from the constant meddling of civil servants and politicians, and for

1. For German theorists of *Gemeinwirtschaft*, recognising the same development of public enterprise in the Weimar Republic, this was evidence of the 'intrusion of capitalist elements in the Gemeinwirtschaft'; see Winkler, *Preußen als Unternehmer*, op. cit., pp. 128f.
2. See *The Economist*, 9 August 1980, p. 18.

decades now have claimed that it is high time that they were treated 'on all fours with the private sector'.[3] The private firms, on the other hand, point out that the nationalised industries are free from the fear of bankruptcy, leading a sheltered economic life cushioned by government money. They, too, claim that public enterprises should be treated 'on all fours with the private sector', but in the sense that they ought to be exposed to the same rigours of a free market economy.

Conflicts between the sectors, as between individual nationalised industries, centre mainly around the question of prices. Yet while the arguments between two nationalised industries over prices and quantities seem to be more or less accidental, as far as the two sectors are concerned the problem is rather one of conflicting systems. It is a problem, though, that has never really quite developed into open conflict, for the government has fought the private sector's battles. For decades it has used the nationalised industries as a means of supporting the private sector, by dint of supplying goods and services to private industry at low prices (sometimes below operating and replacement costs) and 'buying British' at high prices. The 1961 White Paper revealed that at that time two-thirds of the nationalised industries' sales were to the private sector, at prices which did not cover costs. Its findings, however, did not lead to any significant changes in this respect, for in the name of anti-inflationary policies the economy as a whole went on enjoying a low level of public sector prices. Hence it seems hardly an exaggeration when John Hughes, not mincing matters, talks about the 'economic exploitation' of the nationalised industries.[4] This certainly did not contribute to their economic efficiency; nor did the associated obligation to 'buy British' contribute to the improvement of their technological standards.

The private sector, however, has not always shown proper gratitude for such continuous support, complaining instead that the corporations have used their monopoly power and ignored the interests of their industrial consumers.[5] This refers usually to questions of quality and credit only. It is doubtful, anyway, whether such complaints in general need to be taken so very seriously, for most nationalised industries have developed consultative institutions and procedures (industrial consumers' councils and others) which seem to operate

3. The SCNI (Sub-Committee E), Session 1978–79, *The Relationships between Ministers, Parliament and the Nationalised Industries*, op. cit., p. 2.
4. John Hughes, 'Relations with Private Industry', in Shanks (ed.), *The Lessons of Public Enterprise*, op. cit., p. 126.
5. See, e.g., the First Report from the SCNI, Session 1977–78, *The British Steel Corporation*, London, 1977, vol. I., pp. lxiiiff.; vol. II, pp. 130f.

very smoothly and satisfactorily to both sides. The Industrial Consumers' Council of the NCB as well as the British Iron and Steel Consumers' Council, for instance, both support, more often than not, 'their' corporation against outside criticisms (including any from the government); most corporations seem to be equally happy with the smooth-running consultative arrangements, 'joint working parties' and so on, set up with their suppliers.

So, on the whole, relations between private and nationalised industries, albeit somewhat 'asymmetric', are fairly good — even 'in many respects . . . close and rewarding'.[6] There is a close organisational link between the sectors, for all the public corporations are members of the private industries' business association, the CBI. This ought to come as a surprise, for one expects that 'naturally' a business association in a private capitalist economy would be opposed to the idea of nationalisation, and would regard the public enterprises either as intruders or violators of principle. The CBI's predecessors, however, kept a low profile during the time when most of the nationalisations were taking place, opposing them in a rather lukewarm fashion and probably more from a sense of duty than from conviction. Marked opposition from British business associations came only when the renationalisation of British Steel was at stake. Until then the private sector had cooperated with the existing public corporations, setting up joint working parties over questions of mutual interest.[7]

It might be worthwhile mentioning, at this stage, that the CBI and its main predecessor, the FBI, always have played a role in the British economic and political systems that is slightly different from major business associations in other Western countries. Brought into life, originally, with considerable help from the government,[8] it has remained a two-sided agency, much more than, for example, its German counterpart, cooperating so closely with successive governments that even to its own members it has sometimes appeared to be more an instrument of government policy (or even 'a tool of the civil service')[9] than a pressure group for private industry. With such a 'civil

6. Memo of BISPA, ibid., vol. II, p. 168.
7. As early as 1949 the FBI's General Secretary suggested that 'authority should be given to any F.B.I. Committee to invite the co-operation of National Boards in any matter in which the Committee believes that co-operation to be of advantage, including the right to co-opt representatives of National Boards . . .'' (FBI/CBI Archives, Modern Records Centre, University of Warwick; Papers of Gen. Secr. Douglas Walker, FBI/S/Walker/81/4, p. 9).
8. On the history of the FBI, see Stephen Blank, *Government and Industry in Britain. The Federation of British Industries in Politics, 1945–1965*, Westmead, 1973.
9. Quoted in Wyn Grant and David Marsh, *The Confederation of British Industry*,

service mentality'[10] it is not surprising that on its foundation in 1965 the CBI extended its membership to the nationalised industries — although this did not come about without some opposition from its 'original' members. The opposition was based partly on the argument (expressed as early as 1949, when the nationalised industries' membership of the (then) FBI had already been under debate) that 'we must always remember that the representatives of nationalised industry might be merely voicing the views and demands of their masters whatever government is in power',[11] and hence act as a Trojan horse; generally it was felt that the interests of public and private enterprise were too much opposed for them to be integrated in and represented by one and the same association.

The initiative for this controversial extension of membership seems to have come from Sir Henry Benson who, in 1963, was Joint Commissioner to advise on the integration of the FBI, the BEC and the NABM into a National Industrial Organisation. The leaders of the FBI favoured the idea at once and pushed the Integration Working Party, set up in the spring of 1964 by the three existing organisations, to take it seriously; with the same aim in view they kept in close contact with several of the nationalised industries' chairmen. Eventually the FBI brought its partners (including the reluctant NABM) round to its view and convinced its own members, though the latter aspect required some cautious handling. Since there was 'considerable sensitivity among some FBI members about the association of the nationalised industries with the N.I.O.', FBI president Sir Norman Kipping told the IWP in October 1964 that 'it is important to avoid any charge that the issue was being pre-judged. He recommended therefore, that the nationalised industries should not make any public announcement for the time being'.[12] Even in 1966, when most of the nationalised industries were already members of the new CBI, its Director General John Davies had to tell them that there was 'quite a considerable adjustment of mind to be brought about in the existing membership of the C.B.I. to their new and powerful bed-fellows. I have been working hard at this both in London and in the Regions'.[13]

London/Sydney/Auckland/Toronto, 1977, p. 90.
10. See J. P. Nettl, 'Consensus or elite domination: the case of business', in *Political Studies*, 13 (1965), p. 33.
11. Walter Lines (Lines Bros Ltd.), in FBI/CBI Archives, Papers of Gen. Secr. Douglas Walker, FBI/S/Walker/81/4, p. 23.
12. Minutes of the N.I.O. Integration Committee/Integration Working Party; FBI/ CBI/ Archives; IWP 15.10.1964.
13. FBI/CBI Archives, Papers of the Gen. Secr. John Gough, FBI/GO/83: letter from

What was the motive prompting the FBI leaders to press forward against considerable opposition with their wish to include the public corporations in the CBI membership? Certainly it rested on more than the belief that a real National Industrial Organisation, a merger of all the former separate associations which would allow the nation's industry to speak with one voice, could not afford to exclude such a large part of industry as that represented by the nationalised corporations. It is not quite clear whether or not the founders of the NIO were urged in this direction by the government. What *is* clear, however, is that the corporations' joining the CBI implied a considerable financial gain for the organisation — £40,000 per year, or 5 per cent of the CBI's total income, was the estimate given by *The Financial Times*.[14] Throughout the internal discussions of the FBI and IWP concerning the nationalised industries' membership there were continuous references to the high subscriptions to be expected from them; so there is some evidence that the financial motive was the strongest, after all.

Similarly one might wonder about why the corporations wished to join, for was it not 'fundamentally illogical to expect any nationalised industry to subscribe financially in any form to any body pledged to oppose the whole principle of nationalisation'[15] — especially since, immediately after its foundation, the CBI prepared a paper on the 'Manufacturing powers of the nationalised industries', which was not at all complimentary to them, and started its campaign of fierce opposition to the re-nationalisation of British Steel? Furthermore, like any other large companies the public corporations have direct access to the government and are therefore not in immediate need of an association. Certainly some of them showed no great interest in joining. However, the majority obviously thought it beneficial to be constantly in close touch with private industries, to 'belong' to the greater business community, to be privy to their thoughts and to know the direction in which events would move; and, specifically, they will have felt that in conflicts with the government the CBI might prove to be an important ally — as the Devlin Report put it, 'there are . . . times when a nationalised industry finds it preferable that its views should reach the Government as part of a consensus'.[16]

John Davies to Lord Robens, 13.1.1966.
14. *The Financial Times*, 13 January 1966.
15. FBI/CBI Archives, Papers of Gen. Secr. Douglas Walker, FBI/S/Walker/81/4, p. 2; see, as well, FBI/GO/83.
16. *Report of the Commission of Inquiry into Industrial and Commercial Representation*

The main problem for the public corporations was that originally it was intended that they should be 'second-class members',[17] with no representatives on the CBI council. This was altered in due course: since 1969 the nationalised industries have had full membership rights, with representatives on all committees including the President's Committee; in addition there seems to exist, since the latter came into being, a close cooperation between the CBI and the NICG. The problem of possible conflicts over the question of nationalisation as such proved to be no obstacle to the development of an harmonious partnership between the public and the private sectors within the CBI; it was solved in the pragmatic British way by the corporations' not taking part in any discussions that might be 'embarrassing' for them.

Recently, in fact, the CBI has proved to be of assistance to the nationalised industries. It has supported them in their opposition to the Conservative government's policy of restricting public sector investment by subjecting them to rigid cash limits and, more generally, has criticised the strategy of treating their investments as part of the PSBR. For years now they have asked, instead, to increase the nationalised industries' investment, as one of the most promising means of leading the whole economy back to growth.

That in spite of the many areas of possible conflict the relationship between nationalised and private industry is, on the whole, so friendly is certainly due to the fact that in many instances close personal contacts had been preserved from pre-nationalisation days. Meanwhile new generations of managers have come to the top in both sectors; hence the fact that the good relationship has continued may also be due to the composition of the corporation boards. In the beginning board members were, in the main, either company directors or senior executives from the industries which were being nationalised — they recommended themselves by exhibiting the specific expertise needed for the running of the respective businesses. When the Acton Society Trust investigated the composition of twelve boards in 1951, it found that of forty-seven full-time members thirteen had been company directors and ten managers and engineers;[18] of forty-eight part-time members, as many as twenty-five had been company directors and four managers and engineers. Adding to these

---

(Devlin Report), published by the ABCC/CBI, London, 1972, para. 352.
17. Memo, Melville to Davies, 10.2.1967; FBI/CBI Archives, FBI/GO/83.
18. The rest were: 9 unionists, 4 civil servants, 3 accountants, 3 members of the armed forces, 2 solicitors, 1 member of the co-operative movement, 1 scientist, 1 without classification. See Acton Society Trust, *Nationalised Industry. The Men on the Boards,*

accountants and the members coming from the banking and financial sector, the authors concluded that the boards' composition showed a clear bias towards the private sector. In 1956 Clive Jenkins took another look at the matter and counted (though without discriminating between full- and part-timers) 106 board members — out of a total of 272 — who were directors of private companies and seventy-one who were technologists and professionals; the rest were divided mainly into representatives of the Labour Party, the trade unions and the cooperative movement (47), civil servants (15), and some who were more difficult to classify.[19]

In the meantime the tendency to recruit capable men from the private sector has not been abated. Chairmen, especially, are usually drawn from private companies — not without difficulty, though, for the directors of large companies are not usually prepared to accept a drop in salary; there have even been deals reminiscent of the football business, where players are only to be obtained after considerable sums of compensation have been paid to their former club.[20] Since Clive Jenkins' short study, unfortunately, no new figures have been available as to the private sector background of the nationalised industries' boards.

We have therefore examined the members of the boards of nine major corporations, attempting to classify them as 'private sector', 'government/administration', 'unions', 'career men' (who have risen to the top in their own industry), 'other nationalised industries' and 'other' (including non-classified). Our figures for the year 1979/80 are as follows:

	Priv. sector	Gov.	Unions	Career	Other NI	Other
Total (135)	30	17	21*	51	9	7
Full-timers** (41)	15	3	1	20	2	—
Part-timers** (45)	10	5	17*	5	3	5
Chairmen (9)	3	1	—	4	—	1

* The figures for the unionists are so high because of worker representation in the BSC and the Post Office.
** The figures do not add up to the total as some of the corporations, in the list of their board members, did not distinguish between full- and part-timers.

London, 1951, pp. 6ff.
19. Clive Jenkins, *Power at the Top*, London, 1959, pp. 41ff.
20. The government had to agree to pay up to £1.8m to Lazard Frères, subject to

In addition we have made an extra classification for the chairmen of fourteen nationalised industries, including some ex-chairmen and taking into account some recent changes (up to the end of 1983):

	Priv. sector	Gov.	Unions	Career	Other NI	Other
Total (28)	14	4	—	8	1	1

These figures point to an interesting trend which might not be quite what one had expected. The chairmen, of course, due to the government's strategy indicated above, come mostly from the private sector; but on the boards private businessmen take second place, the dominant group being the career men, bred in their own industry. Only the part-timers, again, are predominantly from the private sector (the unionists can be omitted here as their high number is due to experiments in worker participation). Now, one might argue that the chairmen are the most important men on the boards, in any case. Yet while they certainly are held responsible for the success or failure of a corporation's strategies, they are by no means always the ones who define them. With respect to the latter the full-timers — particularly the deputy chairmen who are frequently the chief executives — are equally, if not more important, and they are the group dominated by those career men who are typically engineers, technicians, 'technocrats'. Hence, on the face of it, one may certainly not talk of a 'private business hegemony' of UK nationalised industries as one might, perhaps, in the case of Italy.[21]

The picture, of course, varies with different corporations. The dominance of the career group is most marked, indeed overwhelming, in the Electricity Council, but this is a somewhat atypical example owing to the specific structure of the council (where all the Area Boards are represented). They represent a majority, as well, in British Rail, British Gas and the NCB, while in other corporations, such as the BSC, the former British Aerospace or the Post Office before the creation of British Telecom, private businessmen seem to have a greater say. Yet the fact remains that the career men are of increasing importance; this finding fits in with the Public Appointments Unit's estimate, in 1979, that 75 to 80 per cent of the full-time posts in the

---

certain performance criteria, to get Ian MacGregor for the BSC.
21. See Alberto Martinelli, 'The Italian Experience with State-Controlled Enterprise', 1979 (ms.), p. 28.

nationalised industries 'are filled by promotions from within'.[22]

The figures about 'background', however, do not by themselves say very much about probable attitudes, and the policies and strategies to be expected from them. It is plausible that board members coming from the private sector will have a 'commercial' outlook and adopt the appropriate strategies, the more so (as has been the case more than once) when a chairman or other executive member of a public corporation is at the same time the director of a private company.[23] Equally it would appear plausible that private sector board members might act as a lobby for their (original) firm or industry, even though apart from Lord Robens' complaint about some of his part-timers[24] there is no real evidence that they actually do so. The point here is that what appears plausible is not necessarily so.

Firstly, the 'lobbying' power of private industrial part-timers is debatable simply because the impact of *any* part-timers is not so very great, in any case. Secondly, under the assumption that a public corporation has specific imperatives of action and a logic of its own, it might force upon its senior management equally specific attitudes and an 'esprit de corps', whatever the background of those men. Just as, for instance, Lord Robens, though coming from the Labour Party, in his position at the head of the NCB insisted upon *not* feeling and acting 'as an extension of a Government department',[25] any chairman coming from private industry might — just — insist upon not feeling and acting as an extension of the private sector.

Thirdly, there is the question of the relevance of the growing number of career men at the top. This is of particular importance in view of the thesis of 'convergence' discussed in Part I, for there exist two possible and equally plausible alternatives concerning their attitudes: either, having been reared in a nationalised industry, they may develop specific (technocratic or other) attitudes which make them resistant to tendencies of convergence; or they may be tempted to adapt even more strongly to the norms and attitudes of private sector businessmen to (over-) compensate for the taint of 'unequal birth', of not originally belonging to the business community. This question, which is paramount for our expectations of the behaviour and prob-

22. The SCNI (Sub-committee E), Session 1978–79, *The Relationships* . . ., op. cit., p. 67.
23. This has been the case with R.L.E. Lawrence, National Freight Corporation, Sir Humphrey Browne, British Transport Docks Board (1979), and (since 1983) Robert Haslam, BSC.
24. See Lord Robens, *Ten Year Stint*, London, 1972, p. 116.
25. Ibid., p. 11.

able development of public enterprise in capitalist societies, cannot be decided either theoretically or generally, since the answer would differ from society to society (allowing for such factors as the prevalent values, traditions and the impact of the civil service).[26] Yet any findings on the attitudes and self-definition of individuals in a single public corporation, in a single country, can at least point our way to some suggestive indications.

---

26. For the Prussian public enterprises in the Weimar Republic, H. J. Winkler discovered that the *Bergassessoren* at their top, though not originally from the private sector, developed a marked 'solidarity with private industry' (see Winkler, *Preußen als Unternehmer*, op. cit., p. 134).

III

British Steel: a Public Corporation between the State and the Private Sector

10

History and Organisation of the British Steel Industry

Developments Before Re-Nationalisation and the Role of the ISB and the BISF

This is not the place to deal with the whole history of the British steel industry. One point should be made, however: that, ever since the end of the First World War, this industry has been in a state of crisis. During the 'difficult twenties'[1] it suffered from over-capitalisation, excess capacity, outdated plant and — a factor that cannot be underrated — a lack of efficient management in the (mostly) family-owned firms. This led to a deteriorating financial situation which brought them gradually under the control of the banks (including the Bank of England) who consequently, at the time of the world slump of 1929-34, had gained such a hold on many firms that the boards of the latter were staffed with bank personnel (though usually no more than one or two). They tried to encourage the industry to reorganise and modernise. By 1930, at the latest, it was obvious to the banks, as to nearly everyone concerned with steel, that the industry needed not only reorganisation, but also some sort of public aid or even control; only the steel-masters themselves lacked this conviction. From inside the industry came neither moves nor schemes of reconstruction; the steel-masters' only apparent interest was to protect themselves through pricing associations and high tariffs.

In answer to the industry's claim for protective tariffs the government, in 1929, set up a committee under Lord Sankey to inquire into the current position and future prospects of the iron and steel industry. Its report, published in May 1930, saw the cause of the industry's problems in a lack of coordination among steel-makers as well as in outdated equipment and in the existence of too many small units; accordingly it recommended that the existing firms combine to set up six integrated regional concerns and 'make arrangements with one

---

1. John Vaizey, *The History of British Steel*, London, 1974, pp. 20ff.

another for the development of the industry on national lines'.[2] An alternative scheme for reorganisation was that of nationalisation, put forward by some trade unions since 1931;[3] apart from the divergent views taken on the question of ownership, the model developed jointly by the TUC and the Fabian society, in 1934, was based not on regionalism but on product specialisation: the scattered industry was to be integrated into ten or twelve *product* divisions.

Neither plan was put into practice, although the government had originally intended to link the questions of tariff and reconstruction. In 1932 the industry got the tariff they had asked for and, in exchange, an Import Duties Advisory Committee (IDAC) was established to supervise the promised reorganisation; apart, however, from a few mergers (encouraged by the banks), no reorganisation occurred. Even the mergers that did take place were no more than financial amalgamations and did nothing to remove any of the real causes of the industry's inefficiencies. They did not alter the principle on which the industry was built: that of conglomerates carrying out heterogeneous activities in works scattered up and down the country; they did not lead to the scrapping of old plant; and they did not overcome the firms' stubborn insistence on retaining their individual identities. Not even the system of interlocking directorships imposed on the companies by the controlling banks could improve matters, for the financiers placed on the boards to dynamise the steel managers 'were easily assimilated and often became more like steelmen than those reared among blast furnaces and rolling mills were themselves'.[4]

The only result of the various moves to reorganisation was the founding of the British Iron and Steel Federation (BISF) in 1934. This organisation was brought about mainly through the combined efforts of IDAC and the governor of the Bank of England, Norman Montagu, and forced upon an initially reluctant industry, which accepted it only at the price of a prolongation of the high tariff (which in 1932 had been meant to last no longer than three years). However, the unwilling steel-masters succeeded in keeping the new Federation's powers and tasks, as laid down in its statutes, limited as well as vague. Thus, while intended, *inter alia*, as a means of modernising and coordinating the industry, the BISF found itself restricted to the double role of (a) acting as a spokesman for the industry in negotiations with the British

2. Ibid., p. 51.
3. First published in a pamphlet by the Iron and Steel Trades Confederation, entitled *What is Wrong with the British Iron and Steel Industry?*, London, 1931.
4. Vaizey, op. cit., p. 69.

government and the European steel cartel, and (b) of fixing prices and production quotas — tasks previously performed by the National Federation of Iron and Steel Manufacturers (NFISM), a body which had been very active in drawing up the BISF's constitution and whose director subsequently became director of the BISF. Even within this limited range of functions, the BISF remained ineffective until it was reorganised in 1939. Whether performed effectively or not, however, its tasks were designed to protect the industry from outside competition, and to help to ensure profits from old and inefficient plant. In fact, the BISF became a shield behind which the industry 'organised itself into a complete monopoly',[5] thus rendering a thorough modernisation apparently superfluous: 'Protected by tariffs, exports arranged by quotas, old plant to be kept busy earning money, there was no incentive to build new plant and expand capacity'.[6] For years to come, the BISF seems to have enhanced, rather than fought against the conservative, over-cautious attitude of the average steelmaker — there are several examples of where it effectively hindered, or tried to hinder, the realisation of ambitious projects by the few more enterprising concerns.[7]

During the Second World War the BISF proved to be quite effective, not only in combining the industry's efforts to satisfy the needs of the war economy, but also in fending off direct government control. Though the newly established Ministry of Supply formally took over responsibility for the steel industry, the Iron and Steel Control (ISC) founded for this purpose was virtually staffed by the BISF. So another move to bring the industry into public control ended in industrial self-regulation: 'Control of steel remained, throughout the war, the direct responsibility of senior members of the boards of [the] steel companies'.[8] This basic fact was not altered even when, in 1941, the ISC was reconstructed and restaffed by civil servants and the functions of the ISC and the BISF began to diverge — mainly because of conflicts over prices and profits.

Dissatisfaction over this latter subject again brought to the fore the question of a reorganisation of the industry. While during the war there had been no time to embark on modernisation schemes, plans for measures to be undertaken in the immediate postwar period were

---

5. Wilfred Fienburgh and Richard Evely, *Steel is Power*, London, 1948, p. 50.
6. Ibid., p. 72.
7. See a list of such projects in Dietrich Goldschmidt, *Stahl und Staat*, Stuttgart/Düsseldorf, 1956, pp. 66f.
8. Vaizey, op. cit., p. 93.

prepared from 1943 onwards. The Ministry of Supply commissioned the Franks Report, a new survey of the current situation and future development of the industry, which was completed early in 1945. At the same time the BISF had established a postwar reconstruction committee to make recommendations of its own, so as not to leave the field entirely to the civil service; in 1944, in addition, it appointed an Economic Efficiency Committee to advise firms on proposals involving substantial extensions of capacity and major schemes of reconstruction.

The upshot of all this was a major modernisation plan, shaped into a 5-year capital programme which was approved by the firms, the BISF and the government; it probably gained approval because it did not propose any alterations in the industry's corporate structure. As envisaged in this plan, the government's role was to control coal prices (to keep energy costs down), imports, iron and steel prices, investments, pooling arrangements and the location of new plants. For the government to fulfil such extensive tasks the existing BISF machinery had to be supplemented at official level — or, in other words, a supervising agency was necessary; but the agreement over the capital programme did *not* extend to the question of how this should be constituted. Indeed, an Iron and Steel Board (ISB) was set up in 1946, but by that time a Labour government pledged to a policy of nationalisation had come into office.

The point has already been made that most of the nationalisation bills issued by the new government met with little or no opposition — with the one exception of the nationalisation of steel. Yet the dissension was not over government *control*: it was over public *ownership*. The steel industry had already accepted the need for regular development plans under central coordination and with official government approval. Its senior management as well as its political allies felt that during the war a system of public control over its dealings had emerged that might well be taken as a model for other industries; what the nation wanted to be done was, if 'possible and reasonable', carried out by the industry; so why nationalise? This further step seemed unnecessary and, in the industry itself, met with deep resentment.

The government announced its intention to nationalise the steel industry in May 1946; in September 1946 it established the ISB to safeguard the public interest till nationalisation was accomplished. The BISF, though invited to send two representatives to sit on the Board, declined to do so, in order to demonstrate its opposition to the whole scheme. Since at that time no detailed plans for nationalisation existed, only the pledge to do it, there was at first room for compromise. In 1947 Herbert Morrison, himself only lukewarm on the issue of steel nationalisation, negotiated with Andrew Duncan from the BISF, but the agreement reached between them was repudiated by the cabinet and the talks were broken off. As a result, 'the steel barons felt they had been diddled',[9] and their opposition and resentment became greater than ever. The government, however, had its own cause to feel resentment: the steel industry's first development plan, published in May 1946 and meant to forestall nationalisation by showing the dazzling prospects of the industry and by making far-reaching promises as to concentration, rationalisation, and works' closures, was patently misleading. Soon after its publication the major steel companies announced that they did not intend to be guided by it; the unanimity which both the authors of the plan and the BISF pretended existed in the industry over its further development and over the modernisation/reorganisation issue was obviously far from being a reality.[10]

But when, during 1948, the Iron and Steel Bill was debated in parliament, even the Labour members seemed to have tired of the issue. Hence it is difficult to detect in the Act that was finally passed in 1949 any real determination fundamentally to reconstruct the industry. Unlike the other Nationalisation Acts it did not abolish the identity of the ninety-six companies affected: they were to remain intact, retain their own boards of directors and manage their own affairs much as before. Furthermore the BISF was to continue as an independent entity — one might reasonably ask for what purpose? The Iron and Steel Corporation of Great Britain (ISCGB) — whose establishment was delayed until February 1951 — was nothing but a holding company, equipped mainly with the power to appoint and dismiss the boards of the ninety-six; it also had some other powers of control which it had hardly the opportunity to use during the short period of its existence. The members of the ISCGB themselves were appointed by the government. As there were practically no steelmen ready to serve on the corporation board, its chairman was S.J.L. Hardie, the former chairman of British Oxygen. The steel industry, including the BISF, simply refused to co-operate.

In the autumn of 1951 the Conservatives returned to power and

---

9. Vaizey, op. cit., p. 125.
10. See David W. Heal, *The Steel Industry in Post War Britain*, Newton Abbot, 1974, pp. 43f. See also Vaizey, p. 142: the companies 'did not in any sense meet the terms laid down by the BISF and the Iron and Steel Board for a national plan'.

immediately set about the de-nationalisation of an industry which as yet had not really been nationalised at all. The new act that was passed in 1953 not only gave the companies back into private ownership (a process which in practice proved more difficult than had been anticipated: the selling-off lasted all through the 1950s, and Richard Thomas & Baldwin never returned to the private sector),[11] but envisaged a structure of public control similar to that originally agreed by Andrew Duncan and Herbert Morrison in 1947, with a (new) Iron and Steel Board as supervising agency. The latter's problem — especially concerning the nearly universally acknowledged need of a reconstruction of the industry — was that its powers were essentially negative. Clearly meant not to dominate, but only to supervise the industry, it had no power of initiative concerning investment, but only the right of veto; and it had no power whatsoever to further the re-organisation and amalgamation of firms, or to force closures on them. In composing the development plans of the industry (a habit maintained since 1945) it was in no position to draw up any comprehensive concepts for the future, to say nothing of 'grand designs', but was restricted to compiling the plans for individual firms. Though the ISB itself, staffed with steelmen, was not exactly adventurous in trying to push the industry ahead but tended to support the steel establishment,[12] it was soon frustrated by its narrow terms of reference and more than once asked for reforms and 'for an Iron and Steel Board "with teeth"'.[13] Yet when, in 1963, it submitted a detailed proposal for a public controlling body with powers to force rationalisation on the industry, this was not even discussed by the government.[14]

Hence the main power left to the ISB — in this similar to the BISF of the 1930s — was to fix (maximum) prices for the industry. The idea behind the price-fixing system (which had been developed by the IDAC before the war) was to combine price agreements with an incentive to rationalise. However, this system was not the only thing to be kept from prewar days; there was also the former 'stabilisation fund', whose main task was to make grants to high-cost plants. This meant, of course, that there was no real incentive to hold costs down and to close old and inefficient steel works.

11. 'Over the whole period of 1953 to 1964 . . . the industry's finances were dominated by the problem of selling the shares of the companies in the City' (Vaizey, op. cit., p. 156) — which, incidentally, also lent some power to the Iron and Steel Holding and Realisation Agency which had not been anticipated either.
12. See Vaizey, op. cit., p. 156.
13. Keith Ovenden, *The Politics of Steel*, London, 1978, p. 17.
14. 'This decision on the part of the Conservative cabinet to do nothing . . . is a fine example of what Bachrach and Baratz call a non-decision' (Ovenden, op. cit., p. 17).

Contrary to the new ISB the BISF had, since the war, grown into a powerful organisation. After a further reorganisation in 1945 it now consisted of ten 'conferences', organised on a product basis, of whom eight in turn were federations of manufacturing associations; all in all it represented some 250 firms. In the BISF's council the conferences were represented in order of the sales value of their products; yet council as well as conferences were dominated by the thirteen large concerns: in 1966 these sent thirty-two members into a council of sixty-nine. Hence Keith Ovenden concludes that 'the claim of the BISF to represent the whole of the British steel industry was, politically, hardly true. Politically, it represented and stood to defend the bulk steel producing companies . . . '.[15] Its tasks now were all those a 'normal' trade association would perform; more specifically, it administered the above-mentioned industry fund, advised the ISB on the fixing of maximum prices and was still committed to the task of planning and reorganising the industry's production at national level. Concerning the latter it was more conservative and cautious than the ISB and (understandably, seeing the way it was organised) even less inclined to attack the single firms' autonomy, or to interfere with their managerial decisions.

One might say, therefore, that in this as well as with respect to the pricing policies the BISF dominated the ISB. Yet the question as to which of the two had more power is not of real importance as they were by no means independent of each other, but closely linked through overlapping membership. As Doug McEachern observed, 'the Federation and the Board operated as two parts of a single mechanism for the supervision of the conduct of the individual firms'[16] — or, more accurately, for their protection. The whole edifice of self-regulation and public control, which had been meant to provide an instrument through which the firms would cooperate in rationalising and modernising their industry, proved — as it had done in the 1930s — to be no more than a shield behind which the industry's status quo was maintained and protected; it still operated as a close monopoly.

So once more the development of the industry was left to the individual firms and took place in the usual piecemeal fashion. For throughout all the formal changes of a war-time economy, nationalisation and de-nationalisation, the firms and their managements had remained intact, and were powerful enough to resist all real change in

---

15. Ibid., p. 79.
16. Doug McEachern, *A Class Against Itself*, Cambridge, 1980, p. 148.

their industry. The prosperous 1950s hid for some time the negative effects of the managerial conservatism of the steel industry; but when the situation worsened in the early 1960s, the system described above was revealed as the 'fair weather edifice'[17] it was, and its weaknesses were plain. The British steel industry, compared with its competitors in the world market, was technically backward — it had taken little or no interest in the technical developments made in the rest of the world (such as continuous casting, electric arc steel-making, or the L-D process); its growth rate and the rate of investment were behind those of its competitors while its labour costs were generally higher; the average capacity of plant was lower even than in the 1950s, and the index of capacity increase lower than that of all its competitors; its productivity rose more slowly, and its costs faster, than abroad.[18] All in all, the industry's record was characterised by a 'sluggish performance'[19] which may well be ascribed to allocational inefficiency, the specific system of price control and the failure to rationalise and modernise. As a result, by the mid-1960s the industry was in financial trouble as well, and its leaders decided that the only solution was to obtain a large amount of public money according to an overall concept of coordinated development (unlike the previous rather patchy attempts, which had led the government to support various schemes by individual companies, such as the grants given to RTB and Colvilles to build a new strip mill each in 1960).

The Re-Nationalisation of 1967

By this time the Labour Party had been returned to power and was determined once more to nationalise the steel industry. This re-nationalisation was as controversial as nationalisation had been, although it seemed hardly possible to argue, as had been done in the 1940s, that the industry had a good record and was well capable of the necessary re-organisation and could bring about recovery by itself. Even the leaders of the private sector, hastening to support the steel industry in its fierce battle against Labour's plans, admitted, in a joint statement by the FBI, BEC and NABM on the Steel Nationalisation White Paper in May 1965, that they could not 'subscribe to the view that the

---

17. Heal, op. cit., p. 106.
18. See Anthony Cockerill and Aubrey Silberston, *The Steel Industry: International Comparisons of Industrial Structure and Performance*, Cambridge, 1974, pp. 8–53.
19. Ibid., p. 53.

steel industry is 100 per cent efficient', yet, somewhat lamely, maintained that it was not quite as bad as the government had made out.[20]

Instead, opposition now rested mainly on the argument that, with nationalisation, things might be even worse. For instance, due to lack of competition, prices would be 'likely to rise faster than under a free enterprise system' (though, as should be clear from the above, under private ownership there had not been much price competition to speak of, nor could there be, with maximum prices held to such a low level); there existed no guarantee for any increase in efficiency 'simply by aggregation'; 'further, the impersonal nature of a nationalised concern may well cause a severe loss of morale'; there would be no real safeguarding of the steel customers' interests, for the nationalised industries' Consumers' Councils had proved 'notoriously ineffective'; and, by way of diversification, the projected state concern might prove a threat to the remaining private sector.[21] Finally, there was the clinching argument that 'there is no need to own an industry in order to control it'[22] — an argument apparently proved wrong by the developments of the past twelve years. While thus arguing in public, the FBI was preparing its stance for a possible compromise with the government. Any compromise solution should, it decided: (a) 'provide for the retention of the separate identities of the companies, of their full operational autonomy, and for the maximum possible degree of managerial control . . . ' (that is, repeat the mistakes made in the first nationalisation); (b) 'create a strong control authority, without a direct ownership stake in the companies but with considerable powers to lay down guide-lines on matters of broad policy' (in a note added to this it was admitted that such an authority ought to have some more powers than the existing ISB); (c) introduce a new system of pricing giving due regard to the dangers of 'wholly unrestrained competition in steel' (that is, the argument about price competition quoted above was obviously not to be taken at its face value); and (d) 'make provisions for some degree of State ownership' (in the sense of selling shares to the state, in order to obtain the much-needed public money).[23]

The results show that the government was not prepared to compromise on these lines. The steel industry itself, and the BISF es-

20. FBI Archive, Papers of Sir Peter Runge; Box FBI/P/Runge/4, File FBI/P/Runge/9/8, p. 8.
21. Ibid., pp. 8ff.
22. Ibid., p. 9.
23. FBI Archive, Papers of Sir Peter Runge; Box FBI/P/Runge/5, File FBI/P/Runge/14/1, pp. 16ff.

pecially, was not ready to compromise either, but persisted in 'intransigent antagonism'.[24] It undertook, however, to convince the public that nationalisation was unnecessary, by setting up an Industry Development Co-ordinating Committee (the Benson Committee) to develop (once more) plans of its own for reorganisation. The Committee recommended: (1) the closure of 65 per cent of the then existing steelworks; (2) the loss of 100,000 jobs; (3) the write-off of 9m tonnes of capacity (almost one-third of the then existing capacity); (4) an expansion of total capacity by 3.5m tonnes; and (5) a consequent need to build 12.5m tonnes of new capacity (mainly in five integrated coastal steel works).[25] The plan — nearly identical with the 10-year development strategy the BSC was trying to implement during the 1970s — was to run from 1966 to 1975. While this plan could be agreed to by all those who for decades had asked for a thorough modernisation and rationalisation of the steel industry (though it may be debated whether, when it was finally produced, its demand forecasts were not over-optimistic), it came, first of all, too late (that is, in 1966, when nationalisation was well under way); secondly, the committee had omitted to assess its total costs; and thirdly, it did not show how such a radical restructuring was to be implemented under the existing ownership structure. Sir Monty Finniston could, some years later, rightly argue that the Benson Report, so far from showing that nationalisation was unnecessary, had proved just the contrary: 'To implement the Benson recommendations on investment and the associated unavoidable closures would . . . have required monies on a large scale', and the industry 'would have been unlikely to have provided or attracted the funds from private sources . . . . And if the monies for implementation of Benson had had to come from Government to the private companies, the industry would have been covertly if not overtly nationalised . . . . The conclusion to be drawn is that if the country needed its own independent steel industry then on purely commercial grounds nationalisation was the simplest and most immediate way of providing a future . . .'.[26]

Neither the (only partly-published) Benson Report, nor the BISF proposal, in May 1966 (!), to restructure the ISB into an authority 'with teeth', put the government off its course. In the autumn of 1966 it appointed an Organising Committee to advise it on the organisation

24. Ovenden, op. cit., p. 80.
25. See R. A. Bryer, T. J. Brignall and A. R. Maunders, *Accounting for British Steel*, Aldershot, 1982, p. 23.
26. Sir Monty Finniston, in *Steel Manager*, October 1975, p. 19 (quoted in Bryer et al., op. cit., pp. 45f.).

of the future public corporation; all ten members of the Committee were subsequently appointed to the board of the BSC. Five of them came from the steel industry, including, in the person of Niall Macdiarmid, one of the most outspoken opponents of nationalisation; his appointment seems to have been one of the methods used by the government to allay suspicion of its schemes and to induce the industry to cooperate. More generally, the selection of the members of the Organising Committee obviously was the government's way to compromise: no Socialist was to be found amongst them, only those 'entirely devoted to the notion of a commercial approach to the management of the renationalised industry'.[27]

The Committee proved quite influential, for the Labour government, like its predecessor in the 1940s, though pledged to renationalisation still had no very clear ideas about the shape and character of the new public corporation. Thus, given the industrial and commercial bias of the Committee, the likely outcome of their deliberations, and their advice to government, was a structure which minimised the extent of government control. Especially since they themselves were to sit on the board of the future corporation, they had a vested interest in designing an organisation that could develop as free from government 'interference' as possible. Interestingly enough, the Committee's ideas were not opposed by the Cabinet. The Chancellor of the Exchequer, James Callaghan, seems to have been rather lukewarm on the project; the Treasury view was to delay if not abandon the whole thing: they foresaw problems with the compensation payments at a time of continuing economic difficulties; and, according to Ovenden, the Minister of Power, Richard Marsh, 'was aware . . . that whereas his organising committee would have to live with the consequences of their work, he, as a politician, would not have to live with the consequences of his'.[28] Hence the final Iron and Steel Act and the BSC itself were shaped very much along the lines suggested by the Committee. So, once again, it was mainly the industry itself which made the plans — not ambitious politicians or civil servants (to say nothing of Socialists) developing 'grand designs' and forming an instrument with which to implement comprehensive policies in the 'public interest'.[29]

27. Ovenden, op. cit., p. 135.
28. Ibid., p. 139.
29. 'The Government has hardly bothered to argue for its ritual nationalisation of steel — nor, certainly, to hint what changes it has in mind to make in the industry'. *The Economist*, 8 May 1965; quoted in R. Kelf-Cohen, *British Nationalisation 1945–1973*, London, 1973, p. 103.

It is due partly to the composition, work and influence of the Organising Committee (which, incidentally, was supported by the ISB!) that the public debate on steel nationalisation was characterised by a singular lack of traditional ideological arguments: it was restricted to questions of profitability, efficiency and to organisational problems; even the main argument in favour of nationalisation was that it was inevitable in order to enhance the industry's profitability. But if, as Ovenden remarks, public opinion on this issue 'was consistently without force or expression',[30] this was due furthermore to the hesitant attitude of the Treasury as well as of the Conservative Party, which seemed not very happy to be in honour bound to support the CBI and the BISF in their opposition. Obviously the Conservatives could not help feeling that since de-nationalisation the steel-masters had singularly failed to reconstruct a healthy industry and that their case would have been much more convincing if they had produced plans of their own, on time, for the necessary radical re-organisation of steel production.

Thus the Iron and Steel Act was passed in March 1967, with fierce opposition coming only from the BISF. On vesting day, 28 July 1967, the British Steel Corporation was set up and took over the major private steel concerns and the state-owned RTB; the process of the takeover and merger of the fourteen companies and nearly 200 subsidiaries was accomplished within ten months.

The new Iron and Steel Act was, in most parts 'a faithful copy of the Iron and Steel Act 1949',[31] the main difference being that now only the biggest steel companies were affected. Those fourteen companies, in 1967, employed some 70 per cent of the total manpower of the industry and accounted for over 90 per cent of the industry's production of iron ore, pig iron, oxide carbon steel, heavy steel products, sheet and tinplate; a small but sizeable part of the industry remained in the private sector. Otherwise the Act was purely formal, like all the other Nationalisation Acts, outlining the agencies which were now to deal with steel, and their powers (including those of the minister); the tasks of the new public corporation were kept vague and general, as usual. Above all, the Act was silent about the envisaged organisational structure and about the re-organisation of steel production — all this was left to the corporation itself, which submitted its own proposals (heavily based on those of Benson and the Organising Committee) in a first Report on Organisation in August 1967 (see below). That is to

30. Ovenden, op. cit., p. 106.
31. R. Kelf-Cohen, *British Nationalisation 1945–1973*, op. cit., p. 103.

say, re-nationalisation as such changed nothing but ownership, 'and all this achieved was the transfer of a risky investment from private shareholders to the public'.[32]

Yet this, in the beginning, purely financial transaction was in itself interesting and important enough. The former owners were generously compensated — so generously, in fact, that free enterprise orientated economic journals showed themselves agreeably surprised.[33] This generosity left the BSC with a fixed-interest debt of £834m[34] and the implication that it had to live with a rigid financial structure which was the more problematic since (a) the corporation had to function in a market known to be cyclical and (b) it was clear that, to reorganise its assets, the BSC in its first years would incur high losses. So the foundations for the subsequent various and much-debated capital write-offs and conversions of debt into Public Dividend Capital (the first in 1969!) were laid on vesting day.

Organisation and Reorganisation

Following its First Report on Organisation, the BSC grouped its steel works into four regional divisions (Midland, Northern and Tubes, Scottish and North-West, and South Wales), each under its own managing director; the managerial structure was completed by five 'functional directors' responsible for finance, engineering, marketing and commercial, personnel and social policy, and research and development. This initial structure perpetuated the investment policy of the private industry, with each regional (and otherwise heterogeneous) group submitting its own plans. Since it encouraged local autonomy, at the expense of central investment and rationalisation planning, and hence ran directly counter to the aim of building up 'a unified business entity',[35] it was soon abandoned. In 1970 (following the Third Report on Organisation, issued in December 1969) it was replaced by one based on the principle of product specialisation. The corporation was now divided into six product divisions (general steels, special steels, strip mills, tubes, and the two subsidiary divisions of chemicals and construction engineering). Each of them was seen as a 'profit centre',

---

32. Bryer et al., op. cit., p. 69.
33. Even abroad! See 'Mr. Wilson's falsche Doktrin', in *Der Volkswirt*, 14 May 1966, p. 877. According to Bryer et al., the assets the BSC took over were over-valued by £345m (op. cit., pp. 14f.).
34. David W. Heal, *The Steel Industry in Post War Britain*, op. cit., p. 148.
35. The First Report on Organisation, quoted in Ovenden, op. cit., p. 148.

that is, as a separate financial unit, and consisted of a number of 'working' units spread all over Britain. In abolishing the separate identities of the original companies this reorganisation was the first major step towards centralisation and integration. As such it may be seen (as Ovenden does) 'to represent a victory on the Board for Melchett and the "technocrats" over the "steel barons"'[36] (like Macdiarmid, for instance) who still clung to their old way of life and who, together with the management personnel taken over from the old companies, first had to be reconciled to their new environment before more radical changes could be undertaken.

This first success, however, was in serious danger of being overthrown as soon as it had been achieved, for the Conservative government who returned to power in 1970 intended· to split up the corporation and re-sell parts of it to the private sector. During the ensuing battle between the BSC and the DTI relations between them were, understandably, 'very strained indeed';[37] it ended with another victory for the corporation: in the summer of 1971 John Davies, the Secretary of State, renounced the Conservative reorganisation scheme.

The structure that the BSC arrived at in 1970 and fought to maintain against the new government does not seem to have justified the expectations put into it, for in 1976 another reorganisation was under way, switching once more from product to regional divisions.[38] As a consequence of plans to build multi-product works (and also due to some disappointment with the performance of the first years) the product divisions now seemed inappropriate. Overall financial, operational and commercial control, strategic planning, purchasing of major supplies and pay policy remained, however, under central control, while decisions on investment projects costing up to £2m were made the responsibility of the divisions; that is, an important part of the corporation's decision-making was again placed at the regional level. Another major change in the 1976 reorganisation was that, under the leadership of the managing director of the commercial division (one of the five functional managing directors, who was sitting on the board), five product units were set up, for the sole purpose of controlling sales and plant loading; hence, with the object of bettering the corporation's commercial position, the responsibility for selling the bulk of the BSC's products was centrally controlled and

36. Ibid., p. 171.
37. Ibid., p. 176.
38. The grouping was slightly altered from that of 1967; the regions now were Scottish, Scunthorpe, Sheffield, Teesside and Welsh.

separated from the responsibility for manufacturing them.[39] It may well be thought that this attempt to solve the BSC's problem, in its turn, posed new problems of coordination; furthermore, it shows some ambivalence and indecision concerning the whole question of whether or not to centralise.

It will not come as a surprise to learn that this slightly contradictory structure set up in 1976 was not the final one. Partly because the multi-product works envisaged in the development strategy were not built, after all, in 1980 the pendulum swung back to the principle of product specialisation (see below). Meanwhile, however, important changes had been made in the composition of the BSC's main board. Up to 1978 it had consisted of the chairman, two deputy chairmen (one of whom was the chief executive, heading the regional divisions and 'profit centres'), one or two of the five functional managing directors and a handful of non-executive members, drawn from the City and the business world to give their 'expert' advice. In 1978 the board was considerably augmented by the addition of two government representatives (one from the DoI and one from the Treasury) and six shop-floor workers (nominated by the TUC); all in all a total of twenty-one, including the chairman. Before this alteration, the board had already been mainly a policy board, for executive matters were 'kept outside the Board and . . . dealt with by the Chief Executive's Committee'.[40] With the new additions to its membership, the board grew even more into the role of a policy or supervisory board, and the BSC's top structure came very near the two-tier system of continental joint-stock corporations — with all its well-known drawbacks. One may well speculate as to whether the position of the chief executive (and his committee, consisting of the managing directors) was not strengthened by this measure.

At the same time, it is a debatable point as to whether the employees gained very much by having 'worker directors' on the board. Certainly in 1981 the latter complained bitterly about not having been informed in time about Ian MacGregor's Corporate Plan ('the current plan was developed and determined unilaterally by the British Steel Corporation management'),[41] and about not being placed on the

39. See the BSC Top Management Chart, in BSC, *Organisation Guide*, June 1977, Appendix IV. For comments see J.J. Richardson and G.F. Dudley, *Steel Policy in the UK: The Politics of Industrial Decline*, Strathclyde Papers on Government and Politics No. 10, Nov. 1983, pp. 45f.
40. BSC Memorandum, in First Report from the SCNI, Session 1977–78, *The British Steel Corporation*. Vol. III, op. cit., p. 17.
41. Tom Crispin, TGWU, in Fourth Report from the Industry and Trade Committee, Session 1980–81, *Effects of the BSC's Corporate Plan*, Vol. II, London, 1981, p. 168.

same footing as the other board members: 'We do not know what contacts the Corporation have with the other part-time directors but our people are left pretty much in an isolated position . . . '.[42] Dissatisfaction with this situation prompted the Steel Committee of the TUC to wonder whether recent changes in the organisation of the board had not brought about a 'diminution' of the role and status of the board itself, 'which appears to have a lesser function than that of a rubber stamp, in that issues of major importance are not even put before Board members to be stamped'[43] — a suspicion not unfamiliar to those who have some experience of the practice of supervisory boards of joint-stock corporations organised after the two-tier system.

This leads us to the question as to whether the civil servants appointed to the board were in a position significantly better than that of the worker directors. To have government representatives sitting on the nationalised industries' boards had been one of the various reform proposals brought forward in the 1970s, meant to be 'an important step in the processes involved in creating trust between nationalised industries and government, in improving the general level of understanding . . . '; this device was to be mainly a 'channel of communication'.[44] Yet it was only in the BSC that it was put into practice; and though it may, in some ways, have been the wished-for channel of communication, it certainly did not convince everybody of its benefits, for in the summer of 1983 the two civil servants were removed from the board — partly because of problems of double loyalty and possible clashes of interest, but partly (as was to be heard in the DTI) because 'this government does not believe in civil servants on the board'. Their removal, incidentally, formed a part of the revision which followed Ian MacGregor's leaving the BSC and which further strengthened the chief executive's position: the new chairman (Bob Haslam) is a part-timer only (serving at the same time as the chairman of Tate & Lyle), and the board's secretariat, which was quite influential during the reign of Robert Roseveare, was slimmed down considerably. Still under MacGregor (to whom 'industrial democracy is as dead as a dodo . . . ')[45] the number of worker representatives on the board had been reduced from six to two and, when the term of office of those two expired, in August 1983, to nil; hence the board

42. Bill Sirs, ISTC, ibid., p. 169.
43. Memo from the TUC Steel Committee, ibid., p. 154.
44. SCNI (Sub-Committee E), Session 1978–79, *The Relationships between Ministers, Parliament and the Nationalised Industries*, op. cit., p. 18.
45. Bill Sirs, in Second Report from the Industry and Trade Committee, Session 1982–83, *The British Steel Corporation's Prospects*, London, 1983, p. 59.

now approaches its initial composition again.

The last major change in the structure of the corporation as a whole occurred in 1980. When, in 1979, Sir Charles Villiers had proposed a further decentralisation of the BSC's management, his plan had been turned down by his own board. But his successor, Ian MacGregor, had hardly been appointed when he suggested a restructuring on (at least in principle) very similar lines: the BSC was to be split up 'into small profit centres, taking away management decisions from the head office and leaving local managers free to make and sell steel as best they can'.[46] The new organisational structure completed by the end of 1980 was, once more, based on product specialisation. At top level the divisions, each headed by a group chairman (two of whom sit on the main board), were regrouped into General Steels (comprising the businesses of BSC Special Steels, BSC Sections and Commercial Steels and BSC Plates), Strip Products, Tubes, and BSC Holdings (comprising BSC Stainless, BSC Forges, Foundries and Engineering, BSC Cumbria, and BSC Light Products).[47] The businesses bound together in these operating groups are to act as separate profit centres, responsible not only for the manufacturing of the products concerned, but furnished with the commercial responsibility for them as well. In the words of MacGregor, they are to 'work back from the interface with the market to the production facilities': to identify their own market, quantify its extent, from thence determine their production facilities and capacity and do their own selling, with only the supply of raw materials being left as 'common service'.[48] Hence the corporation itself is once more reduced to the role of a mere holding — but now of a completely reorganised industry.

The new organisational split-up needs to be seen in close connection with the Conservative government's privatisation policy and with the alterations the Iron and Steel Act of 1981 previews. This new Act, in its first section, does an astonishing thing in that it abolishes the corporation's statutory duties — which were, according to the 1967 and 1975 Iron and Steel Acts, mainly 'to promote the efficient and economical supply . . . of iron and steel products, and to secure that those products . . . are available in such quantities, and are of such types, qualities and sizes, and are available at such prices, as may seem to the Corporation best calculated to satisfy the reasonable demands of the persons . . . who use those products for manufacturing purposes

---

46. *The Economist*, 6 September 1980, p. 52.
47. For the new management organisation see Appendix I.
48. Ian MacGregor, in Fourth Report from the Industry and Trade Committee, Session 1980–81: *Effects of the BSC's Corporate Plan*, op. cit., pp. 19f.

and to further the public interest in all respects.'[49] Though this stipulation bound the BSC only in so far as it defined its sphere of activities and otherwise left a wide range for the exercise of managerial autonomy, it is, from the point of the state enterprises' *raison d'être*, of major significance that *now* a big public corporation is robbed of even the vaguest public purpose, and given the dubious freedom to allocate to itself whatever purpose and activities it sees fit. On principle, to declare a public enterprise to be without any public purpose means to declare that there is no jurisdiction for its existence.

The freedom that the new Act gives to the Corporation with one hand, it takes away with the other, in that it puts it much more under the direct control of the minister than the 'arm's length' concept envisaged. The minister is now furnished with enhanced powers 'to direct' the corporation — and especially with the power to give directions to the BSC 'to discontinue or restrict any of their activities or to dispose of any of their property, rights, liabilities and obligations',[50] that is, with the power to denationalise, which heretofore had been the prerogative of parliament. Hence, while the corporation itself is free to withdraw from the steel business, to do something else or to go into liquidation, the Secretary of State, in his turn, is free to sell parts or all of it to the private sector or to liquidate it. This is the most radical change imaginable in the status of a public corporation, for one might say that, *de jure*, this status has gone with the wind.

Obviously the organisational split-up is meant to complement this legal upheaval, for whereas it must be recognised that it is nearly impossible to sell or even to liquidate a centralised state-owned giant, it is quite easy to do so with free-standing portions of it. Accordingly Ian MacGregor, before the Industry and Trade Committee in 1981, talked about the possibility of transforming the BSC's profit centres, especially those 'around the periphery of the basic iron and steel making and rolling facilities', into Companies' Act companies that might then be privatised;[51] and the then Secretary of State, Sir Keith Joseph, announced his intention 'to slim down a nationalised organisation so that it can either become competitive or can in part be sold or can in part be liquidated'.[52]

As yet (1984), seen quantitatively, not much has been done in this line.[53] Still, the changes in organisation and legal framework brought

49. Iron and Steel Act 1975, Part I, Section 2 (1a).
50. Iron and Steel Act 1981, Section 2 (4a).
51. See Fourth Report from the Industry and Trade Committee, Session 1980–81, *Effects of the BSC's Corporate Plan*, op. cit., pp. 28f.
52. Ibid., p. 111.

about during 1980–1 have been the most important and radical ones in the BSC's history, since they constitute a threat to its very existence.

Fighting for the Ten-Year Development Strategy

One might say that, on principle, this new state of affairs is one where the corporation's power, in its relationship with its owner, has reached its nadir. This power is seen, by most observers, to have been at its zenith when the BSC won the battle over its 10-year development strategy, early in the 1970s. The BSC's initial strategy had been the 'heritage' programme, introduced, like the initial structure of the corporation, as a means of conciliating the managements of the recently nationalised firms, and an inducement to them to cooperate. Based on the plants inherited from the private companies, and on the investments the latter had planned, the heritage programme was necessarily short-lived, since nationalisation had taken place with the express purpose of overcoming the fragmented structure and piecemeal planning of the industry. Hence, in 1970–1 the corporation worked out a long-term strategy, looking ahead to 1980 and envisaging a great leap forward, from the steel-making capacity of 26 to 27m tonnes achieved under the heritage programme to a final capacity of about 40m tonnes per annum. This radical expansion of capacity was to be brought about by a giant new 'green fields' works, capable of producing about 15m tonnes a year alone, and to go hand in hand with a concentration of the remainder in five large coastal plants (Teesside, Scunthorpe, Ravenscraig, Llanwern and Port Talbot); thus the strategy included an equally radical programme of closures of existing plant.

The strategy's similarity to that of the Benson Committee is immediately apparent, the main difference being that the latter did not project the major green fields plant (an idea which the BSC's new leaders brought back from a visit to Japan) and envisaged an annual capacity of 'only' about 32m tonnes. This is not to say that the

---

53. Since 1982, the following new companies have been formed as BSC subsidiaries: British Steel Service Centres Ltd (the BSC's stockholding organisation); Stanton and Staveley Ltd; Pipework Engineering (PED) Ltd; Whitehead Narrow Strip Ltd; Fox Wire Ltd; Tinsley Bridge Ltd; six companies in the Tubes Division; and Tube Stockholding. Of these, Pipework Engineering and Stanton and Staveley have already been sold, as has RGC Offshore Ltd. Other businesses have been merged into joint ventures. Redpath Dorman Long and BSC Chemicals, which had formed BSC's fifth group in the period up to 1983, have also been 'hived off'.

Benson plan was significantly less bold than the new strategy: starting from 1966, it looked ahead to the mid-1970s, and for that period its demand forecasts (not allowing for the oil crisis and the ensuing recession) were as over-optimistic as those of the BSC proved to be.[54] The over-optimism in both cases was due to the fact that up to the early 1970s the British economy's situation was characterised by a scarcity rather than an abundance of home-produced steel; besides, at that time the steel industries in other European countries also believed in the need for capacity increase.

Though the BSC's long-term plan was in many points identical with what the private steel industry had planned shortly before its nationalisation, the government was not easily convinced of its necessity. This, however, had only partly to do with the situation, problems and prospects of the industry itself. The new government that had come into office in 1970 was averse to any expansion of public sector investment and pledged to a reduction of state involvement in the nationalised industries and to the 'hiving off' of as much of them as possible to the private sector again. It has been mentioned already that the DTI under its new Secretary of State, John Davies, planned to split up the BSC, selling its peripheral activities to the private sector and dividing the remaining bulk iron- and steel-making into two separate corporations. With such ends in view, the government was not likely to look at all benignly at the BSC's ambitious expansion programme, however well-founded it might have been.

The Department's first — and typically institutional — response, when confronted with the development plan, was to set up a Joint Steering Group to discuss its merits and drawbacks. The Group consisted of civil servants from both the DTI and the Treasury, some senior members of the BSC, and a 'neutral', in the person of the deputy chairman of ICI, and was chaired by a DTI official. In addition, in an attempt to overcome the disadvantage of its own lack of expertise, the government asked a firm of private consultants (McKinsey's) to provide it with a detailed analysis of future trends in the world market for steel, being conscious of the fact that the BSC's projected 'great leap forward' was a great leap into the dark. Perhaps it was even then aware that the BSC, in working out its grand plan, had considered and financially evaluated only one option (that of steady expansion via big integrated works) and omitted to consider other

---

54. The forecast consumption for 1975 was 30.9m ingot tonnes, whereas actual consumption in that year amounted to only 21.26m tonnes (see Bryer et al., *Accounting for British Steel*, op. cit., p. 38).

technological options open to it; the planners were, for instance, committed to the belief that substantial economies of scale were available in the steel industry and ignored any use that might be made of mini-steel works.[55]

Understandably, the BSC was not altogether happy with the steps undertaken by the government, because they meant delays and implied that the industry had, for the time being, to operate under conditions of great uncertainty. They openly admitted (before the SCNI, in 1972) that they were hostile to the JSG since, in their eyes, through this Group the Department had tried to 'second-guess' the corporation to an unusual degree and had, in sort, invaded their own territory.[56] They gave vent to the belief that there was no 'function for the Board of this Corporation if it did not have responsibility for setting the plans for the Corporation itself in commercial, technical and financial terms'.[57] Were this belief commonly held, any attempt at effective *ex ante* control of public enterprise would appear to be illegitimate; what possible legitimation would then remain for public enterprise itself?

The BSC was, of course, equally hostile to McKinsey's inquiry, since it seemed to represent, on the part of the government, a deplorable lack of faith in the collective expertise to be found within the corporation. Experts wish to be accepted as unquestionable authorities; they take offence once their wisdom is doubted. Consequently, the government's measures led to an alienation of the management and to a serious deterioration of the relationship between the corporation and its sponsoring department.

After prolonged negotiations (from March 1971 to March 1972) the government announced, in May 1972, that the JSG recommended a 1980 BSC capacity of between 28m and 36m tonnes — a wide range which indicated the lack of consensus between the DTI and the BSC on the question of the industry's future prospects. In their report, in fact, McKinsey's had advocated a capacity target of only 23m tonnes, or less than what was already in existence. At that point further negotiations reached a deadlock which was only broken when, in October 1972, John Davies, Secretary of State of the DTI, was succeeded by Peter Walker who, contrary to the cautious Mr Davies, seems to have had a penchant for bold solutions and was, therefore, inclined to look more favourably on the BSC's plans for the future

55. See the criticism of Bryer et al., op. cit., pp. 81ff., 88ff.
56. SCNI, Session 1972–73, *The British Steel Corporation*, London 1973, paras. 748, 774.
57. Ibid., para. 796.

than his predecessor had done. The government eventually accepted the BSC's (slightly revised) 10-year development strategy, published it in a White Paper in February 1973,[58] and gave the signal for the BSC to go ahead. The plan now foresaw:

(1) a continuous planning process with high flexibility, from now on, 'avoiding premature commitment to fixed tonnage targets and dates' (in fact the BSC then switched to a 5-year 'rolling' system of investment planning);

(2) the corporation's capacity was to be raised from its present 27m tonnes to 33m to 35m tonnes of liquid steels by the late 1970s, and to 36m to 38m tonnes during the first half of the 1980s;

(3) within those ranges, the five existing major steel-making plants at Port Talbot, Llanwern, Scunthorpe, Lackenby and Ravenscraig were to be brought up to their optimum capacity;

(4) a start should be made as soon as possible on a new steel complex located on the south bank of the Tees and, 'perhaps', two new small electric arc steelworks should be built;

(5) many of the remaining existing works were to be closed; the reduction of manpower was estimated to be about 50,000 (but due regard was to be given to compensation payments and/or provision of new jobs in the areas affected . . .);

(6) the costs of the investment programme were estimated as amounting to £3,000m within ten years.[59]

The government's commitment to this ambitious strategy certainly represented 'a great act of faith';[60] in fact, it had even accepted a capacity target that lay at the upper limit of the JSG's somewhat undecided recommendation. Though some authors argue that this capacity target had again been a 'triumph for compromise and caution',[61] things may well be seen the other way round. For the strategy to prove successful, several conditions would have to be met:[62]

(1) that the ambitious programme could indeed be financed;

(2) that the total concentration of steel-making at coastal plants could be economically justified;

(3) that the drastic programme of closures was politically feasible (which, as the Beswick Review and its consequences show, it soon

---

58. *British Steel Corporation: Ten Year Development Strategy*, Cmnd. 5226, London, 1973.
59. Ibid., paras. 19, 20, 36, 41.
60. Richardson and Dudley, *Steel Policy in the UK* . . . , op. cit., p. 32.
61. David W. Heal, *The Steel Industry in Post War Britain*, op. cit., p. 177.
62. For the following see Richardson and Dudley, op. cit., p. 20.

proved not to be);
(4) that the new investment could be brought 'on stream' and achieve maximum efficiency within a very short time;
(5) that for the greatly enlarged capacity a reasonably high domestic demand would really exist;
(6) that sufficient external demand would exist to absorb increased exports;
(7) that the BSC would soon be internationally competitive.

Some of these conditions were unrealistic from the beginning; others proved to become so, more and more, when the British economy slid into recession and the world market for steel collapsed. Let us not be unjust, however, and admit that the latter developments were not to be foreseen at the time. Still, in the light of the conditions enumerated (which may even not be complete), the 'act of faith' theory appears to have a lot more in its favour than its 'triumph for caution' counterpart.

Richardson and Dudley explain the BSC's ultimate victory in the battle over the 10-year development strategy not only as an act of faith, but also by a tendency in government 'to shift responsibility'. When the DTI finally accepted the high risk embodied in the strategy, it did so because it did not feel finally responsible — after all, 'the Government could gain comfort from the knowledge that should things go wrong then the Chairman of the BSC and his senior executives were always expendable'.[63] Evidence for this thesis is the attitude the government took (prior to the Beswick Review) to the closures implied in the plan: they were happy to entrust the BSC with the responsibility for authorising the closures, and preferred — from understandable reasons of electoral policy — not to be too closely involved in the necessary discussions. At any rate, the BSC's victory may be said to mark the point at which the BSC had gained a certain amount of autonomy to define and pursue its own strategies as well as a certain degree of authority over its sponsoring and 'controlling' department.

This does not mean that from then on things were always to run smoothly, nor that the BSC was allowed, without further questioning, to go ahead with everything its management had taken it into their heads to do. There were, for instance, quarrels over the government's policy of price restraint (which patently contradicted the renunciation of the government's right to control steel prices, laid down in the 1972 Iron and Steel Act, prior to Britain's entry into the

63. Ibid., p. 35.

Common Market). Though this policy was aimed generally at holding down the rate of inflation, it had, in the case of steel, the additional object of supporting the private manufacturing industries by holding down the cost of steel.[64]

The other main cause for quarrels with politicians was the BSC's policy of plant closures. When the Labour Party regained power in 1974, and the unions gained in political strength, this policy was much opposed. The new Secretary of State, Tony Benn, lost no time in appointing a committee headed by Lord Beswick to review the BSC's proposed closures. The Beswick Review, published in February 1975, recommended the closure of several plants (subsequently known as 'Beswick plants') to be delayed.[65] Though it appeared to demand relatively small concessions from the BSC, one of its results was a stormy battle fought in public between Sir Monty Finniston and his sponsoring minister. Tony Benn went so far as to declare that it was high time 'to socialise existing nationalised industries', and Sir Monty answered in the same vein, with Alf Robens from the National Coal Board entering the lists to support the latter, complaining about the government's 'unwarrantable interference' and asking of the public at large whether the Secretary of State wanted 'fifth-rate rabbits', instead of capable chairmen, to run the nationalised industries.[66] Public opinion also tended to support Sir Monty, who seemed to be in the better position through being able to refer to the BSC's statutory duty to produce steel as efficiently as possible, and 'to behave commercially'. Hence the BSC emerged from this new battle essentially unimpaired. The only concessions it had been forced to make over the 'Beswick plants' soon proved to be of little practical relevance: when steel demand began to drop, during 1975, the BSC could, without much further opposition, start to push through with a programme of closures not very different from those originally intended. By September 1978 all the Beswick plants, with the exception of Shotton, had gone.[67]

While one major result of the BSC's victory in the battle over its 10-year development strategy had been the increased autonomy of the corporation's management, its other result was that the BSC soon found itself saddled with serious problems of over-capacity, which showed more and more plainly from 1975 onwards. However, no-

64. See, e.g., Andrew Glyn and John Harrison, *The British Economic Disaster*, London, 1980, p. 66.
65. For details see Bryer et al., op. cit., p. 250.
66. See BSC, *Daily News Summary*, No. 1731, 29 April 1975.
67. See the list in Bryer et al., op. cit., p. 259.

body forced the corporation, in the light of new developments in the steel market, to alter its strategy. Had there been any further proof needed for the thesis of the strength of the BSC's position, it may be found in the fact that it was still allowed to go ahead with its planned projects. In 1977 it decided by itself to abandon the strategy — not in favour of a substantial slimming down, but of the slightly more modest capacity target of 30m tonnes by 1982. The government took a year longer to adapt to the new facts of life; in its 1978 White Paper on the BSC[68] it opted for the deferment of some of the BSC's capital projects and relinquished all specific capacity targets.

The Remaining Private Sector

While the BSC's battles were going on, and were very much in the public eye, one might have been forgiven for forgetting the remaining private steel companies. Yet they still existed — originally there were about 200 of them — and managed (for the greater part) to survive; there have even been some new companies who have successfully entered the British steel market after nationalisation (Sheerness Steel in 1972 and Manchester Steel in 1973, both subsidiaries of foreign firms). The ISB and also (contrary to the 1951 nationalisation) the BISF had been disssolved, but that does not mean that the private firms were now left alone and without organisation: some 110 of them founded the British Independent Steel Producers' Association (BISPA) to safeguard their interests and to act both as their spokesman and, in a certain sense, as their link with the nationalised giant.

Originally, the fourteen steel companies that were to form the BSC in 1967 united about 90 per cent of Britain's crude-steel-making capacity; the remaining 10 per cent appeared negligible. Most of the companies left in the private sector were specialised producers, in any case, and could be expected to depend on the BSC as their main supplier of crude and semi-finished steel. While the BSC struggled with its teething troubles, however, the private steel companies made good a lot of ground, such as doubling their own crude-steel-making capacity, and pursuing a policy of continuous investment in equipment for new steel-making techniques that made them strong enough to compete with their 'big brother' in all areas of product overlap. As a result, the BSC's deliveries of semi-finished steel to the private sector fell from a peak of 3.8m tonnes in 1970 to 1.8m tonnes in 1977,

68. *British Steel Corporation: The Road to Viability*, Cmnd. 7149, London, 1978.

and its share of the market for ingots, billets, blooms and slabs fell from over 80 per cent (1967) to about 50 per cent from 1974 onward.[69]

Until the second half of the 1970s the private steel companies did remarkably well. Of course, the rapid decline in steel demand from that time on hit them as much as it did the BSC, but again some of them managed to profit from the latter's troubles, bettering their market share when the BSC, early in 1980, was paralysed by a seemingly endless strike. Hence, in its Annual Report of 1982, the BISPA stated, not unproudly, that its member firms had been able to maintain a market share of finished steel products of more than 25 per cent of the total UK tonnage and a share in turnover of about one-third of the whole market, and had even improved their share of crude steel production to nearly 16 per cent.[70] Moreover, this satisfactory result had been achieved even though some of the firms had been forced to close down and others (like GKN) had successfully shed their steel-making facilities.

The subsequent loss in capacity is mirrored in the decreasing number of BISPA members, from a peak of about 130 in 1973 to eighty-five in 1982. Not counting the subsidiaries, which in BISPA's lists figure as members in their own right, BISPA membership in 1984 was down to fifty-two companies. It should be noted, however, that the association's coverage of the independent steel firms has never been total. In the first place, it has never included tubes, cold-rolled sections, drop forgings or castings within what may be called the extended steel industry. Secondly, the two big steel-making companies Sheerness and Alpha (both in foreign ownership) and one large re-rolling concern, Glynwed Steels Ltd, are outside BISPA. Thirdly, within the product range that the association does cover, some fifteen to twenty smaller firms have never entered it. Even so, the number of companies (about seventy to seventy-five) that have survived until the present (1984), both inside and outside BISPA, is, when compared with its European competitors, remarkably high. No real concentration took place in the independent sector; as in pre-nationalisation days, rationalisation in the private sector of the industry occurred within, rather than across company boundaries; the industry's inherent conservatism and fragmentation, though seemingly challenged by nationalisation, has continued to prevail.

The relationship between the BSC and its colleagues in the private sector has proved to be by no means simple, being at the same time

69. See Bryer et al, op. cit., pp. 142ff.
70. BISPA, *Annual Report 1982*, p. 6.

one between a supplier and his customers, and one between competitors. Hence, whatever the BSC did and however it behaved — especially with regard to its pricing — it would be certain to cause resentment, for example, being accused of either overcharging or underpricing. To complicate matters still further, from the very beginning, and long before the advent of the Phoenix schemes, certain plants had been in joint ownership (such as Round Oak, Templeborough), thus putting the BSC in the position of competing with its own subsidiaries. In order to straighten the 'ragged frontier'[71] between the two sectors of the industry there have been various attempts to sort out the areas of overlap, that is, to keep the BSC out of the market for finished steel products and to restrict it to bulk steelmaking. The first such attempt was the Conservative government's plan, in 1970, to strip the BSC of its so-called peripheral activities, including substantial elements of its special steels division. We have already seen that this plan came to nothing, being heavily opposed by the BSC itself which, understandably, was very much averse to being robbed of its most profitable activities and reduced to a sort of 'public utility' to the private sector. But the BISPA has not tired of demanding such measures, and eventually found a sympathetic ear with the present (Thatcher) Conservative government which has, meanwhile, undertaken both legal (with the 1981 Act) and practical steps in this direction, having fitted a programme to deal with the overlaps into its general policy of privatisation.

Such a programme has, of course, become particularly urgent in recent years, now that the private steel companies are suffering increasingly from the world-wide steel crisis. In 1981 the only British steel firm still showing a profit was said to have been Sheerness Steel,[72] whose management in that year left BISPA on the grounds that they could not agree with the association's policy of asking for state subsidies for its members, feeling their own company to be sound enough not to need state support. The other firms are all more or less in the red and forced to reduce their capacity but (in some cases at least) rather loth to do so. They would much rather get rid of the awkward competition from the state-financed giant rival and exert pressure on the government to achieve this result, not entirely without success.

---

71. David W. Heal, *The Steel Industry in Post War Britain*, op. cit., p. 182.
72. See *The Economist*, 7 February 1981, pp. 68f.

The Steel Industry in a Declining Market

One of the arguments in the private steel-makers' favour seems to be that for the better part of its history, the BSC has been a loss-maker.[73] Blame for this undeniable fact, however, cannot be laid wholly at the BSC's door. Firstly, that part of the industry which the BSC had taken over on vesting day has been acknowledged to be in bad shape and was not to be expected to show a profit immediately. Secondly, the long overdue rationalisation, modernisation and reorganisation the BSC was obliged to undertake meant that for a considerable time to come it had to live with high capital spending and high costs. Subsequent governments contributed to the latter by delaying, not once but several times, the necessary process of rationalisation, specifically the closures inevitably connected with it.

Thirdly, the BSC was saddled with the high debt incurred at nationalisation, as a result of the generous compensation paid to the former shareholders. Though with the 1969 Iron and Steel Act the greater part of the high initial capital debt was charged into 'public dividend capital' (PDC), for the high amount of capital that was needed to finance the modernisation programme, and had to be borrowed from the Exchequer, the BSC got a gearing ratio (of PDC to fixed interest debt) of only 55:45 (the BSC had asked for 70:30); in 1976 this ratio was worsened still more into one of 45:55. As Bryer, Brignall and Maunders have pointed out, of the BSC's high cumulative losses, which do so much to impair the corporation's stance in public opinion, about 73 per cent are accounted for by its interest payments and, hence, 'are just as much a product of the Treasury's inappropriate financing policies towards BSC as they are a product of BSC's trading results'.[74] Only in recent years has the high interest burden been alleviated by capital write-offs.

Fourthly, the BSC's financial problems, serious as they were from the beginning, were exacerbated by government policies of price restraint, which were intended to support the private manufacturing industries. The BSC and the British Iron and Steel Consumers' Council (BRISCC) have estimated that government intervention on

73. Only in the early 1970s was the steel market such that the BSC 'could not help making profit' (DoI). In 1973–4 the corporation made a profit (after tax and interest) of £39m, in 1974–5 of £70m.
74. Bryer et al., op. cit., p. 166. According to BRISCC, between 1974/5 and 1979/80 the BSC received £2,870m in PDC and other government funding, of which interest charges paid to government accounted for £435m (BRISCC, *Cost Competitiveness in ECSC Steel Industries: The Effects of Government Policies*, London, 1981, pp. 2f.).

prices up to 1974 cost the corporation about £750m of lost revenue — 'which it then had to borrow from Government at interest rates varying between $7\frac{1}{2}$ and $16\frac{3}{4}$ per cent'.[75]

Finally, the BSC is operating in a declining market where, since the mid-1970s, losses are made in nearly all the 'old' industrialised countries, by private as well as by public concerns.[76] The emergence of relatively efficient 'new' steel producers, who are rapidly increasing their share of the market as well as the total available steel-making capacity,[77] combines with the world-wide recession and subsequent fall in demand for steel, to leave the old steel producers — who, in addition, typically operate at higher costs than the new ones — with a disastrously high excess capacity. Since the situation is similar for nearly all West European steel producers,[78] what is briefly outlined here for the United Kingdom may be taken as typical: the home demand for steel — which ought to be the main outlet for a country's output — in the UK declined steadily from over 18m tonnes in 1973 to 12.18m tonnes in 1982;[79] with smallish growth rates, or none at all, predicted for the years to come, there is little hope that the home demand will increase again. In this context one must remember that the BSC's 10-year development strategy was originally laid out for an annual capacity of 40m tonnes by the late 1970s, and that at the time of its birth the British steel industry was by no means the only one which was optimistically bent on expansion.[80] With a steel-making capacity considerably above that required for satisfying the home demand (even though the BSC's capacity target has been drastically reduced meanwhile), and under the necessity of maintaining a certain minimum of steel output to keep the mills profitable, the steel producers are faced with the alternative of either embarking on further closure

75. BRISCC, op. cit., p. 3.
76. The US steel concerns, for instance, in 1982 and 1983 incurred losses of $4.7 billion. See *The Economist*, 1 September 1984, p. 49.
77. In 1960, 19 countries were able to produce 2m tonnes of crude steel; by 1981, that number had risen to 33. In the same period, total world output doubled from about 345 to 707 bn tonnes (see the note by T.A.J. Cockerill, in Second Report from the Industry and Trade Committee, Session 1982–83, *The British Steel Corporation's Prospects*, op. cit., p. 108). For development of the shares of single steel producers in world production see Appendix II.
78. On the German 'steel crisis', for instance, see Josef Esser, Wolfgang Fach and Werner Väth, *Krisenregulierung*, Frankfurt, 1983.
79. See H. Darnell, Tudor P. Miles and M. Campbell Morrison, *Steel: The Future of the UK Industry*, London, 1984, pp. III, 9.
80. In the EEC, crude steelmaking capacity rose after 1973 by about 15 per cent due to earlier investment decisions. Capacity for finished steel products increased even more. The resulting over-capacity is estimated to reach 30 per cent in 1985. See ibid., p. 38.

programmes, or of finding other outlets by increasing exports. As most steel-producing countries have tried to take the latter course the world steel market faces chaos and is in serious danger of becoming the playground of new 'beggar-my-neighbour' as well as protectionist strategies.

In the European Community the Davignon Plan for some years now has tried to solve the problem by fixing production quotas for the steel industries of the member countries, thereby limiting possible increases in their market shares; by fixing minimum prices; and by pressing the countries to reduce their steel-making capacities. The Plan for years met with indifferent success: (1) most of the member countries feel that it should be the others, rather than they themselves, who reduce capacity; (2) there is constant quarrelling over the actual quotas as each member wants to get as high a quota as possible, while some companies (for example, Klöckner, in the FRG) simply ignore their quota; (3) the prices — if one is to believe the complaints, especially from the British — are fixed on too low a level, that is, they still allow for 'dumping' policies; (4) the Davignon Plan cannot solve the problems arising from competition by non-member countries. Japan, though, has practically withdrawn from the Community market, seemingly intending to avoid trade disputes.[81] By contrast, the USA is not at all averse to such disputes, embarking, in recent years, on protectionist schemes and declaring a 'steel war' on all its competitors.

Within the various European countries different strategies have been utilised to find ways out of the steel crisis. The most typical (as well as traditional) way seems to be cartellisation (for example, the *Walzstahlkontore* in the FRG), the cartels fixing internal production quotas and so on, and also (yet with but indifferent success) going so far as to coordinate investment and closure programmes. There has been further concentration — even across national borders — in a traditionally already highly concentrated industry, to reduce the number of competitors; some forms of concentration (especially in Germany) have implied integration with consumer industries to secure a stable and continuous demand. Nearly everywhere there have been (more or less open) massive state subsidies to help the industry out of its problems — mainly to help it restructure, concentrate and modernise; in France, in 1982, the industry was nationalised with this end in view. However, neither government activity nor the steel firms' own endeavours have as yet achieved the capacity reduction that seems to be the only answer to the development of the world steel

81. See ibid., pp. 19f.; Esser et al., op. cit., pp. 36f.

market and to the bleak future 'prospect for steel'. On the contrary, the French steel industry, for instance, in the early 1980s, was determined to maintain an annual capacity of 26m tonnes, although this figure considerably exceeded its home demand; Italy's state-owned Finsider only recently increased its capacity and its many privately-owned 'mini-mills' still expand.[82] Even where plant closures are, indeed, planned, they have frequently been held up by the intervention of governments who find themselves under severe political pressure — be it in France (where the Lorraine steelworkers, in the spring of 1984, marched on Paris), in Germany (where, with ARBED Saarstahl, the future of the whole *Land* seems at stake), in Britain or elsewhere.

In the light of these developments it may be that the BSC has, after all, done better than British public opinion is inclined to acknowledge — especially if we take into consideration the fact that the government, as the BSC's controller, not before 1978, realised that with the steel market in the state that it was, it could not go ahead with its steel policy as before. It woke up to this fact only, it seems, when the BSC's losses had reached the remarkable height of £443.4m in 1977/8. Even so, in its 1978 White Paper *The Road to Viability* (see above) it did not suggest any radical measures to tackle the new problem. This was left to the government which took office in May 1979: the Secretary of State, Sir Keith Joseph, boldly announced that the government would not finance any of the BSC's losses after March 1980. Such a target was, of course, so utterly unrealistic, for the BSC's position continued to weaken, that it was soon abandoned: instead of stopping all government finance for this lame duck in March 1980, the Treasury raised the corporation's borrowing limit to £5.5bn.

Meanwhile, while the BSC's losses climbed from £309.4m in 1978/9 to £545m in 1979/80, the BSC's management itself embarked on drastic policies. In December 1979 it informed the steel unions that 60,000 jobs were to go within a year, which led to the thirteen-week steel strike in early 1980. This did not better the BSC's position, since during that protracted stoppage it lost considerable ground to imports, ground that afterwards was difficult to recover.[83] In May 1980 Ian MacGregor succeeded Sir Charles Villiers as the BSC's chairman

82. See summary in Darnell et al., op. cit., pp. 34f.
83. The BSC's home market share in finished steel dropped from 70.4 per cent in 1970 to 52.9 per cent in 1979 and 47.5 per cent in October 1980, the share of imports climbing over the same period from 5.5 per cent to 21.0 per cent and about 25 per cent (see Fourth Report from the Industry and Trade Committee, Session 1980–81, *Effects . . .*, op. cit., pp. xiff).

and immediately started to push through a massive programme of closures and de-manning and to prepare the corporation's reorganisation into decentralised profit centres that has been described above. The government assisted his plans to put the BSC on a sounder basis by writing off £1.5bn of its debt, and allowing its cash limit to be overrun by £400m; on the other hand it undertook to subject the corporation to much closer and more detailed scrutiny than any other nationalised industry was subject to, monitoring it on a monthly basis. In February 1981 the BSC's borrowing limit was lifted once more (to £6bn); when the 1981 Iron and Steel Act wrote off a further £3.5bn in loans and capital, the borrowing limit could be reduced to £3.5bn. In that year, the government's total aid to the BSC eventually amounted to £1.121bn.

Aided by this massive help, and due also to its own endeavours, the BSC regained some of its lost ground and by January 1981 had again reached a 52 per cent share of the home market. Its main efforts, though, were devoted to the programme of capacity reduction, and here it achieved, compared with the rest of Western Europe, outstanding results: numerous, even modern and efficient, plants were mercilessly closed, and the work-force, 186,000 in 1979, was reduced to 120,000 in the year 1980/1, 103,700 in 1981/2 and 81,100 in 1982/3. Liquid steel-making capacity was run down to 14.4m tonnes per annum, and was meant to stay at that level, though the actual output of liquid steel, 14.1m tonnes in 1981/2, dropped once more to 11.7m tonnes in 1982/3 (while steel deliveries, home and export, were a meagre 9.3m tonnes).[84]

BSC losses 1977–84 in £m[85]

	1977/8	1978/9	1979/80	1980/1	1981/2	1982/3	1983/4
Lost before interest	261.3	119.7	356	482	223	275	105
Loss on ordinary activities					358	386	105
Exceptional items (rationalisation costs)	(69.5)	(47.6)	(1,239)	(352)	146	483	79
Loss before taxation	441.7	327.4	544	521	261	318	174
Total loss	443.4 (512.9)	309.4 (357.0)	545 (1,784)	668 (1,020)	504	869	256

84. For the figures see BSC, *Annual Report and Accounts*, 1982/3, p. 4.
85. See BSC, *Annual Report and Accounts*, 1977/8–83/4.

A further success was that during the 3-year period 1981–4 the BSC managed to stay within its external financing limits (though those for 1982/3 were increased from a previous £365m to £575m). But the one thing the BSC did not achieve was to break even (to say nothing of showing a profit): including 'rationalisation' costs (that is, of closures), its losses rose, in 1982/3, to the dizzying height of £869m.

The BSC's Corporate Plan of 1981 had offered some grounds for optimism that the corporation was now well on the way to overcoming its financial problems and, in fact, losses were brought down considerably in the first half of the financial year 1981/2. But 1982 saw a new slump in the steel industry: the combined output of twenty-nine countries reporting to the International Iron and Steel Institute fell from 449m tonnes in 1981 to 387m tonnes in 1982, a reduction of 13.9 per cent.[86] The home steel market contracted further (not least because of increased imports of manufactured goods, at the expense of British manufacturers, the BSC's customers); increased steel imports (those from third world countries amounting to a share of 8.7 per cent, those of EEC member states rising from 14 to 18 per cent) further reduced the BSC's market share to a meagre 46 per cent;[87] and the protectionist policy of the USA closed the door on one of the British steel industry's traditional export markets. In this newly worsened situation even the BSC's drastically slimmed down capacity of 14.4m tonnes is 'excess'. Once more, Ian MacGregor's reaction was to cut down, this time by closing Ravenscraig, one of the five major integrated plants which had been the core of the 10-year development strategy. Again the government — this time a Conservative one — hindered the corporation's taking the next step towards the cutting of its losses; at the time of writing (1984) the debate on this subject is still going on (Ravenscraig, meanwhile, 'breaking productivity records', as is freely admitted within the DTI). In spite of this unsettled dispute, the BSC managed to decrease its work-force by a further 10,000, and have ended the year 1983/4 with losses of 'only' £256m, its best result since 1977.

Yet one cannot help wondering where the BSC's chosen strategy will eventually lead. Though the 1981 Corporate Plan had been named the 'Survival Plan' it seems doubtful where the policy of capacity reduction, so vigorously started, is to stop, and whether a 'British Steel Corporation' worth the name will be left over. When examined by the Industry and Trade Committee in October 1982,

86. See Second Report from the Industry and Trade Committee, Session 1982–83, *The British Steel Corporation's Prospects*, op. cit., p. vii.
87. Ibid., pp. ix, 1.

MacGregor committed himself to a capacity 'something less than the $14\frac{1}{2}$ million tonnes we have now', since 'the market dictates' it, and hinted that, for the same reason, the capacity might 'in the long run' be run down to zero![88]

Furthermore, and it was not only *British* ministers who raised this point, no other West European country had reduced its capacity as drastically as had the BSC and it was considered only fitting that other member states of the EEC should contribute their share to the overall capacity reduction that all countries agreed, 'on principle', to be necessary. In the early 1980s, as the Secretary of State, Patrick Jenkin, pointed out to the Industry and Trade Committee, the United Kingdom had 'borne the lion's share of capacity cutbacks in Europe';[89] the bulk of obsolete capacity, overshadowing the prospects of the entire industry, lay elsewhere. It was only at the end of 1984 that the British government could rest assured that closures in the rest of the Community matched those in the UK; after a European capacity reduction of about 20m tonnes in 1984, the EEC commission felt that it must not press for any further closures on either side of the channel.

To conclude: the BSC was, for many years, remarkably successful in its dealings with the British government, but was much less successful — due to its own shortcomings or not — in the economic sector. Of course, since the mid-1970s, it has had to operate in a singularly unrewarding market. The latter drawback it has shared with most of its West European competitors, and it has dealt with the situation at least as well as they have, whether they were privately- or state-owned concerns. In many ways, indeed, the BSC seems to have adapted itself to the declining market more quickly and thoroughly than its European counterparts. It is, of course, arguable that this is not necessarily an achievement to be proud of. It was, at least, what was wished for politically.

---

88. Ibid., p. 10.
89. Ibid., p. xiv.

Ministerial Control and the Industry's Decision-making 11

Statutory Rights and Duties

We have already mentioned that the Iron and Steel Acts of 1967 and 1975 showed a certain reticence concerning the exact meaning of a 'public purpose'; the duties of the BSC, as laid down, do not go beyond the definition of its sphere of activity (to supply the nation with iron and steel in an efficient manner and to satisfy the needs of the manufacturing industries), and placing it under the comprehensive, although vague, obligation 'to further the public interest in all respects'.[1] These general stipulations were not meant seriously to restrain the corporation's commercial freedom to act, for subsections 4 and 5 of both Acts state that 'nothing in subsection (1) above shall be construed as imposing upon the Corporation, either directly or indirectly, any form of duty or liability enforceable in any court'; nor shall any of the Act's provisions 'be construed as imposing on the Corporation any duty to carry on, or to secure the carrying on . . . , of iron and steel activities except to such extent as the Corporation think fit . . .'. From the very beginning the corporation's management concluded, not unjustly, that it was statutorily bound to behave 'commercially'.

During the 1970s governments (of either colour) do not seem to have elaborated in any way on the theme of 'public purpose' or 'statutory duties'. The present (1985) Conservative government, believing neither in public enterprise nor in the notion of the latter's 'serving the nation', abolished the BSC's statutory duties altogether when it passed the 1981 Iron and Steel Act. Only one stipulation is now left: whatever the corporation sees fit to do, shall be done 'in the most efficient manner'.[2] Hence, by statute, the BSC is reduced to a 'normal' enterprise.

Of course, the BSC's management have always — in public at least

1. Iron and Steel Act 1975, Part I Section 2 (1a); see above, pp. 127f.
2. Iron and Steel Act 1981, Section 2 (1).

— maintained that they lead a 'normal' commercial enterprise, and have successfully fought against government intervention with the argument that 'unwarranted interference' was against the statutes. It would be mere speculation to wonder whether more specific statutory duties, and a precise statement of 'public purpose' in the Acts, would have made any difference in their behaviour, by providing real checks on the managerial autonomy the existing Acts allowed to develop.

While the Acts did not provide the BSC with a binding obligation, they have been more precise in defining the ministerial powers of direction, approval and control. These are not essentially different from those of other sponsoring ministers relative to their nationalised industries.[3] According to the 1967 and 1975 Acts the minister has, first of all, the power (after consultation with the corporation) to issue 'directions of a general character as to the exercise and performance by the Corporation of their functions. . . in relation to matters which appear to him to affect the national interest' (sect. 4 (1)).[4] Secondly, any 'substantial change' in the carrying out of its activities, any reorganisation or work of development which involve substantial outlays of capital, any take-over or acquisition of interests in other companies, any expansion into fields of activity other than iron and steel, as well as any sale of parts of the corporation, or any decision to discontinue any of its activities, are subject to ministerial consent (sect. 4 (3–5)). These rights of approval extend to a degree of joint planning, cautiously worded as that 'the Corporation shall act in accordance with a general programme settled from time to time with the approval of the Secretary of State' (sect. 4 (4)). Thirdly, the minister has the right to review the corporation's affairs 'so often as occasion seems . . . to require it', and has the right to be fully informed about any of the corporation's property and activities (sect. 5 (1, 3)). Fourthly, there are the financial powers of the minister, covering a wide range, from the power to determine the rate of return on net assets (financial targets), including the direction of the corporation as to the 'application of any excess of the combined revenues of the Corporation', to those of direction relating to the management of the general reserve, the terms on which loans made by the government are to be repaid, the transformation of fixed interest debt into PDC and to the rate of dividend to be paid thereon; in short, any borrowing by the corporation requires ministerial consent. The same is generally *not* required, however, for the corporation's investment,

3. See above, Part II (pp. 54ff.).
4. All quotations are from the 1975 Iron and Steel Act.

Control and Decision-Making

for 'any sums in the hands of the Corporation which are not immediately required for the purposes of their business may be invested in such manner as the Corporation thinks proper' (sect. 22 (1)). Finally, the minister has the power to appoint and dismiss members of the BSC main board. Some further rights — concerning research programmes, pension schemes, compensation payments and suchlike — may, in comparison with those enumerated above, be considered marginal. The major alteration the 1981 Iron and Steel Act made in these powers is that it added to them the ministerial power to direct the corporation to dispose of its assets (which before had been restricted to assets/activities other than iron and steel) or go into liquidation altogether.

At first sight, these powers seem straightforward enough. A second look reveals some ambiguities. There was, for instance, the power (now repealed by the 1981 Act) to give directions of a 'specific character' in order to ensure that the BSC carries on its activities, 'so far as regards the direction thereof, in the most efficient manner' (sect. 4 (2)). While this could mean that the secretary of state had a say in the (formal) management organisation of the corporation, if it appeared to be operating inefficiently, it might well be interpreted in a more extensive way, so as to shift the responsibility for the actual running of the industry entirely onto the minister. On the other hand, powers deemed most important to gain influence over the corporation, such as those of issuing general directives, fixing financial targets and appointing board members, are qualified by the requirements of previous consultation with the corporation itself and/or of obtaining the Treasury's approval, thus rendering their application a matter of consensus, and linking it to the 'expert' information only the corporation is able to provide.

While such provisions may be expected to curtail the minister's power of control, transforming it into a matter of joint decision-making, the application of other powers (the majority of them, in fact) is linked to prerequisites no more precise than 'as he [the Secretary of State] sees fit' or 'as he may require it' or as he thinks that 'the situation' requires it. While no act can define exactly all future situations in which certain powers may or may not be applied, to omit reference to *any* conditions for their application leaves a wide field of uncertainty. Since the powers of the corporation itself are qualified by the same stipulation — 'as they see fit' — the statutes themselves can be said to have provided the source for that blurring of responsibilities so often complained about by the public. The general provision made in the new Act — that 'the Secretary of State shall not give any direction. . . unless he is satisfied that the giving of it will further the public interest' (sect. 2 (5)) — is certainly not clear enough to alter the somewhat unsatisfactory division of statutory powers, nor does it contribute to a clearer definition of the dividing line between ministerial rights and the corporation's day-to-day management. At the same time, these ambiguities make it difficult to determine how far-reaching the statutory powers of the minister are. While heavily biased towards commercial freedom, the Acts contain powers that, generously interpreted, allow for a wide range of government intervention.

The corporation itself, when asked about the statutory provisions, though maintaining the necessity of 'a clear written distinction between the respective responsibilities of the Government and the Corporation', thinks 'the broad statutory relationship' is, on the whole, 'satisfactory'.[5] The reason for this is, of course, the Acts' bias towards commercial freedom, which the corporation consider their most essential feature. Concerning the matter of the government's responsibility for the corporation's viability, which is not materially specified in the rather formal Acts, the corporation undertakes to clarify the statutory provisions in allotting to it, as its rightful place, the two areas of finance ('in particular the Government needs to satisfy itself on the case for the borrowings it provides or guarantees') and of the regional and social consequences of the BSC's activities. In fact, the latter does not go beyond the concern a government ought to show towards any big enterprise, especially one in a near-monopoly position, dominating a considerable part of the nation's economy.

Turning to the acknowledged specific responsibilities of the government, the corporation feels that there should be no attempt to direct the BSC's activities, rather a restriction of its role to the appointment — 'after full consultation with the Chairman, as the statute requires' — a strong and effective board: 'This should be the main way in which the Secretary of State discharges his responsibility for the efficiency and longer-term viability of the industry. . . . Having appointed the Board the Government should rely on it for those matters within the Board's jurisdiction — particularly issues of technical, commercial and financial judgment'. This is certainly a much narrower view of the ministerial powers than that foreseen in the Acts. But then the relationship between the government and the BSC, in the latter's

5. According to a paper circulated within the BSC. In the interviews, no particular references have been made to the alterations in the 1981 Act. In the following chapters, quotations (unless otherwise stated) are drawn from interviews between 1980 and 1984 with members of the BSC, the DoI/DTI and the Treasury.

eyes, should not be regulated primarily by statutory provisions; much more important is the 'close and continuous dialogue between them both' — a state of affairs that does not allow for the attribution of distinct responsibilities to each (but will lead to a degree of 'understanding' which will minimise the need for formal power to be applied).

Since the corporation attributes such paramount importance to the government's powers of appointment and dismissal (which had also been the main ministerial powers in the original Morrisonian concept), it seems worthwhile to look more closely into the way these are applied. According to the statutes, the board members are to be chosen — after due consultation with the chairman — 'from amongst persons appearing . . . to have had wide experience of, and shown capacity in, the production of iron ore or iron or steel, industrial, commercial or financial matters, applied science, administration or the organisation of workers' (sect. 1. (4, 5)). But the government has always experienced some difficulty in searching out such persons; on the other hand there have been many complaints about the dubious channels (or 'old boy networks')[6] through which appropriate names and information reach ministers, and about the lack of expertise in ministers which precludes their ability to judge the competence of the persons proposed through those channels.

In the 1970s the government established a Public Appointments Unit (with a staff of 13!) to replace the old-boy network by a more open system of information. Yet from the list of some 3,500 persons the PAU had acquired by 1979 they did not really know — as PAU members freely admitted before the SCNI — who of those were actually available; they also admitted that, concerning twenty chairmen appointed in 1977/8, they had been asked for information but had not themselves provided names.[7]

The NICG thought of another remedy to the problem of finding suitable candidates for the boards.[8] To minimise the danger of political patronage (which no doubt has been exaggerated) it recommended a 'more professional approach' with a strong 'independent element', the latter meaning that the chairmen and their colleagues ought to have a major say in the selection procedure. For this purpose the chairman and the Permanent Secretary were to work out a 'joint list',

---

6. Sir Arthur Hawkins (ex-chairman of the CEGB), SCNI (Sub-Committee E), Session 1978–79, *The Relationships between Ministers, Parliament and the Nationalised Industries*, op. cit., p. 29.
7. Ibid., pp. 67, 71.
8. In a Memorandum, ibid., pp. 83ff.

with the minister being obliged to consult the chairman once more before making his final decision; the minister should also be under the necessity — especially in the case of executive board members — to look first in the industry itself: 'a Corporation should seek "to grow its own management"'. In practice, chairmen already dominate the process of the selection of board members since the government soon found out that it could not force board members upon 'unwilling chairmen'; usually (as in the case of the BSC) the proposals come from the chairmen themselves.[9]

The BSC provides a good example, too, of the difficulty the government experiences in finding suitable chairmen. Ever since the time of Sir Monty Finniston (who, as deputy chairman, succeeded Lord Melchett when the latter died before the end of his term of office) the government has been at a loss as to where to find a likely successor. For some time it wished Sir Charles Villiers to go, but no capable industrialist could be interested in taking his post. Finally, the search was extended to the United States and a high 'transfer fee' was paid to get Ian MacGregor. When in 1983 the question of his reappointment arose, the Secretary of State for Energy tried to get him for the NCB, an aim which eventually met with success — obviously after some opposition from the DoI. The problem then was who was to succeed Ian MacGregor? He himself was prepared to chair both those giant public concerns (perhaps slightly overrating his own abilities), but the government did not, initially, relish the idea of a half-time chairman for so problem-ridden an industry as the BSC. Nor did it wish to promote the deputy chairman and chief executive, Bob Scholey, who, to an outsider, would have appeared as the likeliest solution, and who himself would have been perfectly willing. Probably the government feared that with such a confirmed steelman heading the BSC it would experience the same difficulties over cooperation, and have to fight the same battles as a former government had had with the 'technocrat' Sir Monty.[10] Though the DoI explicitly looked out for 'some really experienced industrialist from the private sector', they did not wish for one who was too much 'house-trained' in steel. The result of their search was Sir Alistair Frame of Rio Tinto Zinc, who eventually did not accept the steel post but became chairman of RTZ itself. There are two slightly divergent versions

9. In the DoI this is put slightly differently: asked about who made the proposals, one DoI official said '*We* do — but we take advice'.
10. The — not altogether different — version that went round the BSC as well as Whitehall was that Mr Scholey, not being 'diplomatic', had offended some people in Whitehall.

about the reasons for this outcome: the BSC suspected that the DoI had leaked Sir Alistair's name in order to put pressure on him to accept — which he obviously did not relish; the DoI's version was that preparations for Sir Alistair's change to the BSC were well under way and the deal nearly completed, when some unknown mischief-maker leaked it, to alert RTZ to renew its own claims on him. In the end the government, unable to find a better solution, had to be content with a half-timer after all. Now Robert Haslam, chairman of Tate & Lyle, divides his time between the sugar giant and the BSC.

However, there is not only the problem of finding capable board members (though that one seems to be less difficult with the non-executive members). When asked what the government could do if a nationalised industry did not act as the government wished it to, a senior civil servant replied promptly 'sack the chairman' — although obviously this is much more easily said than done. The same official, when coming to what actually happened, had to admit that Sir Charles Villiers, for instance, was not 'sacked': he only 'retired in ignominy . . .'. The latter is not even true: Sir Charles had wanted to leave when his appointment expired in 1979, but had to be re-appointed for a year owing to lack of a successor. In the eyes of most executives and civil servants, 'pressure to retire' is the only way to get rid of board members, especially chairmen; and if such pressure does not succeed, then the only other way (as in the case of Sir Monty) is 'not to re-appoint' them — not a very effective weapon against an obstinate chairman! In private companies, by comparison, the weapon of dismissal seems to be a lot more effective.

Aims, Policies, and Joint Planning

Though the Iron and Steel Acts made it quite clear that the minister shares responsibility for the industry's viability they did not ascribe to him the one power he needs to live up to it: the power to identify the corporation's objectives (other than financial) and to clarify its purpose and duties. A ministerial writ concerning aims and policies is only implicitly contained in the negative power to give or withhold consent to or from general programmes, major works of development and so on.

Whatever the legal framework, the BSC itself starts from the correct assumption that 'for the Corporation to operate effectively, it is essential for its objectives to be clear'. For any government to provide its public industries with clear objectives it is necessary to work out broad-based and long-term concepts about their purpose and future development and, if possible, fit them into the general socio-economic policies, to avoid a zigzagging which cannot but seriously impair the industry's efficiency. However, as both the government's academic critics and government officials themselves have pointed out, initially neither party knew what to do with the nationalised industries, thus leaving them in a conceptual vacuum which they were free to fill with ideas of their own. Over the years two opposing and rather abstract concepts emerged, the Labour Party wishing to prove that nationalisation 'worked' and that public enterprise could operate efficiently, and the Conservatives that nationalisation was superfluous if not downright nonsensical. Interestingly enough, those contradictory views resulted in much the same policies: the Conservatives' tendency to ignore any difference that might exist between private and public enterprises, and Labour's decision to make them efficient, both led to a bi-partisan approach, 'to treat the nationalised industries in as commercial a way as possible', and to restrict the government's role to 'establishing the financial framework' (DoI).

While this generally commercial outlook has been a 'constant trend' (DoI) for at least two decades, there have been a lot of differences in questions of detail, varying over time and from minister to minister, rather than from party to party. The opinion of one DoI official that 'of course' there were consistent concepts, only each party had its own, is highly debatable. Where the parties' concepts differ has never developed in any significant manner beyond the abstract pro- or anti-nationalisation attitude. It is only in recent years that the Conservative anti-nationalisation stance has been transformed into what may rightly be termed a consistent overall concept, applied to virtually all nationalised industries. The Labour Party's pro-nationalisation stance still lacks such a transformation; the socialising of public ownership is, as yet, no more than a catchword.

Even with the Thatcher government's determined de-nationalisation policy, officials in the DoI and Treasury, when interviewed in 1981, were not totally convinced that their government really had a consistent concept of the nationalised industries — perhaps because the change of government had taken place not very long before. Hence the statement that the concepts were 'very much *not* consistent' and varied from one government to the next (Treasury). Some officials felt that it was not the cabinet's task, anyway, to develop policies, since the cabinet as such was not concerned with the nationalised industries; it was up to their sponsoring ministers to do this (DoI). And why should the government have concepts for the nationalised industries if it did not have an overall policy concerning any sector of the economy (DoI)? Rather, steel was given as a good example of the results of not thinking about the industry in broader perspective, for the overall policy of the early 1980s to make the nationalised industries efficient and then sell as much of them as possible to the private sector, comes up against the difficulties that the industry is experiencing as a whole: a growing efficiency of the BSC in a declining steel market where private companies are selling out justly raises the question of 'creeping nationalisation' — 'so it's embarrassing for [the government] to see private sector steel go down' (DoI).

The same inconsistency is apparent when the government's economic and fiscal policy is taken into consideration. Though 'Conservative ministers would say' that both the broader economic policy and the policy towards the nationalised industries 'are very consistent', following the same principle of 'disengagement' as well as that of relieving the PSBR (Treasury), there is, nonetheless, a 'subtle conflict' between them, in that the monetarist policy produces an economic climate which renders privatisation impossible (DoI). Yet it is felt generally that such contradictions had been much more pointed in the 1970s when the macroeconomic policy of price restraint ran directly counter to the policy of making the nationalised industries viable and efficient and of treating them commercially.

As these statements show, government officials do not really believe that the government as a whole has the consistent concepts needful for the successful running of a number of large state industries; they do not have much to contribute, either, as to whether their own department has one for their single nationalised industry. In the DoI you hear either a succinct 'no', a 'definitely not. We are working on a short-term survival strategy', or a meagre 'BSC has to be efficient' (which is no more than its statutory duty, after all). Survival is, of course, the BSC's nearest and most urgent objective. From a ministry responsible for a nationalised industry for more than fifteen years, however, one might expect a more forward-looking approach as to *why* it wants the industry to survive and what to do with it once it has survived. That this policy of having nothing but the first step in view was born out of caution and in reaction to the BSC's 'unrealistic investment strategy' of the early 1970s, is hardly a convincing justification; it is just possible, after all, that the BSC might not have pushed through with its 'unrealistic' programme had its sponsoring department, at the time, had its own concept of the future of the steel industry. Instead it thought only of splitting the organisation and re-selling parts of it to the private sector; when that scheme had failed it left nothing but a vacuum concerning the 'surviving' corporation's possible objectives.

The Treasury — itself 'by nature sitting in the background, taking a detached and slightly sceptical view', and hence feeling justified in 'not having its own view' on the nationalised industries (whom it none the less has to finance) — is equally pessimistic about the existence of long-term approaches toward the industries in the sponsoring departments. The Departments of Energy and Transport, being concerned with nothing but nationalised industries, might have such an approach (though a look into those departments might prove just the contrary),[11] but certainly not the DoI or DoT which are responsible for so many other things; besides 'here is much less continuity, because people are moving around to other jobs' — nobody is dealing with a single nationalised industry for a long period of time. Thus where the question of 'concepts' is concerned, things look rather bleak. Not untypical, perhaps, is the resigned comment, 'I have a clear view of what we should do, but I don't know if we do it. . .'(DoI).

The answers BSC board members give when asked about the government's concepts are still more damning. Apart from 'to become profitable' none exists in their eyes. Policies towards the nationalised industries are seen as 'absolutely inconsistent', varying not only with the colour of the government but additionally with the views of different ministers within the same government; and even single ministers 'have difficulties in sticking to their objectives'. There is no input coming from government concerning the corporation's general policies — 'they refuse to give it nowadays'. Sir Monty commented bitingly on this lack of guidance: 'Nobody has yet learned in this country how to run a nationalised industry!'

The only overall concept that concerns the nationalised industries being, at the moment, one of a purely negative nature, they are left alone when it comes to formulating their aims, policies and strategies for future development (and feel justly incensed when afterwards the government complains that their strategies were unrealistic). In this context it is worth noting that no general directive was ever issued to the BSC. All the interviewees, whether from the government or from the BSC, agreed that the government did not really participate in the process of defining the corporation's objectives (other than financial)

11. See, for example the well-known lack of coordination in the policies of the three fuel industries in the DoE (a fact freely admitted in an interview with two DoE officials in March 1980).

— apart, perhaps, from influencing them 'in a rather subtle way' via 'private meetings of executives and senior level civil servants' (BSC), whose impact it would be difficult to assess. Afterwards, of course, when the corporation itself has decided on its strategies, these are 'discussed' with the government, which then contributes a few details, mostly concerning questions of regional and/or social developments (asking the BSC not to close a certain plant, not to buy imported coal and so on). In the latter case the government 'explains rather than gives an input' (BSC) — explains, mainly, why they wished a certain development not to take place — for even regarding social/regional/structural policy there seems no clear government strategy from which specific 'social objectives' for the corporation might be deduced. In the DoI this surprising reserve is regarded 'as a matter of principle': the principle of formulating objectives in exactly the way in which it would be done 'for any private company, which means financial'. While it may be debatable that private companies do not follow any objectives that are not financial, by adhering to such a principle the government ignores the fact that a public enterprise may well differ from a private company in several important details and will certainly require different treatment.

Apart from the ministerial say in the matter of financial targets there have been discussions about parameters and criteria (why to pursue a certain strategy or undertake a certain investment), but those, too, are mainly of a financial nature. A third subject for joint discussion is the performance indicators, introduced only lately. Here again the department's role is passive and reactive: though it had wished for such indicators it waited for the corporation to develop them.

So, while the final decision may rest formally with the government (which has to approve general programmes), the corporation's plans and policies are essentially those of its management — 'we propose, they dispose' (BSC). And however much they are discussed and negotiated, and though 'in the end it is for government to say' (Treasury), 'I don't think objectives can be imposed': rather than imposed they will be rubber-stamped by the department (DoI) — which then hopes that they will not prove inaccurate or unrealistic too soon. Of course, 'the best situation' for the DoI and the Treasury is 'if you get a proposal that is entirely acceptable' (Treasury); yet how, and with what criteria, will 'acceptability' be judged, and are not a nationalised industry's experts, in most cases, in a position to present their proposals in such a way as to make them 'acceptable'?

For this is the essence of the joint planning: 'We are dependent on the industry for setting the objectives: they have the information, and know what is reasonable and what not' (DoI). Ten years ago, according to the NEDO, the only nationalised industries to have 'formally agreed statements of strategy with government' had been the BSC and the NCB (in the case of the BSC this had been the 10-year development strategy), but the joint exercise did not extend to continuous joint reviews of those strategies in the light of altered circumstances; generally the government showed 'a detached attitude until the pressure of external events dictates some positive reaction'.[12] Although in the second half of the 1970s some sort of joint corporate planning seems to have become a more common practice, in 1977 the SCNI still saw fit to demand urgently 'that an integrated strategy for steel should be agreed between the sponsoring Department and the Corporation'.[13] Obviously the joint planning practised until then was not what the SCNI and other critics felt it ought to be. The SCNI found fault especially with the role the department played in it; hence 'the Secretary of State should take urgent steps to improve the procedures for ministerial decision-taking'.[14]

The last corporate plan of the BSC of which the public had definite knowledge was the survival plan of 1981 (at the time of writing, in 1984, a new one was said to be in preparation: a 3-year plan, with a possible extension to five years). The way the DoI dealt with it is described in the Memorandum sent to the Industry and Trade Committee in March 1981.[15] According to that, the DoI first waited for the BSC to work out its plan and then 'assessed' it. The only action it took before it received the plan was to find out, 'from a number of independent sources', the probable future trends of the steel market, and to send a document to the BSC ('Prospects for Steel: the Steel Market');[16] the DoI's estimate of the future trend was 'broadly consistent' with, though admittedly 'less optimistic' than, the estimate it received from the BSC. After receipt of the plan, it was discussed, as a first stage, with senior staff at the BSC; in a second stage the DoI required further information from the corporation 'about particular aspects' (not specified); in a third stage the plan was once more 'assessed' and 'discussed' at meetings which included officials 'from the other Departments concerned' (not specified). The discussions centred

12. NEDO, *A Study of UK Nationalised Industries*, op. cit., p. 26.
13. First Report from the SCNI, Session 1977–78, *The British Steel Corporation*, vol. I, op. cit., p. lxxiv.
14. Ibid., p. lxxv.
15. See Fourth Report from the ITC, Session 1980–81, *Effects of the BSC's Corporate Plan*, op. cit., vol. II, pp. 68ff.
16. Ibid., p. 70ff.

around the following questions: (1) closures and other capacity reductions; (2) the risks of the plan; and (3) its financial consequences. In judging the plan with respect to these questions the DoI was handicapped by the fact that 'we were not able to consider alternative proposals, since the BSC themselves had not prepared alternative strategies . . . In principle, the Government would have preferred to be given a choice between alternative strategies: in this case, however, we were able to accept the BSC proposals as forming a short-term survival plan'.[17]

This description shows several major deficiencies in the joint exercise that the corporate planning really ought to be: (1) the DoI's estimate as to the future prospects of steel differed from that of the BSC, but the department allowed its own judgment to be overridden by that of the latter, explaining, somewhat lamely, before the Committee that the discrepancy was still 'within the bracket';[18] (2) admittedly, the DoI was in no position to assess accurately any details of the plan; it had to leave all the 'particular judgments to the management of the BSC', in fact, believe what it was told, and restrict itself 'to ensur[ing] that the basic economic assumptions which lie behind the whole of the Corporate Plan are not ones from which we would dissent', thus providing 'an independent check on the Plan'[19] (as shown under (1), even within these limitations it did not operate wholly successfully); (3) the DoI was not left any choice, because no alternative strategies had been prepared and it made no attempt to develop any alternatives of its own (the latter being 'a proper management function of BSC').[20] That the plan was one for survival cannot justify this omission, since it is just the urgency of securing survival that should have prompted an especially close scrutiny and thorough appraisal. Still more lame, but at the same time illuminating was the explanation, given to the Committee by Sir Keith Joseph, that to ask the corporation for an alternative plan 'would have been to challenge their judgment . . . '.[21] The Committee did not find this convincing either; it concluded that 'in our view the appraisal to which the Plan was subjected was minimal'.[22]

Yet the department is not wholly to blame. When Ken Binning, then head of the DoI's Iron and Steel Division, told the Committee

17. Ibid., p. 69.
18. Ibid., p. 80.
19. Ibid., pp. 80, 83.
20. Ibid., p. 84.
21. Ibid., p. 105.
22. Ibid., vol. I, p. xv.

that 'there were no [other] options which were known to us',[23] he hinted at the problem that corporate planning can be a joint exercise only in so far and so long as there is sufficient information available from *both* sides. The Benson Brochures, agreed between BSC and DoI in 1971, prescribe, for the necessary flow of regular information, annual 5-year projections, quarterly progress reports and monthly financial statements; of those, the 5-year projections were characterised by the BSC as having been the 'cornerstone of BSC/Government relations' during the 1970s. While this system appears fairly comprehensive, the SCNI, in 1977 and 1978, criticised the BSC's information policy as being insufficient: 'The Chairman of the British Steel Corporation did not see fit to inform his sponsoring Secretary of State at a confidential meeting four days before a major debate in the House that the prospective losses by the Corporation . . . were likely to exceed those forecast in the previously agreed Annual Operating Plan by at least £93 million, and to exceed the most pessimistic assumption implied in the forecast he was to give in public the next day by some £188 million'.[24] It also criticised the 'failure by Ministers to press for proper information', and concluded therefrom a deplorable 'lack of communication and mutual confidence' between corporation and department; apparently, both were 'determined to follow the normal process of formal communication regardless of the nature of the crisis', neither of them being ready 'to talk frankly about the problems until there was no choice but to do so'.[25]

Accordingly, government officials, asked if they were sufficiently informed, responded freely; 'Not always . . . . You never have the information you want, and you never can probe deeply enough. There is a problem here' (Treasury). They confirmed that the corporation 'have been reluctant sometimes in the past' to pass on the necessary information (Treasury) but suggested that since 1980 the information flow had improved significantly (DoI);[26] still — it's just the way the information is presented' (Treasury) that may pull the wool over the government's eyes. Of course, the government does not always feel obliged to give full information about its future plans to the nationalised industries — 'I

23. Ibid., p. 87.
24. Fifth Report from the SCNI, Session 1977–78: *Financial Forecasts of the British Steel Corporation*, London, 1978, pp. xf.; see also Second Report from the SCNI, Session 1977–78. *The British Steel Corporation*, op. cit., pp. xff.
25. Fifth Report. . ., op. cit., p. xiii.
26. When the BSC, in November 1979, cut back its workforce by 15,000, this measure does not seem to have really been discussed with the government beforehand, but was more or less 'announced' shortly before the event — 'but I don't think that will happen again' (DoI).

don't go trotting around telling all that I'm thinking . . .' (DoI).

This statement is echoed by a 'we do not think there's any point in constantly thinking aloud in public', from the nationalised industries.[27] It will not come as a surprise that the latter are normally little inclined to provide more information than they are specifically asked for — 'you get only the information you push for!' (BSC); why should *they* be blamed if the government does not ask the right questions at the right time? Even if the right questions are asked, though: 'Board members are greatly irritated by questions put to them by civil servants' for, as they see it, not all the answers are fit for the public ear (NCB). Furthermore: 'There are only 365 days in a year and by the time you have had consultations with the unions and consultations with the employee directors and consultations with the Government and with Select Committees . . . the time available is limited'.[28] And, finally, 'total information' is bound to lead to a 'second-guessing' of the management by the department which clearly is not its task. The government certainly should not receive any more information than a bank or the shareholders in the private sector do, that is 'none about details', only about 'whether you're reasonably on course' (BSC). In 1977, however, the BSC seems to have withheld even that limited amount from the government (though, not unnaturally, the BSC's view is different: according to them, it was not a matter of withholding information from the DoI, but of the BSC and DoI together trying to withhold certain information from the SCNI — for 'telling them things would mean telling the press').

The conclusions to be drawn from what could be discovered about the crucial processes of determining the goals and policies of a nationalised industry, and of its 'joint planning' with the sponsoring department, are that: (1) there is very little input from the government. Lacking any consistent long-term concepts of its own — apart from such general ones as 'support the private sector', and the financial as well as purely formal one 'to break even' (which each year is postponed to the next) — the government's role in the planning process is restricted to waiting for the corporation to develop the programmes, and then reacting to them; (2) for the same reason its reactions can be only piecemeal and arbitrary; (3) the sponsoring department's ability to react rationally and assess the corporate plans properly is marred furthermore by there being no guarantee that it will be kept fully informed; finally, even where the department acquires information from other sources, so as to be better equipped to assess the plans, it is

27. Interview with two senior staff members of the NCB, in March 1980.
28. Sir Monty Finniston, in First Report from the SCNI, Session 1977–78, *The British Steel Corporation*, op. cit., vol. II, p. 63.

prone to let its own judgment be overruled by that of the corporation's experts.

Hence the 'joint planning', that has been the subject of so much public discussion and that is considered to be of paramount importance for the (*ex ante*) control of public enterprise (and, in fact, has been thus considered by SCNI and NEDO alike), is fictitious: the planning is all done by the corporation itself. While this has been established beyond any doubt in the case of the BSC, there is little hope that there exists any 'joint planning' more worthy of that name in any other nationalised sector. However, if we take into account the losses the BSC has made and its generally rather desperate situation, there is no other nationalised industry the government has dealt with so closely.

Power on the Board

Since from 1978 to 1983 the government was represented on the corporation board with two part-time members, it could be maintained that joint planning did exist, as government officials were incorporated into the BSC's decision-making structure. This leads us to the question as to precisely what the board's role and functions are, and how the authority to influence decisions is distributed amongst its members.

Since the board's restructuring in 1977-8 (described in Chapter 10 above) the majority of its members have been part-timers, representing the three groups of private sector businessmen, 'worker directors' and civil servants. Generally, and irrespective of their background, the part-timers' contribution to the corporations' policies is, according to the NEDO, 'very small because of the confusion about what they are there for'; this is one reason (the other being the unclear relationship between board and department) why private sector managers appear to have little interest in being appointed as part-time members.[29] Yet of all the part-timers those from the private sector are the most favourably placed since they are brought in specifically to offer the expert advice they are able to give on all matters connected with the running of commercial business; they also have the specific function of forming the Audit Committee.

While the BSC's executive board members are all career steelmen,

29. In First Report from the SCNI, Session 1977-78, *The British Steel Corporation*, op. cit., vol. II, p. 402.

'reared in the industry' (BSC), its private sector part-timers are all from businesses *other* than steel and hence have not been appointed to give their advice on matters specific to the steel industry — or to further the good relations between private and public sector steel. Nor does the furthering of relations with BSC's industrial consumers seem to have been of major importance in their selection. Those who have been part-time members of the board between 1979 and 1984 were: a director of Marks & Spencer (and former finance director at ICI); a managing director of the Beecham Group; two directors from engineering companies (Davy Corporation and Fairey Holdings); a chartered accountant; and a consultant and former BNOC executive, who had resigned that post 'in protest'. When asked why they thought they had been chosen their replies revealed a background of 'successful businesses', 'well-managed companies' and personal records of success in their fields — as 'a well-known marketing person', as being knowledgeable on all questions of energy, as having collected experience in a company with a particularly good 'accounting structure' or, simply, 'because I knew a lot about Wales'. But the main reason why they sit (or sat) on the board is to bring in 'the broad knowledge and experience of industry', and to plead 'the business point of view'.

However, apart from forming the Audit Committee, these part-timers do not see themselves as performing any specific functions, but as being there merely to discuss matters brought forward by the executive, and 'to ask questions' (if possible intelligent ones). While this rather vaguely-defined role may not cause any problems for the private sector members,[30] who in general can expect their judgment to be valued by BSC executives and who do not typically represent interests in conflict with those of the corporation's management,[31] the situation is entirely different for the employees and civil servants on the board — who are equally furnished with the non-specific function of 'asking questions'. The frustration of the BSC's worker-directors has been described already: they obviously felt superfluous. On the other hand it appears that they themselves rarely tried to better their uncomfortable position, or undertook to fulfil their likeliest 'specific function', which was to exert pressure on the executive on behalf of the employees' interests — the six of them, after all, formed the largest single group within the board. According

30. But one of them dismissively remarked that the BSC only got such private sector part-time members as were 'foolish enough to accept', which hints at some frustration.
31. In fact, according to all evidence, 'likely conflicts of interest are taken into account' in selecting candidates for the board, to avoid 'embarrassment'.

to all available evidence, the board's discussions in those years were never controversial and its decisions have always been taken 'by consensus' (with the one exception of the board's rebellion against Sir Charles Villiers when he wanted to restructure the corporation); the unmistakable conclusion is that the employee representatives did not take an active part in discussions[32] — not even during the steel strike. Instead, as a BSC employee somewhat maliciously told the *Sunday Telegraph*, 'they have attended board meetings, and taken their glass of red or white wine afterwards, and then they've gone home for a little solidarity. They've never said, as a block, "this is rot, enough is enough", they've never said they wanted to see the Secretary of State . . . . They don't matter any more'[33] — having let themselves become paralysed by the problem of double loyalty.

The latter problem might be expected to have paralysed the two civil servants on the board as well. Various chairmen have thought the notion of the government being directly represented on the boards 'a bad suggestion because the civil servant must owe his first allegiance to his Minister', whereas 'if he is a member of the board his responsibility and allegiance must be that to the board'; as a result he would end up with a 'split personality'.[34] When asked about the role of government representatives on the BSC main board DoI and Treasury officials unanimously insisted that they did not sit there as spokesmen for the government's interests, but merely 'to improve the flow of information' — though, in point of fact, board members were not expected to inform the outside world about the board's discussions, to pass on board papers, and so on; hence their proper role was further reduced to that of 'removing misunderstandings' and generally 'improving relations'. Of those who actually sat on the board themselves one saw no problems or disadvantages whatsoever in this but, optimistically, advantages for both sides, since he now knew not only what was afoot in the corporation but was, furthermore, in the position 'to provide the board with a clearer impression of external pressures'. Another, while maintaining that he could furnish the government with 'early warnings' as well as inform the board about the probable reactions of the government, had a slightly more sceptical view on the matter: 'I myself ask these questions' (about the benefits and problems arising out of the civil servants' membership).

32. In all these years, I was told, they only once gave an 'open dissent'.
33. *The Sunday Telegraph*, 23 March 1980, p. 22.
34. Sir Henry Marking (British Airways), SCNI (Sub-Committee E), Session 1978–79, *The Relationships* . . ., op. cit., p. 42. See, too, Sixth Special Report from the SCNI, Session 1977–78; *Comments* . . ., op. cit., p. 11.

He named as potential problems firstly, the uncertainty of how much information he might be allowed to pass on to his staff ('in a filtered sort of way') and, secondly, the conflict of interest: 'As a board member I may agree to something — as a civil servant I may have to stand back . . . but of course there is a lot of muddy water in the middle'.

Opinions on this matter within the BSC itself range from 'I think it's a thoroughly good thing', since it 'very much improves the communication and mutual understanding', to 'they have a peculiar role, and I would say an impossible one' (and should not sit there at all). Interestingly enough, the first (minority) view is based on the assumption that as 'they don't have a role' (!) the problem of dual loyalty will not arise. Others are more susceptible to the 'very delicate position' of the government's part-timers who 'wear two hats'; the civil servant 'has to think of his political master — what he wants might be contrary to what is good for the company'. Of course, the civil servants actually sitting on the board were 'very supportive', 'but that can change with persons', and a device whose advantages, and even feasibility, rests on personalities cannot be considered a good one. The implication in such statements is that it is preferable to have a board with only 'independent' non-executive directors (meaning those from the business world) — 'and I expect we shall return to it'.

Stressing the supportive attitude of the two civil servants must, from a different angle, be regarded as rather a damning judgment. It is further said that, compared with the independent part-timers, 'they restrict themselves and their comments, are very cautious of going too far', 'speak only in accordance with their brief from their department', and, hence, 'as individual members . . . are not very valuable'. Thus, according to the evidence, their position seems to have been very similar to that of the worker-directors: paralysed by dual loyalty, they cannot be ranked with executives and 'independents', but are in effect third-class members. Rather than having a 'decision-making helping role' they are reduced to providing the 'link to the government' which can come in very useful 'with an industry in trouble'; but even as such they appear to have been accepted only because (and as long as) they remain quietly in the background. It should be noted that this view has not been contradicted by the civil servants themselves, who have stressed their essentially passive role. Consequently, the deficiencies found in the system of joint planning are certainly *not* made up for by the government's placing some members on the board.

Meanwhile (in July 1983) the government decided that it no longer wished to be represented on the board and the DTI's representative formally asked for his Treasury colleague's resignation. It has been said that the removal took place entirely at the government's instigation, the BSC wishing things to say as they were; yet in the light of the statements quoted here this must remain in doubt. The one advantage the DoI's and the Treasury's representation on the board had had — to strengthen the link between BSC and government and 'improve the flow of information' — has been retained, for both civil servants continue to attend board meetings; but they do so by invitation only and have no vote. Hence it is now made quite clear that no government representative plays any part in the board's decision-making.

One former DoI official has remained on the board, however. When Solly Gross retired in 1980, and consequently had to resign his seat on the board, Ian MacGregor invited him to stay (and induced the Conservative government to reinstate him), obviously finding him so knowledgeable that he wanted to retain his advice. This had certainly not much to do with Mr Gross's (former) capacity as a civil servant, but with his personality and individual competence. In a sense he is now a truly independent (i.e. disinterested) part-timer — perhaps the only one on the board.

Though officially it is maintained that all board members are equal, it is obvious from the above that they differ considerably in rank and status. One might say that the distribution of decision-making power follows a three-class system: firstly, there have been the civil servants and worker-directors, sitting quietly in the background and having no real impact on the board's decisions. Secondly, there are the private sector part-timers, expected to contribute their experience from other fields of business and to give their advice; their impact on the final decisions will vary with the nature of the decision as well as with personalities. They sit on the Audit Committee, and sometimes even do 'odd jobs for the chairman', but have nevertheless neither the amount of knowledge nor the access to information to keep up with the executive members. Finally, there is the group comprising the deputy chairman (and chief executive) and the two other executive directors who, with the managing directors (after the new organisational formula the 'group chairmen' and the 'functional directors') *not* sitting on the board, form the Chief Executive's Committee. Together with the chairman's, theirs is the major influence on the board's decisions, the relative impact of chairman and chief executive again varying with personalities. With the chairman himself now being a part-timer there seems to be no question whose voice will carry the greatest weight, whereas in the reign of Ian MacGregor it was he who was said to have been the dominant figure. In a way, this three-class system might be compared with the German two-tier corporation structure, including workers' co-determination at board level (*Mitbestimmung*).

The board members interviewed mostly gave a similar description, distinguishing the three groups on the board, but would not see them as three factions and rather avoided talking about hierarchies. Although, of course, 'the executives obviously have more to do with the business', while the part-timers usually are 'not well enough informed': 'we have to rely on the executive members, the information they give'. Hence the equality of board members exists 'only legally': 'What clearly you haven't got is equality in information, that must limit the impact of the part-timers'; 'full-timers have the power of information — part-timers can ask intelligent questions . . .' Most board members hastened to add that, firstly, this was quite a normal thing, common to all companies; secondly, the managers did their best to keep the part-timers informed; thirdly, the part-timers, though not so relevant on the board 'as such', did valuable work in its committees; and, finally, they gained in importance 'in times of stress': 'outside directors take a much stronger stance if a company is in trouble'; so they were, at the moment, less reduced to merely rubber-stamping the management's decisions in the BSC than in other (private) companies. One part-timer stated quite freely, however, that the non-executive's role, in the corporation's decision-making, 'looks like rubber-stamping, in the majority of cases'.

Not even the full-timers seem to be of equal status. Nearly unanimously the board members indicated that the chairman ('of course' — and frequently named in second place) and the chief executive (who is 'best informed') played the major roles. There is a clear and hierarchical relationship between the 'Chief Operating Officer' on the one hand and the five 'functional directors' and three group chairmen on the other, the latter reporting to the former who then passes on their reports and proposals to the board. Those two managers who sit on the board themselves, as executive directors, consequently appear not as the equals of the COO, but 'as a sort of interest representatives'. As to the relative position of chairman and chief executive the general distinction is made 'that the policy-making strategic influence was predominantly the chairman's', whereas in all technological matters specific to the steel business the chief executive (with his long experience of the industry) was most influential. Yet, since he provides a chairman coming from the outside with the information needed for his 'strategic' decisions, it is difficult to see how the chief executive's judgment can be overridden. Hence, as in all large companies, routine as well as policy decisions can be said to be coined by the executive management (who make the proposals, after all); and the 'role of the outside board is merely to check on the management occasionally'.

In the reign of Ian MacGregor it was he, and not Bob Scholey, who appeared to the outside world as the BSC's 'strong man'. But this was the impression created by his external relations — especially with the government. In this latter respect, he is said to have had 'more power than any of his predecessors' since, after having paid such a high transfer fee to obtain his services, it was 'difficult for government to disagree with him publicly.' His internal influence is less easily assessed. Though a metallurgist by training, who had had some experience of the steel business as a young man, he will have had nonetheless to rely on Scholey's superior knowledge about the BSC; both were, of course, in 'continual dialogue'. Bob Scholey, on the other hand — an 'idealistic man' and emotionally involved in the steel business — seems to have taken great pains always to remain at the very centre of things, hating 'normal routine' (things not going over his own desk), and thus establishing a superior position as the one who knew about everything. Under the new reign of Bob Haslam who, as a part-timer, only 'does the chairman sort of things' (chairs board meetings and represents the BSC to the outside), Scholey's internally exceptionally strong position has been further upgraded; it is he who is now, to the outside world as well, the BSC's recognised 'strong man'.

The way the board as a whole currently operates strengthens the impression of the executive's dominance and the reduced role of the 'outside board'. The management (naturally) makes the proposals and prepares the decisions to which the board 'reacts' and, formally, has the last say — 'the executive proposes, the board disposes'. The final decision is usually taken 'unanimously' and 'by consensus', not by vote ('I don't think we've had a vote. In general the chairman will get the feeling of the meeting. . .'). Dissenting minorities are evidently seen as a problem to be avoided at all costs (as 'a matter of style'); rather than run the risk of open conflicts on the board the chairman would 'withdraw the item', postpone the respective decision until, in informal discussions outside the board meetings, the cause for dissent had been removed. But such postponements occur only rarely; one statement was to the effect that within one six-months period only one decision had been referred back to the management; another informant said (in 1981) that during the previous thirteen years (that is, throughout the BSC's existence) it had happened fewer than five times that the final decision had differed significantly from the management's proposal.[35] Hence the board members' proper function of 'modifying' those proposals in the light of their wide experience is seldom exercised, or only in minor detail. This is seen not as a deficiency but an achievement, as a sign of the prevailing harmony of interests as well as of the skill of the management (for 'if the executive have done their homework', postponements, as a result of the board's discussions, 'should not happen'). The reverse side of this search for harmony is that board discussions are probably led less openly than one might wish for; where it is held that, 'as a matter of style', there are 'virtually no circumstances where members would wish to record their dissent', it will be difficult to utter conflicting views. Not even dissenting views from the BSC's subdivisions are brought before the board: they are 'sorted out by Mr Scholey' (which may not always be to their advantage).

So, on the whole, the main board's role is a limited one: it is a 'reactive board', not quite reduced to a 'rubber-stamp' but coming very close to it. All the possible arguments take place before board meetings, the board then merely ratifying what the executives have previously discussed. In this it much resembles a continental supervisory board, though its members themselves do not relish the analogy, preferring the expression 'policy board'. While admittedly 'not equipped with the necessary information to be a real executive board' ('executive matters are kept outside the board') they maintain that its function remains to define the corporation's policies. Since these are worked out by the executive, however, and presented in such a way that dissent is difficult, it is actually 'not a policy-making, but a policy-ratifying board'. This may fall somewhat short of what the inventors of the public corporation had envisaged, but is certainly in line with the experience made in normal joint-stock companies.[36]

Financial Control

While there is almost no joint planning and this deficiency has, apparently, not been made up for by appointing two civil servants to

---

35. One such case was the rejection of Sir Charles Villiers' reorganisation plan. A more recent one concerned the removal of the BSC headquarters from Grosvenor Place to the Albert Embankment (the executive had proposed a place north of the river).
36. Asked by the ITC, 'Would it be fair to say that the board itself has precious little influence over management decisions', Ian MacGregor answered, 'I would say it is *no less* [italics mine, H. A.] than any managing board' (and added that the presence of government representatives had constituted 'a supervisory board approach').

the board, the system of financial control has been much elaborated upon; all the energy the government could spare for the nationalised industries seems to have been concentrated on that field: 'the primary concern from our point of view is what are the *financial* [italics mine, H. A.] implications for the public sector of the pattern which is developing'.[37] Generally (as has been described in Part II) this system comprises the three elements of financial targets, investment appraisal and cash limits. Of these, Treasury officials still judge the 'medium-term financial targets' the most important instrument of financial control, though in the case of the BSC it is somewhat difficult to find out what they are — apart from the general (and optimistic) one to 'break even', which has never yet been reached and is always postponed from one period to the next. The last Corporate Plan contained estimates as to the expected losses, but these have not been declared as 'financial targets'; anyway, the 'planned loss' for the year 1981/2 (£318m) was overdrawn by £40m, that for the year 1982/3 (£80m) by as much as £306m, and only in 1983/4 did the 'loss on ordinary activities' remain under the 'target loss' of £181m.[38] There are certainly no targets in the sense of 'average cost profit earned on net assets' over three years, as they exist for other nationalised industries. Whatever else there may be (in the sense of limits to the trading loss) is not fixed for a medium period, but 'continually discussed' — and varied, it seems, according to the ever worsening situation, from one quarter to the next. It is important to note, in this context, that whatever the targets are they are not imposed but 'a matter of real bargaining' between the Treasury, the department, and the corporation.

The other instrument of financial control to be subsumed under the heading '*ex ante* control', the investment appraisal or annual 'investment review', is *not*, interestingly enough, named as one of the more important ones. Originally, within those reviews each investment project costing above £50m(!) had to be specially appraised and approved,[39] but for many years now there have been no such projects. When big investment projects still existed, there was also considerable dissatisfaction about the appraisal; for example, in 1977 the SCNI demanded that, should a government reject a project, it should inform the corporation of the reasons 'by formal procedures', and the latter was to publish the same in its Annual Report; it should also publish

---

Fourth Report from the ITC, Session 1980–81, *Effects* . . ., op. cit., vol. II, p. 201.
37. Mr France (Treasury), First Report from the SCNI, Session 1977–78, *The British Steel Corporation*, op. cit., vol. II, p. 108.
38. See the BSC *Annual Report and Accounts*, 1981–2 and 1982–3, pp. 7 and 8.
39. See NEDO, *A Study of UK Nationalised Industries*, op. cit., p. 29.

details of the cost incurred through the delays caused by the process of appraisal and approval.[40] The DoI, in its written answer to the questions the Committee had put to them before coming to this conclusion, had tried to play down the role of the appraisal process by maintaining that 'it is not the Government's function to duplicate BSC's planning process when considering investment proposals submitted by the Corporation'.[41]

So the investment review, in practice, does not seem ever to have been a truly *ex ante* control, nor was it meant to be, even by the SCNI. In scrutinising the single projects 'in general it is very difficult to say no' (Treasury), since that means openly contradicting the combined expertise of the corporation. The switch from the TDR (test discount rate of return) to the RRR (required rate of return) system in itself can be said to have been a step from *ex ante* to *ex post* control, and even as such is deemed to be rather ineffective. The Treasury now has a tendency to look at the aggregate rather than at the details — although 'you cannot understand the aggregate if you don't know anything about the details'. Try as they may, Treasury officials cannot evade the problem of how to acquire that knowledge, for 'we see little, and what we see is rather haphazard'. Not being able to solve it, they see their role reduced to that of 'improving appraisals that the nationalised industries themselves should do, improving their system' — in the hope that afterwards they 'can rely on them'; thus, in the final analysis, this instrument of control does not amount to more than trying to ascertain that investment appraisals *by the corporation itself* have been properly done.

Nor has the DoI been in a position to appraise all the projects that are relevant to the corporation's strategy. Though they still think a 'careful scrutiny' of all major projects sensible as well as necessary (especially since they have detected a 'tendency to over-investment' in the nationalised industries) they admit freely that it 'could not work'. In any case, the sole criterion for their appraisal would have been a project's profitability, not its position in or necessity for the strategy, to say nothing of any wider socio-economic aspects which might play a significant role in an investment control system worthy of the name.

Such an investment control would be certain to be opposed vehemently by the corporation, already irritated by the investment review: 'I think that it's wrong because it is too detailed' (!). As BSC members see it, the trouble with the government is that it 'always tries to

---

40. See First Report from the SCNI, Session 1977–78, op. cit., vol. I, pp. lxxvif.
41. Ibid., vol. III, p. 93.

double-guess', and 'do the same as the board did, only coming to different decisions', a policy which led to delays that impaired the corporation's efficiency. They cannot see any sense in having 'two people doing the same thing, one after the other', especially since civil servants 'cannot judge the matter', not being experts ('otherwise *they* should run the Corporation!'). It is really 'not their job' to appraise investment, whereas 'management is paid for it'; hence the 'government should make up its mind: give money (to a limit) and leave the Corporation to make the best use of it' — in other words, should refrain from meddling in the latter's business. In the event of managerial error, the government can, after all, apply the final sanction of dismissal. Although, if civil servants 'cannot judge the matter', how can they ever be in the position of being able to pass such a verdict?

So we are back at the problem of information. Usually, when having to approve investments, the minister will have to rely on the information the corporation itself is prepared to give, and the question is then as to whether that is sufficient. 'They get what the board gets' — but as its part-timer members admit, that is 'only a summary'. On the other hand there is the rather cynical view that 'they get as much detail as they can understand: you feed them information until they get indigestion'. Either way it is hard to believe that those charged with the control of a nationalised industry's investment are adequately equipped for their task.

As for managerial 'errors' that could lead to dismissal, one would have thought that investment control — in whatever form — had been designed to prevent misinvestment, not merely to react after considerable resources had been squandered. But the BSC maintains in the teeth of all public criticism that during its existence there have never been cases of 'real misinvestment'. Instead, 'on the whole the direction the corporation took turned out to be right'. That eventually 'the scale of operations proved to be too high' was caused by a number of things — amongst them the oil crisis and the decline of British manufacturing industries — which, at the time, had been 'unpredictable', so that the fault was one of inaccurately forecasting the future (which other steel industries had committed as well), not of wrong investment. At any rate, in the eyes of the public steelmen, it would not have been avoided by more thorough and detailed investment control — in which assertion they may well be right, considering all the problems described above.

More controls would even have been detrimental, causing still more delays than those the corporation already had to suffer. 'Delays through controls' are a favourite subject with members of the BSC,

Sir Monty Finniston going so far as to express his belief that his 10-year-development strategy might well have proved successful, had it not been delayed by negotiations with the government that lasted for more than a year. Yet such delays have occurred much less frequently than the corporation likes to admit. Apart from the 10-year-development strategy (which the government had every right to scrutinise carefully since it involved a greal deal of public money) the longest delay caused by the necessity of gaining the government's approval happened over the Port Talbot scheme. In this case, however, the BSC itself had taken time — years, it is said — to come to a decision, hence there appeared to be no obvious need 'to react quickly'; and when the government had finally given its agreement, in 1976, the BSC cancelled the scheme. The next longest delay concerned the development of Redcar, where the government took eleven weeks to give its approval. In any case the argument that, as a manufacturing industry, the BSC must make quick decisions on investment projects without being hampered by the time-consuming procedure of attaining ministerial approval, has little to recommend it. In the private sector also major projects are appraised very carefully, by the banks, for instance, and hence delayed: large investments are not usually made as the result of snap decisions.

The complaints about delays do not pinpoint the real cause of dissension but serve to underline the corporation's general dislike of government control. The same applies to another complaint: having to consider the government's view before being allowed to take a decision on any single project would necessarily lead to 'low competitiveness'; companies in the private sector are equally obliged to take outside factors into account and to listen to those who bear the risks. It is, after all, the government who must pay if the corporation's plans misfire; it is only reasonable, surely, that they should have a say in major decision-making.

The one instrument of financial control that seems to be entirely acceptable to the corporation — albeit much opposed by several other nationalised industries — is that of cash limits. The annual EFL set by the government is aggregated and does not distinguish between the operating cash-flow, the investment cash-flow, and 'exceptional items'; thus the latter are, in principle, no excuse for the corporation to overspend. Whether or not the BSC stays within its EFL, therefore, depends on how 'realistically' the limit is fixed. The experience of recent years has been of obviously *un*realistic limits, since the BSC has experienced great difficulty in staying within them. In 1980/1 the EFL was set at £450m, but 'in the light of the serious deterioration in trading conditions and the Corporation's actions to meet the situation, the Government increased the limit to £1,121 million'.[42] In 1981/2 the BSC 'for its own direct operations' stayed within its EFL of £730m, yet was asked by the government to meet the financing costs associated with the creation of the first Phoenix (Allied Steel and Wire) and consequently overdrew by half the 'exceptional costs' incurred thereby.[43] In 1982/3, the initial EFL of £365m had once again, 'in recognition of the deterioration in trading conditions', to be raised, this time to £575m.[44] Furthermore (see Chapter 10, pp. 138ff.) several capital write-offs and extensions of the borrowing limit eased the BSC's financial burden. Only in 1983/4 did the BSC manage, for the first time, not to overdraw its EFL of £321m; at the same time its external financing requirement was, at £318m, the lowest since 1974/5.[45]

Hence, the EFL has not been as 'immutable'[46] as originally described by the present (Thatcher) government, and perhaps not quite the 'healthy discipline' for which it is praised within the Corporation. Still, both government and the BSC maintain that a cash limit is the ideal instrument of overall control, affecting all the corporation's activities, and operating with 'a certain beauty of simplicity', 'just controlling the bottom line and leaving you to decide' (BSC); it is said to be 'effective' (for example, in curbing the nationalised industries' 'tendency to over-invest') as well as 'powerful', and the only really workable 'pressure to efficiency' (Treasury). Scepticism as to its effects, as voiced in other nationalised industries, comes from the government rather than from the BSC. While it does not accept the argument that the EFL hinders economically-justified investment — for in times of recession the private sector is also forced to cut back on investment — the Treasury sees the danger that 'a rigid cash limit might render it impossible for a nationalised industry to meet its financial targets'. The BSC does not express such fears, probably because there have been no financial targets for them to meet in the more recent past. There is just a cautious hint at the possible disadvantages arising from the EFL, by comparison with conditions in the private sector ('this has caused a few problems. . .'), but otherwise the corporation appears wholeheartedly to 'welcome the cash limits as a

42. BSC. Annual Report and Accounts 1980–1, p. 7.
43. Idem, 1981–2, p. 7.
44. Idem, 1982–3, p.8.
45. Idem, 1983–4, p. 7.
46. Ian MacGregor, when asked about the EFL by the ITC, coolly remarked that 'in human affairs, there is nothing in the future immutable.' (Fourth Report from the ITC, Session 1980–81, *Effects of BSC's Corporate Plan*, op. cit., vol. II, p. 47).

discipline', mainly because they 'tighten the discipline within the machine' — that is, strengthen central management's position *vis-à-vis* the corporation's divisions and subdivisions.

Perhaps this is the major advantage to be obtained from the EFL. From the above it should be clear that the BSC, as a whole, has never really suffered from a 'harshened régime' of rigid cash limits. If the consequences of conformity would be 'too drastic', then the BSC can inform the department about them and ask to discuss alternatives; and though a possible course, if a nationalised industry does not keep within its limits, might be for the government to 'fire the board, or liquidate the corporation' (BSC), the first and most sensible one is, of course, 'to raise the cash limit'. This would have been negotiated with the corporation in the first instance, in any case, in order to make it 'realistic', using a process of 'continuous dialogue' derived from the annual investment review (which, in the case of the BSC, is more of a closures or loss review). So it would appear that in this case, as in the others discussed above, the corporation has a major voice in the structure and application of the instruments of financial control.

The same holds true for the new control instrument, the performance indicators, invented in the early 1980s with the express purpose of preventing a nationalised industry from meeting its targets (including the EFL) by raising prices, rather than by lowering costs and increasing efficiency. These indicators were not developed by the DoI or the Treasury, both of whom asked the BSC's managing director of finance (then Mr Colin Barker) to do it for them, saying that they were ready to accept any indicators he suggested as long as they were 'tough enough'. Mr Barker, incidentally, undertook this task not only to satisfy the government, but also to improve the corporation's own information system (and would perhaps have done so even without the government's request) — 'so *now* the Board as well as the Department are really well informed' (DTI).

The performance indicators (first published in the BSC's Annual Report and Accounts 1982–83) are as follows: utilisation of furnace capacity in blast; fuel rate (kg. of coke and oil consumed per tonne of iron produced); utilisation of actual manned steel-making capacity; utilisation of planned manned steel-making capacity; liquid steel production by oxygen process, by electric process, and steel production continuously cast; energy consumed per tonne of liquid steel; man hours worked per tonne of liquid steel, employment costs per tonne of liquid steel, and per employee; total corporation employment costs as percentage of value added. The majority of the figures given show that the BSC's performance in these fields deteriorated slightly in

1982/3 in comparison with 1981/2, but improved if compared with the results of 1980/1. As is the case with the EFL, the figures for 1983/4 show a further improvement. What has *not* been published, however, and obviously was not fixed previously with the department, are performance *targets* against which actual performance (as described by the indicators enumerated) could be measured. So this new device is, in fact, a means of obtaining information rather than an instrument of (*ex post*) control: it does not allow for judgment on the rate of target fulfilment.

In spite of this shortcoming the indicators should be seen as a step in the right direction. Whereas before the department had monitored only the corporation's financial performance, monitoring now — at least as far as obtaining the relevant information goes — extends to economic and technical performance as well. Concerning these last two, the stress lies, at the moment, on factors such as capacity utilisation, cost reduction and manpower efficiency (in this the indicators show clearly the prevalent technological interest of their deviser). Could the new system be expanded to cover, for instance, pricing, quality control, the degree to which consumer demands are met, and the social costs of production, the controllers would eventually get an adequate picture of the corporation's overall performance, and be better equipped to fulfil their proper role in the joint planning as well as in all other forms of control.

Finally, something must be said about the entire process of monitoring the corporation (of which the performance indicators now form a part). Ideally, it should be a continuous process, the department constantly watching the corporation's progress towards the targets set for it. In 1977, though, the SCNI criticised the system of supervising short-term performance, which by then consisted mainly of quarterly reports to the DoI, on the grounds that these took too much of the management's time, and recommended its abolition; 'The Corporation should not. . .be required to maintain a continuous reporting system to the government'.[47] Now that the BSC is so obviously in crisis the government has a different view on the matter: the Conservatives, ideologically pledged to non-intervention and to 'leaving the public corporations alone', shifted the emphasis from quarterly progress reports to 'day-to-day financial control' (DoI). In part this is literally true, staff members being in touch on a day-to-day basis; at a higher level monitoring occurred, according to Ian MacGre-

---

47. First Report from the SCNI, Session 1977–78, *The British Steel Corporation*, op. cit., vol. I, pp. lxxiif.

gor, 'literally week by week',[48] while the DoI talks of monitoring performance, especially progress against the corporation's forecasts of capital expenditure, on a monthly basis. In interviews, officials from both sides confirmed the impression that they were continually in close contact with each other. So the flow of communication, at least, has much improved during the last years; it now appears to be constant as well as more detailed.

This is, of course, due to the BSC's present catastrophic situation. Most people inside and outside the nationalised industries agree that monitoring as well as financial control is considerably less intense when corporations are profitable: 'You are not asked so many questions!' (BSC), and 'given a lot more freedom' in spending and investment decisions (Treasury). Though formally exposed to the same system of control (the EFL then being a 'negative' one by which the government tries to lessen the degree of self-financing by taking money from the industry), profitable corporations are said to be better able 'to resist it' (BSC). Yet since it is obvious that the loss-making BSC has been able to evade tight control for some time, the real difference between profitable and loss-making nationalised industries would appear to lie in the frequency of contact and intensity of communication rather than in the effectiveness of control.

As for the variability of controls over time, and from one government to the next, most of those interviewed, rather surprisingly, have not seen much difference: 'The system of control has changed very little', for it had been revised already under the previous government, with the 1978 White Paper (so 'here is a factor of continuity'); 'my guess would be that, despite the philosophy of the present government, the degree of intervention is as great as ever' (Treasury). Some board members feel that controls, on the whole, have lessened, the present government relying more on market forces ('let market forces work!') than on anything else; it is only the EFLs that have become more stringent (which seems debatable, from the above), but rather owing to the general 'shortage of money' than to the government's intention to tighten controls generally. Hence the relaxing or intensifying of financial control is seen as almost entirely dependent on the economic situation, of the individual nationalised industry as well as of the economy as a whole; it is 'less a problem of ministerial policy than of economic conditions' (Treasury).

We may conclude, then, that the present system of financial control

---

48. See Fourth Report from the ITC, Session 1980–81, *Effects* . . . , op. cit., vol. II, 57.

over the BSC is more stringent in theory than in fact. Its most characteristic feature is that its methods — targets, EFLs, indicators and so on — are the subject of negotiation between government and corporation, with the balance on the side of the latter. Its weakest point seems to be the investment review — not least because this is the instrument most resented by the management. But even the EFLs, which are usually held to be the government's most effective method of bringing a nationalised industry under control, have not fulfilled their promise: firstly, in order to make them 'realistic' the corporation needed (and achieved) a major say in their determination; and secondly, the thresholds still had to be raised, again and again, when the corporation found it impossible to stay within them. Nonetheless the new addition to the system, the performance indicators, in improving the flow of information to the department, may well prepare the ground for more effective control, always providing that the government is willing to go further along this particular path. The same can be said about the present very close, detailed and continuous monitoring of the BSC's performance — which is without precedence in the history of ministerial control. Thus, while not actually 'steering' the industry and influencing its policy, the present government at least tries to hold the BSC firmly to its own targets and objectives. If nothing else may be expected from the present system of control, it is realistic to hope that it improves the BSC's internal discipline.

Government Interference

Whatever form 'ministerial control' takes, it is frequently regarded by the corporation as being one with 'government interference' and resented as such. In fact, the dividing line between them is particularly finely drawn; if the government, exerting its right to control, delays an investment scheme or plant closure, then it obviously 'interferes' with the running of the industry. The famous and acrimonious dispute between Sir Monty Finniston and Anthony Wedgwood Benn, in the mid-1970s, over the Beswick Review, and the subsequent postponement of several plant closures, arose out of the government's wish to assert its authority over the BSC, as shareholder, banker and controller. For once it attempted *ex ante* control to prevent damage to the industry, rather than to mourn after the event and then to pay the bill; the laudable intention in this case was to reconcile the necessary rationalisation and reconstruction of the steel industry with the social need to maintain employment in already depressed areas. If the 'public accountability' of a nationalised industry has any meaning at all, the government's stand was perfectly reasonable, on the grounds that the BSC should be accountable for not only the commercial results of its activities, but also for the social consequences. Yet the BSC's chairman pugnaciously tried to fend off this 'unwarrantable interference', arguing that the statutes under which the corporation operated required it to maximise efficiency and nothing else, and that the government had no right whatsoever to require anything further. We have already established that the legal position is not quite that simple; the point at issue here is that Sir Monty implied that *any* form of control which resulted in the corporation having to alter its plans, or even postpone them, was interference with day-to-day management and as such unacceptable. This is, indeed, a somewhat radical view of the line between 'control' and 'interference', leaving almost no legitimate field for 'control'.

The position of the SCNI has been similarly restrictive. It demanded that the corporation 'should not...suffer continual interventions in matters which are strictly the prerogative of management', a phrase which it meant to be understood in the narrowest sense since, ideally, after having appointed the right men to the board and approved of the corporate plans, there should be no 'need for ad hoc interventions by Departments on particular issues'.[49] If, however, the government considered it necessary to use the corporation 'for political and social ends', the BSC was to be 'fully and adequately compensated'; furthermore, the minister was to have 'set out the general circumstances under which he may intervene in the affairs of the Corporation, and the procedures to be followed', in order to remove any element of uncertainty[50] which might force the management unexpectedly to alter its schemes.

While rather more cautious in its conclusions the NEDO, in its 1976 Report, likewise criticised the government's apparent inclination to intervene in the corporation's affairs. While to some extent appreciating the necessity of intervention, arising from the increasingly strategic role of the nationalised industries in a low-growth economy, the Report adopted the boards' viewpoint that interventions were far from beneficial since they 'delayed decisions, disrupted previously agreed plans, invalidated criteria for planning and assessing perform-

---

49. First Report from the SCNI, Session 1977–78, *The British Steel Corporation*, op. cit., Vol. I, p. lxxii; Second Report from the SCNI, Session 1978–79; *Further Comments on the Government White Paper on the Nationalised Industries*, op. cit., p. viii.
50. First Report from the SCNI, Session 1977–78, *The British Steel Corporation*, op. cit., Vol. I. p. lxxii.

ance, resulted in financial deficits, and damaged the corporate morale of management'.[51] Apart from probable delays, however, government interventions do not inevitably produce such results; they will do so only if they are made on an *ad hoc* basis, are not embedded in consistent policies and if they are accompanied by 'the lack of prior consultation, the inconsistency with agreed procedures and guidelines and the...unwillingness...openly to carry the responsibility for their interventions'[52] that previous governments had been accused of.

With regard to this last-named requirement the NEDO (like the SCNI) hinted at the desirability of public explanation and the making of compensatory payments by the government in the case of intervention. While agreeing with the first requirement the BSC — and, more outspokenly, Sir Monty — judged the second to be 'inappropriate' in view of the corporation's 'commercial nature'. If, for example, the government wished to deviate from the management's commercial judgment and to keep a plant open, undertaking to pay workers' wages, it 'could do that indefinitely, but you would never have an efficient industry, and then [the situation] becomes confused. You do not know whether you are running a commercial organisation or providing a social service. You have got to make up your minds'.[53] Hence, if compensatory payments are unable to undo the damage that government interference does to a nationalised industry's efficiency, then the government had better abstain wholly from any form of interference.

Those who are inclined to sympathise with this reasoning should pause for thought: firstly, the board takes the view that *any* exertion of its right of control by the government which causes delay, comes under the heading of 'interference'; secondly, it should be remembered that, if there is any sense at all in public enterprise, it must be held (and rightly) accountable for all the consequences of its activities; thirdly, the assumption underlying the board's reasoning is that all its decisions make a maximum contribution to its efficiency, so that any alteration imposed from outside can only diminish that efficiency. Yet there may have been cases when this simply was not so. When the giant plant at Redcar was planned the government wished to get an independent commission to make a cost/benefit analysis before granting its approval. Anticipating this, the BSC prepared its own analysis to lay before government, hoping thus to prevent a long delay. The govern-

51. NEDO, *A Study of UK Nationalised Industries*, op. cit., p. 35.
52. Ibid., pp. 35f.
53. Sir Monty Finniston, SCNI (Sub-Committee E), Session 1978–79, *The Relationships* . . . , op. cit., p. 62.

ment accepted this and did not further try to acquire independent information; had it done so, and probed more thoroughly into the matter, it might well not have approved the scheme — which, in the view of some members even of the BSC, would have proved beneficial in the long run. Soon afterwards it became clear that, with a declining market in steel, to build a plant with a capacity of 10m tonnes had been an unwise decision which had singularly failed to enhance BSC's overall efficiency.

The areas concerning which the BSC complains about too much interference are, of course, the main areas of conflict between the corporation and government. The subject of closures has always been predominant in the BSC's history, and is given preeminence by corporation officials. Here the governments' views have deviated most from the 'business point of view' and here, likewise, the 'informal processes come in', for 'one avoids complete confrontation' (though Sir Monty and Tony Benn have been not far from it). Next in importance, as a sensitive point, comes the question of prices. The BSC's resentment over price interventions is somewhat justified, not only because they lost it so much money (£750m in lost revenue between 1967 and 1973) but because, in contrast to withheld approval to major investments or plant closures, they are not even statutory. Since Britain joined the EEC, however, this problem is less relevant. The subject of wages is named as a 'potential' area of conflict: though 'government has tried to influence wages', it has done so 'without great arm-twisting' and the Thatcher government has, in this respect, 'withdrawn wholly from intervention'. Instead, there seem to have been further sharp exchanges over the general structure of the industry and the question of diversification: while the BSC wanted to behave 'as a normal enterprise', Conservative governments have been bent on preventing such 'back-door nationalisation'. With the present privatisation policy just the reverse of 'cold nationalisation' is happening but now, apparently, no longer opposed by the BSC. Finally, there are government attempts to force corporations to 'buy British'. This is said to have been a problem for other nationalised industries rather than for the BSC, though there always has been some conflict over the importation of coke from the continent.

These areas of conflict cover a wide range — in fact most of any enterprise's activities. Surprisingly, what have not been mentioned in this context are investment policy and overall strategy; here relations are even called 'satisfactory'. This suggests that in the eyes of the management — Sir Monty's complaints notwithstanding — succeeding governments have shown great discretion in these areas, leaving the corporation to decide these vital points more or less on its own. At the same time, even the most obstinate of chairmen must admit that for the government to have a say in the major policy decisions of a public corporation really cannot be classified as 'illegitimate' interference — even if his personal preference is for the government to restrict itself to the negotiation of cash limits.

While the present government is, ideologically, pledged to a policy of non-intervention, the fact remains that the department is more closely involved in the minutiae of corporation business than ever before. Accordingly, opinions about the government's recent behaviour range from 'at the moment we are desperately non-intervening' (DoI) to 'the non-interference policy of this government is moonshine!'[54] For the public the latter view seems to prevail: '"Non-intervention", says a BSC main board director ironically, "is a 24-hours-a-day, seven-days-a-week business for this government. It's not a question of not being involved, just a question of not giving directives. They still nudge and push non-stop"'.[55] Again, such verdicts are rooted partly in the uncertain use of the word 'interference'. Obviously, fixing the BSC's EFL at a level that seems low in relation to its huge losses is felt to be interference: 'Beating BSC down to £450m was in itself intervention', complained *The Economist*, criticising the department for 'telling the BSC what to spend its money on, and what not to use it for' (covering losses), and concluding therefore 'that non-intervention breeds its own form of interference'.[56] However, trying to keep a nationalised industry, particularly a loss-making one, to a cash limit is (apart from the EFL's proving less rigid in practice than in theory) certainly a comparatively mild type of control and can hardly be classified as interference (with its usual connotations of 'illegitimate' and 'unwarrantable').

There certainly seems to have been intervention in at least one case. The government had stood back when the BSC closed plants or slimmed down their work-force in South Wales (one of the plants affected being Port Talbot where, in the mid-1970s, the BSC had planned a major expansion); nor did it oppose the closure of the reputedly efficient Round Oak plant — rather, it seems to have urged it on. But it expressed serious concern when, in 1982, Ian MacGregor proposed the closure of Ravenscraig, one of the five major steel plants (and the only one in Scotland) on which the BSC's long-term strategy

54. Interview with two senior members of the NCB in March 1980.
55. *Sunday Telegraph*, 23 March 1980, p. 22.
56. *The Economist*, 16 February 1980, p. 69.

was based. The corporation's argument in favour of the closure is that, the steel market being what it is, it has 'one (at least!) strip mill too many' and that, with the general decline of Scottish manufacturing, the closure of Ravenscraig — modernised and efficient though it is — suggests itself. The government's counter to this is that the closure of Ravenscraig would have dramatic effects on employment in Scotland which has been a 'depressed area' for sometime now; the Report of the Committee on Scottish Affairs[57] painted such a dreary picture of the region's future that, as the BSC itself acknowledges, *any* government would have felt obliged to prevent the closure.

Not being allowed to go ahead as he wished, MacGregor tried to find another solution to his problem of minimising losses by negotiating a deal with the United States Steel Company; the idea was to close the finishing end of Ravenscraig but to 'keep the heavy end' to supply US Steel with ingots. Unfortunately the deal did not come off; since the end of 1983, therefore the question of closure is again under discussion. Meanwhile Ravenscraig 'is breaking productivity records' (DTI). Throughout, this case has been regarded as one where an *economically* correct decision has been opposed on political grounds: at the present level of steel demand the closure of Ravenscraig would save the BSC an estimated £100m a year, hence keeping it open would considerably increase the BSC's need for external finance. On the other hand, if steel output were to rise again (as the department seems to hope) the extra costs of keeping all five major plants open would be much lower. Another economic argument of the department is that, while the closure would cut operating costs, under current circumstances it would increase the cash requirements for redundancy payments and associated costs of closure. The Industry and Trade Committee, supporting the BSC, concluded that this view by the government was a short-term (and short-sighted) one, that failed to reflect the burden of operating costs placed on the corporation for as long as the present operating structure is maintained.[58] It is doubtful, however, whether an opposing of long-term (the corporation) and short-term view (the department) is wholly justified: in holding that the steel market cannot stay as bad as it is for ever, the government is certainly considering long-term aspects as well, not unreasonably arguing that, in the light of possible future developments, it might be unwise to close one of the BSC's best works; a big site like that cannot

57. Second Report from the Committee on Scottish Affairs, *The Steel Industry in Scotland*, London, December 1982.
58. Second Report from the ITC, Session 1982-83, *The British Steel Corporation's Prospects*, op. cit., pp. xif.

easily be kept in mothballs!

The Secretary of State, Patrick Jenkin, stated to the House of Commons on 20 December 1982 that 'if there were no prospect of an increased output, there could be no economic justification for retaining all five integrated steelworks', but expressed his conviction that the position was 'not as bleak as that'. He also pointed to the fact that the British steel industry had already made far greater cuts in capacity than any other EEC country, and that it was unreasonable to expect all the necessary cutbacks to be made by the British while the other European steel industries continued as they were. Both factors led him to believe 'that it would be wrong to take irrevocable decisions on future steel capacity at a time of such major uncertainty'.[59]

Hence the government's opposition to the closure of Ravenscraig does not rest on entirely political grounds. The facts do not confirm *The Economist's* supposition that the government opposed the decision simply because they feared that the Tories would lose their electoral support in the south-west of Scotland.[60] In the DTI, at least, the determination to save Ravenscraig is backed by more profound considerations. In any case the whole affair, up to now, has not been one of 'interference': the government did not meddle with the management's prerogatives *ad hoc* and without statutory legitimation, but exerted its right to withhold approval in a matter where such approval is prescribed by the statutes.

There is only one conclusion to be drawn from this discussion of intervention, and that is that, during the last few years, there has been no real problem for the BSC with 'government interference'. Those government officials directly concerned with the corporation do not, in any case see anything out of the way in 'interference': 'From our point of view all interference is reasonable!' (Treasury). What with the economic importance of a large nationalised industry, the amount of resources needed and so on, 'pressures' on the management were 'inevitable: they *must* expect a lot of interference' (Treasury); after all, such pressures obtain with every big company (DoI).

The board members interviewed also agreed that a certain amount of interference is both necessary and inevitable and did not seem inclined to make an issue of it — apart, that is, from their ex-chairman Sir Monty, who still grumbles on even while admitting that even in his time there had been very little interference in day-to-day management, only on 'the major issues'. Of course, the government is always

---

59. See Hansard, Vol. 34, 20 December 1982, pp. 672f.
60. *The Economist*, 20 November 1982, p. 50.

more closely involved than one would like it to be — especially when 'there are signs that we are not living within our cash limits' — wishing the corporation to do this or that (mainly in the fields of privatisation and the setting up of joint ventures) and prepared to withold approval in other cases (although there seem to have been none apart from Ravenscraig). While the board members generally regretted that they had 'to live in a goldfish bowl: everybody in the country has the right to look in', they did acknowledge that they still enjoyed a considerable degree of autonomy, praising the 'refreshing return' to a policy of non-interference in day-to-day management. So, for once and for the time being at least, government involvement in industry is accepted as a correct and lawful exertion of control.

The Impact of Policy Changes

Any government's involvement in industry is, understandably, the more resented the more adversative the succeeding government's policies are. Complaints of this nature from public sector chairmen, in SCNI reports and the like, seem to abound; yet if one looks more closely, it is rare that any actual policy changes are named. Even Sir Monty could think of only one case: that of the incoming government, in 1974, revising capital investment which had been approved and establishing the Beswick Committee to revise the planned closures (though he did not say that those closures had also been agreed by the previous government). In view of this single event, the conclusion that his board 'had gone through so many hoops that it is almost unbelievable' is surely somewhat of an exaggeration.[61] Both Sir Monty and Lord Robens, another chairman famous for his harsh criticisms of government, never tired of enumerating the various ministers they had had to deal with (Sir Monty counted nineteen, while Lord Robens ridiculed the Labour government for having 'maintained its average of a new minister a year'),[62] but did not find it quite so easy to point out actual disruptions of policy resulting from the change of personnel. Though the frequent change of ministers has been (and not in their eyes only) 'one of the greatest weaknesses' of the British system of ministerial control — 'No private or public business could possibly escape bankruptcy if the men at the top were

61. Sir Monty Finniston, SCNI (Sub-Committee E), Session 1978–79, *The Relationships* . . . , op. cit., pp. 60f.
62. Lord Robens, *Ten Year Stint*, op. cit., p. 174.

changed so frequently' — its effect seems to have been toned down by the 'continuity of thinking' provided through the civil servants: 'They made sure [that policies] remained the same'.[63]

In fact, the policies of successive governments towards the nationalised industries have been less contradictory than might have been expected from the 'adversary politics' the British political parties are renowned for. The two main parties have, of course, always disagreed over the principle of nationalisation. Yet however much their attitudes toward the existing nationalised industries may have differed, in actual practice these have resulted (as we have already shown) in surprisingly similar policies of treating them 'commercially' and emphasising their financial viability. It is often argued that there should have been a major difference, with Labour wishing to use the nationalised industries for social purposes and the Conservatives stressing a purely commercial outlook. While such differences may well have existed on the conceptual/ideological level, they do not seem to have had great practical relevance. In the mid-1970s not even a Conservative government could have afforded *politically* to stand aside entirely when the BSC announced its drastic closure programme; it does not do so ten years later when faced with the proposed closure of Ravenscraig. On the other hand, there is not a great deal of evidence that the Labour Party, while in office, was so very successful in implementing its social objectives via the nationalised industries — either because of the managements' quiet resistance to the pressure, or because the politicians became convinced that the *overall* economic situation would not allow it. On the whole, it appears, there has been little room for manoeuvre.

Most of the policy changes that did occur were those of overall economic policy rather than of policies specific to any one industry; they, in their turn, were typically 'forced' on governments, of whatever political colour, by changing economic conditions. Stop-go policies, or anti-inflationary policies of price restraint, however embarrasing their effects may have been for the nationalised industries (and not only for them!), were rarely caused by changes of government. Not even the incoming Thatcher government has provided an exception to this rule: with its inflexible monetarist policy it may have appeared to have turned its back on the policies of its predecessors. We must remember, however, that the system of cash limits had already been introduced by the latter, in answer to the worsening recession and the precarious financial situation of the government.

63. Ibid., pp. 148, 174.

Since its inception in 1967 the BSC has experienced three major policy changes. In 1970 the newly-returned Conservative government brought its entire existence into question when the new Secretary of State, John Davies, threatened to split it up. Though his scheme may have caused some trouble within the corporation, it aroused less of a public stir than the subsequent struggle over the 10-year development strategy. In spite of having won the latter the corporation was not long allowed to go ahead as it wished; the 1974 Labour government withheld its approval to some of the most ambitious projects (albeit for only eleven weeks, in the case of Redcar) and specifically opposed the numerous plant closures connected with the expansion programme. Yet again the BSC was forced, in the end, to make very few concessions; so the major result of this change of government was that it caused delays. A third policy change has occurred since 1979, with the incoming Conservative government, firstly, subjecting the corporation to much closer and more detailed monitoring than ever before and, secondly, renewing plans to hive off parts of the corporation and return them to the private sector.

Only the first of these policy changes can be said, unequivocally, to have been caused by a change of government. In the second case it is quite likely that the Heath government, had it stayed in office, would in the end have been forced to take a similar attitude to the closures. In the third case the closer scrutiny and (attempted) tighter financial control would clearly have been forced upon any government by the general crisis in the steel industry and the heavy losses thus incurred. This does not hold, of course, for the present privatisation policy. But the conclusion to be drawn here is that ideologies, party politics and changes of government have had an impact only on the *principle* of nationalisation or denationalisation. What may otherwise look like the effect of a policy change has been the result of altered circumstances; of the government's having, in the course of implementing a strategy, to take into consideration other interests (such as those of the workers who are threatened with unemployment or of the private steel companies who may be forced out of the market); even of the government's feeling compelled, by the way schemes were developing, to take a more thorough look at its strategy.

Apart from changes of government a change of minister appears to have led to altered policies, not always in a manner disadvantageous to the BSC. Peter Walker, who succeeded John Davies as Secretary of State of the DTI in 1972, was much more inclined to look favourably on the BSC and its strategy; Eric Varley, as successor to Tony Benn, was more inclined to compromise; and there are hints that Patrick

Jenkin has been somewhat easier to deal with than Sir Keith Joseph. Hence policy changes brought about by a change of personnel should not be the subject of too much complaint, since more than once they have had the effect of making the government bow to the corporation's wishes.

When asked directly about the impact that changes of government have had on their industry, members of the BSC voice a variety of opinions, ranging from 'no direct impact' to 'you never stop having to persuade the government'. 'That's the problem of the public sector: government keeps changing its objectives' (thus rendering long-term policies on part of the industry impossible). 'The policies of the Corporation had to be altered, not because it was necessary but because of changing political philosophies, which makes it impossible to run the Corporation commercially'. There is even the (minority) view that varying governments 'quite rightly' exerted pressure on the BSC 'to justify its plans' since they had such 'large-scale political effects' and could not be carried through 'in total autonomy'. The majority view, however, is that the main factor which leads to altered policies is not a change of government but the economic situation and 'the pressure of the market'; most policy changes were but 'necessary adaptations to the outside world'. In this context, some more critical (non-executive) members felt that, so far from pressuring the corporation to alter its strategies, the government had left it alone too long to work on its 10-year development strategy; even Sir Monty states (with some pride) that, in spite of all the government pressures he has been so critical of in public, the corporation had been well able to carry on with this strategy — 'and the chairmen now are still carrying out what was laid down in the [1973] White Paper'. It is generally thought that the Thatcher government, too, 'continues the policies of the previous government'; the main difference (apart from the privatisation issue) being that it acquiesced with the BSC's wish to buy cheap coke on the world market, instead of being forced to buy from the NCB — a change of policy that can give the BSC little cause for complaint.

On the whole, and in spite of the changes of government and the even more frequent changes of minister, there seems to be 'much more continuity than people think'. On occasion, such changes are said to have had 'a much more subtle impact', through a new government's attempt to alter, via its right of appointment, the attitude of the board itself. There have been no instances, though, of 'political' appointments. The main difference between Conservative and Labour governments, in their appointment policy, has been that the latter have favoured the idea of worker directors and civil servants on the boards; as we have already seen, the relevance of these last for the boards' decision-making may well be doubted. Another problem named is that of not having advance knowledge of the probable policies of an incoming government; the early-1970s policy of price restraint, for example, so much resented by the corporation at that time, was pursued by a Conservative government which no one would have suspected of embarking on so interventionist a policy. Equally, the Thatcher government's declared policy of restricting control to the cash-limit system — wholeheartedly welcomed by the BSC since, while 'controlling the bottom line', it apparently left them free to make all other decisions — was in practice accompanied by close monitoring and a policy of near-interference that was not entirely expected. Finally, the impact of government changes is said to vary with the personalities involved. Depending on how a chairman and his new minister get on together, 'the mood can change a lot', which can be 'extremely damaging'.

The general conviction, however, is that most of the possible negative effects can be mitigated as long as the civil servants dealing with the corporation stay and the personal relationships are unchanged. Civil servants are seen as the main element for continuity and the safeguards of the stability that a nationalised industry so badly needs. This may explain in part why *all* the members of the BSC who were interviewed stated that their relationship to government had not deteriorated under the Thatcher government, even though the latter's determination to denationalise, and its original intention to withdraw public funds from the BSC, might well have (and still may) put an end to its existence. With a side glance at other nationalised industries, they concede that life is not altogether easy 'with a shareholder who wishes you did not exist'. 'It is not very constructive, and does not improve the relationship!' Yet, while detecting in Margaret Thatcher a 'reluctant acceptance but continuing dislike' of the nationalised industries, they do not appear to have similar problems with their sponsoring minister, nor with the civil servants with whom they keep in constant touch. Certainly, at the moment, they do not fear being denied further public money; in this instance the facts of economic life soon forced a U-turn on the government; neither do they appear to resent plans to privatise parts of the corporation via joint ventures with the private sector, since this may turn out to be one way of evading the cash limits, at least in part. In other respects the board agrees openly with this government's policies, especially with the notion of 'more freedom and more exposure to the market', which is 'much in line with what MacGregor wanted'. 'We want to be left to sink or swim according to our own efforts.'

Interestingly enough, most of the civil servants interviewed thought that a change of government did have some impact on policies, and that this was particularly true of the 1979 change. What appeared to the board members as continuity, certain civil servants saw as 'the greatest policy change concerning the nationalised industries that had occurred since 1945' (Treasury). At the same time, the majority visualised themselves as mediators, who prevent industrial policy becoming 'a political football'; 'I would like to think that we do have a bit of that influence' (Treasury). 'Politicians slogan-ise things'; civil servants then 'bring in the facts', lest the actual policies take on a 'switch on/switch-off' character (DoI). Though not all of them seem to relish the idea of being viewed by the public as buffers between government and their particular nationalised industry (they are, after all, officially obliged 'to implement what an incoming government wants'), their aim is still that of successfully advising each new minister 'that it is usually very difficult to change the world within three months' (DoI).

The civil servants' view that there was 'hardly an area' where changes of government made such an impact 'as [in] the nationalised industries' looks, in this context, rather like an assertion of their own importance — for, this being so, '*we* naturally look for a certain degree of continuity' (Treasury). On the other hand they are, in common with the members of the corporation, convinced that the managements are pretty well able to resist any major changes they object to: 'they carry through policies almost in spite of changes of government'. However great the pressures on them to alter their strategies, 'it will take a decade to make a real difference' (DoI).

Sponsor Department and Treasury: a Source of Conflict

One of the reasons for the unexpectedly small impact of government and/or policy changes on the nationalised industries may be that such changes are partly neutralised by the rivalry that exists between sponsoring departments and the Treasury. Whereas the Treasury, with the present government at least, is bent on implementing the Prime Minister's policies (in former governments it played a somewhat different role; for example, the Treasury's reluctance, in the mid-1960s, to fall in with Harold Wilson's plan to re-nationalise steel), the sponsoring department is, typically, more inclined to align itself with its industry — which, surprisingly, holds true even for the DoI under Sir Keith Joseph, who previously had acted as Margaret Thatcher's 'moral tutor', defining her strictly monetarist strategies for her.

The tasks the Treasury has to perform in the system of ministerial control are of major importance, albeit its role is a slightly detached one; it formulates the overall policy for the nationalised industries and sets the financial targets for each one. As for the former, the fact that the Treasury appears to have been the only government department concerned with taking a wider view of all the nationalised industries goes far to explain why whatever broader concepts there are, are of a financial nature. As for individual corporations, the monetary targets are fixed after due negotiation and a 'real bargaining' (Treasury); initially, and most importantly, with the sponsoring department and only then with the industry itself. Chairmen are known to have complained about the lack of direct contact with the Treasury, and have insinuated that decisions between department and Treasury were taken over their heads; Treasury officials, on the other hand, talk about 'reasonably frequent contacts'. Of course, men from both sides do meet, if only because a Treasury nominee attends board meetings, but generally this happens on a casual basis ('in an informal sense, we certainly do meet individuals'; 'we like to know the people from the industries'; are sometimes even 'on Christian name terms with them . . .'). There are also contacts at staff level. Most of these are, however, mediated through the department, the typical procedure being that the department arranges monthly meetings with the corporation's finance experts and a member of the Treasury is 'usually present at such meetings' (Treasury). Apart from such monthly reviews, the majority of contacts are 'mainly bilateral' (DoI) — and either between corporation and department, or department and Treasury: the corporation–Treasury contact is the exception rather than the rule ('in a purely formal sense there are hardly any contacts with the boards'). The Treasury appears anxious not to irritate the minister in question.

Such discretion may appear a trifle over-maidenly in the light of the major influence ascribed to the Treasury. Though officially involved only with the immediate financial concerns of a nationalised industry it can exert influence over the latter's long-term strategies simply by supplying economic forecasts; and though all non-financial objectives are a matter for the sponsoring department, 'we tend to be involved in nearly all the major policy questions'. While the Treasury may have the laudable intention of not meddling in matters that are the responsibility of the sponsoring minister, to claim that it is just 'staying in the background' (Treasury) while exerting influence in this way does not aid a clarifying of responsibilities — particularly if Treasury and department act on the basis of conflicting views and interests.

A third task the Treasury performs for the nationalised industries is that of coordination. There is, for example, the Nationalised Industries Policy Committee, which meets in the Treasury. With each sponsoring department represented on it, the committee discusses questions common to all the industries (and thereby contributed greatly to the 1978 White Paper), but not questions concerning either their individual policies or matters of agreement or conflict between them. Hence its 'coordinating' role has been rather limited; at the moment it seems reduced to the level of purely technical financial matters.

For some time, under the Thatcher government, the Central Policy Review Staff (in its last year headed by David Green from ICI) had been concerned with the same general policy questions, as well as with the reviewing of corporate plans and with monitoring the corporations' performances. If this was meant to further a coordination of their policies it did not meet with any noticeable success. Its main achievement seems to have been its 1981 Report (see p. 86 above) on how to improve the system of ministerial control; though not even published, most of its recommendations were immediately rejected by the public as well as by all those concerned. In the summer of 1983 the CPRS was abolished; 'all their good work about the nationalised industries is now forgotten' (DoI), and the policy questions are back with the Treasury — including that of a coordination which never seems to happen.

Though Treasury officials themselves admit to their 'overall coordinating role' — it is even 'the chief function of the Treasury' (!) — they don't give many details as to how, in what areas, and so on, it is actually performed. The main instance given is that of privatisation, where they 'make suggestions', whereas individual measures are, as before, the departments' responsibility. Yet the present (1984) privatisation policy does not look coordinated, either; nor does it seem to be well adapted to the investors' market, and appears to be in some danger of degenerating into one of 'cheap sales', with the City 'quietly making a fool of the government'.[64] So all that the Treasury's coordinating activity amounts to is the fixing, in advance, of the total amount of the public corporations' budget, and then leaving it to them and their sponsoring departments to bargain over their shares. Hence the BSC's opinion that there were 'no attempts to coordinate at

64. *The Economist*, 30 June 1984, p. 19.

all', and the DoI's fatalistic admission that there were, certainly, 'not as many as there should be'.[65]

Treasury influence on the dealings of an individual nationalised industry would be the subject of less discussion, not to mention criticism, if, firstly, the Treasury undertook more in the nature of coordination and, secondly, if it could achieve a more harmonious relationship with each sponsoring department. As it is, Treasury and department see themselves as separated by a barrier and, indeed, admit to 'plenty of conflicts, inherent in the nature of our work' (Treasury). They are regarded as being based on 'natural' conflict between a nationalised industry and the Treasury; the former's 'natural good entrepreneur's animal instinct, . . . making claims on resources . . . which will conflict with other claims', while the latter, euphemistically, is 'trying to reconcile various demands with each other and with the macroeconomic development' (Treasury), or 'will minimise resource use' (DoI). The sponsoring department's position in this basic conflict is 'somewhere in between', attempting 'not to be on anybody's side, but to make sure that what the BSC puts forward is reasonable' (DoI). In the eyes of the Treasury this is mostly siding with the industry. In some cases this has led, indeed still leads (as with British Gas), to fierce battles between the two branches of government, of which the outcome is uncertain ('the Department of Energy defends British Gas against the Treasury and sometimes they win, sometimes not. . .'),[66] and which leave the industry concerned in an uneasy position. In other cases there is said to be, for 'most of the time,. . . a remarkable convergence of views' (DoI), which is probably dependent on the particular situation of that industry: in the BSC's present crisis, once DoI and Treasury have agreed that the corporation is not to go into liquidation immediately, they may feel that there is little choice in the short-term measures necessary to keep it alive and, if possible, make it viable. Conflicts inevitably sharpen as soon as there is investment to be financed; then the short-term view of the Treasury, aiming at a low annual PSBR, will clash with the longer-term view of the industry and its 'friend at court' (DoI), the department. This might then lead, in the words of Alf Robens, to the 'ridiculous . . . spectacle of Ministers complaining and worrying about the lack of investment in the economy as a whole, while at the same time the Treasury is engaged in holding back investment . . .'.[67]

65. The only thing that really *is* coordinated at the moment seems to be the pay of board members.
66. Interview with a British Gas staff member, March 1980.
67. Lord Robens, *Ten Year Stint*, op. cit., p. 148.

The conflict over the use of scarce resources seems to be as natural as the one between short-term budgetary considerations and long-term considerations of industrial policy, and as inevitable. It should be noted though, firstly, that the Treasury, in taking its task of maintaining a balanced macroeconomic development seriously, needs to have a long-term orientation as well — and a less particularistic one than a single industry; and, secondly, that the sponsoring departments do not usually follow long-term industrial policy concepts of their own but defend what has been presented to them by 'their' nationalised industry. Thus the difference between short- and long-term perceptions might not be so great, after all, since both partners lack a truly long-term outlook. It is just that one is better at concealing the fact than the other.

In the DoI (where there is regret that, with the abolition of the CPRS, questions of policy have been returned to the Treasury) a third source of conflict has been named; that of the Treasury's marked tendency 'to treat all the nationalised industries alike'. Surely, though, this is a natural result of the importance the Treasury is in duty bound to place on financial targets and financial control? The DoI, however, contrasts this role to the Think Tank's view that the government should act as a holding *vis-à-vis* the state industries, treating each on its apparent merits. This reasoning closely resembles that of the corporations themselves, whenever a reform of the system of ministerial control has been under discussion: that the new control devices might indeed have their merits, but are not suited to the specific needs of *their* industry. While it may be understandable that the corporations use such a ploy to fend off attempts at tighter control, it is less easy to understand why a government department should use it. For all rivalries with the Treasury notwithstanding, it ought to be a task of government to surmount the particularistic policies of the individual industries, bringing them in line both with its overall policies and with social needs: a task which implies a considerable degree of 'treating them alike'. Once start paying attention to 'specific needs' and you will soon be lost in a jungle of particularistic interests; granting a 'specific' privilege here will immediately lead to the granting of privileges elsewhere. The fact that the sponsoring departments are apparently following this latter line is an indication, not only of the lack of overall policies, but also of a tendency to let individual industries' particularistic interests invade government territory. Not even the presence of the Treasury is a safeguard here, for it has frequently responded to a demand for specific treatment, agreeing to widely differing forms of investment approval, for example, or relaxing the strict bounds of the cash limits.

In actual practice, the Treasury is by no means the unrelenting monster in the background, bent on thwarting the plans of industry and department alike, as has sometimes been claimed by frustrated chairmen. There may be battles before financial targets, capital expenditure programmes and cash limits are agreed, with the Treasury trying to bring its more cautious attitude to bear on ministers' inclination to identify with their corporations' wishes to go ahead with ambitious projects — there have been, after all, several incidents of over-investment, and not only in the BSC! But there seem to have been few cases where the Treasury has actually curtailed previously approved investment, and even fewer of open conflict. In recent years, such cases of conflict have been either about the negative EFL (especially of British Gas), by means of which the Treasury attempts to limit the self-financing rate and hence to maintain a modicum of control over the profitable industries; or about its suggestions to sell parts of them, as a means of implementing the cabinet's privatisation policy. Neither here, nor with the policy of cash limits, however, has the Treasury been able to follow the strict line towards the nationalised industries that the government announced when it came into office. In fact, at intervals since 1979, several newspapers have accused the government of U-turns in this respect, *The Economist* going so far as to detect a tendency by the nationalised industries, via their sponsoring ministers, to undermine both the position of the Treasury and Mrs Thatcher's control over her cabinet.[68] Apparently the sponsoring departments have known very well how to guard their own interests and have frequently succeeded in prevailing over the Treasury's wishes.

To return to the BSC; it does not seem to have experienced any problems, either with the Treasury or the DoI, during recent years. In these times of stress, the Treasury has raised its cash limit repeatedly, working very closely with the DoI/DTI to save the corporation. Not even Sir Monty has been able to complain about interference from the Treasury; probably he was, in his time, too much infuriated with his sponsoring minister (who, uncharacteristically, refused to identify with his plans) to recognise additional adverse influences from other quarters. At any rate the view sometimes heard, that the nationalised industries are the 'innocent victims' of unsolved tensions within the government system,[69] does not now hold true for the BSC.

68. *The Economist*, 20 June 1981, p. 14.
69. Interview at Ashorne Hill, the Iron and Steel Management Training College,

The Treasury, however, is not the only potential troublemaker within the system. Other conflicts are rooted in the divergent interests of the various nationalised industries. This is one of the subjects on which government officials tend to be reticent. When asked about their usual procedure in the case of conflict between the BSC and another nationalised industry (hence, probably, with another department), the first answer from the majority of those interviewed in the DoI, was, quite simply, that they did nothing; it was up to the nationalised industries to solve their problems on their own, via the market and without departmental help. Only one admitted from the start that the department was the corporation's 'friend at court when they have got problems' and, as such, would mediate between the BSC and another government department; although this certainly did not imply that the department would defend the corporation in every case.

Closer questioning of the informants provided some corroboration of this statement. Thus it appears that the more serious conflicts — in the case of the BSC these are mainly with the NCB — are transferred from the corporations to the respective departments. Unfortunately there is no government machinery for the solution of such problems: this merely underlines the deplorable lack of 'horizontal coordination' of the policies of the various nationalised industries, which in the end may become rather costly. For in such cases one or other of the 'contestants' is bound to lose financially, leaving the government to pick up the bill. The only feasible method is to go through informal channels — to try, as a last resort, to 'exert pressure on the respective chairmen'. One may well speculate as to the probable outcome; doubtless the winner will be the chairman who stands best with his sponsoring minister.

Causes of conflict between the BSC and the NCB have been the price set for coal and the problem of coke imports; here the steel industry's interests have prevailed. However, the DoI lost its battle with the DoE over Ian McGregor, who left the BSC without 'finishing his job with steel'. Instead, McGregor went to the NCB where he embarked on a (now notorious) programme of pit closures similar to the drastic slimming down at the BSC. Other, milder, clashes have arisen from time to time when the DoI have attempted to induce other sectors to 'buy British' steel.

Interestingly enough, Treasury officials do not ascribe much importance to such conflicts ('there are not many direct conflicts, and

---

March 1979.

they are not very important'), since they have been 'commercial matters that the government does not want to get involved in' — thus upholding the professed principles of the Thatcher government's policy. To them the main and most disturbing conflicts are still those 'between the coordinating centre [the Treasury] and the single departments', a conviction that may be born out of their irritation at being constantly besieged by sponsoring departments on behalf of individual industries.

Members of the corporation tend to favour the Treasury's view. Though they can enumerate a list of conflicts with their fellow corporations (and detect between them, furthermore, 'an unhealthy relationship, sharing our misery with each other'), these were not normally transferred onto the government: 'We try to resolve them between ourselves', on an 'entirely commercial' basis — or by talking to the other chairman, and 'making a lot of noise'. As in the Treasury, the principle is to 'keep the government out': its involvement would lead to 'too much government interference in the day-to-day management'. Since there is always 'lots of conflict between various departments' ('they never agree with each other!'), it is better not to add to them. 'The big exception is coal, which is a politically explosive subject'; in the mid-1970s it had been the cause of sharp tensions between Eric Varley (DoI) and Tony Benn (then in the DoE) which still linger — though '*we* did not put it to the Government, the Coal Board did'. This is a sure indication that the more serious such conflicts are, the more likely it is that an entirely commercial solution will be abandoned in favour of support from the sponsoring department and, hence, of government intervention. Unfortunately, since the government appears incapable of coordination, this shifting of responsibility does not automatically ensure a rational solution, but is more likely to exacerbate existing governmental rivalries.

Conflict or Harmony: the General Relationship

By now it will have become obvious that it is almost impossible to determine an individual industry's *general* relationship to the government, since it must react differently to its sponsoring department, to the Treasury and to those whose interests are in direct conflict with its own. In the first instance, which is of most importance in the present context, the relationship is reputedly much improved since the late 1970s. During the first part of that decade there seems to have been a great deal of resentment — possibly on both sides, though openly expressed by the managing boards — as to interference, 'arm-twisting', overbearing demands and the like; in the case of the BSC, for example, the SCNI in 1978 still detected 'a grave lack of communication and confidence'.[70] Within a year or so, however, most chairmen reported to the Committee that 'our relations with our parent departments . . . have been excellent';[71] and the 1979 change of government does not appear to have altered those 'extremely good' relationships — with a few exceptions, of course. Sir Denis Rooke of British Gas would certainly raise a dissenting voice . . . .

It is not easy to determine why this improvement should have taken place, for between 1976 (the year of the NEDO Report) and early 1979 there were no major alterations in the institutional make-up, nor had the proposals for reform contained in the Report and the 1978 White Paper been put into practice. The only actual alteration had been a reformulation of the financial framework — including the introduction of the cash limits with which the majority of corporations were not altogether happy. Could it have been the abundance of proposals (starting with the 1968 SCNI Report), rather than the implementation of any of them, which induced the change of mood? Each of them had given rise to the fear of a turn for the worse; rather than risk that, most of the corporations seem to have decided that their relations with the government were, on the whole, tolerable.

Under the present system, the industry/government link is primarily 'a clear person-to-person relationship' between the chairman and his sponsoring minister,[72] which most chairmen felt should be maintained — probably on the grounds that such an intimate relationship gives them a very good chance of making the minister listen to reason; the fewer intermediaries and the less publicity involved, the easier to reach agreement. It is said of Lord Melchett, for example, that 'once his dominant position was established [he] could do anything with the government'. A state of affairs, however, where everything depends on the character of individuals and on personal relationships between senior people always bears the risk that personal animosities can render any rational intercourse between a corporation and its sponsoring department impossible. This was obviously the case when Sir

---

70. Fifth Report from the SCNI, Session 1977–78, *Financial Forecasts of the BSC*, op. cit., p. xi.
71. Sir Derek Ezra (NCB). Sir Peter Parker (BR) regarded the 'NEDO report as being the Old Testament of the relationship — . . . and the New Testament is, frankly, positive and constructive'. SCNI (Sub-Committee E), Session 1978–79, *The Relationships . . .*, op. cit., p. 89.
72. Sir Henry Marking (BA), ibid., p. 40.

Monty and Tony Benn were thrown together, forced into a close person-to-person relationship they both must have deeply resented. Their 'impossible personal relationship' (spiced, it is said, by Sir Monty's having only 'contempt for Benn') led to an estrangement that affected all levels of the organisation; a former senior staff member of the BSC intimated that the head office went so far as to forbid all informal contacts with the DoI — 'you were forbidden even to talk to civil servants'. With the removal of Tony Benn the relationship improved — even to the extent of Sir Monty admitting that it was 'reasonably satisfactory'. On the same occasion the DoI told the SCNI 'that there now existed a close and happy working relationship between the Department and the Corporation'.[73]

At the time of writing it appears that the BSC considers its relationship to the DoI to be 'pretty good'. The DoI appears to feel the same way, the 1979 change of government and the more recent changes at the top of the DTI notwithstanding; 'everybody is trying to achieve the same object of survival . . . we work together to solve the problem'. The current absence of irritations and personal problems is fortunate, in view of the fact that, over the last four years, contacts between the two have been almost on a day-to-day basis. Perhaps it is this closeness which has improved relations and led to a more relaxed atmosphere, an 'old-boy' style of relationship[74] (to which, however, neither side will admit). In the DoI's words it is 'a relaxed professional relationship', while BSC members have described it as 'a complex combination of formal lines of communication (sometimes *too* detailed), of occasionally differing requirements, and of informal relations which are sometimes quite productive'. Treasury officials are more critical, maintaining that, however good relations are on a personal level, the general situation is 'not an easy one . . . rather a bumpy ride'.

Future developments will be, for the majority of those involved, 'determined by people, not policies', no matter what changes occur in the latter. Both DoI and Treasury agree that the impact of changes 'depends on the personalities of ministers'. For the staff at the BSC, 'personal confidence' between themselves and their Civil Service colleagues is the deciding factor in any corporation/government relationship.

It is perhaps surprising that it is the personal factor that is perceived

---

73. First Report from the SCNI, Session 1977–78, *The British Steel Corporation*, op. cit., Vol. I, p. xxvii, Vol. II, p. 69.
74. As a DoE official characterised his department's relations with the NCB in 1980.

as the main determinant in the relations between a nationalised industry and its sponsoring department — rather than government policy, economic performance or actual conflicts. 'Two years ago I would have said economic success was a big influence', confessed a member of the board in 1981, but the experience of the British Gas Corporation at that time gave rise to serious doubts about the relevance of that particular factor: belief that it is economic success, and economic success only, that enables a nationalised industry to achieve the happy state of freedom from interference and, hence, freedom from conflict, is no longer possible. In fact, the profitability of an industry lessens the government's (especially the Treasury's) possibilities of control, and thus has proved to be, in itself, a new source of conflict.

This indicates that, no matter how satisfactory relationships on the personal level appear to be, the *general* relationship between the government and the nationalised industries is still dominated by a series of conflicts; thus, there is resentment, either in Whitehall (when a nationalised industry successfully evades controls) or in the corporations (over government interference). Perhaps it is only when a situation is as desperate as the one that the BSC is presently in, with both sides obliged to work together closely and energetically in order to salvage as much as possible, that the conflicts retreat into the background.

The main sources of conflict, according to the corporation, are in the areas where the BSC has experienced the greatest number of, or the most irritating, government interventions. Yet apart from the issue of closures few of such areas are relevant in the mid–1980s. There has been no interference with prices or wages for some years, and the conflict over the importing of coke has been resolved, for the time being at least. A more recent source of potential conflict, in the opinion of the DoI, is privatisation — in the shape of, specifically, the Phoenix schemes. The position here is not entirely clear, however. The government is obviously interested in the BSC's entering into joint ventures with private steel companies which are, in effect, returning parts of the industry to the private sector; it encourages the corporation, because this is 'politically desirable'. But the new companies need public money as starting capital, which means that the DoI wishes to retain some control over them. Since this is difficult over a private company registered under the Companies' Act, the situation is a tricky one. At the same time the BSC management team, while resenting this hiving-off, must see the possibilities of further cut-backs in capacity and the erasion of their cash limits. Since both of these advantages depend on successful negotiations with their partners in the private sector, the desirability or otherwise of the whole scheme rests on how well they are able to deal with them. This is exactly the area where conflicts with the government will arise: how much support will the BSC receive from the government or will there be pressure on the corporation's management to accept the unacceptable? Hence this new source of conflict links conflicts internal to the government and to the BSC with those between one or both of them and the private sector. This creates a complex situation which has already been the cause of much resentment, as will be shown below.

The nature of these specific conflicts will vary a great deal with time and varying circumstances. They are all rooted, however, in money, time, and the 'schizophrenic attitude'[75] of public sector managers, who expect the government to finance their schemes but then resent the latter's wish to have a say in the running of them. For government officials, all the really serious conflicts are financial — mainly, as they see it, by the corporation's lack of 'financial discipline'. Corporation members also recognise another major source of difficulties in the delays connected with ministerial control — 'they resent the time that is taken' (Treasury), usually 'grumble about it' (DoI) — and in the different time scales of politicians and industrialists.

This question of time-scales indicates a structural conflict, politicians being accused of always taking the short-term view and of never looking beyond the next election (as one board member remarked sarcastically, politicians' usual time horizon ranged 'between forty-eight hours and one week'), whereas an industrialist needed to look ahead for a minimum of several years: 'The time horizons are completely incompatible [which] has made the running of a public enterprise a very difficult business', and might even be the 'most crucial' problem in the entire framework (BSC). Yet the contradiction between short-term and long-term orientation cannot be taken entirely at face value. For however much interventions based on short-term political considerations may derange an industry's longer-term strategies, it could also be shown that changes in policy (one of the main reasons for short-term intervention) have had less of an impact on the corporation's policies than might have been expected (see Part II), and that the BSC had successfully resisted pressures to alter its strategies, even being supported in this by the DoI, against the allegedly short-term budgetary considerations put forward by the Treasury. Obviously the influence of politicians has been limited; hence their short-term outlook must have been of limited relevance, as well. It is

75. Interview at Ashorne Hill College, March 1979.

doubtful, in any case, whether the political aim of maintaining employment in depressed areas by delaying plant closures should be classified, somewhat derogatorily, as short-term. On the other hand, it lacks credibility to claim a long-term outlook while complaining about an eleven weeks' delay caused by a sponsoring minister looking closely at a major investment project before granting his approval. This robs the supposed antagonism between long- and short-term interests of much of its structural character.

The DoI, however, appears able to regard all such complaints as indicative of the generally (and personally!) unsatisfactory relationship between the BSC and its sponsoring department in the mid-1970s. While the Treasury, being obliged to keep the annual budget and PBSR in view, accepts that differing time horizons are 'a real problem', the DoI's view is that 'it's not a fair complaint — that's life!'. The department also likes to make the point that it was the BSC's inflexibly long-term outlook that caused most of the problems that the corporation and the DoI are now trying to overcome together — while being restricted to radical short-term survival policies. Our evidence, at any rate, shows that the disruption of long-term investment by short-term expenditure control has never been a serious problem for the steel industry.

In the end, according to the BSC, it is all a question of the 'conflict between what is commercially desirable and what is politically desirable', the contents of both varying with changing circumstances. While there is something to be said for this view, on a theoretical level, as far as actual practice is concerned it is only part of the truth; throughout most of the BSC's existence, the DoI staff have been more than happy to identify with the industry's commercial outlook. At the moment, especially, though there are the political objectives of privatisation and of restricting public expenditure, the overriding aim of both the DTI and the Treasury is to bring the BSC back on the road to viability, and this is more than merely 'politically desirable'. The final conflict is also, and essentially, between a public corporation which is trying to avoid the consequences of its status (public accountability) and a sponsoring department attempting to carry out its particular function of control.

In the past the BSC has been reasonably successful in creating the impression that, in fending off government influence, it has done no more than fight back extra-legal practices. While there have certainly been 'occasions where the board have resented the use, not of the powers, but of the non-powers the ministers had' (especially concerning the BSC's pricing policy), they have probably been much less frequent than the public has been led to believe. As has been shown above, much of the 'unlawful interference' has been only the exercise of statutory rights of control. Admittedly, the corporation considers even these 'inevitable' rights of government as more or less 'undesirable'.

It is consistent with this attitude to refer to unprofitable industries as 'living in the government's pocket' and of their chairmen as 'tending to oblige the minister'.[76] On the other hand, there is also a wish to avoid open conflict and hence, to some extent, 'do the government's thinking for it', anticipate its wishes, in order to forestall intervention as well as the more formal use of ministerial powers. While to some this would appear to be a cynical view, the majority of board members feel that they are being merely pragmatic ('not weakness but prudence') and do what any responsible private sector management would do as well. 'But (of course!) we still stick to our plans': it is only a tactic, part of the general striving to keep the relationship as easy and as informal as possible. Though, in order to clarify areas of responsibility it is sometimes preferable for the government 'to use its powers formally' (DoI), both sides wish to avoid the latter course — 'Boards prefer to comply rather than to be ordered' (DoI), and the department prefers it that way too. So we are back at the informal, personal relationship once more, claimed to be of major importance and covering but not sufficiently hiding the underlying conflicts. When conflicts are avoided, however, and are not brought out into the open, how can they be solved?

With such importance attributed to the personal factor, the general relationship between the BSC and the DoI, though pregnant with conflict, looks outwardly harmonious — and is certainly honestly felt to be so by both sides, for the moment at least. Small wonder, then, that the DoI has frequently been seen, by both parties, as 'promoting [the BSC's] interests within government'. Even those Treasury officials who deal with the nationalised industries see themselves in this role: while 'the Treasury's role comes nearest to that of a banker', and additionally ought to be that of 'a guarantor of public interest', it is, at the same time, that of a 'friend at court' — 'more often than the nationalised industries themselves recognise!' The role of banker, though, is specified as that of banker 'in the German or continental sense', British bankers being seen as having less influence on company policy. Two other subjects of public debate have been whether the government's proper role towards the nationalised industries is

76. Interview at Ashorne Hill College, March 1979.

(1) that of 'overlord' or (2) consists in acting as the corporations' holding (CPRS); neither is favoured in the Treasury nor in the DoI: for the former, their powers are too limited and for the latter, it is felt that they 'don't know enough about the business' (DoI).

The BSC sees the actual role of its sponsoring department in a very similar light. In a formal sense the DoI is its banker and shareholder, albeit 'of a very special kind: monitoring, not interfering in the business'. It certainly is there to safeguard the public interest (while its concepts as to what this might mean, in varying circumstances, differ somewhat from those of the government) and, therefore, is 'partly a supervisor'; 'sometimes it tends to be a controller . . .'. Its position is frequently likened to that of the owner in a family company. But mainly it is felt to be, again, the BSC's friend at court and the BSC would even 'expect it to be: to fight for our money [against the rest of the government]'; only *afterwards* should the department act as a shareholder-cum-controller. When all is said and done it is, of course, 'a little bit of everything: friend at court, fussy aunt, tutor, treasurer, sergeant-major . . .' — and it is this that makes the relationship 'so complex'. It would be much simpler if the DoI were to restrict itself to the first of these roles, that of friend!

Job Rotation and the Amount of Expertise

The friendly atmosphere that (at the time of writing, at any rate) characterises the relationship between corporation and department depends, to a large extent, on good personal relations between the corporation's management and civil servants; the latter's ability to fulfil the role of controller rests largely on the amount of expertise they can bring to the battles that must inevitably occur, even in the friendliest of atmospheres. However, both the personal confidence so necessary to a good working relationship and the gaining of the essential expertise are somewhat impaired by the British civil service's practice of job rotation.

During the period of the present investigation (1980–4) several changes occurred in the BSC's sponsoring department. In 1983 the Department of Industry was merged with the Department of Trade, and is once more (as in the early 1970s) the Department of Trade and Industry. The Iron and Steel Division was then transformed into the Minerals and Metals Division, with a considerably widened area of responsibility.[77] While it was the ISD its staff had totalled forty-two (including clerical staff); yet of these only three (not counting clerical staff) had been concerned directly with the BSC. Other branches, each headed by an Assistant Secretary, had dealt with the private sector, with EEC matters and with technical matters. The division had been headed by an Under Secretary, who was changed four times (once, though, because of illness); the Assistant Secretary with specific responsibility for the BSC was also changed four times. There have been comparable changes in the less senior staff, who are moved to other departments every year or so, as part of their training. Nor is there more continuity in the position of Assistant Secretary for the private sector, one of those interviewed having stayed for less than a year. One reason for this might be that Assistant Secretaries in this particular branch feel that they fulfil a purely political role, being there 'to allay the suspicions of the private sector . . . . otherwise the private steelmen would think that the DoI does what BSC wants . . . . much of our time we spend dealing with private sector complaints . . .'.

Within the Treasury there has been a greater degree of continuity, which may be explained by the fact that civil servants, having rotated through the other government departments, come to rest there. Both the Under Secretary heading the Public Enterprise Group and the Assistant Secretary concerned with (*inter alia*) the BSC have changed only once in the five-year period. In 1984 the PEG had a total staff of thirty-four, of whom three were Assistant Secretaries, each responsible for some half-dozen nationalised industries or public enterprises, five were principals and two were full-time economists outside the hierarchy. Continuity of office is said to be greatest with the last-named, while it is safe to assume that the frequency of change among the principals does not differ much from that in other departments.

While the amount of change in the DoI/DTI has been probably greater than the average, it is considered normal for civil servants to stay for between three and five years in one position. Chairmen of nationalised industries, on the other hand, usually serve at least two 5-year terms, while executives are often appointed more or less for life. This being so, it is difficult to see how the civil service can provide the continuity of contact that the corporations so ardently desire. None the less, the civil service *does* provide a degree of continuity through a general disposition of good will towards the corporations, and hence it can bring to bear 'a moderating influence' on ministers and politicians.

---

77. This, incidentally, is one of the reasons given for the removal of the head of this division from the BSC board: he would now represent 'conflicting interests'.

Government officials, understandably, are little inclined to see a problem in the present system of job rotation. They justify it with the claim that it lessens the danger of civil servants becoming over-identified with the interests of their clientele and thus losing sight of the *commune bonum*. While this seems plausible at first sight, there is the attendant danger — unmentioned and perhaps unrecognised — that they acquire too little expertise, in the time available, to be able to assess the validity or otherwise of the corporations' case or to recognise when they are being manipulated. What they *do* acquire is administrative expertise and skill in working the machinery of Whitehall. This may merely have the effect of aiding the spread of a clientelistic network through the government departments rather than making them resistant to it. There is no fool-proof way of maintaining the *commune bonum* against particularistic interests; the system of job rotation may even be counter-productive in this instance.

Another argument advanced in favour of the system is that it helps to keep the civil service mind flexible — specifically, that it 'keeps them [civil servants] happy' (DoI). The corporations, on the other hand, find the frequent changes rather 'irritating' (NCB) — although this irritation may be nothing more than a ritualistic grumble and, as such, should not be taken too seriously; at any rate, this is the opinion of the DoI. Of course, where so much emphasis is placed on the *personal* element in the relationship between a nationalised industry and its sponsoring department, frequent personnel changes are bound to cause *some* problems — 'you become friends with civil servants and then you lose them' (BSC). Hence the system is judged to be not only 'slightly archaic', but actually 'detrimental' to the whole relationship ('*YES* in big letters!'). Yet while the majority of BSC officials complain about the necessity of having to deal with new colleagues in the department every three years (or even more often), and being forced to start anew with the tricky business of building up that indispensable personal confidence, at least one voice hinted that it might not be all that advantageous if civil servants stayed on in their positions for a longer period: they might then 'begin to think they knew more about the business than we do'.

Quite obviously, in normal circumstances, job rotation and the question of expertise will be closely linked, in a negative sense; to build up the expertise necessary to deal with a nationalised industry is, admittedly, 'a question of time and proximity' (Treasury). The British public, especially the SCNI, have been very critical in this respect, reproaching the DoI on various occasions for the lack of competence shown in appraising the BSC's plans, and for a 'lack of second-guessing ability' which had led, more than once, to the department's being misled by the corporation.[78] The ITC, in recent years, have renewed this criticism; any outsider, in fact, would express similar doubts on hearing that most of the civil servants involved were arts graduates, rather than, say, economists. Two of the principals in the ISD frankly admitted that they 'still knew nothing about steel', and one of the Under Secretaries spoken to somewhat resignedly disclosed that there were no 'over-competent' people amongst his staff, the problem being to find people 'with the right skills for their job ('I cannot choose them, but I can reject . . .').

Other senior civil servants, when asked whether they thought themselves sufficiently expert to judge the Corporation's return forecasts for investment projects replied, with equal frankness, 'I don't think I am', at the same time indicating that it might be possible to acquire that expertise elsewhere: 'I would not rely on what the board says: I would get other advice'. There are hints that, for instance, one could always tap the expertise to be found in the PE Group at the Treasury ('we refer to the Treasury: they have the economic expertise'). The latter, though, counter with: 'We operate through the sponsoring departments', obtaining the necessary knowledge from their 'full-time specialists'.

While themselves critical of the fact that in Sir Monty's time the DoI had *not* been 'sufficiently equipped technically to judge his plans', the civil servants tended none the less to justify their limited experience, by a twofold reasoning. Firstly, they pointed to the fact that, in the DoI as well as in the wider world of Whitehall, they had their internal as well as external advisers ('I should . . . add that in the Department we have available — and, indeed, as part of my division — technical advisers who have been involved in advising on steel, and nothing else, for some years and who, as a matter of fact, were originally in the steel industry.').[79] In the Phoenix deal the department even approached a merchant bank to look at the proposals; they did not, however, find their advice very useful (DoI). 'We have economists and accountants to advise us' (Treasury), to say nothing of the knowledge acquired through close personal contacts within the industry itself ('the best way is to meet people in the nationalised industries' — Treasury). To sum up: 'I would say there is sufficient expertise to discuss major projects' (DoI), especially since their main

78. Fifth Report from the SCNI, Session 1977–78, *Financial Forecasts* . . ., op. cit., p. xiv.
79. Ken Binning, Fourth Report from the ITC, Session 1980–81, *Effects* . . ., op. cit., vol. II, p. 83.

concern was with matters of finance rather than technical problems.

The second point made by the DoI is that, while they were certainly 'not sufficiently expert to *run* the corporation' (DoI), they were not required to do this, in any case. Referring to the statutory provisions, they 'draw a very sharp distinction . . . between the process of monitoring and the process of managing'; their task 'is designed precisely not to interfere with their [the BSC's] day-to-day or week-to-week management decisions on what has to be done in order to produce steel in an efficient fashion, but to identify those areas in which . . . things are not going well . . . . In this case we are not, as it were, second-guessing the management on management decisions, we are hopefully trying to understand the nature of the problem which is causing the variation from what has been agreed'.[80] This is, indeed, rather a modest claim, as well as a restricted view of a sponsoring department's proper tasks; more specifically, it does *not* consider the amount of expertise needed for the process of agreeing the plans and targets the deviation from which is then to be understood! It appears that the DoI is content 'to take for granted' most of what the BSC sees fit to put before them (Treasury), and then to render assistance where the latter's own plans are going awry.

In regarding 'too much' expertise not only unnecessary but even, on occasion, detrimental (in the interests of the arm's-length concept incorporated in the Corporation's statutes, as well as the good working relationship with the BSC) the DoI's views are in agreement with those of the nationalised industries who (1) consider it advisable that the expertise needed for the fulfilment of the department's tasks be provided by the boards themselves, and (2) maintain that it is 'not their function to look at detail', but merely 'to see that the overall policy of the nationalised industry is moving in the right direction' (NCB). None the less, criticism about the low level of civil service expertise has been coming from within their own ranks — sometimes tinged with a mild form of contempt for those who 'knew nothing about the running of a commercial organisation' yet who constantly meddled in just this way (*pace* Lord Melchett and Sir Monty Finniston!). Owing to never having stayed 'in one post long enough to do any real studies-in-depth', and never having been 'trained in the arts' required for participating in, for example, the nationalised industries' 'planning exercise',[81] they are usually 'at a terrible disadvantage' in discussions on investment programmes and such like: the corpor-

80. Binning, ibid., p. 85.
81. Lord Robens, *Ten Year Stint*, op. cit., pp. 74, 230.

ations' experts being able to 'make a proof case' of nearly everything, they were 'completely lost' — at least while technical matters were being debated (BSC).

Sir Monty, asked whether the sponsoring department had sufficient expertise to judge the problems of their own industry, replied, 'No — they needed outside consultants, who were not any better'. Other BSC members, trying to find some good points in their opposite numbers in the department, said that they believed them to be expert 'to a degree . . . they are quite competent to take our plan and analyse it and pass judgment on any divergence from the plan' (since 'most civil servants are intelligent people, though not all of them are wise . . .'); they *may* be able to 'judge whether plans fit into the government policies — if they understand the latter' (!); but they were certainly not competent to advise on what action should be taken. This limitation on civil service expertise is, not unjustly, put into perspective: 'The civil servants dealing with the BSC would have as much expertise as non-executive members of the board' (who, after all, are expected to join in discussions of the corporation's plans and programmes, and whose advice appears to be much appreciated); 'those I've met were well informed'. One board member, however, declined to give his opinion on the subject — 'I couldn't answer, because civil servants change so much!'

Most BSC officials, furthermore, express their readiness to improve their opposite number's knowledge: initially, they may not be experts, 'but we teach them a lot'; 'though they might know more about the subject, it's my job to communicate and make sure that they understand.' Seen from this angle, a certain lack of specialised knowledge appears positively advantageous. It may be irritating to have them ask so many questions (with the consequence that there is 'too much detailed information flowing to and fro'); but it is better, apparently, to answer such questions (and thus limit the amount of information given out) than to have them know 'too much' beforehand. 'A body of experts in the department can, at its worst, second-guess what the management does'; that is, in the eyes of BSC executives, 'not their job'!

Indeed, as Ian MacGregor stated before the ITC, if a civil servant really proved expert in BSC matters, the DoI would no longer be the proper place for him: 'Any time that we see someone in the Department who could be better used in our business, we try to acquire him. In fact, we have done so'[82] (a probable allusion to Solly Gross). In the

82. Fourth Report from the ITC, Session 1980–81, *Effects* . . ., op. cit., Vol. II, p. 24.

end, nearly all those directly concerned with a nationalised industry seem to feel that too much expertise in a sponsoring department is as bad as too little — or even worse! While this attitude is understandable in a public corporation aiming at minimising 'interference', it is hardly justifiable in a department whose task it is to supervise if not direct a nationalised industry's activities. Ian Mikardo, of the ITC, put his finger on the paradox underlying these attitudes: 'For a to monitor b, he has got to know more than b. I want to ask what are the qualifications of the people in the Iron and Steel Division for monitoring the performance of a great industry. If they do not know more about it, if they have no greater expertise than the management of the Corporation, they cannot monitor it. If they have greater expertise than the management of the Corporation, would they not be serving the nation by working for the Corporation rather than for the Department?'[83]

This neatly underlines the whole problem of how to control experts. One would think that there should be an expertise in the controllers at least equal to that in those controlled, for how otherwise can their performance be judged? There must be a considerable expertise necessary merely to *understand* what the 'experts' submit. Yet the problem is not only how to acquire that expertise; there is the other problem that controllers sufficiently expert to 'control the experts' are in danger of identifying with the latter and making common cause with them, thus losing sight of their initial object. The British answer to the paradox has been to rotate their civil servants between departments at certain specified intervals; as we have seen above, this answer is no more than 'fair-to-middling'.

The Effectiveness of Control — Seen from Two Sides

The system of ministerial control, at least as operated in the case of British Steel, does not appear to be particularly effective. It is difficult, if not impossible, to assess the effectiveness of the system as originally envisaged, owing to the ambiguities of the statutory provisions (see above, pp. 145ff.). Apart from this, the weaknesses of the present framework are quite easily detected. Firstly, there is no *ex ante* control to speak of, since the government seems to have little conception of what to do with a state-owned key industry such as iron and steel, as well as a marked reluctance to involve itself in what, on both sides, is

---

83. Ibid., p. 85.

seen as the management's prerogative. Hence there is no real joint planning — 'the corporation proposes, the government disposes', in the sense that all the planning is done by the corporation and then presented to the department in such a way that it is difficult for the minister to do more than 'rubber-stamp' the proposals. Nor does joint decision-making come in at the back-door, so to speak, through the presence of government officials at the board meetings: even when they were there as part-timers, equipped with a vote and all other rights of a board member (but with none of the functions), civil servants appeared to have no more impact on the board's decision-making than the hapless worker-directors.

While no government has intended to exert *ex ante* control on British Steel, energy has been concentrated on financial control. According to our evidence, however, the present system of financial control is less effective than the public is led to believe. Of its three main elements, the target date by which the BSC shall be free from all state aid has been pushed repeatedly further into the future (at the time of writing, in late 1984, it was the end of 1985); the investment review is of little practical relevance at a time when there *is* no investment; besides, civil servants (for reasons that we have discussed above) usually lack the expertise necessary to judge any projects submitted to them; even the cash limits do not provide the 'harsh discipline' they are often praised for, since they are negotiated with the corporation itself and are raised as soon as the corporation shows any signs of being in financial difficulty.

The overall performance of the controlling agents, then, cannot be said to be at all impressive. Indeed, the few successes the BSC has had, during the time of its existence (concentrating, rationalising and modernising production techniques and then adapting to the declining steel market by a radical cutting of its capacity) have been achieved partly in the teeth of government supervision. This result is the more devastating as no other nationalised industry has been monitored so closely, continuously and in detail as British Steel since 1979. Since one cannot, in the case of financial control, argue that the shortcomings of the actual system were caused by a lack of purpose — there has been every intent to keep a tight grip on the corporation's financial bearings — the only explanation left is that the civil servants responsible were inadequately equipped to provide any real check on the corporation's management. This, in turn, is only partly due to the system of job rotation: it is part of the more general problem of how to control the experts.

However, all is not unremittingly bleak. There is, for instance, the obvious and persisting determination of the DoI/DTI, in recent years, to improve their system of monitoring and the flow of communication and information. Furthermore, as we have already mentioned, the invention of performance indicators has proved to be a step in the right direction, and might prepare the ground for a more effective control system in the future. As yet the indicators do not constitute the much-needed efficiency control, since they are isolated sets of figures, unrelated to any previously fixed performance targets. Still, there is now reasonable hope that the BSC can be held more firmly than before to its own targets, at least. Were this newly-emerging system to be extended (covering more areas where performance is measured), and to be completed by the setting of actual targets, it could provide the factual basis necessary for any effective control. Unfortunately, it would first be necessary for the government to overcome their reluctance to spend time on the question of the industry's purpose, aims, and policies — an unlikely occurrence, it seems.

One would expect those involved to take a different view of the matter. Surprisingly enough, there is a general scepticism as to the effectiveness of ministerial control, even among government officials. As has been shown, the latter are slightly over-optimistic about their own expertise and their ability to do their job as controllers; or they define this job in such a way as not to have to admit to the major weaknesses of the whole framework as well as of their own performance. To give an example: if the decision on a nationalised industry's policies is defined as being the management's prerogative, with the sponsoring department not taking any part in it as 'a matter of principle', then the department cannot be reproached for leaving the industry without an input of its own. So, on the whole, civil servants think they work reasonably effectively and have done a good job — even with the tricky business of the investment review.

The question of sanctions brings scepticism to the fore. In the last resort, most civil servants feel that there is no way to force an obstinate chairman into compliancy — or a loss-making corporation into one that breaks even. It is all very well to speak of 'sacking the chairman!' (DoI) — this, obviously, is not 'done'. In the case of the BSC, the DoI tried to compensate for this by linking Ian MacGregor's salary to the corporation's performance. More precisely: the high transfer fee was to be paid back in case MacGregor did not manage to reach the break-even target. But (one is tempted to say 'of course') when Ian MacGregor left the BSC, the target had not been met, nor was the fee paid back. 'In the end there is *no* effective means of control': 'we don't have enough sanctions' and so can do hardly more than 'threaten' (Treasury). This even applies to the allegedly harsh régime of the EFL, for there can be no effective sanction if a public corporation does not stay within limits: 'Cash limits must be varied if the Corporation does not meet them; there is nothing else the government can do' (DoI), since it 'cannot let the nationalised industries go bankrupt' (Treasury). To admit that the government will have to pay in the end, whatever a nationalised industry does, while at the same time it is 'very difficult for government to get its way' (DoI), is a devastating verdict by civil servants as to the function they are supposed to fulfil. Neither does it enhance a sense of responsibility within the industry.

Nor does the government itself — in spite of its having to bear the costs — appear to feel really responsible for what happens within the industry. They are not willing to accept responsibility, for instance, in the case of misinvestment, since 'we see so little of the project!' (Treasury), especially when their opinion on the project had been 'overruled'. The DoI, cautiously, indicates that it could not be held responsible in the case of failures that could not have been foreseen — which, as far as the BSC is concerned, can be maintained in all the instances where its critics have spoken of 'misinvestment'. Hence the notorious blurring of responsibilities, which is usually blamed for many of the shortcomings of the present system of ministerial control, is, more precisely, an avoiding of responsibilities: 'There are times when we are wary of [the blurring] happening'; and 'in important matters [plant closures] we try very hard to make responsibilities clear' — that is, that the corporation is to take the blame (DoI).

In the end 'there is no real difference' between the government's dealings with a large private firm and a nationalised industry: 'We don't influence [the former] — but the line is: we don't even influence BSC!' (DoI). In fairness it must be said that this statement represents a minority view among those civil servants interviewed; others tended to stress the 'important differences of form' (DoI), the 'political dimension' (Treasury) (which has been shown to be of much less relevance than could have been expected, from the massive public criticism it has received), and the 'fundamental difference that the nationalised industries are financially controlled very closely' (DoI) — of which, however, the effectiveness is in doubt. Finally, of course, 'private companies can go bankrupt' (DoI); but even here the realisation is dawning that this difference is less real than originally, the last fifteen years or so having demonstrated that the government cannot afford to let a large private concern go into liquidation any more than a giant nationalised industry. While it may not effectively *control* either of them, it must 'pick them up if they go bankrupt . . .' (Treasury).

According to most of the evidence, then, those in control are not entirely convinced (much as they would like to be) of the effectiveness of the existing control system; with Treasury officials (due, no doubt, to their generally more detached attitude) rather more sceptical and critical than their colleagues from the sponsoring department. Both are trying to take a philosophical view of the matter, however; things are as they are, 'that's life', most of the problems of control are 'only natural' (DoI) — hence there is little point in attempting to change the system.

The BSC members' views on the subject are much more ambivalent than those of their counterparts in Whitehall. They have to maintain that controls are really tight and effective since they have so often publicly expressed resentment of ministerial powers, on account of the delays, wrong decisions and general irritation they have caused. Hence the insistence that it is actually the government that, 'as the owner of the business. . .has the last say' on all important matters, while the board, in the end, 'can do nothing' against the 'overriding powers of the Minister' — except resign from their posts. In their eyes the government is not without real sanctions against obstinate boards; it has, after all, 'the power to liquidate the Corporation', and to 'sack the whole lot'. The ministerial power of dismissal is seen as a strong weapon — even though it has not been used as yet — the only member admitting to scepticism on this head being a former civil servant who expressed some doubts about the feasibility of a government's 'going on sacking chairmen'.

The main effect ascribed to those 'overriding' ministerial powers of control, however, is not that of the minister's overruling the corporation's 'commercially sound' decisions but, characteristically, only that of the delays they cause ('they can introduce whatever delays they wish, for reasons which I find difficult to understand').[84] That the corporation cannot, apparently, point to any more impressive effects is one indicator of the ambivalence of the views its members have on the matter. For while their resentment of all ministerial control prompts them to make it look effective — even dangerously so — they know as well as their controllers that the latter's powers are really rather limited. They know, for instance, that however much they may praise (or condemn) the EFL as 'harsh' or 'healthy discipline' the

---

84. Finniston, First Report from the SCNI, Session 1977–78, *The British Steel Corporation*, op. cit., vol. II, p. 91.

government has few means with which to enforce it: that if the corporation does not observe it, there is little the government can do except 'raise the cash limit. . .or liquidate the Corporation'. They also know that the government has hardly any alternative but to pay 'if we are in a mess', no matter what the targets have been or how far the corporation is from meeting them. They know that, if it is difficult to keep a loss-making industry under control, it is impossible to do so with a profitable one: 'once a corporation needs no money there is hardly a way to control it'. Furthermore, this knowledge is tinged with a suspiciously low opinion of the minister's and his civil servants' competence in dealing with them: in the words of Sir Monty: 'Why should the government, who are ignorant of steelmaking, make better judgments than we do?'! Hence the rather complacent statements that the corporation 'usually got its way', and that any chairman 'worth his salt' could twist his minister round his little finger.

At the same time this is not regarded as in any way unusual, happening as it does in any large company where management expertise normally convinces outside directors (to say nothing of the shareholders) of the wisdom of following the board's proposals, the said proposals then being implemented by the executive directors without any outside 'meddling'. In the corporation's view, the problem of control is 'structurally' the same in public and in private enterprise: 'you need a strong management' and both the government and the outside directors should 'leave managements alone'; 'the policies must be agreed, but afterwards the management must go on'. Running an industry is mainly 'a matter of confidence', in any case, for there is no other way to control the experts than to 'make sure they know what they are doing, and then let them do it'.

Having stressed this basic similarity with the private sector, the corporation feels that it is at a comparative disadvantage: in public enterprise there is 'less incentive for the management to work efficiently' (which must be attributed to the ineffectiveness of ministerial control, though, *not* to its existence); there has been government interference which 'prevented us from being efficient'; and there is generally much more 'political pressure'. On the other hand, there is the advantage that 'private companies usually go into liquidation, or are taken over, and public corporations do not'. On the whole, however, BSC members, like some government officials, recognise that the differences in government treatment of large private and public enterprises are being eroded. From time to time, both are under political pressure ('ICI and Shell would say there is no difference') appear not to be susceptible to effective influence, but are 'helped. . .in case they get into trouble'.

Thus, while differing in opinion on questions of detail, both the controllers and the controlled tend to agree on the question of the general effectiveness of control, and the related question of 'who is in power': it is certainly not the minister, nor his Under-Secretary, but the corporation's chairman and/or (depending on personalities) the chief executive. This is the more surprising since the numerous complaints made in public by the chairmen of nationalised industries have led many observers to believe it to be the other way round: that, as *The Times* put it, 'the will of the sponsoring minister not infrequently prevails over the commercial judgement of the state industry chairman'.[85] The SCNI seemed inclined to take the same view. Most of the authors, however, who have investigated BSC's history have come to the conclusion that the government's attempts to influence the corporation's policies, so far from 'prevailing over the commercial judgement' of its management, have had 'only a limited impact' on the BSC's strategies,[86] and that the most characteristic feature of the relationship between the BSC and the government was the BSC's highly developed 'ability to act autonomously':

> Although the BSC is officially accountable to the Minister...the power balance of the relationship has undoubtedly favoured the management of the Corporation. The most obvious facet of the BSC's power is its specialized expertise, which both Ministers and civil servants have challenged only occasionally and tentatively. As a result of this official passivity, the development of steel policy is largely a story of BSC autonomy interspersed with spasmodic bouts of relatively ineffectual intervention by government'.[87]

Members of the corporation would, in public, deny very strongly holding such a view and would deny that it had anything in common with the reality they had experienced, pointing, not unjustly, to the many battles they had fought with 'interfering' ministers. Yet they cannot deny that, no matter how much they may have resented those battles at the time, they have usually ended with victory for the BSC (with the notable exception of price restraints in the corporation's

---

85. *The Times*, 27 August 1976 (see First Report from the SCNI, Session 1977–78, *The British Steel Corporation*, op. cit., Vol. II, p. 65).
86. Geoffrey Dudley, 'Pluralism, Policy making and Implementation: The Evolution of the British Steel Corporation's Development Strategy with Reference to the Activity of the Shelton Action Committee', in *Public Administration*, vol. 57, Autumn 1979, p. 267.
87. Richardson and Dudley, *Steel Policy in the UK*, op. cit., p. 3.

early years). Even Sir Monty conceded, rather proudly (albeit only after his years in office) that, despite all its efforts, the government had not managed to have the BSC alter its strategies: the corporation had always followed the path it had originally decided upon — with the government lacking the confidence to say a definite 'no.' This state of affairs is not the exception but the rule, the chairmen of other nationalised boards also maintaining that, in spite of the government — 'arm-twisting' and all — 'we have not done a single thing. . . . which we had no intention of doing'.[88]

Where power is as unevenly distributed as it is, apparently, between a public corporation and its controlling minister, the question of defining the proper dividing line between policies and day-to-day management (which had been of paramount importance in the Morrisonian arm's-length concept) loses much of its relevance. Accordingly it does not, at the moment, seem to be a question seriously debated in boardrooms in Whitehall or by the critical public. In Whitehall, there is a general recognition that a clear demarcation should exist and that the notion that policies and day-to-day management are different things should be retained — if only because 'you have to limit the class of things you get involved in' (Treasury). Those involved would, however, have difficulty in drawing the dividing line — 'the demarcation changes' (DoI), for instance, and 'there is bound to be an overlap' (Treasury). While still clinging to the necessity of such a distinction, they 'don't think it possible' to define it (Treasury, DoI).

Members of the Corporation, by contrast, have somewhat clearer ideas as to where the line should be drawn — with the government, for example, 'just controlling the [financial] bottom line', otherwise 'leaving us to decide'; or the government agreeing the general objectives but going no further, so that it is the executives only 'who take the decisions concerning the business'. But the matter is not considered really important. In reality there will always be a grey area, since plans are constantly updated, and there will always be situations where the management will have to consult government on details — 'and from time to time it will forget to ask about policies (maybe even deliberately)'; 'you can't have fixed lines: that's not an important issue'. What matters, instead, is that both sides 'take the sensible view' and have 'a general understanding — in an atmosphere of tolerance'.

This relaxed attitude may come as a surprise, considering the vehemence with which the corporation used to fight back against

---

88. Sir Arthur Hawkins (CEGB), SCNI (Sub-Committee E), Session 1978–79, *The Relationships* . . ., op. cit., p. 27.

unwarrantable interference, a notion which one would expect to have been derived from a distinction between 'legal' control (policies) and 'illegal' meddling with the day-to-day management. But as we have seen already, the corporation's executives tend to perceive *any* form of control as unwanted interference. Hence it is not only that they deem the dividing line to be of but little importance, but a clearer definition of the legitimate areas of government control/intervention would render it more difficult for the corporation to fight, publicly resent or quietly evade every attempt by the government to gain influence and, for once, to get its way.

Where there is no clear distinction between rights and duties, blurred responsibilities are the natural outcome — with every possibility of each using the other as a scapegoat. There have been hints, in the interviews, from both sides that their counterpart (of course) might try to 'exploit' the 'unavoidably' unclear responsibilities (Treasury), also complaints from each side about attempts to shift the responsibility for, e.g., closures; more especially, there has been 'no minister who, when something has gone wrong, has stood up, admitted responsibility and resigned his position'[89] — nor (one should add) has there been a chairman who has done so. Since, obviously, there are advantages for both sides in a situation of 'confused responsibilities', neither side necessarily wishes the situation to be altered (although, as Sir Monty observed in a flash of insight, this state of affairs might easily result in the corporation's being controlled by *nobody*, either from without or within).[90]

None of this sounds very much like the implementation of the arm's-length concept envisaged by the early nationalisers. The government, avowedly, still holds to it, and still thinks of it as a useful concept, finding it convenient (contrary to the public image of meddling civil servants) not to be too closely involved in the running of a nationalised industry: 'a closer relationship might have a lot of drawbacks' (Treasury) — for example, in terms of responsibility. It appears necessary to cling to the *principle* of arm's-length control, at least, to be able to adopt a detached attitude, to blame the other side in the event of things going wrong, and to conceal one's own lack of power. The practice can be more difficult than the principle at times: 'It's all right if you can get it'; unfortunately, it is not really practicable with loss-making industries (DoI). Of those government officials who

---

89. Finniston, SCNI (Sub-Committee E), Session 1978–79, *The Relationships* . . ., op. cit., p. 60.
90. Ibid.

were interviewed, only one openly dismissed the concept as 'a myth, really', saying definitely that it was of no use whatsoever, being 'too simple a view of life' (Treasury); he avoided, however, any definition of the relationship that existed instead.

According to members of the corporation no such arm's-length relationship has ever existed. To them, it would have meant that the government restricted itself to appointing board members, and at the very most 'agreeing' the latter's programmes; any attempt at greater control would have violated the principle. Since real life violations did not imply the thwarting of the corporation's plans, they are easily able to resign themselves to the fact that the degree of government detachment that they wish for ('in principle') is not really feasible. Hence, and for the time being, 'arm's-length' is not an active issue for the BSC, although it is occasionally useful, when it becomes necessary to apportion blame.

In reality, the concept has come under pressure in a twofold way. It has been led *ad absurdum*, firstly, by the lack of a dividing line between the two spheres of commercial management and political control, a lack which results — paradoxically — less from the politicians' urge to meddle than from the governments' actual *unwillingness* to deal with the nationalised industries, in terms of concepts, and from their *inability* to deal with them, in terms of expertise and power. The other major influence has its roots in the growing losses some of the large nationalised industries have incurred. These forced upon a (reluctant) government, for budgetary reasons alone, a closer monitoring of the loss-making giants than had ever been originally envisaged. This monitoring is, as yet, only financial, and its effectiveness has yet to be proved; nevertheless it has resulted in the development, in the case of the BSC at least, of a closeness which makes the corporation, its 'commercial' stance notwithstanding, something of a half-way house between the public and the private sectors, between state and capital.

The BSC and the Private Steel Companies

12

An Involved Relationship

The BSC's situation between the public and the private sectors, however, awkward as it is in the eyes of its management, is rendered yet more difficult by the existence of a private sector in the same industry. There is, of course, the possibility that the latter can ease the problems arising out of the BSC's position as a halfway house between the two sectors. To a considerable degree, this depends on the attitudes of the people at the top of the public sector giant and of the private sector companies: whether they favour an intimate relationship of cooperation, stressing their similarities and the interests of the industry as a whole and thus skirting the public/private divide (and with it, the state's controlling influence over the public sector) — or whether they foster an atmosphere of resentment, envy and hostility, stressing the conflicts and widening the divide. Both attitudes can result from the very closeness of the two sectors, and both actually occur — in varying degrees. This is precisely what makes the public/private sector relationship in the British steel industry intricate and interesting. It is all the more surprising that as yet no research has been done on the subject.

As has been described in Chapter 10, vesting day in 1967 saw the thirteen major steel companies, plus the state-owned RTB, transferred into the BSC — assets, subsidiaries, shares (in other companies) and all — while some 200 smaller firms remained in the private sector. An impressive number of private-sector competitors for the newly-founded public corporation! However, they were by no means all competing directly in the same businesses, since many of the remaining private companies were steel *processors* rather than producers and, hence, customers rather than competitors of the BSC. In fact, the BSC, representing in the beginning about 90 per cent of the total crude steel-making capacity, was the private sector's largest supplier by far. Competition was reduced to specific finished steels (where the

BSC's share in the market was much lower), mainly in the re-rolling business. This is a limited area, especially since a number of finished steels — notably high alloy, high speed, tool, and stainless — have been produced virtually only in the private sector.

The situation has changed slightly over the years. During the 1970s the private sector managed to double its crude steel-making capacity, and to increase considerably its share in the market for ingots, billets, blooms and slabs (see Chapter 10, p. 136), while any fall in the private sector market share in special steels was due to imports rather than the corporation's activities. The relationship between public and private sector steel is now, more markedly than in the late 1960s, the complex and intricate one of competitors as well as of supplier and customers, with both aspects frequently occurring in the BSC's dealings with a single company. The relationship is complicated further by the fact that the BSC had inherited a stake in a number of companies who belonged otherwise to the private sector, and which were now owned jointly by the state concern and its competitors/customers.

How involved the relationship can be, in individual cases, is shown by the example of Tube Investments and its steel tube division. Tube Investments and BSC were joint owners, on a 50:50 parity, of Round Oak, one of the steel producers left in the private sector (manufacturing carbon and alloy bars and sections). While Round Oak was still in existence (TI sold its share to the BSC which eventually closed it down) it was chaired alternately, year by year, by a representative from TI and one from BSC; of its board of six directors, three came from TI and three from BSC. It was in the composition of the board that the involvement became evident. One of the TI (non-executive) directors, K. G. Webley, was the managing director of TI Weldless Ltd, which had been the major customer of Round Oak; one of the BSC directors, John Pennington, was the managing director of BSC's Sheffield division, 'a main supplier of TI, in competition with Round Oak'.[1] The BSC is the main supplier of most of TI's steel tube subsidiaries; TI Weldless was not only the main customer of Round Oak (until the latter was closed) but also bought from BSC, while being in direct competition with the state giant: in the types and sizes of tubes they produce 'there is exact overlap with the BSC Tube division'. It has been said also — albeit not specifically — that TI steel

---

1. Quotations in this part, if not explicitly stated otherwise, are drawn from interviews with chairmen and/or executive directors of the steel companies visited in 1981.

subsidiaries in some instances even supply the BSC, for the latter's downstream production. 'This is a very complex relationship indeed, and probably manageable only in England (certainly not in France!)'; 'we may be more involved than others, but this complex relationship is quite typical'.

In fact, the overwhelming majority of the steel firms visited owned to being both a large customer and a competitor of the BSC; two others were, at the same time, partners of the BSC in joint ventures which, in their turn, were in the same involved relationship with both their 'parents' (these were Templeborough Rolling Mills, owned by BSC and Bridon, and Alloy Steel Rods, owned by the corporation and Lee Steels). In short, 'there is a lot of untidiness about . .. ..'. Apart from the few new steel companies, which are foreign-owned, there seems to be hardly a single British firm which can claim, with Sheerness Steel, that they are 'wholly independent' of the corporation. It is in this same company, incidentally, that the personnel were heard to comment, rather maliciously it may seem, that it could take 'a week to explain' the intricacies of some of their competitors' relations with the BSC.

The Personal Relationship or: Remnants of the Past

'Of course, these are all informal relations that should not exist' — they even run counter to EEC rules on competition, a fact that is admitted quite freely — but they are, after all, inherited from pre-nationalisation days. Many links seem to have been inherited from the past: those of ownership, of close commercial connections, of personal ties. As has been described above (pp. 112ff.), prior to nationalisation the steel industry had been organised in a system of interlocking directorship; at the head was the BISF, itself dominated by the fourteen major companies and closely connected, by overlapping membership, to the supervising body, the ISB.

When the steel industry was being re-nationalised, the system of thus providing close personal links — from company to company, from companies to organisations, and from past to future — was continued: half of the ten members of the Organising Committee (see pp. 120f.) came from the steel companies; all ten were subsequently appointed to the BSC board. Other personal links were introduced less formally. The personnel of the BISF (which was dissolved with nationalisation) was distributed between the new public company and the remaining private sector. Jim Driscoll and James Siddons, for instance, changed sides and accepted appointments within the BSC, while Alec Mortimer became in due course director-general of the newly founded BISPA. There were, of course, managers of the nationalised firms who stayed on in their posts but kept their contacts with colleagues in the private sector, and those who preferred to leave and take a post in one of the remaining private firms while keeping links with their colleagues in the BSC. The outstanding example of such twofold exchange of personnel is what is termed 'the United Steel Mafia'. United Steel had been the largest company before nationalisation, with a particularly good and well-renowned training centre and research department. They nurtured a whole generation of bright and capable steelmen, who now occupy leading positions in the BSC and in private steel firms. It was quite remarkable how many interviewees from both sectors of the industry admitted to belonging to this Mafia. Moreover the exchange of personnel is not just something that had happened only on vesting day. Steelmen still go to and fro; Herbert Morley, now an executive director of Bridon Ltd., who had been a BSC man before, provides but one example.

The relevance of these links from the joint past is judged differently by those concerned. There have been the references mentioned above to the United Steel Mafia having created 'first-class' personal relations, whereas the after-effects of membership of the former BISF are sometimes doubted — albeit mainly on grounds of time passing: 'it's beginning to wear thin' — the old (BISF) generation leaving, and a new generation rising to the top. Still, 'the steel world is small': its members seem to know each other reasonably well, with or without the joint past; 'there are still a lot of old friendships that have prevailed', guaranteeing a constant and beneficial flow of intercommunication. Even those who hold that the past is past are convinced that the tensions evoked by nationalisation would have been considerably greater had not the individuals concerned known each other so well. Others maintain that 'you can't destroy relationships that have existed for a long time', for 'humans change more slowly than organisations', and that, therefore, the shared past has not yet lost its 'significant impact on policies'; 'most commercial decisions [after all] depend on personal relations'.

Among BISPA members, one even hears the complaint that relations were not *quite* what they might have been, with something like the old BISF continuing to provide a forum for the whole industry. The blame is laid, not only on nationalisation as such, but explicitly on Lord Melchett (who had not wanted the BISF to survive) for having destroyed so many of the close relationships that had bound the industry together in pre-nationalisation days. (The BSC, of course, think that this complaint is unjust, since Lord Melchett had tried his best to bridge the gulf that had opened with nationalisation.)

However that may be, most of the steelmen, from both sides, judge their own relationship with the other side to be fairly good ('we call them by Christian names'), 'harmonious' or even 'first class' (though 'not necessarily from pre-nationalisation days'). Relationships are undoubtedly helped by the frequent lunches and other social activities; then there are institutions like the Metal Society, which 'as the great meeting place' permanently contributes to the 'camaraderie and club feeling' that has always characterised the industry. The strongest link, though, that had traditionally guaranteed the cohesion of the industry, that of interlocking directorship, does not, now, number among the devices used to build a bridge between public- and private-sector steel (except in the case of the joint ventures). From those firms visited there was just one (Bridon Ltd., in which the BSC has a 10 per cent share) that had two BSC representatives on its board of directors; Sir Monty sits on the board of GKN, but he has left the BSC long since. Right at the beginning Lord Brookes, from GKN, was on the BSC board; yet his presence there obviously caused embarrassment because of the manifold conflict of interests, and he soon left.

Since then, it has been considered — albeit mainly by the private steelmen, BSC members apparently not having any firm opinion on the subject — 'not wise [for the BSC] to have non-executives who are too closely linked commercially with the firm', and 'very embarrassing' as well as 'not compatible' with their duties to have those who are competitors; in fact, 'I would not invite a direct competitor to sit on *my* board!' There is only a small minority who still think interlocking directorship a useful ploy — not only to better commercial relations between private companies, but to improve those between private companies and the public corporation: 'I suggested to Scholey that that would be a very good thing to do, and he agreed. I even suggested a name — but it never happened . . . '. The BSC is said, indeed, to have supported such schemes and itself to have made moves in that direction. The DoI, however, perhaps wisely abstained from using this institutional device, since it could well aggravate the tensions already existing within the private sector which is (as will be seen below) far from united over the question of what stance to take toward the public giant.

Conflicts — Past and Present

However friendly personal relationships may be, there are still many causes for tension between the two sectors of the steel industry. Characteristically, it is the private steelmen who complain about the BSC rather than the other way round. A major cause for complaint, throughout the BSC's history, has been its pricing structure, even though their views may be contradictory: as customers the private sector favours low prices, as a competitor it accuses the BSC of under-pricing. Apparently the former has been the lesser problem, since it is in just this area that friendly personal relations between the principals can prove so valuable. Furthermore, in the early 1970s the government, as part of its policy of supporting private industry generally, forced the BSC to charge lower prices than it would otherwise have done. In the interviews, there have been only two explicit references to BSC products being too expensive; more specifically, one customer accused the corporation of charging more for the billets it sold to outside customers than for those sold to its own re-rolling plants — simultaneous charges of overpricing *and* unfair competition! That this was possible was due to the monopoly position that the BSC held for billets in the UK; as a consequence the customer in question had started to buy billets from German suppliers at 20 per cent less than the corporation's price.

As far as the pricing policy of the BSC is concerned, this was the only reference made to its monopoly position. Otherwise such comments were more concerned with the quality of the BSC's deliveries and service and specifically with the 'take it or leave it attitude' which only monopolists can afford. The poor quality of the corporation's products and the 'inadequacy of BSC's performance as a supplier' (which the BISPA reported to the SCNI in 1976)[2] was seen as partly due to that inefficiency automatically ascribed to public enterprises by many staunch believers in free enterprise, but mostly because the BSC was not forced to oblige the customer — 'they didn't care at all for a customer!' Apparently it was not possible to order supplies from the plant that you preferred; if complaints were made, the BSC took little action to remedy their cause; during the steel shortage in 1974, especially, 'they let us down very badly . . . . I told Bob Scholey then that we would never again place everything with BSC'. It seems, indeed, that during the 1970s several of the corporation's steel proc-

---

2. First Report from the SCNI, Session 1977-78, *The British Steel Corporation*, op. cit., vol. II, pp. 164f.

essing customers switched over, at least partly, to foreign suppliers; two of those interviewed even gave figures disclosing that the share of the purchases that they made from the corporation had fallen from 80 per cent to 50 per cent, and from 100 per cent to 65 per cent respectively. Others, however, judged the BSC's commercial and technological performance as quite up to standard and 'found them satisfactory to deal with'; 'if we weren't, we would buy somewhere else!'; 'all things being equal, we would buy British, and most times they are equal'.

To return to the question of prices: much more numerous than complaints about overpricing are those about the BSC's policy of *under*pricing. In the early 1970s BISPA was publicly airing the problem of the 'squeeze' on re-rollers' margins occasioned by the corporation's pricing policies. The problem then was that there were differential increases in the prices of semi-finished (billets) and re-rolled (billet-derived) products. This led to the Hirshfield Inquiry of 1972 (commissioned by the DTI) which, in three out of the four cases submitted by BISPA, considered the complaints about the BSC's unfair competition justified, consequently recommending that prices for the products in question be increased.[3] When Britain joined the EEC the issue receded into the background — not least because of the provisions against 'abuse of dominant position' made in Art. 66.7 of the Treaty of Paris; for the rest of the decade BISPA never found cause to invoke these provisions against the BSC.[4] As BISPA officials themselves admit, up to 1979 'the BSC was extremely careful to give due weight to private sector opinions on the question of margins'.

Things changed, however, with the recession in the steel industry and with Ian MacGregor's energetic attempts to put the BSC back on the road to viability. Generally, problems such as the one at hand are very much a function of 'bad times': in an industry as closely interconnected and as prone to cartellisation (open or veiled) as the steel industry has been, it would be normal for the firms in competition to have 'a sort of general understanding' about prices. There will be much less of it in a declining market, with imported steel forcing its way in. To make matters worse the long steel strike caused the BSC to lose more than its fair share of the market, leading to redoubled

---

3. The products were reinforcing bars, soft wire rods and hot re-rolled bars and sections. See the Extracts from Lord Hirshfield's Report, in: BISPA, *Annual Report*, 1972, pp. 48ff.
4. BISPA mentioned the problem to the SCNI, however, in 1976 (See First Report from the SCNI, Session 1977–78, *The British Steel Corporation*, op. cit., vol. II, pp. 160ff.).

efforts, on its part, to recover at least some of what it had lost. Hence the renewed and reinforced complaints made in the early 1980s now less about differential pricing than about the BSC's 'deliberately undercutting the private sector prices': it 'is charging very much lower prices than we are' — up to 30 per cent, it is said — and so 'has been encroaching on our recognised market'!

Frequently the accusation of undercutting is mollified by an appreciation that the BSC must, somehow, match import prices: 'I must say that in fairness: *they* do not lead the price down'; rather, it has been the imports starting the undercutting business. The BISPA, in a Memorandum of April 1981, told the ITC that they 'do not believe that the Corporation is deliberately seeking to destroy independent companies by price-cutting. We do, however, point out that even a sincerely expressed intention to "roll back imports" and to "regain market share" is, given the indivisible nature of the steel market, bound to have the same effect. It could not be done without access to public funds, and it cannot be done without damage to private producers'.[5] This is the sharpest thorn in the private steelmen's flesh, and what causes the most resentment: that the BSC, backed by government and supported by public funds, can, indeed, afford to meet import prices which the private companies, some of whom in recent years have lost even more of their market share to imports than have the BSC, are unable to meet. At the root of their difficulties and their conflicts with the BSC lies the fact 'that the flow of public money may enable the BSC to behave uncommercially in its pricing', and that it 'can establish market prices which are unrealistically low and which can jeopardise our profitability and our future'; for how can they have any chance against 'a competitor who has a seemingly bottomless purse'?

Apparently several of the private steel companies have tried to tackle the problem of underpricing by entering into direct negotiations with the BSC: 'I discussed it with Scholey, but he gave me an evasive answer. He claims that they've been fair . . .'. Since these have not met with the wished-for success — and since, at any rate, the main fault lay not with the BSC but with the government's 'continually subsidising it' — the BSC's competitors have taken to pressing their point in Parliament (via individual conservative MPs)[6] as well as in the DoI (via BISPA). As it seems that they were able to make out a

5. Fourth Report from the ITC, Session 1980–81, *Effects of the BSC's Corporate Plan*, op. cit., vol. II, p. 125.
6. See, for instance, the debates on the occasion of the Steel Bill, February 11 and 18, 1981.

sufficiently plausible case of being 'driven to the wall', and that the private steel sector was in imminent danger of extinction, the Conservative government, pledged to privatisation, cannot take this risk. The government has thus promised that any public money given to the BSC was to be used exclusively for redundancy payments and restructuring but not 'for an aggressive under-pricing policy';[7] it has delegated a Parliamentary Under Secretary to play 'the role of "conciliator" on any specific cases where unjustified market aggression is alleged',[8] and to take the BSC to arbitration; and Ian MacGregor promised to deal personally with complaints from the private sector.

Meanwhile the BSC itself seems to have thought such complaints, together with the public uproar about under-pricing, much exaggerated. The 'amount of direct competition is', in their eyes, 'rather limited'. This relaxed attitude may be considered typical of a giant concern towards the bickerings of its smaller competitors. For the latter, however, what for the giant is only 'a small amount of competition' may be for them vital to their very existence. While quantitatively the BSC is more the private steel firms' supplier than their competitor it is in this comparatively narrow area that the sharp conflicts arise — the more so as the size of the cake to be distributed diminishes. Hence the many recent complaints about product overlap[9] between the BSC and the private sector. But here again opinions are at variance. Whereas some steelmen maintain that 'it's not a bad idea to have a bit of overlap' because 'it's probably the best spur to efficiency' (one must bear in mind that 'overlap' is hardly more than a new expression for 'competition', after all!), others think overlap both unfair — since the BSC is that much bigger and funded by the government — and irrational, especially in the context of international competition. The latter group (which includes BISPA) propagate schemes of 'tidying up' the public/private boundary, which 'was a bit haphazard', to say the least. In future the demarcation should follow more functional lines — in that the BSC should operate the blast furnaces and big rolling mills which private firms cannot afford any

---

7. Roger Moate in the House of Commons (BISPA, *Extracts from a Debate in the House of Commons*, 11 February 1981, p. 5).
8. Fourth Report from the ITC, Session 1980–81, *Effects* . . . , op. cit. vol. II, p. 125.
9. According to BISPA, this area amounts to about 20 per cent of the BSC's business. The products involved are: semi-finished steel for re-rolling and forging, heavy forgings, tubes, cold-rolled narrow strip, hot rolled bars and light sections, wire rod and coiled bars, reinforcing bars and rods, stainless bars and wire, and tool steel (ITC, ibid.). According to other sources, however, stainless bars and tool steels are produced virtually only in the private sector (see, e.g., BSC, *Annual Statistics for the Corporation*, 1980/81, p. 18).

more, and the private sector should produce all the finished products.

Such had been the plan of John Davies in the early 1970s, when he proposed to split up the BSC and re-sell parts to the private sector (see p. 130, 137). The BISPA now is concerned rather less with the question of public or private ownership but 'advocate that BSC production in the overlap areas be removed as soon as possible from the mainstream of BSC's business' either by (1) selling the respective assets to private sector buyers (which at the moment it is hard to find); (2) forming joint companies (the Phoenixes, see below); or (3) by the formation of Companies Act companies still owned by the BSC 'but managed and financed entirely at arm's length'.[10]

While these plans seem to be supported by the majority of private steelmen, they meet with severe criticism from some of those who still favour competition — and are, apparently, still strong enough to face it. In their eyes the tidying-up of overlap is either an attempt by private companies to leave the steel business altogether, or an (equally to be scorned) attempt 'to get their hands on those parts of the BSC that are efficient'. In both cases the demand to remove overlaps was nothing but 'special pleading', coupled with 'a fair amount of prejudice' against the BSC.

Such prejudice, such resentment against 'big brother', recurred everywhere during the interviews. Whatever the subject under discussion — pricing, wages, investment, exports, or fighting back imports — there is nearly always a strong undercurrent of feeling that the BSC has 'unfair advantages'; it is backed by public money, it cannot go bankrupt, it can realise projects and implement strategies its private competitors cannot afford to: 'We are just not able to adopt their policies'. Resentment of this type, of course, will be felt equally by all the small competitors of ICI. It is always preferable to be a complementary to a giant, rather than its rival.

We have already noted this resentment and that it has been growing in recent years, with the worsening of the steel market and the private steel companies' financial situation. After having overcome the first shock of nationalisation most of the steelmen in the private sector began cultivating friendly relations with their opposite numbers in the public sector, who they had known 'all their [working] lives'. While there had been initial conflicts — mostly about high prices, differential pricing, and the unsatisfactory quality control described at the beginning of this chapter — these could be solved 'by negotiation' and were not of a nature to cause serious resentment; the situation in the early

10. ITC, ibid., p. 126.

1970s was, after all, characterised by a general confidence in the future of steel, and the belief that there was room enough for all, for the BSC as well as for the private sector. Unfortunately, in the second half of the decade this belief was shattered; the private producers now fear they will get squeezed out of the market.

Most of the private sector's subsequent losses in the market, though, have been due to increased imports rather than the BSC's 'unfair competition', and had already taken effect when, after the 1981 steel strike, the huge public outcry about the BSC's price-cutting started; furthermore, the most drastic losses have occurred in businesses where the BSC does not compete at all.[11] The truth is that the BSC is both nearer and easier to attack than the importers. Thus much of the recent economic frustration, only part of which was caused by the BSC, has been turned against the corporation — a new and perplexing experience for the latter.

The corporation's view of itself was that it had always done its best to maintain friendly relations with the private sector, and that these efforts had been fairly successful; moreover it underrated its competitive role. Instead, it saw itself as the 'helpful big brother', believing that others saw it in the same way. Accordingly, in public as well as in the interviews, BSC executives tried to play down the problems: there was nothing more to them than that, at a time when the steel industry as a whole was facing difficulties and most companies were losing money (with the honourable exception of Sheerness Steel) relations between the two sectors had become a little 'difficult'. It seems impossible for those in the public sector to appreciate the fears of those in the private. This is not wholly unjustified, for, as we have seen, the private sector lost out to imports rather than to the BSC. The steel strike occasioned a further misapprehension in that it temporarily concealed the fact that demand for steel had collapsed, for while the BSC was paralysed private companies did comparatively well; when, after the strike, they felt the full impact of the slump they were quick to lay their losses at the corporation's door.

While defending themselves against the private steelmen's accusations, BSC executives have no complaints of their own against their 'little brothers'. This is not altogether unexpected since, as we have seen, the BSC does not really regard the smaller companies as competitors, but as customers — and you don't usually complain about

11. According to a statement from BRISCC (28 July 1982), imports of high speed and tool steels, and stainless bars — products of the private sector — achieved a market share of about 60 per cent in 1981/2, compared with a share of only 25 per cent in ordinary steels, where for most products BSC is the dominant supplier.

those ('they're customers, so we have to be nice to them . . .'). Suppliers are a very different matter, but these are mostly other nationalised industries. Hence BSC executives have more to say on the subject of conflicts with their fellow public corporations (the NCB especially) than on the conflicts within the steel industry.

The government has been eager to act in an attempt to solve the conflicts between the two sectors — responding to pressure, no doubt, since those in the private sector, when experiencing difficulties with the corporation, are quick to bring their problems to its owner, the government. In the case of policy differences — so BISPA — 'we don't deal with the BSC, but go to the government', the latter being 'the only body who can tell the BSC to alter its policies'. On principle, this ought to place the Thatcher government in an awkward position, for it is against its expressed principles to ask the corporation to alter its price structure and, though it might be supposed to influence the corporation's overall policies, that would not be in line with its own professed policy of disengagement, and of treating the BSC as an entirely commercial body; it is certainly not treating a corporation 'commercially' to tell it to raise its prices because its competitors wish them to be higher. The government has tried to escape from this tricky situation by arranging for the BSC to submit to arbitration over its pricing. This device has proved successful; those in the private sector accept it and those in the corporation do not complain.

The government, however, went further. After the private steel firms had complained for some time about the unfair advantage to the BSC of being funded by the state ('we were in continuous dialogue about it with the DoI, but so far to no avail . . .', BISPA), the government started to subsidise the private firms as well. As the Secretary of State, Patrick Jenkin, told the House of Commons in December 1982: 'We have already announced a £22m scheme for the private sector. That sum will be increased to over £34m to allow for all the applications that have been made and we expect to give additional assistance under section 8 of the Industry Act 1972, so that the total help available for the private sector will be nearly £50m'.[12]

That sum (which does not include the financial assistance granted in connection with the Phoenix schemes, see pp. 234ff., below) looks small if compared with the huge losses that the BSC made and which had to be funded by the government, the amount of debt written off, and so on. Still, by demanding and receiving state subsidies most of the independent companies have now lost their innocence, and cannot

12. See Hansard, vol. 34, 10 December 1982, p. 677.

claim any longer (as Aurora's chairman did in 1981) that 'the only really independent steel companies in Europe are the British independent steel producers (you can quote that as my belief)'. One of the few to remain genuinely independent of government aid is Sheerness Steel, which left BISPA not least on the grounds that the association had promoted the policy of state subsidies for the private sector. From many of the other companies, complaints about the government's U-turns — when, contrary to its 'ideology that private steel companies should thrive' it continued to spend money on the BSC, and that 'whilst talking about privatisation the government has continued to give money to BSC to use it to decimate the private sector' — do not sound altogether convincing. 'It goes against the grain to see so much public money spent on steel' — but, apparently, only if it is spent on public sector steel. One might conclude, maliciously, that granting subsidies to private firms removes one major cause for the resentment private steelmen have felt towards their public counterpart, and is one way to restore harmony to the industry.

Joint Interests and Joint Ventures

It should be emphasised, however, that neither the conflicts nor the resentment are shared by all private steel companies. Nor should conflicts and resentment — albeit having grown in recent years — be given more than their due: there are still many areas of joint interest between the two sectors, where 'conflicts are very minor', where 'mostly we're working in harmony', and 'many areas where we combine forces'. In most technical matters, such as standards, for instance, both have worked happily together; for years now they have combined to produce demand forecasts, market surveys and such like; they are united over most EEC matters (and especially over the question of steel prices in the Common Market and, hence, import prices); and they take the same stance, and do some joint lobbying, on energy costs — where, incidentally, the corporation sides with the private sector against its fellow nationalised industries. In all these areas the BSC is seen as 'simply a big steel company' with whom one is 'acting together like normal companies do'. Opinions vary as to what form this 'acting together' takes, ranging from 'we have mutual interests but approach government separately' to a freely-admitted 'lobbying together', developing joint strategies towards government and exploiting the advantages of a division of labour — where resources are needed, or 'in writing up economic scenarios', the private sector is happy to participate in the BSC's superior facilities, while 'we can attack government more easily' (BISPA).

Generally, then, 'concerning steel as a whole BISPA would line up with the BSC'; in all such matters 'we are as one'. It is interesting to note, though, that this feeling is said to be stronger, and the 'lining up' easier, under a Conservative government. With Labour in office, 'the private sector felt itself under threat' and at a continuous disadvantage. Another interesting point is that BISPA leaders are more ready to discuss joint lobbying, and are more emphatic about their joint interests with the BSC, than many of their members. They have even hinted occasionally at the possibility of helping the BSC, supporting it over some of its specific problems (for instance in its dealing with the government). The BSC themselves, like BISPA, attach considerable importance to the joint interests of both sectors — as the BISPA president, Mr Lee, once remarked: 'It is good to have some common issues, to build up some sort of relationship . . .'. They go, however, a step beyond naming those mutual interests enumerated above, and place some emphasis on the fact that they are both 'part of the business community', generally sharing the same interests and troubles ('whether you're public or private, your pride is to make the company efficient').

This being so, BSC members are convinced that government cuts in the nationalised industries' finance, for instance, are also a matter of joint interest, since they weaken the corporation's purchasing power and thus affect private industry. Most private steelmen do not agree with this — on the contrary: they feel that the nationalised industries get too much public money rather than too little — nor are they inclined to support the BSC against government. When BISPA showed signs of wanting to do just this, some of them openly disagreed with their own association. Except for the few staunch independents who, as a matter of principle, would never make common cause with a nationalised industry, and for those to whom any support for the BSC would automatically equal acquiescing in its being granted state subsidies, this reserved attitude seems to be a matter of expediency rather than a lack of sympathy. 'We try not to enter into the conflicts of BSC and government', but 'we always sympathised with them'[13] and thoroughly appreciate their striving 'for more freedom . . . to act commercially'.

There was certainly such sympathy in the early 1970s, when the

---

13. Such statements were made even by steelmen who would, they declared, never support the BSC 'because I can see no sense in the policies of the BSC at all!'.

government would not allow BSC to raise its prices. This led to 'artificially low prices' which not only ruined the corporation's profitability but, moreover, rendered the British manufacturing industries 'less cost-conscious than they should have been' (and induced them, probably, to demand the same low prices from the private steel companies: this goes far to explain their strong feelings on this point). There are hints that, on this issue, the BISPA put some pressure on the government. Another example given is employment policy, where private steelmen still feel that the government should not have interfered with the BSC's commercial judgment — especially when the corporation wanted to tackle the problem of over-manning by dint of plant closures (another issue that directly affects the interests of the private sector, for the more plants the BSC closes down, the less are other companies able to reduce their capacity). Even in the case of the BSC's 10-year development strategy, which is otherwise attacked as unrealistic to the point of fantasy, some private steelmen think that the government would have done better to have stood back, for it *'might have been successful if realised in time'*. In short: 'We couldn't have run this company under such conditions successfully'.

Any support that there is for the BSC seems to be mainly 'atmospheric' and not of much immediate help to the corporation, who would not rely on it, in any case. 'We fight our own rows with the government, and we are quite used to it by now.' None the less, one should not underrate the pervading influence of such atmospheric support, especially not on Conservative governments which are particularly prone to listen to the opinions and feelings of private industrialists. It may easily have the long-term effect (may indeed have had it already) of the corporation's being granted ever more commercial freedom.

Whereas support has been of a rather indirect and delicate nature from one direction, from the other there have been cases of a much more direct approach. This has taken the shape of the corporation's buying plants from private steel firms in order to close them down. For the private firms this had the double advantage of sparing them the costs (such as redundancy payments) of any inevitable capacity reductions, as well as providing a special bonus in the form of the price they received for the assets. It is debatable whether Duport falls under this category of massive financial help for the private sector. When the Duport Group, in early 1981, was in imminent danger of bankruptcy, BSC bought its steel subsidiaries to prevent the rest of the group from collapsing. At the time the plants in question were said to be only 'parked' with BSC until they could be lodged in one of the proposed Phoenixes. But Duport's steel-making plant at Llanelli (considered by some to have been one of the most modern in Europe) was shut down immediately, and London Works, the re-rolling plant, closed at the end of 1982; only Flather Bright Steel was saved, being merged with similar GKN companies to form British Bright Bar Ltd. This looks a clear case of the BSC buying assets that it could not use in order to help a private company (Duport) out of dire financial straits and helping them to avoid the ignominy of bankruptcy. The BISPA, however, took a different view of the matter, at least in public. It was suggested that, in negotiating the price for Duport's plants, the corporation had exploited the latter's difficulties. The association also argued that the BSC would not have been forced to help Duport if it had not (*inter alia*) been responsible for the group's difficulties in the first place: 'If the Corporation had been subject to the same disciplines, *they* might have gone out of business before Duport. It is because they were not permitted this luxury of going bankrupt that Duport went instead of them'.[14]

The case of Round Oak is more straightforward. Though said by all to be 'a really good plant', modern and highly efficient, in 1981 TI felt that it provided excess capacity. However, instead of negotiating its immediate closure with the other owner, the BSC, TI actually sold its half to the corporation, who bought it 'virtually on the instructions of the government' (DoI), leaving the awkward business of closure, in 1983, entirely to the latter. One of the government's reasons for 'instructing' the BSC, thus postponing the actual closure, may well have been the fact that Duport had disappeared from the market only recently; another one certainly was to help the ailing private sector — at the expense of the BSC, which was afterwards to blame for its high 'exceptional costs' and its huge losses. In this deal the management of Round Oak seems to have been left in the dark to quite an astonishing degree. Even when the sale to the BSC had gone through they still believed either that they would become part of the next Phoenix or that they would be integrated into the corporation; their only worry appeared to be that, in the latter case, they would lose the managerial autonomy they had enjoyed while still serving two masters. They did not foresee the obvious snag: that in negotiating the details of the next Phoenix the inevitable question would be whether to close Brymbo (from GKN) or Round Oak, and that in this case GKN held the better

14. Alec Mortimer, from BISPA, Fourth Report from the ITC, Session 1980–81, *Effects* . . . , op. cit., vol. II, p. 134. There had been a public outcry by the private steel companies that Duport, 'the most modern steel plant', had to be closed. Others, however, privately say that 'this is a nonsense'.

cards.

More recent still is the example of Hadfields, which had been bought by Lonrho in 1979. In 1981 Lonrho hoped to bring it into a joint venture with the BSC, but for once the corporation had made its agreement conditional on Hadfields closing its plants and making the redundancy payments for 2,600 workers. Consequently the deal did not come off. Lonrho then closed one of the two Hadfields plants, but managed to keep the Hecla Works open,[15] though not for long: it was finally closed in 1984, after having been bought jointly by the BSC and GKN.

Hence to speak of the 'joint interests' of the two sectors means that the BSC — with government backing — must have the private sector's interests very much at heart, helping them to solve their major problems, one way or another, and easing the process of closure. The primary method used to achieve this has been, of course, the Phoenix projects, to which frequent reference has already been made. Before discussing them in detail, however, the point should be made that joint ventures are nothing new. They have been in existence since the BSC was established, mostly inherited from pre-nationalisation days, although in the case of Round Oak things were not quite that simple. In 1967 it was intended that Round Oak should be fully integrated into the BSC, and it was only after massive protests from TI that 50 per cent of the company was returned to the private sector (BSC chose to give this out as an example of Lord Melchett's attempts 'to build a bridge' between the public and the private sectors). As for Templeborough Rolling Mills, owned 50–50 by BSC and Bridon, the BSC stepped immediately into the shoes of United Steel; meanwhile the corporation has a stake of 10 per cent in Bridon itself. A further link between Bridon and the state giant is through Tinsley Wire Industries, of which 40 per cent is owned by Bridon, 20 per cent by the BSC and 40 per cent by a Belgian company. The third major example of inherited joint ventures is Alloy Steel Rods, in which the BSC originally held the shares of English Steel, later taking over the shares of Firth Brown, which increased its stake to 50 per cent; the other 50 per cent was owned by Lee Steel. It was only in 1972 — as a result of the Heath government's first attempt to tidy up any overlap — that the BSC cooperated with Lee Steel, in Lee Bright Bars Ltd. In November 1981, however, Lee Steel bought the BSC's 50 per cent holding in Lee Bright Bars, in exchange for 30 per cent of its shares in Alloy Steel Rods (now 80 per cent owned by the corporation) and a

15. See *The Economist*, 25 April 1981, p. 83.

cash payment of £487,500, a transaction obviously meant to contribute to the general tidying up. Alloy Steel Rods has since been in the same complex situation as other joint ventures, supplying rods to Lee Steel and to the BSC for the production of wire with which they afterwards compete. Simply moving blocks of shares around could not alter what was basically a rather delicate situation, as long as it was still a joint venture, but in January 1984 Lee duly exercised an option to sell its remaining 20 per cent holding in Alloy Steel Rods.

The involved relationship between the BSC and the private steel firms, which has been described at some length above, is certainly rounded off by their joint ownership of steel companies which supply, buy from, and compete with their mother companies. At the same time, joint ownership is bound to strengthen the idea of 'joint interests', as well as the informal links between the two sectors, since representatives of both sit on the boards of the jointly-owned companies, together formulating policies, developing strategies, dealing with costing problems, fighting back outside competition, and so on. To a certain extent, even, the older system of interlocking relationships has been reintroduced.

The Phoenix Projects

At first sight, the more jointly-held companies exist, the more impenetrable the intricacies of this relationship. Yet the Phoenix scheme (a policy of enforcing the formation of joint ventures) was brought into being with the express objects of tidying up and rearranging the public/private boundary.

The first Phoenix actually to fly, Allied Steel and Wire Ltd., was formed in the late June of 1981 after having been under discussion for some three years. The project originated not in government circles but as a result of discussions between BSC and GKN ('it sort of arose . . .'), who in 1975–6 had each completed the building of a new rod mill (at Scunthorpe and the GKN Castle Steel Works, Cardiff). Both had been planned in 1972–3 when steel producers were more optimistic about the future of their industry; there had been even a steel shortage. By the time that the plants were ready to go into service, however, prospects were much less bright, and what had seemed a sensible investment initially now appeared 'a very silly thing' (BSC). Of course (according to a spokesman for the BSC) 'we could have competed and one would have been ruined, but GKN *was* at the same time our main customer'. So both parties soon agreed —

in principle — to 'do the sensible thing' and undertake an overdue rationalisation in tandem.

The problem then became one of obtaining finance for the project and of deciding which of the plants were to be closed, and it was here that the government stepped in (initially a Labour government!) — 'they would not have got anywhere without government help' (DoI). GKN (as they saw it) was bringing to the Phoenix more assets than the BSC, and therefore wanted the corporation to give money to equalise the difference. This proposal was seen as 'far too favourable to GKN' by both the BSC and the DoI, especially since, in the latter's view, GKN was trying to bargain by demanding the book value for loss-making assets — in other words, asking to be paid by the government for leaving the no-future steel business altogether (an interpretation which GKN does not hesitate to substantiate: 'In a way it's true!'). It is small wonder that the ensuing negotiations were protracted and difficult and led to a degree of ill will, not between GKN and the BSC but between GKN and the government, the former complaining about unnecessary delays[16] ('the government's part on the whole was rather negative'), the latter suspicious that GKN might get the better of them. On the other hand, the department proved a valuable ally to GKN, as it was only with government pressure that the BSC could be induced to close Appleby-Frodingham rod mill: 'They did not want to take the rubbish out . . .' (DoI).

The final settlement, in the eyes of government officials as well as of some outside observers, is still very favourable to GKN. (According to Sir Monty Finniston, 'GKN won!'). Though ASW is formally owned by the BSC and GKN on a 50:50 parity, the corporation provided all the cash (the initial working capital amounting to £50m) and was to do so for ASW's first three years, while GKN provided only the management (five out of six executive directors); that is, the new company is run by GKN but — via the BSC — financed by the public. In spite of ASW's being a Companies Act company, and thus supposedly belonging to the private sector, this arrangement does not make it a striking example of real privatisation. Indeed GKN does not see it that way at all, but rather as some sort of nationalisation ('BSC took over the greater share from us'). Accordingly some of the more staunch believers in free enterprise among the steelmen accuse this new scheme of being 'cold nationalisation' (see below). The government, however, thought that it fitted perfectly into its privatisation

16. In fact, the government, which had just come into office, took a year to make up its mind whether or not to support the scheme with public money.

policy, and decided to pursue this strategy further.

Hence Phoenix II was initiated entirely by government, with negotiations starting even before those for Phoenix I had been happily concluded, since the worsening recession in the steel industry[17] attached considerable urgency to all attempts at rationalisation (whether combined with privatisation or not). The original participants in the second Phoenix were to have been Tinsley Park, Templeborough and Stocksbridge (BSC — all electric-arc plants in the Sheffield area), Round Oak, Brymbo (GKN),[18] Hadfields and Duport. Unfortunately Duport had to withdraw from steelmaking soon after the first plans were drawn up, Hadfields closed down about two-thirds of its capacity and (temporarily) lost interest, and Round Oak passed from joint ownership with TI wholly to the BSC. In a way, the recession thus brought about rationalisation without the help of Phoenix II — except that it implied closures in the private sector which the government would rather have avoided.

Eventually the BSC and GKN were once more left as sole participants. Their negotiations soon came to a standstill and in February 1982 appeared to have broken down entirely (leaving, as it was ironically put in the Treasury, 'lots of ashes but no bird'). The main stumbling block seems to have been the question of which plants to close, the BSC favouring Brymbo, GKN Round Oak, and the DoI hovering helplessly between the experts from both sides.[19] There was also the fact that not only GKN but a considerable part of the private sector (including BISPA) feared the growing dominance of the BSC (which was to have put about 2m tonnes of capacity into Phoenix II, compared with a meagre 400,000 tonnes from GKN);[20] 'with the new Phoenix the BSC has an albatross and the private firms are left with swallows' (BISPA).

While the new Phoenix seemed still-born other rationalisations that took place resulted in some fledglings. Glynwed took over Ductile Steel (1982); Firth Brown and the BSC River Don Works formed the 50:50-owned Sheffield Forgemasters (1982), and GKN and BSC the

---

17. In the financial year 1980–1, Sheerness Steel appears to have been the only UK steel company still to make a profit. Hadfields' problems have been mentioned already; Johnson & Firth Brown had to shed 1,250 workers and even GKN 'plunged into loss' (see *The Economist*, 7 February 1981, p. 68; ibid., 25 April 1981, p. 87; *The Financial Times*, 3 March 1981).
18. Incidentally, Brymbo had belonged to BSC and only in 1974 was bought back by GKN.
19. 'BSC tells us since 1979 that Brymbo is inefficient and should be closed down — but GKN disagree, and so do our technical advisers . . .' (DoI).
20. See Richardson and Dudley, *Steel Policy in the UK*, op: cit., p. 67.

60:40-owned British Bright Bar Ltd (1983). There were other smaller mergers: with TI (Cold Drawn Tubes Ltd and Seamless Tubes Ltd); W. Shaw Ltd (Clyde Shaw Ltd); Faber Prest Holdings (Flixborough Wharf Ltd); and, very recently (1984–5), Caparo Industries (United Merchant Bar), Hepworth Ceramic Holdings (G. R. Stein Refractories Ltd) and Afon Tinplate, with BSC shares varying from 25 per cent to 74.5 per cent. Finally, GKN and the BSC combined to acquire as much as remained of Hadfields — 'as part of Phoenix II arrangements'[21] — and afterwards (1983) closed it down.

It would seem then that Phoenix II was not dead but dormant. The cooperation apparent over these smaller projects, but primarily the closure of Round Oak, prepared the ground for an agreement over a jointly-controlled British Engineering steel group, for which the BSC and GKN jointly presented the Bill to the government, in March 1984. In order to merge four of BSC's Sheffield plants (Tinsley Park, Stocksbridge, Templeborough and Aldward) with GKN's Brymbo plant they demanded government aid of approximately £150m, a cash demand somewhat larger than had been expected in the DTI; consequently, after an original negotiating period of some three years, months of negotiation between the BSC, GKN and the government followed, with the Treasury not at all enthusiastic over the sums involved.[22] The proposed aim of this ambitious merger is to produce 'a competitive £500million-a-year private sector steel business',[23] — combined, of course, with a considerable slimming down: two plants of those merged will be closed, reducing capacity by some 40 per cent.

Capacity reduction (going under the name of rationalisation) is indeed one of the main objects of all the Phoenix projects, including the 'little Phoenixes' (the forming of Sheffield Forgemasters, for instance, 'saved' 1,100 jobs). But who covers the costs? Though information to the public about who pays what in the transactions has been meagre throughout, that which *is* available for Phoenix I, as well as the cash demand for Phoenix II, indicates that it is either the government directly or the BSC (the public sector again), which bears the greatest share, paying for the private sector's closures and/or easing its troubles. At any rate it is misleading (if not actively mali-

---

21. BSC, *Report and Accounts 1983–84*, p. 13.
22. Another reason for the government's apparent lack of urgency in this respect is that most of the BSC assets earmarked for Phoenix II were in the Sheffield area which was hit severely by the miners' strike of 1984–5. The government were very wary of announcing anything that would have caused the Sheffield steelworkers to align themselves with the miners.
23. *The Guardian*, 30 March 1984.

cious) when representatives of the private sector complain in public about the way in which the BSC drives private companies into liquidation with the purpose of 'then pick[ing] up the parts he [MacGregor] wants for a sop'.[24] Perhaps the question of who pays the piper will be answered soon, as the Phoenixes continue to make losses; ASW, for example, has spent nearly half of its £50m reserve already.[25]

The other major aim of the Phoenix projects, as stated repeatedly by various members of the government, is that of privatisation. Opinions on this matter, from those involved, are as contradictory as those on the question of 'who pays?', which should come as no surprise, since the two matters are closely connected. According to the then Minister of State in the DoI, Norman Tebbit, the joint ventures are to be 'free-standing companies' and should 'not. . . be dependent upon subsidy' and 'not have recourse permanently to injections of capital from the public sector'[26] — but this, of course, is exactly where the doubt lies. If, however, the Phoenix ventures are but a clandestine method of pumping public money into the private sector (any support that the BSC gives to one or other of its subsidiaries does not have to be declared as a state subsidy), it is doubtful if the whole scheme can, in truth, still be termed 'privatisation'.

Yet there is more than one aspect to the question of whether or not this *is* privatisation. Firstly, which side puts more, and more valuable, assets into a particular venture? Some critics (mainly from the trade unions) fear that since the BSC is apparently selling its few good and profitable plants,[27] Phoenix is nothing but a series of 'back-door denationalisation' schemes[28] — with the further drawback that public money hitherto going to the BSC will in future be diverted to the private sector, with a subsequent loss of public accountability. Others — some, but not all, from the private sector — feel that the boot is on the other foot, with some of the private sector's best and most profitable plants coming to be dominated by the BSC. The corporation itself, incidentally, takes a relaxed view of the matter: if some people call it nationalisation and others denationalisation, 'then we obviously did the right thing . . .'.

A second aspect, not to be underrated, is that of the legal status of

---

24. John Osborn in the House of Commons, 18 February 1981 (BISPA, *Extracts from a Debate in the House of Commons*, p. 16).
25. Allied Steel and Wire Ltd., *Reports and Accounts, 18 months to December 1982*, p. 7.
26. BISPA, *Extracts from a Debate in the House of Commons*, 18 February 1981, p. 3.
27. See, for instance, Tom Crispin, TGWU, Fourth Report from the ITC, Session 1980–81, *Effects* . . . , op. cit., vol. II, p. 163.
28. Ibid., Gavin Laird, AUEW, p. 164.

the new companies: as Companies Act companies they definitely belong to the private sector. Whatever their internal composition, and whoever finances them, they are acting under 'normal market conditions', on an equal footing with all other private companies, and are 'responsible for their own losses', since they have no automatic recourse to taxpayers' money. This is exactly why the government, as well as BISPA (see above, p. 227), strongly favour the formation of Phoenixes as well as the splitting-up of the BSC into as many free-standing companies as possible. What BISPA seems to have overlooked, especially in the latter case, is the (theoretically) essential fact that Companies Act companies, even if owned 100 per cent by the BSC, are not under ministerial control and have no public accountability whatsoever; to this extent, therefore, the Phoenix projects (and allied schemes) may indeed be classified as 'privatisation'. The point has already been made that the BSC was not altogether averse to either Phoenix or to the strategy of transforming parts of the corporation into 'free-standing' companies: always provided that its management retained its influence, such schemes provided a method whereby the corporation could escape control, especially in the matter of cash limits.

Neither BISPA, who favours this policy, nor the private steelmen who oppose it see the problem at all systematically. Not seeing how close it comes to true privatisation, they complain about the U-turns of the government's privatisation policies ('They came into office with the promise of supporting the private sector, but they are the best nationalisers I've ever known!'), seeing in the Phoenix business only the threat of their giant public competitor overwhelming the private sector, and 'taking over the whole thing'. It is also said, however, that if this *were* to be the outcome, the blame would attach not only to the corporation and the government, but also to the private steel firms — which are either wholly dependent on the BSC or which aim 'to extract from the steel industry as much capital as possible' (a strange argument, coming from a capitalist!), before leaving the business.

At the moment, most private steelmen — as well as most other observers — unite in the view that the first Phoenixes are half-way houses, 'hybrids', with a future as yet undecided. But on what this future will be, the private sector is split (although the majority seem to support these projects, for one reason or another): 'Phoenix could be a new means of state control, instead of privatisation'. On the other hand it is also a means whereby private investors in steel can avoid bankruptcy; it is a way of weakening 'big brother' by hiving off the most profitable parts; and, in the long run, 'these hybrid companies could spread further into the BSC' and lead to 'the total hybridisation of BSC and the end of public ownership'. The ISTC sees it this way, too: 'Side by side with the collapse of the old private sector, there is a new private sector fashioned out of the body of the British Steel Corporation'.[29]

During all the discussions on privatisation or non-privatisation the initial reasons that had prompted BISPA to favour the Phoenix schemes (that they were a means of 'tidying up overlap' and making the industry more 'transparent') had drifted into the background. While the first effect can be achieved in the end (though this might rob the industry of a 'spur to efficiency'), the latter result must be doubted since the increase in joint ownership will inevitably add to the already manifold complexities that characterise the corporation's relationship with the private sector. Nor will a reinforced system of interlocking directorships — an equally inevitable result — make for greater clarity in dealings within the industry. One further effect, however, that has so far been spoken of only by BSC executives, must be discussed later: that the Phoenixes might induce 'both public and private parts of the UK iron and steel industry' to recognise 'the need to see the industry as a whole'.[30]

Cooperation, Coordination and the Role of BISPA

Despite all the joint interests, joint ventures and the much-vaunted 'good relations', this is precisely what has been missing up to the present: an appreciation of the needs of the industry as a whole. The necessary cooperation and coordination appear to occur only too rarely. There is some cooperation concerning EEC matters[31] and international trade; the need for joint representation in Eurofer (to be able to speak there 'with one voice') prompted the forming of the British Steel Industry Group (BSIG) as an informal institution where European steel policy can be discussed and a common stance be found. Otherwise, cooperation is restricted to technical problems, standards, statistics, environmental protection; it does not yet extend to joint research (an attempt was once made but was soon abandoned).[32] There have been hints at a joint lobby over energy

29. Paper submitted by the Iron and Steel Trades Confederation, Second Report from the ITC, Session 1982–83, *The British Steel Corporation's Prospects*, op. cit., p. 33.
30. Bob Scholey, Fourth Report from the ITC, Session 1980–81, *Effects* . . . , op. cit., vol. II, p. 28.
31. There is 'a very close alliance there: they sit together on the aeroplane . . . '.

costs, but it was not made clear whether this implied actual cooperation in dealing with the government, or whether it was more a matter of 'having mutual interests but approaching the government separately'.

More specifically, there is no coordination between the sectors on their pricing policies. During the interviews there has been only one slight reference to the BSC having played, in some areas, the role of price leader; at the same time a private company claimed that, in its own product range, it had been the price leader 'during the last two years' and that even the BSC followed suit! But with the Restrictive Practices Act and the Treaty of Paris in the background, the subject of pricing agreements is dangerous ground where you have to tread carefully; it is only natural that statements here are mainly negative (such a thing 'does not happen in the UK at all . . .'). Moreover, with the private sector complaining so loudly about the BSC's underpricing it is improbable that they would accept the corporation's lead in setting prices. It is quite possible, however, that the new system of arbitration, intended to stop 'unfair competition', may result in a new system of pricing agreements. What else can the BSC's private competitors aim at when they claim the corporation's prices are 'unrealistically low', thus revealing the linking of them to their own cost structures?

More open comments were made on the subject of investment and rationalisation policies (joint planning). Though the existence of any 'cartel-type activities' is denied, it is possible to discern a desire that it should be otherwise — up to the point of declaring that the lack of coordination is 'terrible' (Sir Monty); for example, in the mid-1970s both GKN and BSC built a new rod mill, on completion of which one was immediately seen to be superfluous![33] Some private steelmen lay the blame for this on the BSC, claiming that the BISF had been responsible for a great deal of coordination (although this is doubtful — see pp. 112ff. above) but that this beneficial state of affairs had ended abruptly with nationalisation. Since then the 'different feels' in

---

32. In 1970, a joint Research Collaboration Committee had been set up, but the BISPA *Annual Report 1972* was already saying that actually there had been 'little or no new . . . collaboration with BSC in research' (p. 31); in 1973 the Research Collaboration Agreement was not renewed.
33. It is interesting to note that with hindsight Sir Monty, who had been chairman at the time, saw this as a great mistake which he ascribed to the lack of joint planning; while one of the BSC board members maintains that coordination had, in fact, taken place, so that GKN built an electric arc plant and BSC did not. Another view held within the BSC is that the latter took place only after it had become clear that GKN was going ahead anyway.

the BSC and the private companies had rendered any joint planning impossible.

However, the 'different feels' must have abated somewhat, for in January 1981 BISPA and BSC agreed on a joint five-year forecast of steel demand and steel production. Although at the time of writing this has not been followed by any comprehensive joint planning of investment and capacity reduction, it is a first step. Accordingly, 'some very informal discussions' take place when one of the steelmakers or steel processors plans any major alteration such as plant sales or closures. At the moment, unfortunately, coordination can be only negative; yet the more surplus capacity there is, the greater the readiness to acknowledge the need for concerted action. Hence the Phoenixes; hence the fact that even Sheerness admits to 'informal discussions' on matters of rationalisation with the BSC, since 1981; and hence the fact that both sectors recently combined forces to prevent an American company from investing in tubes in the UK, although the plan found favour with the British government.

But there are still many complaints about the lack of joint planning for the reduction of surplus capacity, some supporters of the private sector going so far as to accuse the BSC of deliberately delaying such a joint exercise 'until losses in the private sector force closures'.[34] While acknowledging the problem the BSC, not unnaturally, takes quite a different view of its cause. 'The problem with BISPA members is, they are generally agreed on the need for rationalisation, but no one wants to close *his* plant — however outdated it is.' This is the very same defect which had characterised the steel industry, and caused its many crises, in pre-nationalisation days.

Surely this is a task for BISPA, to tackle this basic problem of the private sector of the industry? Not so; however willing its leaders, BISPA is clearly not the type of organisation needed for the task — a task, after all, which even such a powerful organisation as the BISF had failed to perform. BISPA's primary and 'normal function' is to 'represent the interests of members'[35] to the outside world, especially to the government and the EEC; on such external matters the association spends, according to the evidence of its leaders, 60 per cent of its time and energy. The remaining 40 per cent, spent on internal matters, seems fair enough, but (somewhat unexpectedly) includes dealings with the BSC on such matters as market surveys and the production of statistics. In BISPA's Annual Reports those activities

---

34. Mr Edward du Cann, in the House of Commons (BISPA, *Extracts from a Debate in the House of Commons*, 18 February 1981, p. 10).

(which are the responsibility of its Product Groups) are presented modestly as regular 'monitoring of the changing market situation', 'updating steel demand and product forecasts', and 'keeping abreast of technological developments in their sector of industry, initiating work where required, and ensuring that the standards relevant to their products are satisfactory'.[36]

It is interesting to note that the Annual Reports of the early 1980s do not contain a single word on any internal activities concerning rationalisation or capacity reduction — not even advice to members. In 1982 BISPA stated explicitly that it did not consider this to be one of its proper functions; 'it had of necessity to "stand off" while companies in the various product sectors determined for themselves what rationalisation was practicable and desirable'.[37] Its only action in this respect (on an official level, at least) was 'to assist this process by cooperating with Government in the appointment and briefing of various independent consultants, each charged with reviewing the structure of a particular product area and making recommendations for producer action which Government could support'[38] (that is, for the Phoenixes and other joint ventures). In public, of course, BISPA lent energetic support to 'this process', while restricting its statements to demands that the *corporation* move certain of its plants (those in the famous 'areas of overlap') into joint ventures, and not extending such demands to any of its members.

BISPA leaders explain this reserve by the fact that BISPA is a wholly 'voluntary' association, with a much more 'loose organisation' than its continental counterparts — for example it cannot apply sanctions to any of its members. However, the typical trade association on the Continent has no such sanctions either.[39] Nor is the other problem named by BISPA — that its members have 'divergent interests', 'are in competition with each other',[40] and are 'downstream quite a long way' (with the implied supplier-and-customer problems) — that specific. The *real* problem for BISPA, which prevents it from committing itself on the question of cooperation with the BSC, is that from the beginning it set out to organise and represent an industry

---

35. BISPA, *Annual Report, 1981*, p. 1.
36. Ibid., p. 10; *Annual Report, 1982*, p. 6.
37. BISPA, *Annual Report, 1982*, p.3.
38. ibid.
39. See H. Abromeit, 'Unternehmerverbände', in Manfred Schmidt, ed., *Westliche Industriegesellschaften*, Pipers Wörterbuch zur Politik vol. 2, Munich/Zurich 1983, pp. 454–61.
40. BISPA, *Annual Report, 1982*, p. 3.

which found itself split over the question of how to deal with the state-owned BSC once nationalisation had been completed. Consequently, a substantial part of the time spent on internal matters might be used up by BISPA officials trying to mediate between competitors, between suppliers and customers, and between the 'truly independent' firms and those with closer links with the BSC. This renders BISPA's situation rather more intricate than is usual for a trade association.

It is this intricacy, resulting as it does from such a divergence of interests and attitudes, that makes for immobilism on a number of issues, for whatever line BISPA takes in public, it will be certain of alienating many of its members. Despite its efforts to maintain a modicum of unity amongst its membership, however, BISPA itself is inclined to further a close relationship with the nationalised giant — both for personal reasons (Alec Mortimer and Bob Scholey have been close friends since pre-nationalisation days, for instance) and from the conviction that it is only in this way that the industry as a whole is going to prosper. It sided with the corporation in some of the latter's disputes with the government, when many of its constituent firms would have preferred it to keep a low profile; it favours cooperation between public and private sector steel, supporting particularly the Phoenix schemes as a means of making the British steel industry viable; and it (or rather, in this instance, Alec Mortimer) may even dream of some new Iron and Steel Federation, reuniting both sectors under one roof ('I would like to see the reunification happen' — only 'if it is hurried it would divide the industry').

Its policy of combining forces has already estranged some member firms. In 1981 Sheerness Steel left BISPA, giving as its main reasons the fact that BISPA did not seriously oppose the government's policy of subsiding the BSC, and its own policy of supporting joint ventures, as well as that of asking for state subsidies for the private sector ('Mr Schueppert will have none of this cuddling up to government'),[41] and the personal involvement of its own leaders with the BSC. P. W. Lee, the president of BISPA, to take but one example, had partnered BSC in several joint ventures. How much the latter is felt to be a problem affecting the internal cohesion of the association, is highlighted by the fact that when Alec Mortimer retired in 1983, he was replaced by a complete outsider. There are others, meanwhile, who judge BISPA to be 'nearly dead': since Sheerness left and Duport closed down, there are very few representatives of steel-making companies left in the association. Since the steel-processing majority

41. *The Economist*, 7 February 1981, p. 69.

are largely dependent on the BSC, BISPA is no longer a match for the corporation. Now the independents 'wonder about any useful place in an association dominated by the BSC in one guise or other'.

When asked about BISPA all the member firms stress the problem of divergent interests and the difficulty of achieving internal cohesion — especially where alliances with the BSC are under discussion. At the same time most of them feel that BISPA 'does a good job', be it in the EEC, in policies towards the government or in disputes with the BSC; it is said to be, within the UK, 'a more effective association than most'. Yet whether true independents or allies of the corporation, they all agree that some fundamental change is coming. After nationalisation BISPA was seen as a counterpart of the BSC; the more joint ventures are formed the more this will change, for they will increase the public sector element within the association, tipping the balance towards the corporation and eroding the differences between corporation and association. The more Phoenixes arise, therefore, the nearer the realisation of Alec Mortimer's dream of a reunified, restructured steel industry — though its precise form is difficult to determine and may not resemble the original dream. What is certain is that BISPA in its present form will then be superfluous.

The 'Real Interest Divide' — and the Benefit of Dividing an Industry

While most BISPA members appear to agree with this analysis, they disagree about its valuation. But we have already made it abundantly clear that the private sector is by no means united. Of the two main groups, one is prepared to cooperate with the BSC up to the point of throwing in their lot with it in joint ventures; the other group is strongly opposed to anything that might blur the boundary between the public and private sectors, even going so far as to reject state subsidies for themselves. This latter group appears to be in the minority, though. It can be subdivided into: (1) those rather few companies which see themselves less as customers of the corporation than as its competitors, in which role they feel confident of their viability (they refer to competition rather than to overlap); and (2) a number of comparatively small yet competitive companies in high-alloy special steels. These are neither dependent on nor in competition with the BSC, 'but find this big neighbour decidedly uncomfortable'. Their attitudes towards the corporation, accordingly, range from detached to definitely hostile (see below, Chapter 14); any complaints they make are, perhaps, less about the policies of the BSC than about the support that it receives from the government; they appear to oppose the BSC on principle, and still refer to the nationalisation of a major part of the steel industry as a 'complete and utter disaster'.

The majority is formed by those (mostly smaller) firms dependent on the BSC as their main supplier; by companies which line up with the corporation in order to attract state subsidies, sometimes so that they can close down without making a loss; and by those who have been in joint ventures with the BSC for some time — in short: those whose very involved relationship with the corporation has already been described in some detail. Companies in this last group are, understandably, inclined to be kindly disposed towards the BSC, tending to support it (against government interference), and to defend it (against accusations of inefficiency), and to show sympathy with its management (see below, Chapter 14). Although complaining occasionally about one or other of the BSC's policies, and even, in times of stress, displaying resentment towards their big brother, this group are apparently convinced that most of their problems could be solved by cooperation. They certainly do not wish to see the corporation abolished, taking the line that there are definite advantages for the steel industry as a whole, if part of it is in public ownership.

These contradictory views within the private sector indicate that the real split in the steel industry is not between the two sectors, public and private, but is within the latter. It appears most unlikely that the private sector would unite in the face of conflicts with the BSC: increasingly the groupings are 'BSC plus cooperators' against 'true independents'. The emerging boundary is a little difficult to define since it does not fall along 'natural' cleavages such as that between steel-makers and steel processors (there are few steel-makers left, in the private sector), between competitors and non-competitors of the BSC (there have been few areas where the BSC has not competed), or that between small and large companies. The dividing line seems to be precisely between the groups that have been described above: the comparatively few viable and commercially independent companies who feel strong enough to stay in the market, on the one hand, and those who are commercially dependent on the BSC, who cooperate because they see no future without the corporation, or who want to get out of the steel market before it is too late, on the other.

Hence one effect that the nationalisation of steel did not have was to tidy up the industry by reducing its internal conflicts (merging them all in the public/private divide); rather, it created a further division of opinion over how to behave towards the corporation — whether to oppose it or incorporate it. In the beginning both strategies were equally understandable, for while nationalisation had been vehemently resisted, the management of the new corporation was composed of executives from the private sector. So the ensuing conflict of opinion appears to have developed quite randomly, with the new lines of demarcation being drawn as haphazardly as had those in the public/private divisions in the product areas.

This raises the question of how much sense it made to divide the industry by only partly nationalising it. One of the main reasons for nationalisation had been that it seemed to be the only way to overcome the industry's fragmentation, which had been the major stumbling-block on the way to modernisation and rationalisation. It certainly resulted in some modernisation — not only in the BSC but also in the private sector (which recognised the challenge of nationalisation while being relieved of the political uncertainty of the decade before; see above, pp. 135ff.). Yet it did not succeed in achieving the necessary rationalisation: when the steel market collapsed, in the second half of the 1970s, the old problem of fragmentation remained to block the way to a coordinated reduction of capacity, and with it the way out of the crisis. One might even say (in principle at least) that the fragmentation of the industry had intensified rather than lessened, with the public/private gap an additional bar to progress.

Fragmentation, the engrained weakness of the industry, might have been overcome, even with part-nationalisation, had the selection of the areas to be nationalised followed any functional lines. To select the fourteen largest companies ensured that it did not, for it merely took the conglomerates, each of which contained in itself a miniature world of steel-making and steel processing. Thus the old weakness of the industry was passed on into the new age, and the industry was as untidy as ever. More so, indeed: whereas before nationalisation the private steel companies had been more or less equals, there was now the looming presence of the state-owned giant, towards which they could be expected to gravitate sooner or later. Both fragmentation and imbalance may not have been felt as long as steel demand was high and the industry thriving; both were revealed by the steel crisis, during the course of which it became increasingly clear that the structure of the industry and the demarcation between public and private that had been laid down in 1967 were very unlikely to stay unchanged.

While it did not pave the way for any functional division of labour between the two sectors, the untidiness of the industry after nationalisation had the beneficial effect of throwing them so closely together as to leave little room for alienating strategies, but rather to force them into some sort of cooperation. For most of the private companies, their convoluted relationship with the BSC, joint subsidiaries and all, soon made it difficult to go against the public company and embark on policies that were openly detrimental to it. But the haphazard process of nationalisation has not only contributed to the professedly friendly relations existing across the public/private divide; it has also contributed to that closeness to the private sector which characterises all the BSC's attitudes and policies, and which tends to neutralise its public character. While such closeness is not altogether untypical for public enterprises in capitalist systems, it seems particularly pronounced in the case of the BSC. The corporation management refers explicitly to its very special situation, bound to private firms in the same industry, to justify its determination never to be deterred from its commercial orientation.

However, as has already been made clear, such a friendly muddle is not likely to survive for very long; nor are friendly relations between the sectors sufficient to put the industry back on the road to viability. All the signs (as well as the needs of the industry) indicate the probability of some fundamental restructuring coming about. One possibility, of course, is that the government (as Sir Keith Joseph indicated during the debates on the 1981 Steel Bill) will allow the BSC to go bust; but this is only a theoretical possibility, it being highly improbable that even a government ideologically committed to a free enterprise- and market-orientated economy will be ready to totally renounce having a modern steel-making industry in the country. The second possibility, equally in line with the Thatcher government's economic beliefs, would be wholly to privatise the BSC; this, too, is only a theoretical possibility, since who could be found to buy? Certainly not the private steel companies, which are in a bad enough shape themselves.[42] Besides, the majority of private steelmen are not at all convinced that such a step — even if they could afford it — would be a sensible one to take. They can see definite advantages in bulk steel-making being state-owned, since the level of capital required could not possibly be found by private investors in a comparatively small and economically weak country. The answer in such a case, whether for an up-to-date steel industry or any other equally capital-intensive and high-risk business, must be that 'you cannot

42. 'Sir Keith would like to sell steel back to private hands, if he could find any buyers. But Britain's 50-odd private steelmakers were in bad enough shape before the steel strike; now (losing £10m a week in cash flow) they are even less likely to plunge in where BSC has belly-flopped', *The Economist*, 23 February 1980, pp. 61f.

leave it all to the market': 'money must be directed there by the government' ('to leave us not completely at the mercy of the giants from the (USA. . .'). Generally, it is considered that public enterprise is quite beneficial 'in heavy industry, as a bulk supplier for engineering industries', and to 'provide for the country's basic needs'.

This leaves us with the third, most probable possibility, that of restructuring: privatisation will continue until the BSC is stripped of all its fringe businesses (a lot have been hived off already, in recent years, including BSC's thriving subsidiary Redpath Dorman Long)[43] as well as of most of its down-stream steel activities. The latter, however, will not be sold (for who would buy?) but, after the model of the Phoenixes already flying, will be brought into joint ventures with the private sector, thus achieving three aims at the same time: (1) sorting out all areas of overlap; (2) helping the private sector to concentrate into larger units; and (3) accommodating those private investors who wish to rid themselves of their steel interests. Theoretically, both the fragmentation and the imbalance of the steel industry could be overcome in this way; the industry could be streamlined into fewer but evenly-matched groups and reorganized along functional lines, working towards cooperation instead of competition — a modernised steel cartel, in fact. The remaining public corporation would then be left with 'the heavy stuff' (blast furnaces and rolling mills, more specifically the large integrated coastal plants of the BSC's 10-year development strategy), and would take on the role of public utility to the private sector — or rather, to the public/private sector hybrids thus created.

As has been seen, the first steps in this direction have already been taken. It is uncertain, of course, where the process started in the early 1980s will lead, and whether it will actually result in a streamlined and functionally organised industry; that will depend on the next government as well as on the depth and length of the present steel crisis (which constitutes the greatest pressure for reorganisation), and on how much of the industry will survive (there may not much be left, in the end, to be reorganised). Equally uncertain is the future character of the reorganised industry: whether the hybrids will develop into viable private companies, supported by a state-owned public utility, or whether they will be BSC subsidiaries in the guise of private sector companies — and this is just the point on which the present private steelmen disagree.

One way or other, the restructuring may lead to a reunification of

---

43. See the list in BSC, *Report and Accounts 1984–85*, pp.14f.

the steel industry, either with the BSC itself providing shelter for the remaining hybrids, or the BSC and BISPA combining into some new Iron and Steel Federation. In 1977, indeed, this last was the solution favoured by the SCNI when it demanded that the BSC and BISPA establish a joint 'forum' comparable to the former BISF.[44] This is the ideal state of affairs dreamt of by the directorate of BISPA, who can detect in it advantages not only for the private sector but for the corporation, which would then be 'just an ordinary company' and free from political interference. Not surprisingly there are those in the corporation with the same desires, though to them the exact shape of the future reunification of the industry does not really matter, as long as the organisation is strong enough for effective coordination and rationalisation — an organisation which 'analyses the market, finds out which is the most efficient plant to do what, and then can get the other plants closed'. In their view, a future (and necessary) Iron and Steel Federation should have more positive powers than the former BISF, in order eventually to overcome the rivalries to be found among the private sector's various separate capital interests — the 'class against itself'[45]. These rivalries still dominate the policies of the greater part of the BISPA membership, who agree, in principle, on the need for rationalisation but who wish to avoid the practical consequences for themselves.

In that future restructured industry the public/private divide, which up to now has seemed so arbitrary, will either become neutralised — with the BSC, in the words of one of the 'true independents', directly or indirectly 'taking over the whole thing' — or it will be functionally determined. It is tempting to think that either of those results could have been achieved at the start of nationalisation: it might have spared the industry a lot of trouble. Yet the first, the 'neutralisation of the public/private divide', might easily occur in the sense of public sector steel increasingly losing its character as a public corporation, since the hybrid companies would be under no obligation to be publicly accountable; as for the remainder — BSC could use those hybrids to hide behind and evade ministerial control even more than it has done in the past. The second possibility — the functional division of the public from the private sector — in theory allows for the transformation of what remains from the BSC into a public enterprise truly under public control, able to be used by the government if it wished to influence the development of the industry. But one should not forget

44. First Report from the SCNI, Session 1977–78, *The British Steel Corporation*, op. cit., Vol. I, p. lxviii.
45. Doug McEachern, *A Class Against Itself*, op. cit.

that in this second possibility the interlocked company *relation*ships would in all probability be replaced by a system of interlocking *director*ships (in the hybrids), as well as by a new federation. Hence, in one way or the other, the public/private divide is bound to lose much of its former meaning. In either case there will be little sense in public ownership, other than as a means of subsidising a major British industry.

The BSC and the Private Economic Sector

13

General Relationships

The BSC's relationship to the non-steel private sector has been much less involved, and much less fraught with problems and signs of imminent change: a comparatively simple, straightforward matter of supplier and customers. Though purchasers may sometimes grumble about prices, services or quality, if they are seriously discontented they can switch to private sector suppliers (where any still exist) or to imports.

But it will surprise no one that the BSC's non-steel industrial customers find much less cause to complain about its performance than the BISPA members. Indeed, the evidence of recent years shows hardly any such cause: there have been no complaints. While some motor companies, for instance, had previously criticised inadequacies in quality and service — especially delivery times, apparently a major problem — [1] in 1981 they all told the ITC that meanwhile BSC's performance had greatly improved and was now 'satisfactory'; 'BSC have now established themselves as a competitive supplier'.[2] Specifically, there are no accusations of monopolistic tendencies ('There is evidence that, since the Hirshfield inquiry, the Corporation's monopolistic powers have not been wielded to any great extent . . .'),[3] though it is noted that BSC performance was significantly better wherever the corporation had to face UK competition; nor are there complaints about pricing.

1. In the early and mid seventies, customers used to complain to the SCNI and elsewhere about the BSC's long and unreliable delivery times and its inability to meet quality requirements. According to Richard Pryke, in 1977 a consumer survey showed that 24 per cent regarded BSC's delivery performance as worse or much worse than that of other suppliers, and only 6 per cent thought it better (Richard Pryke, *The Nationalised Industries*, op. cit., p. 196).
2. BL Ltd., Fourth Report from the ITC, Session 1980–81, *Effects* . . .,op. cit. vol. II, p. 212.
3. GKN, First Report from the SCNI, Session 1977–78, *The British Steel Corporation*,

In any case, BSC normally negotiates somewhat long-term supply agreements, with most of its largescale customers,[4] so that all important conditions will be settled to suit *both* partners; any subsequent problems will be 'overcome by personal contact' (GKN). In part, such contacts seem firmer than those with private sector steelmen, even leading to some sort of joint planning. For instance, the last BSC corporate plan was 'discussed in a liaison meeting' between BL's Sheet Steel Sub-Committee and BSC's Strip Mills Product Group; in the same way, British Shipbuilders have set up a joint steering committee with BSC, meeting quarterly.[5] While these two customers are themselves public enterprises, the respective procedures and the general friendliness of the relationships must be judged as typical — according to the evidence from various reports as well as from BRISCC (see below) or private sector companies such as GKN.

GKN especially, although a former competitor, boasts exceptionally good relations with the BSC. Until recently, it was itself a steel company and before nationalisation even a major one, with three plants in Cardiff, Scunthorpe and Brymbo, where it produced between 12 and 14 per cent of Britain's steel. In 1967 the big GKN steelmaking plants were nationalised, leaving it only the re-rolling plant in Cardiff and some 'fringe' activities in special steels. In 1974, however, the company repurchased Brymbo from BSC, which was planning to close the plant, three quarters of whose output went to GKN (before nationalisation 'we had built it up as a supplier for our own needs'). GKN, like most other steel companies, had accordingly found itself in the 'very difficult, very mixed-up position' of being both a competitor and one of the major customers of BSC (at times 12 per cent of the total BSC output was going to GKN). Yet the inherent problems could, according to GKN, always be 'resolved by good personal relations, and the supply agreements'.[6] But then, GKN's conflicts with the BSC had from the start been less serious than those of other steel companies; GKN was a highly diversified concern and not unnaturally reinforced this element after nationalisation, so that its

---

op. cit., vol. II, p. 131.
4. For example, in 1969, GKN had agreed a supply contract with BSC for a term of seven years! After this expired, a new agreement was made, which was still in existence in 1981.
5. See Fourth Report from the ITC, Session 1980–81, *Effects* . . ., op. cit., vol. II, pp. 210, 213.
6. Potential conflicts between the two seem, indeed, to have been neutralised to such a degree that GKN did not enter into the private steel sector's complaints about the BSC's underpricing, but instead 'feels the case has been overstated by the other private sector companies'.

steel interests were no longer paramount for its viability. Such conflicts as arose with BSC related not so much to steel production as to steel stockholding: GKN had moved into this area after 1967, achieving a market share of 20 per cent; BSC had also expanded its stockholding interests to a share of 15 per cent.

Meanwhile GKN has virtually withdrawn from the steel market, having moved the Castle Steel Works, Cardiff and (it hopes) Brymbo into the Phoenixes with the BSC. Most areas of potential conflict have now disappeared (apart from stockholding which, however, became less vexed when BSSC was transformed into a 'free-standing' Companies Act subsidiary of BSC). Nevertheless, the 'good personal relations' remain, originating in the days before nationalisation and reinforced by exchanges of personnel between GKN and BSC on various levels — from lower management up to Sir Monty, who now sits on the GKN board. They will be further strengthened by the joint ownership, and therefore joint board appointments, of the Phoenixes.

The GKN relations with the BSC are certainly special compared with those of the 'ordinary' private non-steel company. However, the possibility must be borne in mind that other steel companies, after having entered into joint ventures with the BSC and thus having got rid of their steel interests, may at some future time enjoy a similar 'special' relationship. The emerging system of interlocking directorships between public and private sector steel may be expected to spread further, thus also linking the BSC to various non–steel companies.

It is hard to find evidence of existing interlocking directorships between the BSC and its private customers from other industries. Apparently the private sector part-timers on the BSC board have not been specifically selected with a view to furthering supplier-customer relations, or to bind the BSC closer to its large industrial consumers. During the past five years, one or two individuals came from engineering companies (see above, p. 161) but none from major customers such as the big motor companies. It may be, of course, that relations are so good, having regard to long-term supply agreements, joint steering groups and the like, that no particular improvement would arise from an additional exchange of representatives on the respective boards (an opinion ventured by GKN).

Another personal link might be constituted if BSC executives had the same background as their industrial customers. But the executive directors are definitely 'career steelmen'. Of its chairmen, Sir Monty Finniston was a metallurgist and in some respects a career steelman; Lord Melchett was a banker; Sir Charles Villiers had been in the brewery industry; Ian MacGregor came from a firm of brokers; and the present chairman, Bob Haslam, had previously been with ICI and Tate & Lyle. It is impossible to detect in this any element of establishing firm links with the private sector industrial consumers, though the chairmen's general private sector background will certainly have strengthened the BSC's 'commercial' orientation.

The Role of BRISCC

Whether or not firmly institutionalised personal links exist, the BSC's relations to its consumers in other manufacturing industries are obviously very friendly — to the point where its customers publicly display great sympathy for the corporation and its difficulties and defend it against critics ('when we were asked to appear before the Select Committee, we did refrain from making any statements against the BSC...'). More often than not, the British Iron and Steel Consumers' Council also proved a valuable friend to BSC (during the strike, for instance, 'they were an enormous help', BSC).

When steel was re-nationalised in 1967, Section 8 of the Act provided for the representation of consumers' interests in a separate Consumers' Council, so following a tradition established with the nationalisations of 1946 and after, when the Labour government had felt that consumers ought not to be left defenceless against the new giant statutory monopolies controlling such necessities as coal, gas, electricity and transport. This is not the place to describe in detail the composition, work and failings of the various consumers' councils.[7] Suffice it to say that — as R. Kelf-Cohen put it — they 'have not impressed the people they were intended to serve'.[8] The main criticisms are that relations between the corporations and these councils are usually 'too close and too good',[9] and that, instead of 'marshalling the consumers' cause', the councils tend merely to a dispassionate assessment of the boards' own arguments. This is largely due to the councils' composition: since consumer interests are usually 'not conveniently organized',[10] ministers have to select appropriate members from other organisations and representative bodies which may be expected to have 'the people's interests' at heart. Hence a high pro-

7. See, for instance, National Consumer Council, Report No. 1, *Consumers and the Nationalised Industries*, London 1976 (HMSO).
8. R. Kelf-Cohen, *British Nationalisation 1945–1973*, op. cit., p. 215.
9. Leonard Tivey, *Nationalization in British Industry*, op. cit. p. 155.
10 Ibid., p. 154.

portion of council members are drawn from local authorities (i.e. from local political parties), from women's organisations, or bodies that generally suggest 'public-mindedness'. On some councils (such as the Coal Consumers' Councils) the board itself is represented: their superior expertise guarantees that the council's discussions and subsequent reports will not run counter to the board's policies. At any rate, the councils are in no position to challenge the board's experts, nor do they have any real powers to do so. The boards have little cause to regard them 'as real partners; rather they are sounding-boards for decisions already reached by themselves',[11] or at best 'moderate and impartial bodies instead of partisans of the consumers'.[12]

A further consumer representation problem has been that most nationalised industries deal with domestic as well as industrial consumers. Hence the NCB, for one, was (until recently) faced with two councils: an Industrial and a Domestic Coal Consumers' Council. The industrial consumers, however, have far less difficulty in making their voices heard; in fact, by comparison they are few enough and sufficiently well-organised not to be in immediate need of such specially institutionalised representation. At present the iron and steel industry has nothing at all to do with domestic consumers, nor is the BSC a 'statutory monopoly'; an Iron and Steel Consumers' Council might, therefore, be deemed superfluous. Nevertheless such a council was established but, as a statutory body, dissolved when Britain joined the EEC.

The existing BRISCC is an entirely voluntary body, without ministerially appointed members, lacking a claim to speak for all BSC customers, and without any statutory functions. It merely 'represents the views and interests' of those steel users who have joined it, 'on issues of policy affecting their steel supplies' not only as regards the BSC, but 'both in the UK and internationally; it is recognised accordingly by the British Government and by the Commission of the European Communities'.[13] In some ways, BRISCC resembles a trade association rather than a Consumers' Council, though it does not itself like to be seen in that way, mainly on the grounds that it deals exclusively 'with broad issues of policy, not with matters which can best be dealt with by its members in direct negotiations with their steel suppliers, eg complaints'.[14] This stress on more general policy matters and the somewhat careful avoidance of the impression that it is a mere

11. Kelf-Cohen, *British Nationalisation 1945–1923*, op. cit. p. 125.
12. Tivey, op. cit., p. 155.
13. BRISCC, *Cost Competitiveness in ECSC Steel Industries*, op. cit., p. 20.
14. Ibid.

successor to the former BSC Consumers' Council, are highly characteristic: both attitudes allow BRISCC to claim greater importance than it actually has, to pursue wider interests than just passing on the bickerings of some BSC customers, and from that comprehensive point of view to make common cause with the BSC. BRISCC 'believes that it is in British steel users' interests that there should be a competitive and ultimately profitable steel industry in the UK. It seeks to work closely with British producers and all others concerned to that end'.[15] At any rate, the Council insists on being concerned not merely with what BSC does, but also to a considerable degree 'with the framework set for BSC by government'.

As an organisation, however, BRISCC appears rather insignificant. There is a chairman (Lord Marsh, who as Richard Marsh, Secretary of State, in 1967 promoted the re-nationalisation of steel; 'he might wish now he had not done it . . .', BSC), and a director (J. F. Safford), but only a minuscule staff; the address is Mr Safford's house. Council members meet four or five times a year; no other body exists to mediate between these meetings and Mr Safford's manifold activities (he even sits on a consultative committee of the ECSC Commission). The membership list of up to 16 members (1981) itself is not particularly impressive. Nevertheless, BRISCC's claim that 'its members include most of the bulk steel using industries of the UK and account for more than half UK steel consumption'[16] may be correct, since nearly half of those members are themselves associations, including the Society of Motor Manufacturers & Traders (represented by a senior member from Talbot and another from Ford). Incidentally, the membership is not entirely made up of private sector companies or associations, since the two public corporations British Shipbuilders and the NCB are also represented.

With such a rudimentary form of organisation and a total lack of statutory provisions, the director-cum-secretary possesses considerable freedom to shape the Council's activities as he sees fit (so long as they do not blatantly contradict members' interests). In fact, BRISCC's role and importance seem to rest entirely on the personality and talents of its director. He maintains contacts with the members, he talks to the BSC and attempts to impress government, he makes the proposals for the Council meetings' decisions, he initiates whatever actions there are for BRISCC to undertake. When in 1975 Mr Safford became director, he at once tried to make the best possible use of his various

15. Ibid.
16. Ibid.

'excellent connections' from his former occupations (in the City, at the Bank of England, in the NCB and as Engineering Director of NEDO), widened BRISCC's range of activities and, at the same time, re-shaped its attitude into something rather closely resembling cooperation (instead of confrontation) with the BSC. Apparently this did not alienate BRISCC's membership.

And this certainly reflects the most interesting feature of the relationships between the BSC and its industrial customers: that for years they have been quite serene, and characterised by cooperation rather than conflict. Of course, every now and then there have been tensions about BSC prices, but these were evidently not difficult to solve; in any case, they are said not to go very deep, since the big steel consumers tend to use higher steel prices to justify their own price increases. There might have been a clash of interest on the high sterling exchange rate which — in BRISCC's rather involved reasoning — was disadvantageous to UK steel consumers because it hindered imports coming in, 'for fear of dumping actions'; in this case BRISCC found no willing ear in government, which (again in the Council's view) sided with the steel producers (fearing even greater losses for BSC), nor could it in any way induce Davignon to react. But this issue, too, is far from essential, since — as BRISCC told the ITC — 'all our members prefer to buy the bulk of their steel from UK sources'; 'there are substantial advantages in convenience and flexibility in buying from a local supplier who speaks the same language and operates under the same conventions'.[17] Hence in most respects BRISCC can admit to a 'close working relationship with BSC', with whom it unites in the 'common interest' of owning an efficient home steel industry.

While on the whole this common objective has been reached already — the quality of BSC products 'is recognised by our members now to be well up to international standards' and the reliability of its deliveries has 'notably improved'[18] — there are still things to be done. For instance, the BSC has not yet made enough efforts to promote continuous casting, and this prompted BRISCC to exert 'positive pressure' on the corporation. Contrary to most domestic consumers' councils, it appears to be quite well informed about such issues. For example, it was 'appalled' that BSC was still investing capital at Consett in 1978, although it was foreseeable that the plant had no future; and BRISCC was all the more appalled that the responsible

---

17. Fourth Report from the ITC, Session 1980–81, *Effects* . . ., op. cit., vol. II, p. 218.
18. Ibid., pp. 218ff.

DoI Under-Secretary had not realised this fact and set to work to enlighten him.

Curiously enough, BRISCC sees Consett as an example of government, rather than corporation, errors; in its eyes, government has been the chief obstacle to BSC's 'gradual adaptation to the market'. Moreover, it was government which had kept the corporation from rapid modernising, by delaying BSC's development strategy; for years it hampered BSC efficiency and cost–competitiveness[19] by interventions in pricing policies[20] and closure programmes, added to an energy policy keeping energy prices high. Therefore, on the whole, attack and pressure should be directed not so much upon the BSC itself as upon the government. Hence BRISCC usually sides with the BSC and supports it against government, believing that this course has even proved helpful, since their contacts in the DoI have sometimes been better than those of the corporation (one DoI Under-Secretary having been 'an old comrade from Neddy days').

Consequently, the general as well as the personal relationship between BRISCC and BSC is at present exceptionally friendly (though 'it wouldn't help either of us to be too close: that would look like a conspiracy'). However, this has not always been the case. Both BRISCC and BSC remember that until Safford became director (and, apparently, as long as the Council was still a statutory body) relations had been far from good. The reason for this lay not only (as BSC members indicate) 'in the chemistry of people' — even though it was mainly Safford who brought about the change — but to a considerable degree in the BSC's view of the Council as superfluous if not irritating: it 'got between us and our customers', alienating them and poisoning the relationship by 'unfair rebukes' and so on. Safford himself recalls a time of 'great hostility' between BSC and BRISCC — 'it took two years to break it down'. Now that BSC is convinced that there is no longer any cause for hostility, it appreciates the benefits accruing from the Council and its work: 'They give us a balanced view of the interests of steel users', give information as to consumers' development plans and on possible consequences of BSC pricing policies; in short, they undertake to keep 'a continuous information flow' — according to BSC, from both sides, though BRISCC says regretfully that BSC does not provide the same extent of information. Yet what the corporation most appreciates is that in recent years the

19. See the relevant BRISCC paper, *Cost Competitiveness in ECSC Steel Industries*, op. cit.
20. These interventions, however, had in the short run rather favoured steel consumers!

The BSC and the Private Economic Sector

Council has been accustomed 'to defend BSC against unfair criticism' (BSC) from whatever quarter it may come.

Indeed, if BRISCC's function had been solely to mediate between BSC and its major customers, BSC feels that it could easily have done without the Council, and this is borne out by the existence of joint steering groups and similar bodies. GKN, for instance, not a BRISCC member, does not believe that the Council could improve their already first-rate supplier–customer relationship with the BSC; it has 'no need of BRISCC: would only complicate the relationship'. This leads to the question of BISPA's position within this only half-organised, yet potentially triangular relationship of steel suppliers and steel customers.

BISPA represents, as we have seen, both steel producers and BSC customers. In the consumer interest, it should sit on the Council, but only TI has become a member: representing suppliers, it ought to be subject to a consumers' council which in public statements explicitly names its tasks as being to deal 'with steel suppliers' and to 'work closely with British [steel] producers' in the interests of a 'profitable steel industry in the UK'[21], clearly including the private sector steel suppliers. However, practice is otherwise: 'our interest concentrates on BSC — not on the private steel industry', on the grounds that BSC is the market and price leader, the others being of secondary importance. Another explanation is, of course, that, as a statutory body, the Council had initially been obliged to restrict its activities to the BSC and afterwards simply continued this tradition.

Yet BRISCC neglect of the private steel industry is only half the story, for there also appears to be considerable resentment between BRISCC and BISPA. The latter (like GKN and also, in principle, BSC) judges additional industrial consumer organisations as 'superfluous', since 'the responsibility for relations to customers rests with the supplier', and in shaping those relations 'we prefer to keep our flexibility'. Apart from this, BISPA views an organisation such as BRISCC as incompatible with the principles of a free market economy; prior discussion with it of possible price increases would be 'something very uncommercial!'. And lastly it considers that BRISCC membership is too small in any case: this hints at some BISPA resentment at the fact that BRISCC members obviously buy their steel requirements from the BSC rather than from private suppliers.

More detachedly, BRISCC, while expressing regret at the absence of cooperation with BISPA, characterises BISPA as 'an extremely

21. BRISCC, *Cost Competitiveness* . . ., op. cit., p. 20.

defensive organisation', an attitude which hampers it in adopting the sensible view of what is the best for the industry. At the same time, the Council has openly supported BSC in its conflict with BISPA on underpricing. At the height of this conflict, it told the ITC in 1981 that BSC prices were still on average 'at least 10 per cent . . . above those charged by their Continental competitors in their home markets', thus putting 'UK users at a substantial competitive disadvantage in world markets . . .'.[22] Such an attitude is bound to strengthen BISPA mistrust about increasing closeness between BSC and BRISCC, and the suspicion of a possible 'conspiracy' which must inevitably seriously undermine private sector viability. It also clearly shows that the industrial steel consumers' interests definitely differ from those still struggling in the steel market in the shadow of their giant competitor BSC. Meanwhile the corporation itself attempts to placate both parties, though in present conditions it will secretly not be altogether unhappy to have a private sector ally in its intricate and at times rather awkward dealings with fellow steelmen in the private sector.

Strategies for a State-Owned Industry in a Private Enterprise Environment

Nevertheless BSC seems to have developed rather a knack of dealing with the private sector and maintaining fairly good relations with most of its customers and competitors, despite their differing interests. The hypothesis may well be put forward that relations with the private sector have on the whole been better than those with other nationalised industries (where dealings are far from harmonious, the BSC itself here being in the unaccustomed position of a customer faced with monopoly suppliers).[23] As we have seen, this has not always been the case, and such a position is by no means inevitable.

Various strategies are open to a nationalised industry in dealing with its private enterprise environment, the choice depending much on the purposes of nationalisation and the objectives it should follow as shown above (see Chapter 1, pp. 17–20). Firstly, if it is really at the commanding heights of the economy, its policies concerning industrial consumers may be so formulated as to steer development of the economy as a whole in a particular direction, thus implementing the

22. Fourth Report from the ITC, Session 1980–81, *Effects* . . ., op. cit., vol. II, p. 219.
23. It has been said for years that relations between BSC and NCB have been notoriously bad. During the miners' strike however, it seemed to be their workers/ unions rather than their managements who were at loggerheads.

government's economic, growth and/or structural (or even planning) policy. Ultimately (and in an ideal world) it may thereby contribute to the political end of achieving a different society and transforming capitalism. In the latter case especially, its policies will be certain to meet hostility from the private sector. Such a reaction, however, is much less probable where all that is involved is restructuring single industries. Throughout the last half-century, the need to restructure parts of the economy has frequently been acknowledged, although the private sector alone has not felt equal to the task, either hampered by the inherent rivalries of separate capital interests, or because of the vast amount of capital involved.

Secondly, a nationalised industry may fashion its policies so as to become a 'model competitor': perhaps in order to support a government's anti-monopoly policies, to counterbalance oligopolistic tendencies or to lead the private sector back to the 'path of virtue' of a free market economy. Alternatively, it may turn itself into a 'model employer', so helping to implement government social policies. Neither variant will be much relished by the private sector and will be judged rather as a disturbance — especially if the nationalised industry is important enough for its own influence to be felt by its compeers.

Thirdly, a nationalised industry may act as a sort of public utility to the rest of the economy, providing the necessary infrastructure, cheap energy, raw materials and so on. This is certainly the alternative most favoured by the private sector — though where the nationalised industry has no statutory monopoly it will inevitably be accused of underpricing.

Fourthly and finally, it is possible for a nationalised industry to behave like any other, 'one of them', operating 'commercially' and trying not to make its public enterprise status too much felt. Though there will always be some complaints of unfair competition — the state-owned company is, after all, state-subsidised — in such a case most of the private sector will tend to accept it and to treat it as any 'normal' enterprise.

The BSC choice among these options seems to have been clear from the start: while accepting the task of modernising the steel industry, and doing its best for the overdue process of its reorganisation and rationalisation, they nevertheless took the fourth option (see below, pp. 278ff.). The government, however, displayed some ambivalence in this respect. Initially, steel nationalisation had clearly been meant as the device for restructuring the industry, but it is equally clear that this restructuring was in no way meant to affect the remaining private companies, their structure or policies, still less those of the wider private sector surrounding the new public corporation: reorganisation was intended for the fourteen companies brought into the BSC and no more. At any rate, there were no significant moves to use the nationalised steel industry to implement any broader structural government policy, since none existed. Nor is there any evidence that it was an instrument for the patchy governmental attempts at national economic planning.[24] These had started in 1962 under the Conservative Chancellor of the Exchequer Selwyn Lloyd, with the establishment of NEDC and the subsequent 'little Neddies'. They continued with Labour's ambitious National Plan for 1965–70. Though the nationalised industries apparently felt obliged to keep to the Plan's optimistic growth forecasts and to use them as a basis for investment decisions (which quickly brought problems of overcapacity), the Plan by its nature could not materially influence their policies, nor did government use it in that way. In any event, the Plan collapsed in autumn 1966 because of a 'crisis of confidence' in the private sector of the economy. National planning has been practically dead since then: hence there was no broader framework left into which the BSC's ten–year development strategy, to give one instance, might have been embedded.

The only area where planning lingered on was prices and incomes policy. At the same time, successive governments' 'battle against inflation' seems to be the only policy area where, indeed, nationalised industries were used as tools,[25] especially by frequent interference with their pricing; complaints to this effect abound, emanating from the corporations and in particular BSC (although the policy of price restraint affecting it ended with Britain's entry into the EEC). Theoretically the private sector was subject to the same policy, yet in their case (as in that of the TUC) they were bound only by entirely voluntary 'self-discipline' (see the 'Declaration of Intent' in 1964, the voluntary wage and price restraint of 1972–73 and Labour's 'Social Contract' of the mid-1970s): the government had no means whatsoever to force them or to forbid price and wage increases. Government's only inducement for private industry to keep prices down was in fact to guarantee low costs where it could exert influence — namely, by keeping the nationalised industries' prices down. Hence in this respect few complaints have been heard from the private sector about government use of nationalised industries 'for political ends' in order to influence private sector policies: they rather relished this sort

24. See Michael Shanks, *Planning and Politics*, op. cit.
25. See, for instance, Edmund Dell, *Political Responsibility and Industry*, op. cit., p. 22

of influence. It is only now that some private businessmen (including BRISCC) criticise this government strategy as far from beneficial for the British economy since it lowered cost-consciousness in the manufacturing industries.

Successive governments have *not* used the nationalised industries, however, in any comparable way to further general social policy aims, despite more than one complaint from their chairmen to this effect: nor have they intended them to be 'model employers'. Only two, rather shortlived experiments with worker directors on the Post Office and BSC boards might have been interpreted as moves in the latter direction, yet, especially in the light of the somewhat lame reaction of even the Labour government to the Bullock Report on industrial democracy, it is doubtful whether they were ever meant to be extended to private industry at some future date. Nor can we attribute some such systematic value to the postponement of plant closures, as in the case of the BSC Beswick plants, since government intervention did not form part of a premeditated social policy pattern, but was a mere reaction to pressures from the affected regions and the plants involved (for example, by the Shelton Action Committee).[26]

On the contrary, most governments — and not just the present one — rather fend off demands for the use of nationalised industries to further more general social or structural policy aims with the argument that as industries they had to be operated commercially and not interfered with for political ends. This tendency has been particularly pronounced in the case of BSC, where governments have made quite a habit of echoing the corporation's own reasoning: that as a manufacturing industry facing tough competition it must behave just as commercially as its private competitors, in fact as any private enterprise. Hence, at least where the BSC is concerned, general government strategy has been the fourth option: to render the public enterprise, *qua* public body, as inconspicuous as possible, and to fit it perfectly into the private enterprise environment.

Yet this line has not been kept through thick and thin. More precisely: the 'one-of-them' strategy has always been modified by the other equally general tendency to use the BSC (as well as other nationalised industries) as a means of supporting the private manufacturing industries. This aim was achieved not only by the price interventions frequently mentioned here; the corporations' selling too cheap was frequently coupled with buying too dear under the constraint of 'buying British' (see above, pp. 99). In recent years the

26. See Geoffrey Dudley, 'Pluralism, Policy making and Implementation . . .', l. cit.

needs of monetary policy, as well as, in the BSC case, private steel companies' loud complaints of underpricing, have induced government to drop the policy of keeping public sector prices low. Instead, as we have seen, BSC is now used to help its private sector competitors out of their troubles, by buying plants they would otherwise have had to close at their own expense and by bearing the losses inevitably connected with the necessary rationalisation and slim-down of the steel industry as a whole.

While government ambivalence between those two strategies may have been somewhat irritating for the corporation itself, it has certainly been welcomed by the private sector. Hence the 'first-rate' relations the BSC enjoys with the majority of its private enterprise environment.

The BSC in the CBI

The private sector, then, obviously had little difficulty in accepting the BSC as 'one of them' — at any rate it was more assimilable than some other nationalised industries which, as public monopolies, may be eyed with some distrust. Prior to steel re-nationalisation in the mid-sixties, the CBI (and its predecessors) had supported the unwilling industry and, briefed by the BISF, had heavily opposed the Labour government's policy in this respect (see above pp. 118ff.). They may not have been altogether happy with the role they felt in honour bound to adopt since, like practically everyone else, they knew that the steel industry was far from efficient and that the private steel-masters were unlikely ever to undertake the long overdue reorganisation. Yet those steel-masters were, after all, part of the 'business community' whose interests the CBI was there to defend. So the CBI valiantly threw itself into the BISF's battle against government, although it may have been slightly more ready to compromise on the issue.

Immediately after nationalisation the BSC joined the CBI, the very association which had done its best to prevent the corporation coming into existence. In fact, according to information given in the BSC, it was the first public corporation not only to discuss the possible merits of joining or formally to announce its entry, but 'actually to join'. But then, the CBI had acted on behalf of those major steel companies now making up the BSC and of BISF, the majority of whose staff had become corporation personnel. Hence, in a way, the BSC's joining was no more than a continuation of the steel industry's former membership, particularly on the personal level. However, there was rather more to it than that. From the start the new corporation, most explicitly, 'wanted to establish that we are a very commercial body'; 'we are commercial manufacturers, so our assets should be part of the business community'. The main motive for joining so promptly (and apparently without internal discussion) was outwardly to play down any essential difference that might exist between a private and a public manufacturing industry, to draw a line between itself and government — and even to distance the public sector (for 'we joined taking our individual interests into account, *not* as part of the "club" of nationalised industries') — and to establish the firmest possible links with the private sector. While this move may be classed as the corporation's attempt at the earliest possible stage to determine its own identity as that of a 'normal' commercial enterprise, it was equally strongly motivated by the desire 'to be associated with industrial power' (BSC). This can only mean that the corporation expected the CBI, in one way or another, to prove an ally against government — or might even (as a BSC part-timer suspected) 'hope that the CBI could pressure government that the public corporations should be treated like private companies'. To some degree, therefore, the BSC seems to have wished for a continuation of the pattern developed before nationalisation: that of the association supporting the steel industry against government.

This does not necessarily mean that the BSC expected the CBI to 'lobby' on its behalf during conflicts with government; it is rather a matter of a climate of support, for we have seen that the corporation is 'quite used to . . . fight our own rows with government'. As a major public concern it is, after all, in a very similar position to that of any big concern which approaches government directly without the need for any intermediary association. Neither such concern in any way depends on the association's help in the event of conflict or in pursuit of specific interests, but joins to stress that it 'belongs' and that to attack one is to attack all. It finds things easier if it can claim that its own specific interests are bound up with the interests of the whole business community and that these are now are at stake.

While the motives prompting the BSC to join the CBI are clear, and the corporation apparently feels quite at home in this association, it is much more difficult to assess the view of the business community just referred to. Initially (as has been shown above, II pp. 101ff.) the rank and file membership of the CBI predecessors were by no means united in wishing to have the nationalised industries amongst them — just the contrary. Unfortunately, CBI officials are not at all forthcoming as to the development of internal relationships after the nationalised industries had joined. There are only hints from the nationalised industries that it might have been 'a mistake of the CBI to have us', since the membership was now too heterogeneous (BSC) and that internal conflict on the point continued. The general device to prevent acrimony within the membership — that public corporations should not participate in any committee discussions that might lead to 'embarrassment' — does not always seem to have sufficed, as indicated by the establishment of 'separate committees patrolling the border between the public and private sectors and promoting better relationships' between them.[27] In 1975 one nationalised industry, the Post Office, even left the CBI for a time, to demonstrate that it did not see its interests properly represented there.[28]

Contrary to expectations in the sixties, the main causes of conflict have not been matters of principle (for instance, expanding or contracting the public sector) but prices: every price increase by the corporations has caused fresh resentment. This problem, however, has proved considerably less weighty in the BSC case than with those nationalised industries which are statutory monopolies as well as a sort of public utility on whom all other industries depend. This is particularly true of the fuel industries: the outcry about high energy costs has been heard everywhere for years on end. Even the BSC complains about them: another 'joint interest' binding the corporation closely to the private sector. Of all the nationalised industries, therefore, the BSC, nearest in character and outlook to private manufacturers, seems to have presented the smallest problems of integration and the fewest conflicts with the CBI's private sector membership

---

27. Wyn Grant, *Representing Capital: The first fifteen years of the CBI*, paper presented for the British Sociological Association Conference on 'Capital, Ideology and Politics', Sheffield 8–9 January 1981, p. 12.
28. See Grant and Marsh, *The Confederation of British Industry*, op. cit., p. 102. In discussions at the International Institute of Management's Workshop on 'Employers' Associations as Organisations' (Berlin, 14–16 November 1979), Grant has hinted that the former Labour government intended to get all the nationalised industries out of the CBI.

Attitudes Towards Nationalisation

14

The Civil Servants' Views: The Controller as Banker

Our findings so far indicate that not only does the BSC try to behave as 'commercially' as possible but that most of those who have dealings with it see it, in many respects, as a 'normal' commercial concern instead of a public body as defined theoretically in Part I. This might surprise in government officials who, after all, could make use of nationalised industries to achieve broader political ends and who, to safeguard popular influence on those industries' policies, ought to lay particular stress on the latter's 'public accountability'. However, leaving the nationalised industries to act as normal enterprises seems so much simpler and spares them so much thought and energy (especially when in any case no broader long-term political ends are in view). Secondly, to insist on specific public accountability would thereupon expose most of the officials' dealings with the nationalised industries to public criticism; the feeling that they receive quite enough such criticism as it is, is another reason for keeping a low profile in this respect — they had rather not take upon themselves too much responsibility. Whilst senior civil servants concerned with the corporations appear to have taken this line practically from the start (contrary to some of their ministers), such an attitude has become still more pronounced under the present government: it is now decidedly a matter of principle.

Among the civil servants interviewed, virtually each and every one emphasised the essentially commercial character of the nationalised industries in general and the BSC in particular, and, even with some force, rejected the idea that a public corporation such as the BSC might pursue any other (*horribile dictu*, 'political') ends than 'to be efficient'. Though at times the nationalised industries seem to be 'a very political subject' (Treasury), this without question does not refer to the way in which they are run, but to the sporadic (re-)appearance

269

of nationalisation or privatisation slogans in party manifestos. Hence the government's abstention 'as a matter of principle' from formulating any objectives other than financial for the corporations; objectives are set up in 'the same way as would be done in the private sector', 'which means [they are] financial' (DoI). Another result is government determination to restrict its own role towards the nationalised industries to that of 'the banker'. Only in one interview was the government also cast in the role of a 'guarantor of the public interest' ('certainly . . .', Treasury), but this was meant to be only subsidiary, the principal role being that of a banker, looking at the corporations primarily 'from the business point of view'.

The stress on this priority ought to place the government officials involved in a somewhat awkward position, since they have admittedly never been trained to make correct judgments 'from the business point of view'. Yet while admitting this lack of expertise, civil servants ignore the consequent asymmetric relationship with the corporations' experts. Rather they veil it (from others, but perhaps from themselves too) with matter-of-fact statements about the inherent limitations of their work with respect to the nationalised industries: their job is definitely not, in their eyes, 'second-guessing' and 'doing the job of the management'; and they see as clearly nonsensical 'the government trying to run the industry, which it can't' (DoI). Much less clear is what remains for them as their proper task, and the task they can actually fulfil. For them it boils down to holding the purse-strings, though even this imperfectly, since they realise their lack of any real sanctions to enforce financial discipline. In the end, there is the slightly cynical suggestion that the difference between government control of a big private concern and of a public corporation is less substantial than is supposed. The difference appears to rest solely in the 'continuous dialogue' government officials profess to keep up with the nationalised industries.

It might be imagined that this is rather a dreary and frustrating prospect for those whose position in sponsor department or Treasury obliges them to exercise 'ministerial control' over a nationalised industry. However, theirs is not a life-long position: they don't stay in it, as a rule, much beyond three years (and in that short time may not always realise all the intricacies of their department's relationship with the corporation in question). Moreover, their various activities, from the 'continuous dialogue' with the nationalised industry's senior staff to 'briefing the minister' for countless debates and hearings are unlikely to leave much room for frustration concerning the limited nature of the job. And finally, the limitations can always be justified by the 'arm's length concept', the general rule for the British system of ministerial control. While most observers judge this concept to be 'a myth', it will live on because departments maintain and cling to it — if only on the grounds that 'you have to limit the class of things you get involved in' (Treasury). Of course, systematically the idea poses certain difficulties, since in principle it demands a clear demarcation between the sphere of ministerial powers and that of managerial autonomy, and this in fact appears impossible ('it's a relationship that you can hardly codify'; 'perhaps one needs a different system for different industries'): hence it is 'certainly not a perfect system'. Real life, however, never provides 'perfect systems' and the present somewhat muddled arrangement of 'arm's length held up in principle, and practice deviating when required by occasion' has the definite advantage of leaving 'a lot of freedom for managements to run their industry', restricting government responsibility and shielding the ineffectiveness of department control.

No one in the departments seems to realise that the latter deficiency and the lack of power over the nationalised industries — even loss-makers such as the BSC — might originate precisely in the lopsided perception of the corporations' character and the civil servants' role in this field. To define the corporations, and the BSC in particular, as entirely commercial bodies with entirely commercial objectives, and their own departmental role as supervision entirely 'from the business point of view', means, as it were, fighting on the enemy's ground, and firmly establishes the management's superiority as experts. Under such conditions, even a determination to maintain at least a semblance of control has no chance to survive long; it will be replaced — as is already partly the case — by a simple belief that management (being after all trained) will do their job properly by themselves — 'The boards try to work conscientiously as far as possible as their own masters (within the given constraints)' (Treasury). But in this context it must be borne in mind that the 'given constraints' are at the moment hardly more than previously negotiated cash limits agreed upon by the various boards.

Things might, perhaps, be different with a less commercial, more political approach. But in view of the attitude described it will come as no surprise that not a single one of the government officials interviewed professed a belief in nationalisation, or said they saw any intrinsic benefit in public enterprise. Instead, and apparently not allowing any non–commercial considerations to creep in, they all tend to take rather a critical view of nationalisation since it worsened the 'commercial [or financial] discipline', or (with respect to market developments) merely 'delayed the inevitable' (Treasury). In their eyes it has 'not (been) a success' (Treasury), particularly not in the case of the BSC, whose history is one 'of unmitigated disaster (partly because they had a grand plan and we financed it)' (DoI); hence 'I'm actually opposed against having *any* nationalised industry' (DoI).

The Private Steelmen's Attitudes: Nationalisation a Benefit or a Disaster?

The above views are echoed by private businessmen but with variations: whilst highly critical of nationalisation, they can still detect some sense in it. As we have seen, this holds particularly good for the private steelmen who, after having vigorously fought steel nationalisation at the time it was happening, have since then in the great majority come to appreciate that nationalisation in fact solved some of the industry's problems (since 'without nationalisation and public funds no reorganisation would have been possible') and had not been so bad after all. From this personal experience they have drawn the conclusion that nationalisation generally could be rather beneficial, if not even 'inevitable' — not only for public utilities (they all seem to agree that nationalisation of fuel and transport industries had been a good idea), but also in some special cases and 'for certain types of projects' in the manufacturing industries. Beyond a certain level of capital requirement and where it is a question of 'providing for the basic needs of the economy', 'you cannot leave all to the market', no matter how strongly you support free enterprise. Such reasoning, it would appear, is prompted not only by 'economic expediency' but is tinged with nationalism or patriotism, for those steelmen obviously abhor the notion of their country being left 'completely at the mercy of the giants' from USA or Japan. Furthermore, 'I have to admit that there might be a time scale where you [as a private enterprise] cannot meet short-term pressures without suffering long-term disasters' and where, therefore, nationalisation would come in useful to prevent, with public funds, the short-term pressures from having that disastrous effect.[1]

Of the steelmen interviewed, only two have declared that they see no sense — 'not in any way!' — in nationalisation ('government could

---

1. The example given (in 1981) was the NCB: 'Had it not existed, the coal mining industry would probably have disappeared completely between 1955 and 1965; but it's a very good thing that it did *not* disappear.'

make much better use of its money . . .'). Another confessed that in his younger days he was much in favour of nationalisation but meanwhile had become 'disillusioned', finding the nationalised industries' 'efficiency most unimpressive'. But then, most of those inclined to ascribe some benefits to nationalisation also find much to criticise in *existing* nationalised industries: 'The biggest failure of nationalisation was the way in which it was done!'. Such statements usually refer specifically to steel nationalisation ('it was crazy!'): one objection was that the unfortunate BSC was created 'too heterogeneous to be managed centrally, by a big head office staff'; 'you cannot run a business that way'. Hence, future nationalisation (where it will still be 'inevitable') should be carried out differently: not by establishing big public corporations (with the danger of bureaucracy creeping in and with it immobilism and inflexibility) but by forming more decentralised public enterprises less open to political influence, the state being reduced to the role of shareholder.

The private steelmen's attitudes to the BSC and their ambivalence between rather close friendship and sometimes very deep resentment has been detailed above. Suffice it here to focus on those aspects where the BSC is seen as a more or less typical example of public enterprise. The few who oppose nationalisation naturally also oppose the BSC as showing all the weaknesses 'inherent in the system', the major faults being 'lack of realism' and absence of 'commercial morality': 'The threat of bankruptcy forces on a private board a certain realism which is not existent in the board of a nationalised industry', whose managers can 'spend money on anything they want to spend it on and don't have to suffer the consequences of wrong decisions', leading to 'a feeling of grandeur'; they believe themselves capable of realising dreams and 'grand plans' which can only result in misinvestment. Accordingly, in this view it is rather 'doubtful whether government can be blamed' for all the BSC's failures, problems and inefficiencies, because at the root of them all was Sir Monty Finniston's unrealistic 'grand plan'. This he could implement without much government interference and so caused the overcapacity from which the whole steel industry is now suffering — 'that is entirely at the door of BSC'. These steelmen do not appreciate that the BSC's 'wild investment' has brought about the long overdue adjustment of the bulk of British steel-making to the technological standard reached by its main foreign competitors;[2] instead they argue — rather forgetting their own recent history — that private steel under the umbrella of BISF would have

2. See Jonathan Aylen, 'Innovation in the British Steel Industry', l. cit.

managed as well if not better had it been left alone without the threat of nationalisation.

Some of those critics go so far as to suspect that the BSC management actually prefer leading a public enterprise to being in the private sector ('a much tougher place'): 'They enjoy the cushioning effect of being in the public sector', where they have 'virtually a civil service type of employment' (and 'get index–linked pensions' which several private steelmen considered a major advantage), and where 'it would require a bloody earthquake to get you sacked'. They point to the exceedingly small number of senior BSC staff members leaving for private companies ('they don't *want* to leave . . .'), and to Finniston and Scholey, both of whom did or do 'enjoy immensely being on top of the BSC', being 'concerned with power' rather than with nasty everyday questions of finance and profit. Hence, when Sir Charles Villiers declared to the SCNI, 'We want to be commercial', 'everybody laughed . . .'. Moreover, 'I have detected changes': 'Initially there were those who said they hated nationalisation', but then adopted 'the career point of view'; now 'there are those who begin to defend it — and this attitude begins to find more adherents. BSC has bred a generation with new attitudes.'

More frequently, though, quite drastic criticisms of the commercially incompetent, irresponsible, over-centralised monster BSC are coupled with considerable sympathy for its management who, after all, have been continually hampered by government interference, delaying necessary action, counteracting commercially sound decisions on entirely political grounds, and so on. 'They've never been allowed to run their business' and have always been 'too much at the mercy of politicians' (although sometimes not even knowing 'who is your real boss'), so it's unfair to 'blame the management for doing the wrong things'. Most steelmen are absolutely sure that the BSC management 'would much rather be operating commercial rules, without interference, and without parliamentary scrutiny' (in short, without all those tedious, time-consuming processes of control) and 'more free to use their own initiative'. There may be advantages such as the index–linked pensions and the greater financial freedom; yet 'on balance, I think the average executive would still prefer to be in the private sector', where he has not only 'greater freedom to take action' but is, at the same time, really 'judged by the results of it'. The reason given is that not being sacked for a mistake has its reverse side in a serious lack of incentive; managers 'can be a roaring success and don't get a reward either'.

Hence it is judged that one of the greatest disadvantages in being in

Attitudes towards Nationalisation

a nationalised industry is that it 'breeds a civil service mentality'. All the same, the managers actually running the BSC are said by the same steelmen to be 'doing a good job' ('they've got some damned good people there!'). Incidentally, just two exceptions are named: Sir Charles Villiers ('incompetent and a total nonentity') who knew nothing about steel or about running a business and had 'no authority, not even on his board'; and 'brilliant' Sir Monty Finniston ('brilliant but in the wrong place: he should have been a professor . . .'), who knew too much about steel, became 'too expansive' and by wishing to implement his 'technological fantasies' had proved 'a catastrophe for BSC'. On the whole, however, BSC management has been 'not worse than management in any other companies, and in some cases better'.

And not only the management is better than its popular image: steelmen kindly disposed towards the BSC maintain that the corporation itself is not half as inefficient as public opinion makes out. Its losses are considered as by no means worse than those of comparable steel companies abroad (the losses being, at present, 'a function of the industry, not of the management, or of the social structure in which they are operating') and it is competitive — so much so, in fact, that several private steel firms are already complaining. Apparently, commercial inefficiency is neither 'inherent in the system' nor inevitable in a nationalised industry. Any real problems of efficiency are ascribed to the BSC's unmanageable size rather than to its public character.

In this context it is interesting to see what private steelmen think their *own* future would have been, had they been nationalised as well. Though in that case their policies 'would have depended on our constitution', they one and all believe that they would *not* have been able to follow the same policies as they have up to now — or rather, '*I* would not have followed different policies, but I believe that other policies would have been dictated'. 'If you sit on the BSC board you simply cannot take decisions that are solely concerned with profitability: it is impossible', since the statutes contain 'a set of references different from that of a private firm' (implying, for instance, the 'social objective to meet the needs of British industry . . .'), and politicians must always be reckoned with. It might have been possible to embark on bigger investment schemes ('without cost counting . . .') than could be envisaged in a private enterprise; on the other hand, 'I suspect that if we had been nationalised, we would not be in existence today', having been 'rationalised away'. Another view is that 'I would be only a general manager, more or less uninfluential, and hence losing enthusiasm and responsibility'. One of the most revealing remarks made, however, is that 'we would have been in a greater mess than BSC is!'

Therefore the obvious general impression is that 'nationalisation matters', one way or other — by hampering an enterprise's efficiency, by enhancing a certain 'social responsibility', or by enabling an industry to modernise and rationalise. The conclusion to be drawn from these considerations on 'What would have happened if . . .' is that public enterprise, contrary to what most civil servants think about it, in some respects differs essentially from private enterprise — not least in attitudes. The differences are easily seen, the list being headed by 'lacking threat of bankruptcy' and 'free credit' via 'access to public funds' ('They ask the government for £5 billion — and they get them, and nobody asks how they are spent'). This, in its turn, 'changes people's attitudes', letting them 'get out of touch with reality' ('we want to be the world leaders', or 'we need a beautiful office building' — and 'only have to ask the government for the money for that . . .'). Another possible change of attitudes — patently running counter to the first one, but apparently depending on individual predispositions — is the emergence of a civil service mentality, lacking 'dynamics', real 'involvement' or identification with their corporation (they 'take their holiday, in the midst of all the BSC's troubles', an unthinkable attitude in a private company): they are 'not forced to succeed', the survival of a public company depending 'on government policy, not on its performance'.

A third major difference is named as government's (or politicians') direct influence, together with the social obligations imposed upon a public enterprise. Notions about these obligations are somewhat hazy; apart from 'meeting the needs of the industry' the one example given is 'to provide employment' (which 'no private firm would do') though the BSC's history makes it abundantly clear that this type of social objective cannot have had much weight on its policies. As for the government's 'over-riding influence', there are those in the private sector who doubt its existence, suspecting rather — not altogether unrealistically — that the BSC is 'virtually autonomous: neither accountable to government nor to their shareholders [that is, the taxpayers]'. They tend, however, to pass over the fact that private enterprises too are not normally strictly controlled by their own shareholders; they maintain what is really an ideal state of affairs, that theirs is 'a very direct accountability'. Nor do they accept that the contrast between the interests of the private shareholder and of public controllers — 'his interest is financial success, their interests are political (the main objective there being: don't upset the voters)' —

has little foundation in reality.

While some of these differences appear rather exaggerated in the light of a public enterprise being run in a private enterprise system, on other points the private steelmen show considerable insight. Particularly interesting is their assessment that nationalised industries breed specific attitudes in their managers, a matter to which we shall return. Yet there are private steelmen who judge the difference between the two types of enterprise to be less essential than appears at first sight. They say that public sector managers 'act commercially if they are given the freedom to act'; especially in the face of competition 'the nationally owned company has to operate the same commercial rules as private ones'. 'In manufacturing industries, I don't think there should be any essential difference'; in that field a nationalised industry 'is forced to behave like a commercial unit, not like a social unit', a view to which even governments have come round 'gradually'. Big private companies like Shell or ICI may still be different because they are 'not embroiled with every politician in the country', but that does not normally lead to essentially different policies or attitudes — they all have 'a similar sort of ethos'. It is not surprising that subscribers to this view are just those who remain unimpressed by the extent of actual government influence on BSC policies. To them, the 'overriding influence' is that of the executive ('the chairman is always struggling to secure a position of influence' — though this might have been otherwise with Ian MacGregor — and 'we can leave out the board'): 'it's the executive who has an effect' and 'plays the tune, even to the DoI!'. This dominance of the executive seems to constitute the most striking parallel with private enterprise, since 'ownership as such has little relevance for the decision–making' of an enterprise, so that there is little difference 'whether it is publicly or privately owned'.

How Public Steelmen Define their own Role: 'Convergence' or an Alternative?

As for the public steelmen themselves, there seems to be no doubt at all on how they define their own job and how they wish to be seen: they 'want to be commercial', theirs is 'the same as any private sector business', their tasks are identical with those of any private sector management — 'to properly employ labour economically . . .; to remain viable; to make a profit at the end of the day; to supply a product; to collar as much of the world market as it can; and to perform in the national interest and in the interest of the corporation'.[3]

As a manufacturing industry, they 'have no future when we're not commercial', for 'the corporation's success in the market requires it to be free to behave as flexibly as its competitors'.[4] Accordingly, their qualification to run the BSC lies in just this commercial outlook: 'None of us is at all a political person. . . . I run the Corporation as best I can, with the help of my colleagues, from a commercial point of view'.[5]

The first conclusion intended to be drawn from this is, of course, that a nationalised industry's board ought to be given 'maximum freedom under the Act'[6] and not hampered by government interference and a profusion of controls. In particular, nothing should be required of the corporation that 'a private business would not dream of doing'[7] — aimed at incessant discussions and consultations, the endless provision of new papers, prognoses and so on for the department, and at the apparently arbitrary delays introduced by civil servants, 'for reasons which I find difficult to understand'.[8] This, in a nutshell, is one of the major problems of relations between a nationalised industry and its controlling minister: the industry's management put so much stress on their necessarily commercial outlook that they pretend not to understand the reasons for all the government controls and connected activities. It is not only BSC which considers that everyone would be so much better off if the government could be persuaded to renounce all its meddling, at best superfluous and at worst detrimental: for in this view the simple truth is that 'if you give good management freedom of action . . . you will get better performance'.[9]

The other consequence of this decidedly commercial outlook, and the reverse side of the BSC's particular closeness to the private sector as described above, is a rather unexpected tendency to emphasise dissimilarities with other nationalised industries, most of whom are 'service industries' as well as 'monopolies'. As a competitive manu-

---

3. First Report from the SCNI, Session 1977–78, *The British Steel Corporation*, op. cit., vol. II, pp. 386 (Villiers), 455 and 463 (Woodeson).
4. Ibid., p. 34 (BSC Memo). The 'no future' remark was made in an interview.
5. Ibid., p. 465 (Villiers).
6. Sir Monty Finniston, *Nationalised Industries: For Better or Worse*, BBC, 16 and 27 February 1977 (ms, p. 7).
7. Villiers, Second Report from the SCNI, Session 1977–78, *The British Steel Corporation*, op. cit., p. 9.
8. Finniston, First Report from the SCNI, Session 1977–78, *The British Steel Corporation*, op. cit., vol. II, p. 91.
9. Sir Denis Rooke, Eighth Report from the TCSC, Session 1980–81, *Financing of the Nationalised Industries*, op. cit., vol. II, p. 180.

facturing industry the BSC feels it has much more in common with any of the large private companies than with its nationalised counterparts, to whom it is linked solely by the 'unhealthy relationship' of 'sharing their misery'. The same attitude, however, seems meanwhile to have spread amongst public corporations, most of whom try, in public at least, to draw attention to their peculiar and altogether 'untypical' situation, so justifying their claim for 'maximum freedom to operate'.[10] This might be expected to create some difficulty for the NICG (see above, II pp. 82f.), since it can scarcely lobby convincingly for the shared interests of the nationalised industries if most of them individually give the impression that they have hardly any interests in common. As a matter of fact, the Group considers this heterogeneity as its major problem, forcing it to keep a low profile on a number of issues. In the BSC, this insight is coupled with a growing rather than lessening unease of several years' standing. Sir Monty, who claims to have been an initiator of the NICG, soon 'found there . . . that the number of things we had in common was a fair bit smaller than the number of things we did not have in common'.[11] In recent years BSC directors have been more sceptical than ever about the NICG since its practice showed that there were, indeed, '*no* real common interests'; 'and not to mince words: I found them tiresome . . .'.

Obviously, the BSC feels less at home amongst fellow nationalised industries than in the greater business community. Yet there are features of private enterprise the BSC would rather *not* share, as indicated in Sir Monty's answer to the question of what the BSC's investment policy would have been, had it been a private concern: 'The answer is that we would have done nothing if we were in the private sector, absolutely nothing'.[12] By this highly interesting remark he referred to the state of the steel industry before nationalisation: too fragmented, too cautious and without enough capital to embark on the modernisation schemes that not only Sir Monty considered necessary at the time. But his reasoning went beyond that: he actually attributed a specific meaning to nationalisation in adding that, since nationalised industries were *not* in the private sector, it was

---

10. See, for instance, a memo by the NFC of 1979 where it was stated to have 'more in common with a large conglomerate private sector organisation than with other nationalised industries, whose position is . . . protected by a monopoly.' SCNI (Sub-Committee E), Session 1978–79, *The Relationships . . .*, op. cit., p. 146 — not long after, the NFC was duly privatised.
11. Ibid., p. 59.
12. First Report from the SCNI, Session 1977–78, *The British Steel Corporation*, op. cit., vol. II, p. 53.

pointless to expect them to behave exactly as if they were; for 'if there is any sense in nationalisation, it is that during periods when life is difficult and when you still have to meet the requirements of a vital industry, vital to the whole economy, then the nation must put its hand in its pocket, it must pay for it'.[13] More particularly, 'the nation' should 'put its hand in its pocket' to finance investment enabling the industry to attain the 'technological standard' it thinks proper and which could not be attained in the private sector: in other words, public money is to finance comparatively higher-risk investment strategies.

This points to a desire in public sector managements not simply to resemble their private sector counterparts but, in a sense, to be *better off*: able to implement 'grand designs' and to reach technological optima — in fact to pursue technological optimising strategies *without* having to bother unduly about finance and risk. In the absence of a specific purpose imposed by the political authorities, they have decided on a purpose of their own — which in most cases is the achievement of technological improvement if not perfection.[14] At the same time, they expect to be shielded from market influences and private sector risks as if they were, indeed, fulfilling a public purpose. In evidence of this, there are hints that the BSC executives' opposition to Sir Charles Villiers in 1977–78 was partly due to his proposal that BSC should adapt its policies to the declining steel market, whereas the executives still clung to their ambitious development programme of the early 1970s.

Other observers — including, incidentally, Ian MacGregor — have criticised the tendency of the 'typical' public sector management 'not [to] regard itself as wholly responsible for its results or failures'.[15] This has frequently been put down to the 'demoralising' effects of government intervention. On the other hand, managements themselves complain that when high losses arose 'who was held responsible? The Minister? Not at all. The Chairman and the Board of the Corporation were held responsible for that loss'.[16] However, chairmen have not

13. Ibid.
14. In a German study of 1983–84 made with a group of students and concerning public enterprise on the local level (in a case study of the Müllverbrennungsanlage Wuppertal), we detected a similar phenomenon on the part of the management and senior staff: the 'technological ambition' (as we termed it) to attain a 'pilot function' in their field.
15. Ian K. MacGregor, *Re-Industrialization. The British Experience*, 1981 Benjamin F. Fairless Memorial Lectures, Carnegie–Mellon University, 1982, p. 21.
16. Finniston, SCNI (Sub-Committee E), Session 1978–79, *The Relationships . . .*, op. cit., p. 61.

really been held responsible — in the sense that they were sacked — nor can it really be maintained that managements have been made irresponsible by frequent government interference. Instead, they have operated in a vacuum allowing them to develop their own objectives; they have defended the pursuit of these aims and shielded their own maximisation strategies against government intervention, by dint of superior (technological) expertise; but at the same time they have used their state-owned and state-financed situation, together with their alleged public accountability, as a protection against the realities, risks and vagaries of market developments.

Needless to say, these matters are hardly ever voiced openly by public sector managements. Yet there are sufficient hints that, for some of them at least, the notion of 'managerial autonomy' includes freedom not only from government control, but also from the controls inherent in the market system. But such an extensive notion of managerial autonomy is not altogether limited to managers of public enterprises: it is a typical feature of large-company managements, and obviously regardless of ownership. Students of big private joint-stock corporation behaviour have long since detected a pronounced tendency in managers, (1) to rid themselves of ownership control (which becomes easier as shares are distributed more widely) and (2) to emancipate themselves from market pressures. At the same time, the managers have been found to identify strongly with the firm itself, whose well-being may or may not be a mere projection of their personal ambitions, chiefly their desire for success and security: these goals suggest, besides the emancipating strategies just mentioned, (3) policies not of short-term profit maximisation but of longer-term expansion and technological optimisation.

Depending on the economic or financial situation and the state of the market, the similarity may well end here. For while public and private sector managers will all *wish* for the same 'maximum freedom to act' unhampered by any external pressures, the likelihood as well as the methods of obtaining autonomy will differ. For a great nationalised industry it may suffice just to neutralise the influence of the minister; as long as consistently high losses are not shown, this will not require much effort. For such an organisation, with no direct threat of bankruptcy, the 'market forces' will in the medium-term, hold less relevance; so that less effort to stabilise them will be required than in the case of a large private sector company which, particularly in the fairly typical oligopoly situation, must carefully build up more or less elaborate strategies to neutralise competition and stabilise its market environment. To achieve such stabilisation — and to satisfy a personal need for security — private sector management strategies will frequently show a certain conservatism, a bias towards risk–avoidance. Of course nationalised industries may adopt similar policies, but in that case, they will originate from bureaucratic inertia (and occasionally from fiscal constraints) rather than be forced upon them by a need to circumvent adverse effects of market pressures. In short, nationalised industries, operating under insufficient control, *can afford* to be more radical and innovative; their managements have more elbow–room for experiment and hence their attitudes and behaviour can be more 'entrepreneurial' than those of their private sector colleagues. The whole history of the BSC (not least its recent attempts to cope with the steel crisis) provides plenty of evidence for this perhaps unexpected suggestion. To prevent any misunderstanding, it may be emphasised that this does not mean that public enterprises are necessarily more innovative than comparable private concerns; but, to repeat what has been said, it simply means that they can more easily afford to be so — and, if not, this is a matter of personalities or internal problems, rather than of external constraints and forced strategies.

This leads back to the theory of 'convergence' referred to twice already in the course of this investigation (see above I, pp. 20ff., II, pp. 106f.). On the surface, public sector managers certainly do show a marked tendency to adapt to the commercial outlook of private sector managements; equally, both groups certainly 'converge' in their striving for managerial autonomy. Yet this is only part of the story. Perhaps from a wish not only to equal but to outstrip their private sector colleagues and to prove that, though dismissed as alien and not up to the private enterprise system, they are at least *as* efficient, public sector managers tend to develop an orientation towards technological achievement, a 'technocratic' attitude that seems rather characteristic. Basically many private sector managements may have a similar orientation, but for two reasons they are less likely to exploit this urge to the full. Firstly, they are less constrained to a continual demonstration of this kind of efficiency to the world at large; and secondly they are less independent of external constraints. It might be said that the public sector managers' desire 'to belong', to be just like the others, prompts them to overtake those others and become *plus royaliste que le roi*. They can do this, however, only so long as they retain their own additional measure of independence: the freedom both from effective ministerial control and from any immediate control through market forces. Their apparent ability to boast this freedom is rather a damning verdict on the practice of public enterprise whose main distinction and *raison d'être* is, theoretically, to be found in its external political guidance.

These are, of course, very tentative conclusions, drawn mainly from studying the BSC and its economic and political environment, and are not to be taken as a 'general theory' on the conduct of public enterprise. Attitudes and behaviour will vary considerably with the size, type and organisational formula of the public enterprise (whether an entire nationalised industry, or a smallish firm organised along the same lines as its private competitors). Nevertheless, the 'technological ambition' suggested here as a typical feature has been detected not only in some British nationalised industries but also in German municipal enterprises (see above, fn 14). Given the characteristic independence of most public enterprises, behaviour will vary greatly with personalities involved and may be further influenced by individual backgrounds (private sector, 'career' or otherwise; see above II, pp. 104ff.), yet the evidence is too slender for any indications on that head. It may be that the 'technocratic' attitude is most strongly developed in the 'career men' reared in the state–owned industry (and hence most used to its peculiarities); but since all the BSC executive directors have fallen into this category, no comparisons are possible.

When asked directly to comment upon the essential differences between a nationalised industry and private enterprise, some BSC members do, in fact, hint at their being able to be 'more radical' in regard to both modernisation programmes and capacity reductions — though, at the same time, 'being much in the public eye, we must be more cautious about changes of direction', as having 'to do so much explaining'. This obligation, coupled with the 'political overtones' always to be reckoned with, are considered a serious disadvantage, which none the less would appear to be outweighed by the fact that they 'can't go bust' or, less racily, by their 'ability to stand a long–term negative cash–flow', the major reason, indeed, why they can afford to be 'more radical'.

Interestingly enough, it is the members voicing these opinions who obviously feel that such advantages cry out for special justification and who consequently point to their necessarily greater 'social responsibility': 'A public corporation has to have a public conscience' — and not only towards its employees but also towards the regions in which they operate (especially in 'areas of economic difficulty')[17]. They also stress 'anti–pollution measures' and the like. Such 'heavy social re-

---

17. Thus they point to having in 1975 formed BSC (Industry) Ltd, without government urging and with the express intent to create new jobs in areas where the BSC was closing plants. Meanwhile this subsidiary has become 'self-supporting' and no longer funded by the BSC (See BSC, *Report and Accounts 1983–84*, p. 18).

sponsibilities' are definitely seen as 'desirable' ('a lot of private sector companies' behaviour is unacceptable!'), although 'this can contradict the need to be profitable: you have to do both, earn profits *and* be socially responsible . . .'.

There are others, however — and, most interestingly, mainly non-executive directors — who maintain that a public corporation ought not to be expected to show any specific social responsibility, 'not more than a private company which has to show it anyway'. In fact, *any* large organisation, public or private, whose decisions were of great importance for the community, should display a responsible attitude, 'but the *chief* objective of a public corporation is commercial efficiency'. Incidentally, the civil servants who at the time of the main interviews still sat on the board were of the same opinion, though with a slightly different reasoning. To them it was not only that the fact of social responsibilities being 'loaded on the corporations' would contradict the rule of minimum cost criterion; over and above that consideration they considered it 'dangerous if the BSC started on other objectives', for, since only government has the common weal at heart, 'it is for government to respond to social consequences' — otherwise you get 'a completely mixed picture'.

Even if there are those who own up to a public conscience it is certainly somewhat far-fetched and an over-idealised view to detect a well-defined motivation of this type in public sector managers, as Richard Pryke did in 1971, in saying that their objective was not profit maximisation, but 'to meet the needs of the consumer at the lowest possible price, to act as model employers and in general to help maximize the welfare of the nation' and that they showed a 'social service orientation' enforced upon them through the 'machinery of public accountability'.[18] It would be truer to say that such an orientation is just what all the devices to obtain public accountability did *not* achieve, for none of them, nor any of the agents of ministerial control, provided the corporations with any clear idea about their own public purpose or about the purpose of nationalisation as such. If some managers do, in fact, show a 'social outlook' this — like the 'technocratic attitude' — is in no way imposed upon them but is a matter of the economic or financial situation, or the state of the market; probably it depends more on personality and 'background' than on any other factor.

At any rate, contrary to Pryke's expectation, none of the BSC members puts the social outlook in the first place. Instead, the 'main

---

18. Richard Pryke, *Public Enterprise in Practice*, op. cit., pp. 460f.

objective' of a public corporation, 'not different from any in the private sector', is in their eyes 'to be commercially successful' and 'to earn a profit'; 'whether you are public or private, your pride is to make the company efficient.' A public corporation is primarily a commercial body, as most of their officials never tire of emphasising; it has 'to be efficient, competitive and profitable', 'otherwise it has no reason to exist'. In this context, only one of all the BSC directors maintained, quite simply, that the 'BSC's first objective is to make steel . . .'. Similarly, only one suspected that, as profitability is the corporation's main objective, privatisation would be the only logical consequence.

This indicates that there are public-sector board members who cannot see any sense in nationalisation, or in their own being in the public sector at all: 'You should ask whether the government should own companies', for if such companies are (as everybody seems to agree) both commercial and commercially successful, then 'there is no reason for the government to own them!' Others appear rather indifferent, finding it 'no different here than in any private enterprise', seeing no particular advantages or disadvantages,[19] and give the seemingly impartial technician's point of view: 'All I say is try and make a success of it once it is nationalised'.[20] But to nearly all of them, if there *is* any sense in nationalisation it is of the 'fire brigade' type: 'You do not nationalise. . .until there is something seriously wrong';[21] then the government steps in to give financial help — there is no more to it than that. Anything else is merely accessory.

---

19. MacGregor, Fourth Report from the ITC, Session 1980–81, *Effects* . . ., op. cit., vol. II, p. 200.
20. Finniston, SCNI (Sub-Committee E), Session 1978–79, *The Relationships* . . ., op. cit., p. 61.
21. Ibid; see also above, pp. 279f.

IV

The Meaning of Nationalisation

Summary 15

Underlying this study has been the idea (outlined in Part I) that public enterprise is inherently distinct from private enterprise in that the former is provided with a public purpose and subject to political guidance, and that its *raison d'être* and the justification for public ownership lie in just this distinction. Starting from this basic assumption, we have endeavoured to investigate (1) the actual operation of the essential processes of public control and joint decision-making, (2) the 'triangular' relationship of public enterprise in a private capitalist environment with government and the private sector and (3) the attitudes of those involved and, more specifically, the relevance of the attitudes of the 'public businessmen' for the actual conduct and character of public enterprise.

The evidence already available (not least in various reports) has concentrated almost exclusively on the first of these questions, and is rather daunting — not only where the British experience is concerned (see I, pp. 75ff., above). As for the British system, all observers — even those within the nationalised industries — agree that its most characteristic feature is the *lack* of effective public control. Most of them unite in naming as the major weaknesses of ministerial control (as described in Part II):

— a general 'lack of purpose and objectives' for nationalised industries individually and as a whole;
— a lack of long-term development concepts;
— a lack of coordination of their policies;
— a lack of economic efficiency and economic and social performance control;
— too many short-term interventions;
— too much financial control, leading (inter alia) to the Treasury gaining a pre-eminent role without being a real partner of the boards;
— a general 'blurring of responsibilities' between the boards and all those concerned with them;

— and finally, a similar general lack of expertise in the controllers.

Hence the general contention that, while the Morrisonian arm's-length concept envisaged guidance (and consequently, a certain closeness) on policies, while keeping a distance concerning day-to-day management, in practice, matters developed just the other way round: into a somewhat contradictory mixture of 'beyond arm's-length' where policies are concerned, in short a lack of policy guidance, and considerable closeness on quite a few aspects of day-to-day management, in other words, a good deal of government 'interference'. The latter is seen as the more damaging because of frequent policy changes and because interventions tend to relate less to the nationalised industries' specific situation than to the various governments' 'day-to-day' economic policies, budgetary needs or considerations of electoral policy. The many reforms undertaken during the last twenty years, according to the same observers, fell short of improving matters since they did not tackle the faults mentioned above but did no more than tighten the financial framework. Though aiming at the invention of a system of 'control by formulae', to circumvent the tricky problems of face-to-face relationships of controller and controlled and to minimise the necessity of 'interference' — an object which most observers thoroughly approve — they are on the whole judged to have been failures both as regards this aim and on the objective of achieving greater financial discipline.

Observers disagree, however, on the question of power balance between boards and ministers. Some maintain that, notwithstanding the general ineffectiveness of control, the main drawback of the present system is the number of short-term political pressures on the boards, 'excessive government intervention', the fact that all too often political considerations by government have prevailed over the boards' sound commercial judgment, thus rendering the nationalised industries commercially inefficient. Due to the chairmen's frequent vociferous complaints, and the support usually given them by the SCNI, this seems at present to be the majority view. Yet every now and then others have thought that the boot is on the other foot, believing that excessive managerial autonomy rather than excessive government influence lies at the root of most problems of ministerial control. Recent exponents of this view are Dudley and Richardson who accuse the departments of passivity rather than of a constant urge to 'meddle', and of a general reluctance 'to challenge the judgment of the NIs' or 'to claim more authority for themselves'; they conclude from the nationalised industries' superior expertise and other advantages (amongst them not least 'the ability of an NI to embarrass a Minister by discreetly circulating stories to the media about his proclivity for "interference" ') that 'bargaining between the government and an NI is rather like a duel between someone wielding a broadsword, and an opponent holding a rapier (with the blood usually being spilled behind closed doors)'.[1]

The findings of the present case study on British Steel has put some of these contentions into perspective and unveiled several not unimportant points of variation from the general impressions listed above. However, the system of ministerial control in the case of the BSC bears out the general report of its ineffectiveness. Neither does the department expend energy on 'policy guidance' or *ex-ante* control, nor is there any real joint planning: the DoI has shown, indeed, a marked passivity so far as any input of its own is concerned, as well as a marked reluctance to meddle with what it calls the 'running of an industry'. Hampered in addition by its lack of expertise, it has been content to leave all the planning and practically all the decision-making to the corporation's experts. This picture of passivity and restraint has not been altered by the fact that for several years government representatives have been sitting on the corporation board: they found themselves rather at the bottom of the power hierarchy there and seem mainly to have listened, adopting the role of a kind of third-class members, simply 'improving the flow of communication'.

Those energies the DoI and the Treasury's PE Group could not spare for thinking about concepts, programmes and policies were directed to improving financial control (in recent years not altogether unreasonably, seeing that the BSC has incurred such heavy losses). Yet financial monitoring, too, has fallen somewhat short of expectations — despite the fact that no nationalised industry has ever been subjected to such close, continuous and detailed monitoring as has the BSC during the past five years. Not even cash limitation provided the tight grip on the corporation's course which might have been envisaged, since (apart from being negotiated with the corporation itself and hence to some degree according to the latter's wishes) it had to be raised every now and again when the BSC found it difficult to remain within the stated limits. Unless the corporation is to go into liquidation, the government has obviously no choice but to yield in financial as well as in most other matters.

This indicates that the power balance between government and even a loss-making nationalised industry is more asymmetric than

---

1. G. F. Dudley and J. J. Richardson, 'The Political Framework', in J. Grieve Smith, ed., *Strategic Planning in the Nationalised Industries*, London, 1984, pp. 112–34.

most observers have tended to believe. In the strict meaning of the word there is no 'balance' at all, but a definite superiority of the nationalised industries' managements over the supposed controllers, who lack real power. The government may be able to force upon the boards lengthy bargaining processes and its much castigated delays, there may even be fierce battles — yet in the end the managements usually win. For the government has only two weapons it can brandish, the power to dismiss and (in the case of the BSC) to liquidate. As somewhat extreme measures, either of these must represent a last resort and consequently both have so far been avoided; they provide no more than an unwieldy 'broadsword', a mere threat. What the controllers clearly lack are more tactical 'middle range' weapons.

The reason for this power asymmetry is to be found not only in the absence of penalties, nor simply in the controllers' lack of expertise and dependence on the boards for adequate information. The overall problem of how to keep the experts disciplined is aggravated by the attitude towards nationalisation found among the civil servant controllers, and by their definition both of the character and tasks of nationalised industries and of their own role in this field. To define the corporations as entirely commercial bodies whose objectives are primarily and almost exclusively commercial, whilst the civil servants' own role is seen as supervision from the 'business point of view', must without fail establish and confirm the superiority of the business experts, and reduce the controllers to rubber-stamping the managements' 'sound commercial judgment'. Civil servants themselves may see such an attitude as alleviating their task, since it obviates the necessity of developing their own concepts about the nationalised industries' purpose and objectives. On the other hand, if they had their own long-term concepts generally agreed to be directed to the common good and fitting into the government's broader policies, they would stand on much firmer ground in dealing with the necessarily particularist views and schemes of those business experts.

The problem of inferior expertise might be shown to be further aggravated by another specific feature of the British administrative system: job rotation, meant to minimise the danger of a client–patron relationship. While it must be seriously doubted that it in fact achieves that end — on the contrary, it may serve the better to conceal tendencies towards clientage — job rotation undoubtedly serves to frustrate the acquisition of adequate expertise. Moreover it leaves civil servants with little incentive to enter wholeheartedly into the matters they have to deal with in such short–lived appointments. Hence this British peculiarity contributes considerably to government passivity towards the state industries, as well as to a more general 'government inertia'.

Inertia and immobility seem to contradict another feature usually said to characterise the British political system: 'adversary politics', or the frequent and (on the surface) radical policy changes resulting from party confrontation. However, apart from causing an extremely short-term orientation making formulation and implementation of consistent programmes impossible — so, in fact, adding up to immobility — 'adversary politics', as found by this case study, proved less of a problem for the nationalised industries than was expected: the impact of policy changes is far less marked than public sector chairmen or critics of the British system of ministerial control have led the country to believe (however traumatic the policy switch involved with the Beswick Review may have been for the BSC). There is, of course, the 'political football' of nationalisation and de-nationalisation, although in the thirty years from 1950 to 1980 this has been a major issue only with respect to steel. On existing nationalised industries, policies of both major parties have been remarkably alike in emphasising their commercial character and financial viability. Most of the policy changes that did affect them (in the case of the BSC there were only three) either arose from overall economic policy forced on governments, regardless of their political colour, by changing economic conditions, or else were reactions to corporation losses or to unforeseen social consequences of its strategies; these too were forced upon governments by altered circumstances. Such adaptations to external changes are inevitable and would have to be accepted by any industry, public or private. As for politically induced changes, even corporation members acknowledge that there is 'more continuity than people think'. The 'pressures of the political market', visualised by some authors as the main problem of state enterprises,[2] pushing them here and there according to erratically changing voter preferences, are obviously neutralised by other factors: by the general ineffectiveness of ministerial control, by government inertia and not least by the managements' highly-developed ability to resist political influence.

It is these same factors which render the much-criticised 'government interference' less relevant than expected: just another case of public opinion being led astray by the biased statements commonly put out by public sector chairmen. In most instances their various complaints have been about the legitimate exertion of ministerial veto rights (with the one exception of interventions in the corporations'

2. See Charles K. Rowley, *Steel and Public Policy*, op. cit.

pricing policies), though even these have often had very little effect. Nor are the famous 'arm-twisting' and 'backstairs pressures' really an issue: in the first place the chairmen themselves usually prefer to negotiate behind closed doors and, secondly, they are perfectly able to resist the pressures. The BSC at least, since Sir Monty's row with his sponsoring minister in 1975, cannot be said to have been forced away from the path dictated by its own 'commercially sound judgment' or to have suffered from a surfeit of interference. The 'meddling politician' is an ogre invented for the benefit of the public: in real life, on the contrary, ministers and senior civil servants dealing with the nationalised industries are much more inclined to stand back, happy if there are no losses or other disasters which leave them no choice but to become involved.

This points to a lack of intent in the matter of control, which we had expected to characterise the controllers. It is certainly in line with the attitude towards the nationalised industries found in the civil servants interviewed; yet, at present, in the case of steel this is only part of the truth. There is still no intent to exert antecedent control in the sense of political guidance, nor to impose concepts evolved by the department itself, nor to meddle with the corporation's non-financial objectives; with the present government this lack of intent is even an explicit 'matter of principle'. But for some years now there has been every intention to tighten financial control and to find ways to establish control over efficiency and performance. The one ray of light shed on the otherwise bleak picture of ineffectual control is the obvious determination of the DoI/DTI to improve the system of financial monitoring and the flow of communication and information, and by dint of the new device of performance indicators, at least to hold the corporation more firmly to its own targets.

However, this study has not been solely directed to problems of ministerial control. Public enterprises in private capitalist economies must reckon with the private sector, and this will influence both their policies and attitudes — all the more so in the case of a manufacturing industry not enjoying a monopoly. Our assumption was that, as a rule, public sector managements will emphasise their nearness to the private sector, try to establish good relations with them and strive to appear as 'one of them'. Hence, indirectly, the private sector might be assumed to exert more influence on a nationalised industry than can the government. In the case of the British steel industry, though, which is only partly nationalised, a rather intricate combination was to be expected, covering highly involved commercial relationships, friendly personal relations and sharp conflicts over policies and principles — a mixture whose impact on BSC behaviour and self-definition would not be easy to predict. The peculiar closeness of public and private sector in this industry might breed friendship and cooperation, that is, might neutralise the public–private divide, or bring about the very opposite, increasing resentment and aloofness and so widen the gap between the two sectors.

The findings show that both possibilities occur, yet in varying degrees and unequal distribution. The BSC's commercial relationship with many of the private steel companies is, in fact, extremely involved, with BSC being at the same time supplier, competitor, occasionally customer and partner in joint ventures which, in turn, supply, compete with and buy from both parent companies. This kind of complexity will even grow for some time to come, with the birth of further Phoenixes and similar ventures, and will lead to solid cohesion between steelmen across the division of sectors. Accordingly most of them stress the extremely good personal relations between them and their help in overcoming all sorts of problems; if the old 'camaraderie' stemming from a shared past (in the BISF, for instance) may have worn thin with new generations coming to the top, its place has increasingly been taken on both sides by the club (or even family) feeling occasioned by close and intricate commercial connections. Nevertheless there are many conflicts (or, more exactly, complaints from private sector steelmen), mainly about pricing and 'overlap', and some resentment against the public 'big brother' who is seen to have substantial 'unfair advantages'. This undercurrent occurs widely among the private sector and reflects the mixed feelings of smaller competitors and business partners contemplating any giant concern.

Though resentment grew in the early 80s with the worsening of the steel market, in most cases it did not lead to open conflict and hostility. In fact, one finding of this study is that the real interest divide is not between the public steel industry and its private counterparts; it is the split within the private sector itself. Most steel firms are ready to cooperate with the BSC to the point of throwing in their lot with it in joint ventures — either because they depend on BSC as their major supplier, or because cooperation is for them a means of sharing in state subsidies, or else because they see in this course a safe chance of getting out of the steel business. Notwithstanding all their complaints about this or that BSC policy, they are rather kindly disposed towards the corporation and inclined to defend it even against government; and they definitely approve a part of their industry — bulk steel-making — being in public hands. Their statements indicate that life would be less easy for them without their helpful if somewhat clumsy big brother; consequently, they visualise the future BSC as a sort of public utility, tailored to the needs of the industry.

By contrast, the minority group see no sense whatever in public enterprise, but attack the BSC as a matter of principle and point out its manifold inefficiencies and 'unrealistic' policies; they also accuse the government of meddling with the rightful sphere of private enterprise and continually subsidising an ailing giant. These are the few large, commercially independent companies, defining themselves as competitors and not customers of BSC (without feeling compelled to complain about 'overlap') and viable enough not to harbour a wish to step out of the steel market by placing part of the burden on BSC's shoulders; joined with them are a number of smaller yet highly competitive firms in special steels with a similar sense of independence.

In point of fact it seems doubtful that this can truly be termed an 'interest divide', since the group is not marked by lines of probable cleavage such as that between steel-makers and steel processors, between BSC competitors and non-competitors or between large and small companies. Rather, the division appears to be one of (perhaps intrinsic) attitudes towards nationalisation. Instead of contributing to the overdue 'tidying up' of the steel industry by reducing its internal conflicts, the nationalisation of a major part created a further conflict on whether to oppose or 'incorporate' the state-owned concern. And this new dividing line appears to have grown as haphazardly as the public-private boundary itself, with respect to product areas. This necessarily raises the question of whether it makes sense to divide an industry by only partial nationalisation. Obviously, problems enough arise in operating a public enterprise in a private capitalist environment; they are multiplied when a single industry is divided into a public and a private sector — the more so if, as in the case of steel, the division does not follow functional lines.

Complex relations such as those described here are of particular importance in considering attitudes and self-definition of public sector managements and the 'public good' aspect of public enterprise — or for the question of convergence. Thiemeyer[3] and other authors consider convergence, more precisely the public enterprises' adaptation to the behaviour of their private competitors, as an inevitable law of development in capitalist economies; competition would force upon all of them the same micro-economic rationality, profit-maximising strategies and 'commercial' attitudes; in other words, though being (in

---

3. See Theo Thiemeyer, 'Privatwirtschaft und Gemeinwirtschaft', l. cit.

principle) 'foreign bodies' within capitalist systems they would have no other chance of economic survival than by assimilation. Since this law would be reinforced by social factors — such as public sector managers quite naturally accepting the caste of private sector managers as reference group and hence adapting to the latter's group norms, status criteria and so on — it must be expected to have more weight in proportion to the closeness of a public enterprise to its private sector environment, and to the number and complexity of points of contact, social and commercial, between the two spheres.

However, this law might be modified by the particular backgrounds of public sector managers. Looking in Part II at the careers of the 'men at the top' in British nationalised industries, we found the interesting (though not surprising) trend of a growing proportion of 'career men' at high levels; amongst the executive board members they now form the majority. This fact may not in any way have significantly influenced their attitudes; on the other hand, it may be that the career men, reared in a nationalised industry, develop particular attitudes and their own *esprit de corps*, making them partly resistant to the tendency of convergence; on the other hand, they may seek to over-compensate for the taint of 'unequal birth' and adapt all the more strongly to the norms of the private business world.

Since there is hardly a nationalised industry in the UK closer to the private sector than the BSC, its attitudes may be expected to be practically identical with those of the private steelmen. At the same time, however, the overwhelming majority of BSC management are what has been termed career men. One interesting finding in this study is that, though outwardly and publicly stressing their 'commercial' character and their 'normal businessman's' outlook, BSC executives do feel somewhat set apart, and definitely appear to develop attitudes of their own. In this way the two possibilities mentioned above may be said to combine: their 'esprit de corps' results, in a way, from a desperate striving to belong to the 'business community'; they try so hard to be as efficient, innovative and 'entrepreneurial' as their private sector colleagues that, by their attitudes (though not necessarily in success!) they outdo them in their clear–cut orientation towards technological achievement. They even evince their own rudimentary 'public conscience', though that is certainly not the predominant attitude.

What is most remarkable about this is that, no matter what particular attitudes exist, they are not a long–term reaction to political guidance; they stem precisely from the lack of that discipline. Such attitudes are rooted in the wide freedom enjoyed by public sector managers: in addition to political autonomy so far as ministerial influence is concerned, the managers are largely free on the economic level. They need not fear bankruptcy and have no need to evolve cautious market-stabilising strategies: accordingly, they can afford to embark on policies of technological maximisation. Unfortunately the technocratic attitude[4] which appears to be growing in nationalised industries was not the original purpose of nationalisation, which would have demanded quite another set of attitudes — strong social responsibility, macroeconomic orientation and the like — which do not grow naturally but have to be politically enforced. In a way, that same technological orientation found in BSC managers is nothing but 'over-convergence'. While in itself not altering the trend to 'cold commercialisation', it does show that convergence is not inevitable and that a different orientation of public enterprise is possible.

Before concluding this summary, the nature of the evidence used in the present study should be considered. There is, firstly, a certain administrative bias since civil servants were interviewed, but no politicians. This procedure appears justified by the dominant role of senior civil servants, who actually carry out all monitoring of nationalised industries. Every incoming minister is briefed by them; any radical policy changes desired by a new minister are usually very much toned down by them; changing posts even more frequently than the civil servants (the DoI/DTI is under the fifth Secretary of State since 1979), ministers have to rely most heavily on their advice and, as a rule, are 'house-trained' by them in no time. Other politicians — MPs, especially — cannot be said to have much influence, in view of the restricted role of Parliament in the affairs of nationalised industries; they can scarcely do anything but criticise policies and performance, or pass on constituents' complaints and demands to the minister. Still, the findings concerning 'government interference' might perhaps have taken on a somewhat different aspect, had we taken into account all the various *attempts* in this field by politicians. Moreover, there is every reason to expect politicians' attitudes towards nationalisation to differ (in one way or another) from those of the civil servants who have to deal with it.

Secondly, the present work has a tendency towards centralism in that it has concentrated on policies and influences aimed at BSC as a

4. Leonard Tivey, one of the very few authors to notice a similar trend, has termed it 'technocratic nationalism'. See 'Structure and Politics in the Nationalised Industries', l. cit., p. 174.

whole, and on decision-making processes on a central level, that of the main board and head office. Evidence of the situation at local level might also have altered the picture painted here — again especially on the issue of 'interference'. But simultaneous investigation of influences, processes and relationships on central, regional and local levels would have been beyond the capacity of a single researcher. Hence it may rest with future studies into those other levels to modify our findings. Nevertheless, we may be allowed to doubt whether local politicians are significantly more successful than central government in their attempts to influence BSC.

Finally, it should be borne in mind that the conclusions here reached about the attitudes of public sector managers rest on a small amount of evidence — on hints given here and there — and are as yet rather tentative. Since the matter of individual attitudes is crucial for any theory of public enterprise not restricted to stating norms of behaviour, much more research remains to be done in this field.

The Future of the BSC and the Nationalised Industries

16

In a way public enterprises like the BSC are hybrids — not so much between the private and the public sector (or 'the state' and 'the market') as between private enterprise and 'public enterprise as it ought to be'. What then will be their future? Will they sooner or later assimilate totally to private companies (as most of the German state enterprises on the federal level have already done), or will they even cease to exist?

As for the BSC, since 1981 the Secretary of State has had the power to liquidate the corporation, judged by some as the best course to take with this seemingly inefficient and loss-making giant. However, the BSC has been much less inefficient than its critics habitually make out. Out of its heritage of a fragmented industry with many out-dated plants, it has achieved a technological standard that compares not unfavourably with most of its competitors within the UK and outside; it is well ahead of many of them in the task of adjusting capacity to a declining market; and its losses which appear so huge at home are by no means greater than those of comparable steel concerns abroad. Hence, in economic and technological performance, the BSC's history is not altogether one of 'unmitigated disaster'. It is not unimportant in this context that most of its customers have for some time found the BSC 'satisfactory to deal with'.

What speaks even more strongly against the likelihood of imminent liquidation is the fact that hardly anyone seems interested either in transferring all bulk steel-making to the private sector, or in wholly renouncing any British steel-making industry. Most of those concerned — particularly the private sector steelmen — deem it impossible as well as undesirable that BSC should cease to exist. Nearly all of them, however, are equally certain that considerable restructuring is necessary and that it is coming, the first steps having already been taken. Some even believe that, far from vanishing, the BSC will in the long run swallow up the rest of the indusry, either directly or through joint ventures; yet this view of BSC's 'taking over the whole thing' is a polemic assessment rather than a factual prognosis of future developments, depending mainly on how the Phoenixes are judged.

This, then, is the most likely course of events. The BSC will almost certainly be stripped of all its fringe businesses (in fact, most of them have gone already) and most of its downstream activities; the steel industry as a whole will thus be reshaped following functional lines into fewer and more evenly matched groups, leaving just the 'heavy stuff' wholly in the public sector. Whereas the fringe businesses are actually privatised, the downstream activities will be 'hybridised' since they will be joint ventures after the Phoenix model: formally in the private sector (as companies subject to the Companies Act) but to a considerable degree run with BSC — and hence public — funds.

There can be no more than speculation concerning the nature of the public-private divide in that future reorganised industry, on how the hybrids will emerge or on what the remaining public corporation will be like. A functional division of public and private sector might allow the BSC remnant — by then a sort of public utility to the private companies — to be transformed into a true 'public enterprise under public control' and to be exploited by government to influence the development of the industry. Unfortunately, this possibility appears merely theoretical, since in the first place the sphere of public influence would in that case be somewhat limited; secondly, there might not be much left of a private sector to steer and influence. Thirdly, reorganisation into a few evenly-matched groups might easily lead to a tight new steel cartel, including BSC. This would bind the public and the private firms more closely together than they already are today and give the BSC better opportunities of evading public control on the grounds not only of economic necessities but of its external agreements. The main snag, however, will probably be the hybrids, which will be closely linked with each other as well as with the BSC by a system of interlocking directorship, thus rendering public control wholly fictitious; the more so since the hybrids themselves, as Companies Act companies, are under no obligation of 'public accountability'. So the most likely outcome is that the meaning of nationalisation will come to be stripped of all connotations of public guidance and control, and will be reduced to a means of subsidising an industry.

As for *all* the nationalised industries and the British system of ministerial control, there has recently been a move to alter the existing characteristically 'muddled approach' (BSC). Some years ago, *The Economist* demanded that 'a choice must be made. Either the management of the industries must be brought far closer under ministerial control with board chairmen seen more as permanent secretaries to their sponsoring ministers or the industries should be privatised lock, stock and barrel'.[1] The present government has always been bent on the second alternative; but finding that privatisation was not to be achieved in a couple of years, that in some cases it was heavily opposed by chairmen, and that it was in any case not possible with every nationalised industry, the government now seems to think it necessary to take steps towards the first alternative as well. In autumn 1984, a Treasury plan was leaked, relating to new legislation on the nationalised industries to replace the various Nationalisation Acts by one single comprehensive Act. The most striking element of the proposals is that sponsoring ministers should be empowered to dismiss chairmen and board members of corporations failing to live up to their targets — or, as *The Economist* suspects, those who disagree with government policy.[2] Secondly, ministers would be able to order disposal of any part of the corporations' assets (whereas up till now, except for the BSC under the 1981 Act, corporations have, by statute, to be kept intact). Thirdly, the vague statutory requirement to 'break even' would be replaced by more specific financial objectives which could then be legally enforced; fourthly, the nationalised industries are to abide by standardised accounting rules.

These plans, obviously leaked prematurely (and probably by the NICG), are postponed, however, for a year at least and will not be reintroduced before the 1985/86 parliamentary session; the general view is one of serious doubt whether the future Bill will have much in common with the original proposal, since the postponement seems to be due almost entirely to the 'angry reaction'[3] from the nationalised industries' chairmen. Their opposition has for more than a decade prevented the implementation of every scheme of structural reform. And their arguments against this new move read the same as before: the proposals 'would infringe their ability to act in a commercial manner and threatened to make them "political pawns" in the hands of ministers',[4] or, in the words of NICG's Jim Driscoll, 'would have meant a substantial shift away from the traditional arm's length relationship between the Government and the state sector'.[5] Any new Bill will now be drafted only after extensive consultations with nationalised industries and the NICG, and is 'expected to be watered down considerably'.[6] Accordingly, while the government for once

1. *The Economist*, 13 June 1981, p. 26.
2. *The Economist*, 22 September 1984, p. 31.
3. See *The Times*, 5 October 1984.
4. Ibid.
5. *The Financial Times*, 5 October 1984.

appears to have acknowledged the need for a stricter curb on state industries (even though its chief motive is all the better to abolish them), its plans are likely to be thwarted by those industries' resistance. This opposition is not, as Dudley and Richardson assume, prompted by an 'understandable lack of enthusiasm for major institutional reform, reflecting a weariness with a long history' of proving such reforms as never coming up with 'workable solutions'[7] (there have not, after all, been all that many reforms of the institutional framework of ministerial control). Rather, the corporations are inspired by a fierce determination to defend the autonomy gained throughout their long existence. They are experienced in such fights and have fended off so many attempts to gain a hold over them by individual measures and by many proposals of reformation, that there is indeed every reason to expect them to succeed once again.

Meanwhile the government tries to press on with privatisation, yet with mixed results. In March 1984 it sold Scott Lithgow, one of British Shipbuilders' shipyards, for a mere £12m (the yard having lost £66m in 1982–83);[8] in June 1984 Enterprise Oil, previously hived off from British Gas, was put on the investors' market where its shares did not reach the price the government had hoped for — this aroused some criticism about its policy of 'cheap sales';[9] the same objection recurred when Jaguar was hived off from BL and sold, critics alleging that this sale would needlessly cheapen the eventual privatisation of BL itself. Early in December the shares of 50.2 per cent of British Telecom were floated with considerable 'technical' success (in fact, it was one of the biggest ever floatations); yet again there was the rebuke of 'give-away prices', a charge that seems not altogether unjustified in view of the 45p premium gained in the 130p shares on their first day in the City. Hence part of the public now complain about 'a depressingly long line of unhappy privatisation pricing', said to have lost the taxpayer '£2.1 billion through the entire five year privatisation programme'.[10] Still to come may be de-nationalisation of the National Bus Company, and the sales of the Trustee Savings Bank, British Airports, further parts of British Shipbuilders and the ordnance factories. The next Phoenix in the steel industry, however, has been delayed for the moment (see above, III, pp. 237f.); and plans to sell

6. Ibid.
7. Dudley and Richardson, 'The Political Framework', l. cit., p. 132.
8. See *The Economist*, 31 March 1984, p. 34. For privatisation implemented before 1984, see the list given in Part II, pp. 89f., fn. 38.
9. *The Economist*, 30 June 1984, p. 19.
10. 'How Maggie sold us out £2bn short'. *The Guardian*, 4 December 1984.

further parts of British Gas (and its eventual total break–up) are at a standstill because of Sir Denis Rooke's firm opposition, in which, incidentally, he is supported by his sponsor department. Nor does privatisation necessarily mean that the companies are off the government's hands: Aerospace, for instance, received a state subsidy of £250m *after* de-nationalisation, in March 1984.[11] Since the government tends to retain a qualified minority stake in most of the companies it has sold or intends to sell, it is likely to continue feeling financially 'responsible'. Hence, as in the Phoenix case, 'hybridisation', rather than privatisation, would be a more precise term for its policy.

Another area where government plans seem to hang fire is that of deregulation and liberalisation. In the case of Telecom, the intention to heighten competition is (despite the creation of Mercury) again somewhat 'watered down' owing to the corporation's resistance (its officials own privately that they 'don't wholly like' the scheme), while 'Nobody is daring to introduce much competition into the gas and electricity industries'.[12] In these instances, the corporations' opposition combines with fiscal interests, for the Treasury may expect a higher price for BT and other state businesses if their monopoly power remains intact: 'So there is a conflict between the short-term wish to cut public borrowing and the long-term aim of a more . . . competitive economy.'[13]

However scanty the information about the processes for or against de-nationalisation, it indicates that the future of the nationalised industries as public corporations or as organisational entities is less in jeopardy than the government's determination to privatise might lead one to expect. Where the government does not succeed in persuading the boards that the sale of assets is the most sensible course, or that they would be better off in the private sector, it is not easy to achieve privatisation, as the British Gas rows show. As public sector executives are wont to stress their commercial character and their desire to be treated 'commercially', not all of them are averse to a transfer into the private sector (witness Lord King of BA and Sir George Jefferson of BT, who obviously like the prospect); nor do they all oppose the hiving-off strategy, since it may help them towards circumventing their cash limits, or provide a means for a long-wanted capacity reduction. But, as in most other respects, it is very difficult for government to get its way against unwilling chairmen.

11. See *The Economist*, 3 March 1984, p. 36.
12. *The Economist*, 10 November 1984, p. 17.
13. *The Economist*, 24 November 1984, p. 16.

What is very much at risk, however, is the 'public enterprise' character of the surviving public corporations, and this is closely linked to governments' ability to get their way and to the effectiveness of public control. The NEDO verdict in 1976 that the nationalised industries are 'not effectively required to account for their performance in a systematic or objective way — whether it be to Parliament, to Ministers, to other legitimate groups or to the wider public',[14] is still valid, even in the teeth of the last two governments' determination to tighten the financial grip at least. In a way the corporations are still left in a 'minimising environment, with few rewards for success and negligible sanctions for failure';[15] however, they need no pity on that score, for they have neatly managed to fill the vacuum with maximising concepts providing their own rewards, or have used their autonomy to behave as 'commercially' as their private sector environment and share its intrinsic reward system.

14. NEDO, *A Study of UK Nationalised Industries*, op. cit., pp. 38f.
15. Ibid., p. 40.

The Meaning of Nationalisation in Capitalist Societies

17

The shortcomings of ministerial control, government's inability to impose strict discipline on the nationalised industries, its lack of sanctions to impose on them, clearly contradict the *Instrumentaltheorie* of public enterprise (see Part I). Not only adherents of that theory, though, but most authors dealing with public enterprise in a theoretical and systematical way unite in the view that public control, political guidance, the fulfilment of public tasks and the direct contribution to the objectives of the society are constitutive for the notion of public enterprise, that this is where they differ from private enterprise, and that without all this, when they are exactly like any private enterprise, there is no justification for their remaining in state ownership. As *The Times* once commented, on the policy of commercialisation of the nationalised industries, 'This in itself makes a strong case for denationalization'.[1] Is this book, then, another vote for privatisation?

In fact, few practical differences still exist between public and private enterprise, where they are similar in size, market position and type of industry. If comparatively small and under competitive pressure, they operate the same 'commercial rules'. If large concerns, both tend to maximise their own particular, internally dictated objectives (market share, 'security', technological achievement and so on) and to emancipate themselves from public, market and all other external control, even from their owners' control; both defend their autonomy with various, and usually successful, strategies and show equal capacity in obtaining public help and subsidies in times of stress. Experts in the subject usually stress the presence or absence of the threat of bankruptcy as the main (in some respects the only) difference between public and private enterprise; but beyond a certain size, level of employment and economic importance, the state cannot afford to let a private concern collapse, any more than a nationalised industry, as the reality in most Western countries shows. Others — mainly private

1. *The Times*, 9 September 1968.

sector businessmen or their allies — maintain that the real difference lies in state industries being even less controlled than private concerns, since they can more easily evade market control and also, because of the 'soft' control system at the top, have a softer internal control system.[2] In contrast, public sector businessmen would lay stress on the 'political concerns' for ever facing them and the endless enquiries and discussions they have to endure; for them, these considerations would represent the actual difference from the private sector and would at the same time constitute their own main disadvantage.

While there is some truth in all these views, in the last resort it seems that the difference boils down to little more than the 'continuous dialogue' which the government tries to keep going with its state industries — and even that only whenever they make losses or otherwise cause trouble. At the same time, the meaning of nationalisation itself comes to no more than subsidising certain industries. If the term has any further meaning, it is to give them a period during which they may force through modernisation or rationalisation — or (to put it in a more pointed and polemic way) a sort of technological art for art's sake. The question may well be asked whether this is sufficient justification for the existence of state industries. Where public enterprise is not endowed with a public purpose but is expected basically to behave like any 'normal' enterprise — and when there is no 'particular benefit . . . in public expenditure, other than in the rate of return it produces',[3] — then there is certainly some logic in privatisation.

On the other hand, as recent British experience shows, privatisation does not seem to make much difference: it does not cancel the need for public funds to support certain concerns or industries, nor does it restore vigorous competition and the healthy discipline of market forces. Hence it may reasonably be argued that as long as neither effect is guaranteed by merely selling public assets to the private sector, the state had better refrain from such a course and so retain a minimum control over the way in which public money is spent. There is also a third view, that 'the technocrats win, whatever happens',[4] whether there is nationalisation or privatisation, attempts to regulate or deregulation; so the whole question might be dismissed as unimportant,

---

2. See, for instance, Rhodes Boyson, ed., *Goodbye to Nationalisation*, op. cit., p. 5; John B. Heath, *Management in Nationalised Industries*, op. cit., p. 10.
3. P. Shelbourne (BNOC), Eighth Report from the TCSC, Session 1980–81, *Financing of the Nationalised Industries*, op. cit., vol. II, p. 17.
4. Leonard Tivey, in a talk to the Birmingham branch of the Fabian Society, 21 March 1980.

except for crude budgetary reasons.

Still, there might be ways to implement some degree of public control and thus partly restore the meaning of nationalisation. In this study, we have repeatedly emphasised the significance of the newly evolving system of performance indicators: this, duly extended, combining the measurement of financial and economic performance with 'social accounting', and backed up by suitable targets, may provide the informational basis for effective control which has so far been lacking; similar considerations have become apparent in Germany regarding a *gemeinwirtschaftliche Rechnungslegung*. Coupled with wider publicity, this kind of specific reckoning could eventually result in forcing a real 'public accountability' on nationalised industries.

Several prerequisites are necessary, however, before public control can be made effective. There must, firstly, exist an intent throughout in the political system to control nationalised industries. The mention of so basic and self-evident a requirement should be superfluous, yet most of the time there has been an obvious lack of such intent, not only in British governments; for the present government, it is still restricted to matters of finance. The second prerequisite is that the nationalised industries' targets should be well-known and clear; this means that governments must overcome both their reluctance to direct their thoughts and energies towards purposes, aims and policies of the industries, and their tendency to avoid public commitment here and elsewhere. Thirdly, governments would have to alter their lop-sided idea of public enterprises as entirely commercial bodies and cease to see the necessary supervision over them as solely 'from the business point of view', a view which inevitably and substantially weakens their position. So long as government defines its own role as that of 'banker', it may reasonably be asked why it does not wholly renounce ministerial control, leaving the job to the bankers who have the proper training. Breaking up this limited view and developing a more comprehensive concept of control is the only way to tackle the problem of handling the business experts. This will in no way provide an instant solution to the overall problem of how the experts are to be controlled, but unless this first step is taken there will be no answer at all. In short public enterprise, which at present is treated mostly as a normal business, rather than as the often-quoted 'halfway house' between the state and the private sector, must decisively be perceived and also dealt with as occupying 'its rightful place in the public sphere where it truly belongs'.[5]

5. W. Thornhill, *The Nationalized Industries*, op. cit., p. 189.

There is no great hope that these prerequisites will be realised or that ministerial control will be made effective in present Western societies, one reason for scepticism being grounded in certain weaknesses of the political system. The shortcomings of the British political system, with respect to the guidance of nationalised industries, have been described in some detail above (Part II, pp. 93ff.) and need not be repeated; it will suffice here to point out the more general features common to most parliamentary democracies. Particularly when coupled with two-party systems, they typically breed a short-term, piecemeal orientation of policies, for party competition forces politicians to look first and foremost to the next election; so that they react to short-term pressures from various sides, without thinking of the more distant outcome. This tendency does not square with the necessary mid- or long-term planning of nationalised industries and makes it unlikely that government will apply thought-out concepts to the industries — the more unlikely since, similarly in the interest of electoral policy, party politicians shun public commitment to comprehensive plans (which inevitably antagonise one group or another).

Another snag deriving from the political arena is that issues such as the operation of public enterprise fall into two categories: either they are of minor significance in voter preferences and, hence, for party strategy (the German case); or else they figure prominently in public opinion and party dogmas (the British case, at least with respect to the principle of nationalisation). The first will result in a failure of intent in dealing with the subject, the second in a lack of consensual policies, both of which will ultimately make for inertia and immobility (although in the latter case this may be concealed by a good deal of windowdressing), rather than for active guidance of nationalised industries (or, more generally, for actively shaping future developments). Charles K. Rowley has argued that it is practically impossible to run state industries efficiently in modern democracies (see Part I) since they would be 'subjected to all the pressures of the political market place', with governments not hesitating 'to intervene to ensure that voter preferences are observed, even at very considerable costs in terms of sacrificed social welfare'.[6] In party democracies, it may indeed be very difficult if not impossible to submit public enterprises to effective public control, but, contrary to Rowley's assumption, this is because of the government inertia they cause rather than because voter preferences will push governments to interfere with them; and, left in a political vacuum, such enterprises seem quite able to operate

6. Rowley, *Steel and Public Policy*, op. cit., pp. 268ff.

in an extremely efficient manner.

It might be expected that such deficiencies would be neutralised by the administrative system, which is said to gain in political influence to the same degree that the parties appear unable to 'govern'. Similar deficiencies are found, however, in the administrative apparatus. Firstly, if it works on the principles of political patronage or job rotation, it looks no further forward than do the politicians; secondly, there are hardly any incentives for civil servants to develop the long-term concepts the politicians fail to provide. On the contrary, left by the latter to deal with nationalised industries, they will tend to choose the course of least exertion (on their part) and least resistance (on the part of their clients), which usually means that they adopt the clients' own ideas. This is a major reason for the prevalent 'commercial' definition of the nationalised industries and makes it particularly hard to overcome. Thirdly, again because they themselves are left without 'political guidance', they will have little inclination to look beyond those interests they are dealing with at any one moment, or to fit their different activities into broader policies. Thus doubly predisposed to identify with the interests in question, they will transfer the particularistic segmentation of society into the government machine, dividing it up into islands of clientage. The outcome is less (as Richard Rose suspects) 'government by directionless consensus'[7] than (non-) government by particularistic and uncoordinated fragmentation, which, again, cannot but lead to immobility. Furthermore, this is not only a matter of aggravating, instead of neutralising, the defects of party government: clientelistic fragmentation here adds to the problem of how to control the experts, that of 'how to control the controllers'.

Yet one should not be too eager to allocate the blame entirely to party democracy: the phenomenon just mentioned is more general than that. We have spoken of the lack of overall political guidance: responsible both for that shortcoming and for the fragmentation is the asymmetrical relationship between state and economy in capitalist societies and the resulting inherent limitations on political action.[8] In economic systems directed by the autonomous investment decisions of (private) capitalists, governments inevitably depend on the latter rather than the other way about, particularly (1) if economic develop-

---

7. Richard Rose, *The Problem of Party Government*, New York, 1974, p. 424.
8. For what follows, see H. Abromeit, *Staat und Wirtschaft*, Frankfurt/New York, 1981, pp. 21ff.; idem, *Theses on the Restrictions of State Capacity to Act in Contemporary Capitalism*, paper presented at the ECPR Workshop 'Industrial Society and Theories of the State', Lancaster Joint Sessions, 29 March–4 April 1979.

ments force political agencies to intervene in the economic process, (2) if a 'commercial' orientation and the consequent norm systems prevail in the society and (3) if the state is seen as responsible for economic failure and success, that is, if its legitimacy largely rests on its ability to deal with economic crises and its promise of economic growth. These factors cast governments in the role of a central coordinator of economic processes; but in fact they are unable to play that role, since most decisions of economic relevance rest with the autonomous capitalists and can only marginally be influenced. Hence the state's regulatory activities will be restricted to sanctioning those decisions or, at most, toning down their negative effects. This limitation is, of course, enhanced by the state's financial dependence in that it has no resources other than taxes.

Yet public enterprises might provide a source of income for the state, so lessening its financial dependence and, if spread further in the economy, might also lessen its other areas of dependence, since it might in that case *directly* influence a number of investment decisions. This, however, is exactly what is so difficult to achieve. For public enterprises to survive economically in a private enterprise environment, they have to adopt a 'commercial' (that is, profit-orientated) stance similar to that of private capitalists (which, as shown in practice, holds good even for most of the state–owned public utilities); if not, they will in all probability draw heavily on public funds, and so sharpen the state's resource problems. At the same time, extending public ownership with the express aim of altering the capitalist logic of the system may provoke reactions from the private sector which will render any such attempt futile long before it has a chance to succeed. It is no coincidence that such state enterprises as do exist in Western societies were typically created because the firms or industries concerned had run into severe difficulties, rather than from any political or 'ideological' reason, and that they characteristically occupy a minority position forcing them to adapt to the majority: either behaving like any private concern, or else supporting private industry, but always settling down as part of the 'business community'.

Consequently, governments face the same problems with respect to private as well as 'state capitalists': both of them act autonomously, largely independent of political influence, both overcome the relatively helpless political authorities by unanswerable arguments of 'economic necessities', and quite successfully exploit (and hence particularise and 'colonise') the administrative machine in their own interests. Ownership, it seems, matters little so long as the logic of the system is intact; and, what is more, ownership alone cannot alter this logic. Instead, the lack of power we have found to be characteristic of sponsor departments in their dealings with nationalised industries is not so much intrinsic to their particular relationship, but rather derives from the general lack of the state's power within capitalism — and this too forms part of the same logic.

At the end of Part I we concluded from theoretical considerations that, from every aspect, the crucial question concerning public enterprise is that of political guidance. Without this guidance there is no hope of a solution to any of the problems of public enterprise, which must moreover in that case run a severe risk of losing its *raison d'être*. Our somewhat daunting conclusion is that, given the existing system, it is exactly this political guidance of public enterprise whose practical possibility is very much in doubt. Little short of an earthquake seems necessary — a major change of attitude at the very least, for to alter the structural inhibitions of public control the first step is to identify the obstacles and look beyond the *status quo*.

Accordingly, this book is not so much a vote for the privatisation of public enterprise as an urgent appeal to find a new meaning for the nationalised industries which will transcend their mere commercialisation, which is, after all, no more than 'back-door privatisation'. Then comes the need for energy in holding fast to their newly-found purpose. In other words, despite all structural problems, public enterprise should be given a fair chance.

Appendix

Appendix I BSC management organisation, April 1985

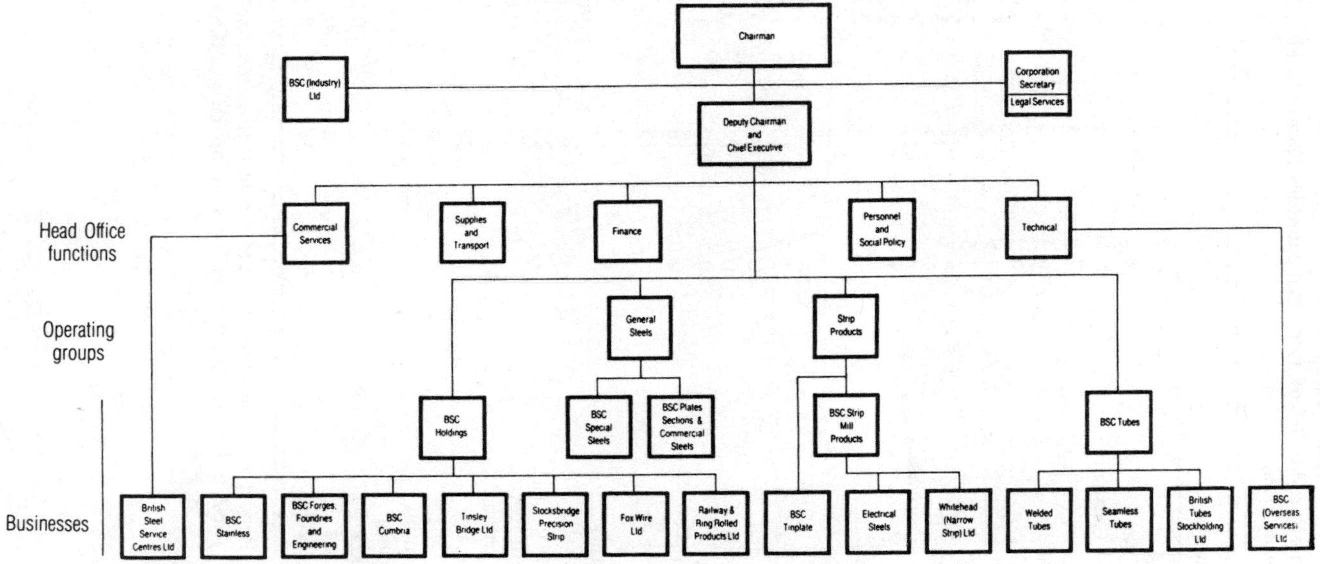

Head Office functions

- Chairman
- Deputy Chairman and Chief Executive
- Corporation Secretary / Legal Services
- BSC (Industry) Ltd
- Commercial Services
- Supplies and Transport
- Finance
- Personnel and Social Policy
- Technical

Operating groups

- British Steel Service Centres Ltd
- BSC Holdings
- General Steels
- Strip Products
- BSC Tubes
- BSC (Overseas Services) Ltd

Businesses

- BSC Stainless
- BSC Forges Foundries and Engineering
- BSC Cumbria
- Tinsley Bridge Ltd
- Stocksbridge Precision Strip
- Fox Wire Ltd
- Railway & Ring Rolled Products Ltd
- BSC Special Steels
- BSC Plates Sections & Commercial Steels
- BSC Tinplate
- Electrical Steels
- Whitehead (Narrow Strip) Ltd
- BSC Strip Mill Products
- Welded Tubes
- Seamless Tubes
- British Tubes Stockholding Ltd

313

Appendix

Appendix II Steel production of individual countries (% of world production)

(Rank)	Country	1960	(Rank)	1981
1	USA	26.1	2	15.4
2	USSR	18.9	1	21.0
3	West Germany	9.9	4	5.9
4	UK	7.2	9	2.2
5	Japan	6.4	3	14.4
6	France	5.0	7	3.0
7	China	4.9	5	5.0
8	Italy	2.5	6	3.5
9	Belgium	2.1	15	1.7
10	Czechoslovakia	2.0	10	2.2
11	Poland	1.9	8	2.2
12	Canada	1.5	11	2.1
13	Luxemburg	1.2	25	0.5
14	East Germany	1.1	21	1.1
15	India	1.0	16	1.5
16	Sweden	0.9	26	0.5
17	Austria	0.9	24	0.7
18	Brazil	0.7	12	1.9
19	South Africa	0.6	18	1.3
	Romania		13	1.8
	Spain		14	1.8
	South Korea		17	1.5
	Australia		19	1.1
	Mexico		20	1.1
	North Korea		22	0.8
	Netherlands		23	0.8
	Hungary		27	0.5
	Taiwan		28	0.4
	Argentina		29	0.4
	Bulgaria		30	0.4
	Turkey		31	0.3
	Finland		32	0.3
	Venezuela		33	0.3

Source: Second Report from the Industry and Trade Committee, Session 1982/3, *The British Steel Corporation's Prospects*, op. cit., p. 108 (note by T.A.J. Cockerill).

Abbreviations

ABCC	Associated British Chambers of Commerce
AG	*Aktiengesellschaft*
ASW	Allied Steel and Wire Ltd
AUEW	Amalgamated Union of Engineering Workers
BA	British Airways
BEC	British Employers Confederation
BISF	British Iron and Steel Federation
BISPA	British Independent Steel Producers' Association
BL	British Leyland
BNOC	British National Oil Corporation
BOAC	British Overseas Air Corporation
BP	British Petroleum
BR	British Railways
BRISCC	British Iron and Steel Consumers' Council
BSC	British Steel Corporation
BSSC	British Steel Service Centres Ltd
CBI	Confederation of British Industry
CEEP	*Centre Européen de l'Entreprise Publique*
CEGB	Central Electricity Generating Board
CPRS	Central Policy Review Staff
C&AG	Comptroller & Auditor General
DoE	Department of Energy
DoI	Department of Industry
DoT	Department of Trade
DTI	Department of Trade and Industry
ECSC	European Coal and Steel Community
EEC	European Economic Community
EFIM	*Ente partecipazioni e finanziamento industria manifatturiera*
EFL	External Financing Limit
ENEL	*Ente Nazionale per l'energia Elettrica*
ENI	*Ente Nazionale Idrocarburi*
FBI	Federation of British Industries
FRG	Federal Republic of Germany
GKN	Guest Keen & Nettlefolds
GÖWG	*Gesellschaft für öffentliche Wirtschaft und Gemeinwirtschaft*
ICI	Imperial Chemical Industries

Abbreviations

IDAC	Import Duties Advisory Committee
IRI	*Istituto per la Ricostruzione Industriale*
ISB	Iron and Steel Board
ISC	Iron and Steel Control
ISD	Iron and Steel Division
ISCGB	Iron and Steel Corporation of Great Britain
ISTC	Iron and Steel Trades Confederation
ITC	Industry and Trade Committee
IWP	Integration Working Party
JSG	Joint Steering Group
MMC	Monopolies and Mergers Commission
MP	Member of Parliament
NABM	National Association of British Manufacturers
NBPI	National Board for Prices and Incomes
NCB	National Coal Board
NCC	National Consumer Council
NEB	National Enterprise Board
NEDC	National Economic Development Council
NEDO	National Economic Development Office
NFC	National Freight Corporation
NI	Nationalised Industries
NICG	Nationalised Industries' Chairmen's Group
NIO	National Industrial Organisation
PAC	Public Accounts Committee
PAU	Public Appointments Unit
PDC	Public Dividend Capital
PE Group	Public Enterprise Group
PSBR	Public Sector Borrowing Requirement
RAG	*Ruhrkohle AG*
RIPA	Royal Institute of Public Administration
RRR	Required rate of return
RTB	Richard Thomas & Baldwin
RTZ	Rio Tinto Zinc
SCNI	Select Committee on Nationalised Industries
TCSC	Treasury and Civil Service Committee
TDR	Test discount rate of return
TGWU	Transport and General Workers Union
TI	Tube Investment
TUC	Trades Union Congress
VEBA	*Vereinigte Elektrizitäts- und Bergwerks AG*
VIAG	*Vereinigte Industrie-Unternehmungen AG*

Bibliography

Abromeit, Heidrun, *Staat und Wirtschaft*, Frankfurt/New York, 1981
—, *Theses on the Restriction of State Capacity to Act in Contemporary Capitalism*, paper presented at the ECPR Workshop 'Industrial Society and Theories of the State', Lancaster Joint Sessions, 29 March–4 April 1979
—, 'Unternehmerverbände', in Manfred Schmidt (ed.), *Westliche Industriegesellschaften*, Pipers Wörterbuch zur Politik, vol. 2, Munich/Zürich, 1983
Acton Society Trust, *Nationalised Industry. The Men on the Boards*, n.p., 1951
Albu, Austen, 'Ministerial and Parliamentary Control', in Michael Shanks (ed.), *The Lessons of Public Enterprise*, London, 1963, pp. 90–112
Aylen, Jonathan, 'Innovation in the British Steel Industry', in Pavitt, Keith (ed.), *Technical Innovation and British Economic Performance*, London/Basingstoke, 1980, pp. 200–34
Backhaus, Jürgen, 'Ökonomik der Sozialisierung', in Gert Winter (ed.), *Sozialisierung von Unternehmen*, Frankfurt a.M., 1976, pp. 25–118
—, *Öffentliche Unternehmen*, Frankfurt a.M., 1977
Barlow, Sir William, 'The Problems of Managing Nationalised Industries', (Lecture to the RIPA), London, 26 January 1981, (ms.).
Barry, E. Eldon, *Nationalisation in British Politics*, London, 1965
Bell, J.D.M. (Electricity Council), 'The Development of Industrial Relations in Nationalized Industries in Postwar Britain', in *British Journal of Industrial Relations*, vol. XIII, 1975, pp. 1–13
Berkovitch, Israel, *Coal on the Switchback*, London, 1977
Blank, Stephen, *Government and Industry in Britain. The Federation of British Industries in Politics, 1945–1965*, Westmead, 1973
Blankart, Charles Beat, *Ökonomie der öffentlichen Unternehmen*, Munich, 1980
Boswell, Jonathan S., *Business Policies in the Making*, London, 1983
Boyson, Rhodes (ed.), *Goodbye to Nationalisation*, Enfield, 1971
Brittan, Samuel, *Steering the Economy*, London, 1969
Brümmerhoff, Dieter and Heimfried Wolff, 'Aufgabe und Möglichkeit einer Erfolgskontrolle der staatlichen Aktivität', in *Zeitschrift für die Gesamte Staatswissenschaft*, vol. 130, 1974, pp. 477–93
Bryer, R. A., T. J. Brignall and A. R. Maunders, *Accounting for British Steel*, Aldershot, 1982
CEEP (ed.), *Les Entreprises Publiques dans la Communauté Européenne*, Paris, 1967

Bibliography

—, *Gegenwärtige Probleme der öffentlichen Unternehmen in der Europäischen Gemeinschaft. Dokumentation: VII. Kongreß CEEP, 16.-19.6. 1975, in London*
—, *Jahrbuch 1981: Die öffentlichen Unternehmen in der Europäischen Gemeinschaft*, Brussels, 1981
—, *Die öffentliche Wirtschaft im Europa der Gemeinschaft — Bilanz und Ausblick. Dokumentation: IX. Kongreß der CEEP Athen '81*, Berlin, 1982
Clegg, H. A. and T. E. Chester, *The Future of Nationalization*, Oxford, 1955
Cockerill, Anthony and Aubrey Silberston, *The Steel Industry. International Comparisons of Industrial Structure and Performance*, Cambridge, 1974
Coombes, David, *State Enterprise: Business or Politics?*, London, 1971
Darnell, H., Tudor P. Miles and M. Campbell Morrison, *Steel: The Future of the UK Industry*, London, 1984. (Ed. by Technical Change Centre)
Dell, Edmund, *Political Responsibility and Industry*, London, 1973
Dudley, Geoffrey, 'Pluralism, Policy Making and Implementation: The Evolution of the British Steel Corporation's Development Strategy with Reference to the Activity of the Shelton Action Committee', in *Public Administration*, vol. 57, Autumn 1979, pp. 253-70
Dudley, G. F. and J. J. Richardson, 'The Political Framework', in J. Grieve Smith (ed.), *Strategic Planning in the Nationalised Industries*, London, 1984, pp. 112-34
Eichhorn, Peter (ed.), *Auftrag und Führung öffentlicher Unternehmen*, Berlin, 1977
—, et al., 'Probleme der Eigenwirtschaftlichkeit öffentlicher Unternehmen', in *Politische Vierteljahresschrift*, Sonderheft 8/1977, *Politik und Wirtschaft*, Opladen, 1977, pp. 65-75
Esser, Josef, Wolfgang Fach and Werner Väth, *Krisenregulierung*, Frankfurt, 1983
Fienburgh, Wilfred and Richard Evely, *Steel is Power*, London, 1948
Finer, S. E. (ed.), *Adversary Politics and Electoral Reform*, London, 1975
Finniston, Sir Monty, *Nationalised Industries: For Better or Worse*, BBC, 16 and 27 February 1977
Fischer-Winkelmann, Wolf, *Gesellschaftsorientierte Unternehmensrechnung*, Munich, 1980
Foster, C. D., *Politics, Finance, and the Role of Economics*, London, 1971
Friedmann, W. G. and J. F. Garner (eds.), *Government Enterprise. A Comparative Study*, New York, 1970
Garner, Maurice R., 'The White Paper on the Nationalized Industries. Some Criticisms', in *Public Administration*, vol. 57, Spring 1979, pp. 7-20
—, 'The Financing of the Nationalized Industries: Note on the Report of the Treasury and Civil Service Committee', in *Public Administration*, vol. 59, Winter 1981, pp. 466-73
—, 'Auditing the Efficiency of Nationalized Industries: Enter the Monopolies and Mergers Commission', in *Public Administration*, vol. 60, Winter 1982, pp. 409-28
GÖWG (ed.), *Entstaatlichung, Verstaatlichung, Status quo — Europa wohin?*, Baden-Baden 1982
—, *Kontrolle öffentlicher Unternehmen*, vol. I, Baden-Baden, 1980; vol. II, Baden-Baden, 1982

Bibliography

Glyn, Andrew and John Harrison, *The British Economic Disaster*, London, 1980
Goldschmidt, Dietrich, *Stahl und Staat*, Stuttgart/Düsseldorf, 1956
Grant, Wyn, *Representing Capital: The first fifteen years of the CBI*, paper presented for the British Sociological Association Conference on 'Capital, Ideology and Politics', Sheffield 8–9 January 1981
—, and David Marsh, *The Confederation of British Industry*, London/Sydney/Auckland/Toronto, 1977
Hanson, A. H., *Parliament and Public Ownership*, London, 1961
Harlow, Chris, *Innovation and Productivity under Nationalisation*, London, 1977
Harris, Nigel, *Competition and the Corporate Society. British Conservatives, the State and Industry 1945–1964*, London, 1972
Hayward, Jack, 'Institutional Inertia and Political Impetus in France and Britain', in *European Journal of Political Research*, 4 (1976), pp. 341–59
Heal, David W., *The Steel Industry in Post War Britain*, Newton Abbot, 1974
Heald, David, '*The Economic and Financial Control of U.K. Nationalised Industries*', in *The Economic Journal*, 90, June 1980, pp. 243–65
Heath, John B., *Management in Nationalised Industries*, Second NICG Annual Lecture (25 March 1980), NICG Occasional Papers No. 2, London, 1980
Himmelmann, Gerhard, 'Gemeinwirtschaft, Wirtschaftsdemokratie, Wirtschaftsplanung', in Joseph Huber and Jiri Kosta (eds.), *Wirtschaftsdemokratie in der Diskussion*, Cologne, 1978, pp. 209–22
Hirsch, Joachim, *Staatsapparat und Reproduktion des Kapitals*, Frankfurt a.M., 1974
Hoffmann, Eberhard, *Zur Aussagefähigkeit von Vergleichen über die Erstellung kommunaler Leistungen durch Verwaltungen und private Unternehmen*, Speyerer Arbeitshefte 51, September 1983
Holland, Stuart (ed.), *The State as Entrepreneur*, London, 1972
Hughes, John, 'Relation with Private Industry', in Michael Shanks (ed.), *The Lessons of Public Enterprise*, London, 1963, pp. 126–48
Jarass, Hans D., 'Der staatliche Einfluß auf die öffentlichen Unternehmen in Frankreich', in *Archiv des öffentlichen Rechts*, 106/3, pp. 403–25
Jenkins, Clive, *Power at the Top*, London, 1959
Johnson, Nevil, 'The Public Corporation: An Ambiguous Species', in Butler and Halsey (eds.), *Policy and Politics. Essays in honour of Norman Chester*, London, 1978, pp. 122–39
Kavanagh, Dennis and Richard Rose (eds.), *New Trends in British Politics*, London/Beverly Hills, 1977
Kelf-Cohen, R., *British Nationalisation, 1945–1973*, London, 1973
—, *Twenty Years of Nationalisation*, London, 1969
Loesch, Achim von, *Die gemeinwirtschaftliche Unternehmung*, Cologne 1977
MacAvoy, Paul W., *The Regulated Industries and the Economy*, New York, 1979
McEachern, Doug, *A Class Against Itself*, Cambridge, 1980
MacGregor, Ian K., *Re-Industrialization. The British Experience*, 1981 Benjamin F. Fairless Memorial Lecture, Carnegie–Mellon University, 1982
Marrati, Marco, 'State/economy relationships: the case of Italian public enterprise', in *The British Journal of Sociology*, vol. I, December 1980, pp. 507–24

Bibliography

Marris, Robin, *The Economic Theory of 'Managerial' Capitalism*, London, 1964
Martinelli, Alberto, 'The Italian Experience with State-Controlled Enterprises', 1979 (ms.)
Mill, John Stuart, *Principles of Political Economy*, London, 1865
Nettl, J. P., 'Consensus or Elite Domination: The Case of Business', in *Political Studies*, 13 (1965), pp. 22–44
Nove, Alec, *Efficiency Criteria for Nationalised Industries*, London, 1973
Oettle, Karl, *Grundfragen öffentlicher Betriebe*, vol. I, Baden–Baden, 1976
Ovenden, Keith, *The Politics of Steel*, London, 1978
Painter, Martin J., 'Policy Co-ordination in the Department of Environment, 1970–1976', in *Public Administration*, vol. 58, Summer 1980, pp. 135–54
Pryke, Richard, *Public Enterprise in Practice*, London, 1971
—, *The Nationalised Industries. Policies and Performance since 1968*, Oxford, 1981
Punnett, R. M., *British Government and Politics*, 3rd ed., London, 1976
Redwood, John, *Public Enterprise in Crisis*, Oxford, 1980
—, and John Hatch, *Controlling Public Industries*, Oxford, 1982
Richardson, J. J. and G. F. Dudley, *Steel Policy in the UK: The Politics of Industrial Decline*, Strathclyde Papers on Government and Politics No. 10, November 1983
Robens, Lord, *Ten Year Stint*, London, 1972
Robson, William A., *Nationalized Industry and Public Ownership*, 2nd ed., London, 1962
—, 'Ministerial Control of the Nationalised Industries', in *Political Quarterly*, vol. 40, 1969, pp. 103–12 (repr. in Friedmann and Garner (eds.), *Government Enterprise. A Comparative Study*, New York, 1970)
Rose, Richard, *Politics in England Today*, London, 1974
—, *The Problem of Party Government*, New York, 1974
Rowley, Charles K., *Steel and Public Policy*, London, 1971
Schaaf, Peter, *Ruhrbergbau und Sozialdemokratie*, Marburg, 1978
Schuke, Andreas, *Theorie des Unternehmens*, Frankfurt/New York, 1977
Seidman, Harold, 'Ministers, Departments and Public Enterprise', Paper presented to the RIPA Research Group on Public Enterprise, 27 June 1980
Shanks, Michael (ed.), *The Lessons of Public Enterprise*, London, 1963
—, *Planning and Politics. The British Experience 1960–1976*, London, 1977
Sheahan, John B., 'Experience with Public Enterprise in France and Italy', in William G. Shepherd et al., *Public Enterprise: Economic Analysis of Theory and Practice*, Lexington (Mass.), 1976, pp. 123–83
Shepherd, William G., *Economic Performance under Public Ownership*, New Haven/London, 1965
—, et al., *Public Enterprise: Economic Analysis of Theory and Practice*, Lexington, 1976
Shulman, James S. and Jeffrey Gale, 'Laying the Groundwork for Social Accounting', in *Financial Executive*, March 1972, pp. 38–42
Silberston, Aubrey, 'Nationalised Industries: Government Intervention and Industrial Efficiency', in Butler and Halsey (eds.), *Policy and Politics, Essays in honour of Norman Chester*, London, 1978, pp. 140–51
Sloman, Martyn, *Socialising Public Ownership*, London, 1978
Thiemeyer, Theo, 'Privatwirtschaft und Gemeinwirtschaft', in Neumann,

Lothar F. (ed.), *Sozialforschung und soziale Demokratie*, Bonn, 1979, pp. 303–20
Thornhill, W., *The Nationalized Industries*, London, 1968
Tivey, Leonard, *Nationalization in British Industry*, rev. ed., London, 1973
—, 'Structure and Politics in the Nationalised Industries', in *Parliamentary Affairs*, vol. 32, no. 2, 1979, pp. 159–75
Tombs, Sir Francis, 'The Role of the Nationalised Industries', Bristol Lecture to the Local Centre of the Institute of Bankers, 11 November 1980, ms.
Vaizey, John, *The History of British Steel*, London, 1974
Vernon, Raymond and Yair Aharoni (eds.), *State-Owned Enterprise in the Western Economies*, London, 1981 ̇
Weisser, Gerhard, *Gemeinwirtschaftlichkeit bei Einzelwirtschaften*, Schriftenreihe Gemeinwirtschaft Nr. 11, Frankfurt a.M., 1974
Wenger, Karl, *Die öffentliche Unternehmung*, Vienna/New York, 1969
Winkler, Hans-Joachim, *Preußen als Unternehmer, 1923–1932*, Berlin, 1965
Witte, Eberhard, and Jürgen Hauschildt, *Die öffentliche Unternehmung im Interessenkonflikt*, Berlin, 1966
Wysocki, Klaus von, *Sozialbilanzen*, Stuttgart/New York, 1981

Newspapers

The Economist
The Financial Times
Guardian
The Times
The Sunday Telegraph (23 March 1980)
Der Volkswirt (14 May 1966)

Reports and Official Papers

Allied Steel and Wire Ltd, *Reports and Accounts, 18 months to December 1982*
BISPA, *Annual Reports*, 1970–82
—, *Extracts from a Debate in the House of Commons*, 11, 18 and 24 February 1981
BRISCC, *Cost Competitiveness in ECSC Steel Industries: The Effects of Government Policies*, London, 1981
BSC, *Annual Report and Accounts*, 1977/8–1984/5
—, *Annual Statistics for the Corporation*, 1980/81
—, *Daily News Summary*, No. 1731, 29 April 1975
—, *Organisation Guide*, London, 1977
—, *Prospects for Steel*, London, 1978
CBI Predecessor Archive, Modern Records Centre, University of Warwick
CBI, *The Manufacturing Powers of the Nationalised Industries*, London, 1966
Committee on Scottish Affairs, Second Report, *The Steel Industry in Scotland*, London, December 1982
House of Commons, *Parliamentary Debates*, Hansard, vol. 19, no. 73, 9 March 1982

Bibliography

—, *Parliamentary Debates*, Hansard, vol. 20, no. 77, 15 March 1982
—, *Parliamentary Debates*, Hansard, vol. 34, no. 34, 20 December 1982
Industry and Trade Committee, Fourth Report, Session 1980–81, *Effects of the BSC's Corporate Plan*, London, 1981
—, Second Report, Session 1982–83, *The British Steel Corporation's Prospects*, London, 1983
Iron and Steel Act, 1975
Iron and Steel Act, 1981
ISTC, *What is Wrong with the British Iron and Steel Industry?*, London, 1931
NCC, Report No. 1, *Consumers and the Nationalised Industries*, London, 1976
NEDO, *A Study of UK Nationalised Industries*, London, 1976
Report of the Commission of Inquiry into Industrial and Commercial Representation (Devlin Report), London, 1972 (published by the ABCC/CBI)
SCNI, First Report, Session 1967–68, *Ministerial Control of the Nationalised Industries*, London, 1968
—, Session 1972–73, *The British Steel Corporation*, London, 1973
—, First Report, Session 1973–74, *Capital Investment Procedures*, London, 1973
—, Second Special Report, Session 1976–77, *Comments by Nationalised Industries on the National Economic Development Office Report*, London, 1977
—, First Report, Session 1977–78, *The British Steel Corporation*, London, 1977
—, Second Report, Session 1977–78, *The British Steel Corporation*, London, 1977
—, Fifth Report, Session 1977–78, *Financial Forecasts of the British Steel Corporation*, London, 1978
—, Sixth Special Report, Session 1977–78, *Comments by Nationalised Industries and Others on the Government White Paper on the Nationalised Industries*, London, 1978
— (Sub-Committee E), Session 1978–79, *The Relationships between Ministers, Parliament and the Nationalised Industries, Minutes of Evidence*, London, 1979
—, Second Special Report, Session 1978–79, *Further Comments on the Government White Paper on the Nationalised Industries*, London, 1978
Treasury and Civil Service Committee, Eighth Report, Session 1980–81, *Financing of the Nationalised Industries*, London, 1981

White Papers

British Steel Corporation: Ten-Year Development Strategy, Cmnd. 5226, London, 1973
Cash Limits on Public Expenditure, Cmnd. 6440, London, 1976
The Nationalised Industries, Cmnd. 7131, London, 1978
British Steel Corporation: The Road to Viability, Cmnd. 7149, London, 1978

Index

Acton Society Trust, 103
'adversary politics', 37, 96, 184, 293
Afon Tinplate, 238
'agency theory', 7
Albu, Austen, 4
Aldward, 238
Alloy Steel Rods Ltd., 220, 234f.
Allied Steel & Wire Ltd., 235f., 239
Alpha Steel, vii, 136
Amersham International, 90
anti-inflation policy, 63f., 264
Appleby-Frodingham, 236
appointments, 55, **149ff.**, 186
ARBED Saarstahl, 141
arm's length concept, **50ff.**, 58, 65, 67, 91, **216f.**, 270 f., 290
Ashorne Hill Management Training Centre, 11f.
attitudes (to NI), 10, 106f., 218, 246ff., 249f., **269–85**, 295f., 297ff.
Audit Committee, 160, 164
Aurora Steel, 230
Aylen, Jonathan, 26

Backhaus, Jürgen, 19
'backstairs pressures', 33, 37, 63, 294
Bank of England, 111
Barker, Colin, 173
Barlow, Sir William, 20
BEC, 101, 118
Bell, J.D.M., 72
Benn, Tony, 134, 176, 185, 195, 196f.
Benson, Sir Henry, 101
Benson Brochures, 158
Benson Committee, 120, 129f.
  Report, 120
'Bergassessoren', 9, 107
Berle, Adolf A., and Gardiner Means, 7, 21
Beswick (plants), 134, 265
  Review, 132, 134, 176, 183
Binning, Ken, 157f., 205f.
bi-partisan policy, 70, 152
BISF, **112–17**, 119f., 122, 220f., 242, 251, 266

BISPA, 11, 100, 135ff., 221, 224–7, 229, 231, 233, 237, 240, **243–6**, 251, 261f.
  cooperation with BSC, 230ff., 241ff., 245
  members' attitudes, 227, 245, 246f., **272–7**
  complaints, 137, 221, 223–8, 243
  market shares, 136, 228
  state subsidies, 137, 229f.
Blankart, Charles Beat, 15
'blurred responsibilities', 37ff., 52, 62, 66, 68, 91, 211, 216
BNOC, 46, 89
BOAC, 46
boards, composition of, 81, **103–07**, 219
Boswell, Jonathan, 8
BP, 89
Bridon Ltd, 220, 221, 222, 234
BRISCC, 11, 100, 138f., 228, 254, **256–62**
British Aerospace, 2, 46, 90, 105, 304
British Airports, 303
British Airways, 64, 90
British Bright Bar Ltd, 233, 238
British Gas, viii, 60, 74, 98, 105, 191, 198, 303f.
British Leyland, 254, 303
British Rail, 26, 105
British Shipbuilders, 26, 48, 254, 258, 303
British steel industry, future of, 245f., **249–52, 300f.**
  history of, **111–18**
  joint interests, 231–4, 235
  private sector, **135ff.**, 153, **218–52**, 246ff., 261, 295f.
  public–private divide, 135ff., 235, 246, **248–52**, 296, 301
  renationalisation, 100, **118–23**, 263f.
British Steel Industry Group, 242
British Telecom, 303f.
Britoil, 89
Brookes, Lord, 222
Browne, Sir Humphrey, 106
Bryer, R.A., T.J. Brignall and A.R.

323

Index

Maunders, 138
Brymbo, 233, 237f., 254f.
BSC, attitudes of, **277–85**, 297
　board, 105, **125f.**, **160–7**
　borrowing limit, 141f.
　capacity reductions, 142ff.
　capital write-offs, 123, 138, 142
　Corporate Plan, 1981, 125, 142f., 156f., 154
　customers (non-steel), **253–62**
　debt, 123, 138
　EFL, 142, **171ff.**, 176, 180
　history, 121ff., 124, 129, 138
　losses, vii, 138, **141ff.**, 168
　'lost revenue', 138, 179
　manpower, vii, 142f.
　market shares, 135f., 141ff., 218f.
　objectives, 145, **153ff.**,
　organisation/reorganisation, **123–8**
　performance, 144, 173f., 223f., 253, 259, 273, 275, 300
　pricing, 63, 223–6, 232, 242, 262
　profits, vii, 138
　relations to private steel companies, 136f., **218–52**, 295
　relations to other NI, 98, 194f., 229, 278f.
　statutory powers (of the Minister), **146ff.**, 200f.
　subsidiaries, 129
　Ten-Year Development Strategy, 120, 125, **129–35**, 139, 171, 186, 232, 264
BSC (Industry) Ltd, 283
BSSC, 129
Bullock, R.H.W., 60, 67
　Report, 265
Bundesrechnungshof, 33f., 78
'buy British', 65, 99, 179, 194, 265

cabinet, 93, 152, 193
Cable & Wireless, 90
Callaghan, James, 121
Caparo Industries, 238
Cardiff, Castle Steel Works (GKN), 235, 254f.
'career men', **104–07**, 160f., 283, 297
cash limits, 81, 91, 184, 187, 193, 240, 271
CBI, 11, 83, **100–03**, 266ff.
Chief Executive's Committee, 125, 164
CEEP, 15, 83
CEGB, 64, 65, 74, 89
Central Electricity Board, 46
Central Policy Review Staff, 86, 190, 192
civil servants, 66f., 93, 95, 184, 187, 188, 203f., 207, 310
　attitudes of, **269–72**, 284, 292
　on the boards, 81, 126, **162ff.**, 209
clientelism, 42, 204, 310

Clyde Shaw Ltd, 238
Cold Drawn Tubes Ltd, 238
Colvilles, 118
'commercial' orientation of NI, 20, 87ff., 92, 148, 152, 249, 263, 265, 267, 269, 271, 277f., 285, 308, 310
Commission du Plan, 76
commitment, 63, 97, 309
Committee on Scottish Affairs, 181
commonweal, 17, 21, 34
Companies Act companies, 51, 198, 227, 240, 300
compensation payments, 177f.
Comptroller & Auditor General, 83, 86f.
Conseils d'Administration, 75, 81
Conservative Party, 47f., 89, 122, 152, 182, 184, 232
Consett, 259f.
consumer councils, 119, **256f.**
continuous casting, 118, 259
Contrats d'Entreprise, 33, 76
control, **32–41**
　ex ante, 28, 32, 35ff., 73, 91, 131, 160, 168f., 176, 208
　ex post, 28, 32, 73, 91, 174
　financial, 33, 59, **61f.**, 66, 87, **168–76**, 209, 291
　by formulae, 34f., 91
　'control of controllers', 39, 41f., 310
　'control of experts', 39, 41f., 208, 308
Contrôleur d'Etat, 33, 38, 76
convergence, 20ff., 42, 106, 282, **296ff.**
coordination, lack of, 35f., 65f., 91, 93, 190f., 194
corporate planning, 60, 89, 156f.
'corporate responsibility', 21
Corte dei Conti, 33
Cour des Comptes, 33
Crispin, Tom, 125, 239
'crowding out', 59, 88

Davies, John, 101, 125, 130f., 184, 227
Davignon Plan, 140
day-to-day management, 28, 51f., 56f.
decision-making (in NI), 7ff., 166f., 277
'Declaration of Intent', 264
'delays', 28, 36, 69, 170f., 178, 199, 212
democratic socialism, 16
denationalisation, 47ff.
Dep. of Economic Affairs, 94
Dep. of Energy, 12, 64, 65f., 83, 93, 150, 154, 191
Dep. of the Environment, 93
Dep. of Industry/of Trade and Industry, 11, 59f., 94, 124, 130f., 133, 150f., 154, 156ff., 181, 197, 200, **202f.**, 205f., 209f., 222, 236, 237, 298
Dep. of Transport, 154
Devlin Report, 102
disengagement, politics of, 48f., 153,

Index

229
dismissal, power of, 55, 149, 151, 210, 212
dividing line, between policies and day-to-day management, 51f., 60, 148, **215f.**
'double-guessing', 67, 71, 159, 170, 270
Driscoll, James, 82f., 89, 220, 302
duCann, Edward, MP, 243
Ductile Steels, 237
Dudley, G.F., and J.J. Richardson, 290f., 303
Duncan, Andrew, 115
Duport, 232f., 237

Economist, The, 82, 97, 121, 180, 182, 193, 301f.
EEC, state enterprises of, 4f.
 steel policy, 140, 144, 182, 242
 steel production, 139
efficiency of NI, **23–31**
 Audit Commission, 86
 comparisons, 29
 control, 68, 91
 measurement, 30
 social, 29
EFL, 35, 61, **87ff.**, 171ff., 176, 211
 negative, 89, 175, 193
electric-arc steelmaking, 118
Electricity Council, 66, 105
English, Michael, MP, 67
ENI/ENEL/EFIM, 77
Enterprise Oil, 303
executive directors, 164ff., 277
expertise, 38ff., 42, 66f., 91, **204–08**
Ezra, Sir Derek, 196

Faber Prest Holdings, 238
FBI, 100ff., 118f.
Finance Act (1956), 61, 79
financial targets, 36f., 61, 80f., 168
Financial Times, The, 102
Finniston, Sir Monty, 120, 134, 150, 154, 159, 171, 176f., 178, 182, 183, 186, 193, 196f., 206f., 212, 213, 214f., 216, 222, 236, 242, 255, 274, 275, 278ff., 285
Firth Brown, 234, 237
Flixborough Wharf Ltd, 238
Foster, C.D., 72
Fox Wire Ltd, 129
fragmentation (of government), 37, 42, 95, 97, 310
 (of the steel industry), 111ff., 117, 129, 136, 248, 250
Frame, Sir Alistair, 150f.
France, public enterprises in, 5f., 33, 38, **75f.**
 steel industry in, 140f.
Franks Report, 114

Garner, Maurice, 50, 66, 86
'Gemeinwirtschaft', 15f., 30, 34, 98
'gemeinwirtschaftliche Rechnungslegung', 308
general directives, 33f., 55, 154
Germany, public enterprises in, 19, 34f., 39, **78**
GKN, 11, 222, 233, 235ff., 242, 254f.
Glover, D.H., 69
Glynwed Steel, 136, 237
goal displacement, 21, 38
goals (of NI) **15–22**, 27
government, inertia of, 42, 94f., 292, 309
 interference by, 28, **62–5**, 68f., 71, 73, **176–183**, 198, 200f., 290, 293f., 298
Granville, Sir Keith, 85
Green, David, 190
Gross, Solly, 164, 207
'guideline packages', 85

Hadfields, 234, 237f.
handicaps of NI, 24f.
Hardie, S.J.L., 115
Haslam, Bob, 106, 126, 151, 166, 256
Hawkins, Sir Jack, 71, 149, 215
Heath, Edward, government of, 48, 185, 234
Heath, John B., 7, 26
Hepworth Ceramic Holdings, 238
'heritage programme', 129
Hilferding, Rudolf, 21
Hirshfield Inquiry, 224, 255
'hiving off', 90, 130
Howe, Sir Geoffrey, 94
Hughes, John, 99
hybrids, hybridisation, viii, 240f., 250f., 301, 304

Imperial Airways, 46
Import Duties Advisory Committee, 112, 116
industrial consumers' councils, 99f., 257
Industry and Trade Committee, 128, 144, 156f., 181, 205
inefficiency (of NI), **23–8**, 275
information flow, 158f., 170, 175, 260
'institutionalism', 94f.
'Instrumentaltheorie', 15f., 306
Integration Working Party, 101f.
interlocking directorships, 112, 220, 222, 235, 241, 252, 255
investment appraisals reviews, **59f.**, 61, 69, 87, 168ff.
IRI, 77, 82
Iron and Steel Act (1949), 115, 122
 (1953), 116
 (1967), 121f., 127, 145ff., 256
 (1975), 127, **145–9**
 (1981), 127f., 142, 145, 147f.

325

Index

Iron and Steel Control, 113
Iron and Steel Holding and Realisation Agency, 116
ISB, 114, 116ff., 120, 122, 220
ISCGB, 115
ISTC, 112, 241
Italy, public enterprises in, 5, 33, 77, 105
   steel industry in, 141

Jaguar, 303
Japan, steel industry in, 129
Jarass, Hans D., 15
Jefferson, Sir George, 304
Jenkin, Patrick, 144, 182, 185f., 229
Jenkins, Clive, 104
job rotation (Civil Service), 70, 95, **202ff.**, 291
Johnson & Firth Brown, 237
joint decision-making, 41
joint planning, **155–60**, 209, 244f., 254
Joint Steering Group, 130f.
joint-stock corporations, 7, 21, 23, 39, 281
joint ventures, 90, 187, 220, 234f.
joint working parties/steering groups (in industry), 100, 254f., 261
Joseph, Sir Keith, 128, 141, 157, 186, 189, 249

Kaufman, Gerald, 56
Kelf-Cohen, R., 256
King, Lord, 304
Kipping, Sir Norman, 101
Klöckner, 140

Labour government of 1945–51, 46f., 114f.
Labour Party, 45f., 48, 50, 58, 96, 152, 184
Lackenby, 132
Lawrence, R.L.E., 106
Lee, Peter W., 231, 245
Lee Bright Bars Ltd., 234
Lee Steel, 220, 234f.
Lévy, D.M.G., 38
liberalisation, viii, 304
Llanwern, 129, 132
Lloyd, Selwyn, 264
LPTB, 50
Lonrho, 234

Macdiarmid, Niall 121, 124
McEchearn, Doug, 117
MacGregor, Ian, 8, 12, 126f., 128, 142ff., 150, 164, 166, 167, 172, 194, 207, 210, 226, 256, 280, 285
McKinsey's, 130f.
managerial autonomy, 10, 20f., 32, 39f., 51, 70, 276, 281, 297f.

'managerial capitalism', 21
'management ethos', 27, 68, 277
Manchester Steel, 135
marginal cost pricing, 79ff.
Marking, Sir Henry, 71f., 162, 196
Marris, Robin, 21
Marsh, Richard, 121, 258
Melchett, Lord, 124, 196, 206, 221f., 234, 255
Mercury, 304
Mersey Docks, 48
Metal Society, 222
Mikardo, Ian, MP, 208
Mill, John Stuart, 23, 40
miners' strike (1984–5), 238
ministerial control general, 28, 52, **54–73**, **91f.**, 308
   'deficits', **65–70**, 97, 288ff.
   reforms (and reform proposals), **79–87**, 91, 196, 290, 302f.
   of BSC, **145–217**, 291, 294
Min. of Nationalised Industries, proposed, 83
Min. of State Holdings (Italy), 77, 83
Min. of Supply, 113f.
misinvestment, 170, 211
'Mitbestimmung', 33, 81, 165
Moate, Roger, MP, 226
Moellendorff, Wichard von, 15
monitoring, 174f.
Monopolies and Mergers Commission, 74, 87
monopolist practices, 40, 223f., 253
Montagu, Sir Norman, 112
Morley, Herbert, 221
Morrison, Herbert 33, 45, 50, 52, 115
Mortimer, Alec, 221, 245
MVA, Wuppertal, 280

NABM, 101, 118
Naphthali, Fritz, 16, 33
National Board for Prices and Incomes, 63, 80, 94
National Bus Company, 303
National Coal Board, 12, 26, 74, 98, 100, 105, 156, 159, 194f., 206, 257, 258, 272
National Consumer Council, 80f.
national economic planning, 45, 48, 264
National Enterprise Board, 82
National Federation of Iron and Steel Manufacturers, 113
National Freight Corporation, 90, 279
National Industrial Organisation (proposed), 101f.
Nationalisation Acts, 47, 54ff., 58, 63
nationalisation, 3
   in Britain, history of, **45–9**, 114
   meaning of, 4, 272, 279f., 307
   objectives, 17f., 58, 262ff., 285

Index

nationalised industries, economic impact of, 5
future of, ix, **301–04**
losses by, 26
performance by, 25f., 74
Nationalised Industries', Policy Committee, 93, 190
Chairmen's Group, 11, **82f.**, 88, 103, 149f., 279, 302
National Plan (1965), 64, 264
NEDC, NEDO, 48, 83, 264
NEDO Report (1976), 25f., 55, 60, 63, 72, 84f., 160, 177f., 305
NORA Report (1968), 76
Nove, Alec, 30

objectives (of NI), 27, 30, 36, 41, 58, 70, 151f., 270
Oettle, Karl, 39ff.
Organising Committee, 120ff., 220
Osborn, John, MP, 239
Ovenden, Keith, 117, 121f., 124
'overlap', 137, 226f., 234, 241
overlapping responsibilities, 94

'paradox of public enterprise', 37
Parker, Sir Peter, 196
parliamentary control, 56f.
part-time directors, 104ff., 160f., 165, 255
party competition, 309f.
Pennington, John, 219
performance indicators, 32, 61, 81, 155, **173f.**, 176, 210, 308
personal relationships, 103, 196ff., 201, 204, 221f., 255
Phoenix, projects, 198f., 205, 227, 233, **235–41**, 255
I, 172, 235f.
II, vi, 237f.
Pipework Engineering (PED), 129
plant closures, 132ff., 179, 180f., 185, 232ff.
policy changes, impact of, 96, **183–8**, 293
Policy Council (proposed), 84f.
political guidance, 19f., 28, 30, 36f., 42, 91, 310, 312
political market, pressures of, 23f., 30, 37, 41, 293, 309
Port of London Authority, 46
Port Talbot, 129, 132, 171, 180
Post Office, 105, 268
power balance (between government and NI), 71ff., 214f., 271, 289ff., 311
price restraint/control, 63f., 80, 99, 133f., 153, 179, 187, 229, 264, 266
price leadership, 242
private sector, relations to NI of, **98–103**, 263, 266, 268

privatisation, viif., 42, 89f., 127f., 152, 190, 236f., 239ff., 302–05, 307
Prussia, public enterprises in, 9, 35, 38, 107
Pryke, Richard, 25ff., 68, 74, 253, 284
PSBR, 61, 81, 88f., 103, 153
public accountability, 19, 36, 41, 51, 90, 177, 200, 239f., 269, 304, 308
Public Accounts Committee, 86
Public Appointments Unit, 55, 105, 149
Public Corporation, 45f., **50–3**, 128
public dividend capital, 123, 138
public enterprise, definition of, 6, 15, 305
distinction from private enterprise, 6ff., 15, 211ff., 213, 270, 276f., 306f.
economic impact of, 4f.
strategies in capitalism, 262f., 311
public purpose of NI, **15–22**, 30, 37, 39f., 145, 264ff.
lack of 58, 60, 67, 91, 97

Raiffa, Howard 27
Ravenscraig, vii, 129, 132, 143, 180ff.
Redcar, 171, 178f.
Redpath Dorman Long, 129, 250
Redwood, John, and John Hatch, 34
Rees, Peter (Treasury), viii
regulatory commissions viii, 78f.
RGC Offshore Ltd, 129
Richard Thomas & Baldwin, 116, 118
Richardson, J.J., and G.F. Dudley, 133, 214
Rio Tinto Zinc, 150f.
Robens, Lord, 82, 106, 134, 183, 191
Robson, William A., 24, 29, 34, 86
Rolls-Royce, 48
Rooke, Sir Denis, ix, 196, 278, 304
Rose, Richard, 310
Roseveare, Robert, 126
Round Oak, 137, 219, 233f., 237f.
Rowley, Charles K., 23f., 30, 41, 309
RRR, 59, 61, 81, 87, 169

Safford, J. F., 258ff.
sanctions, lack of, 210–13, 270
Sankey, Lord, 111
Scholey, Bob, 150, 166, 167, 241, 245, 274
Schueppert, Clancy, 245
Scott Lithgow, 302
Scunthorpe, 124, 129, 132, 235, 254
Seamless Tubes Ltd, 238
Select Committee on NI, 28f., 34, 39, 56f., 63, 68f., 71, 83f., 156, 158, 159, 168ff., 174, 177, 196, 204, 214, 251
Shanks, Michael, 48
W. Shaw Ltd, 238
Sheahan, John, 76

327

Index

Sheerness Steel, 135f., 137, 220, 230, 237, 243, 245
Sheffield Forgemasters, 237f.
Shelbourne, P., 88, 307
Shelton Action Committee, 265
Shepherd, William, 25f., 68
short-term interventions, 63ff., 68, 70, 181
short-term orientation of politics, 96, 192, 199f., 293, 309
Shotton, 134
Siddons, James, 220
Sirs, Bill, 126
Social accounting/audit, 30f., 34
  costs, 31
  indicators, 31, 37
  obligations, 29
  responsibility, 283f.
'Social Contract', 264
socialisation, 45f.
Society of Motor Manufacturers, 258
'soft management control', 26f.
'Sondervermögen', 78
specific directions, 85, 147
sponsor departments, 54ff., 62, 72, 87, 97, 153f., 156, 188–95, 201f., 205f., 270f.
Stanton and Staveley, 129
state holdings, 33, 35, 77, 82
state in capitalism, 310ff.
statutory powers/duties, **54–7**
steel, demand for, 130, 134, 136, 139, 156
  world market for, 139ff., 143
  stockholding, 255
  strike, 141, 162, 224, 228
G.R. Stein Refractories, 238
St John Stevas' Bill, 86f.
Stocksbridge, 237f.
'strategic objectives', 86
Sunday Telegraph, The, 162, 180
supervisory boards, 35, 39, 167
supply agreements, 254
'survival strategy', 153, 157

targets, sets of, 33ff.
Tate & Lyle, 126, 151
TDR, 79ff., 169
Tebbit, Norman, 239
'technological achievement', 280ff., 283, 296f.
Teesside, 124, 129

Templeborough, 137, 220, 234, 237f.
Thatcher, Margaret, 187, 193
  government, 48f., 57, 74, 93, 97, 137, 152, 180, 184, 186f., 229
Thatcherite system of ministerial control, **87–90**
'theory of the firm', 7f., 21
Thiemeyer, Theo, 295
time horizons, 199f.
Times, The, 21, 214, 306
Tinsley Bridge Ltd, 129
Tinsley Park, vii, 237f.
Tinsley Wire Industries Ltd, 234
Tivey, Leonard, 30, 297
Tombs, Sir Francis, 70
trade associations, 244, 257, 267
Treasury, 11, 59, 61f., 66, 68, 70, 72f., 82, 88, 90, 93, 94, 97, 121f., 154, 169, **188–93**, 195, 203, 205, 238
Trustee Savings Bank, 302
Tube Investments, 219f., 233f., 238, 261
TUC, 83, 126
two-tier organisation, 33, 78, 84, 125f., 165

United Merchant Bar, 238
United Steel, 221, 234
  'mafia', 221
Upper Clyde Shipbuilders, 48
USA, public enterprises, 78f.
  protectionism in, 143
  steel industry, losses in, 139
US Steel Co., 181

Varley, Eric, 185, 195
VEBA, VIAG, 78
Villiers, Sir Charles, 127, 150f., 255, 274, 275, 277f.

Walker, Peter, 131, 185
Walzstahlkontore, 140
war economy, 47, 113
Webley, K.G., 219
Weisser, Gerhard, 15
Whitehead Narrow Strip Ltd, 129
White Paper, (1961), 79f., 99
  (1967), 79f.
  (1978), 81, 85, 175
  (1978) (BSC), 135, 141
Winkler, Hans-Joachim, 9, 35
worker directors, 104f., 125f., 161f., 265
workers' control, 45, 50